Iris Biometrics

Advances in Information Security

Sushil Jajodia
Consulting Editor
Center for Secure Information Systems
George Mason University
Fairfax, VA 22030-4444
email: jajodia@gmu.edu

The goals of the Springer International Series on ADVANCES IN INFORMATION SECURITY are, one, to establish the state of the art of, and set the course for future research in information security and, two, to serve as a central reference source for advanced and timely topics in information security research and development. The scope of this series includes all aspects of computer and network security and related areas such as fault tolerance and software assurance.

ADVANCES IN INFORMATION SECURITY aims to publish thorough and cohesive overviews of specific topics in information security, as well as works that are larger in scope or that contain more detailed background information than can be accommodated in shorter survey articles. The series also serves as a forum for topics that may not have reached a level of maturity to warrant a comprehensive textbook treatment.

Researchers, as well as developers, are encouraged to contact Professor Sushil Jajodia with ideas for books under this series.

For further volumes:
http://www.springer.com/series/5576

Christian Rathgeb • Andreas Uhl • Peter Wild

Iris Biometrics

From Segmentation to Template Security

 Springer

Christian Rathgeb
University of Salzburg
Salzburg, Austria

Andreas Uhl
University of Salzburg
Salzburg, Austria

Peter Wild
University of Salzburg
Salzburg, Austria

ISSN 1568-2633
ISBN 978-1-4899-8619-1   ISBN 978-1-4614-5571-4 (eBook)
DOI 10.1007/978-1-4614-5571-4
Springer New York Heidelberg Dordrecht London

Springer is part of Springer Science+Business Media (www.springer.com)

Research starts with inspiration. This book is dedicated to our families and friends, who are our source of motivation in everything we do. We greatly appreciate their love, support and encouragement.

Foreword

It is marvelous to encounter the enormous depth and breadth of material presented in this work, which is the first large monograph devoted entirely to iris recognition. Its three Salzburg-based authors have given us a deeply insightful and creative presentation, whose mastery, diversity, and orchestration seem inspired by that other most celebrated son of Salzburg who wrote some 230 years ago.

This book provides a comprehensive review of the field of iris recognition as it has developed in its short 20-year history, together with important new advances by the authors themselves in areas such as matching and biometric security protocols. With more than 600 references, it offers the most complete bibliography available today for those seeking a survey of existing ideas and developments in a single source. In addition, this book presents a large number of very comprehensive experiments that the authors have performed on many aspects of iris recognition, equivalent in content to dozens of journal papers. For example, the detailed analysis of several possible compression scenarios in Chap. 8, including systematic parametric investigation of alternate compressors and quantisation tables, is far more comprehensive than any extant in the literature. The same may be said of the experiments on biometric cryptosystems and iris template protection in Chap. 14. (Incidentally, Figs. 14.7 and 14.8 have seriously enlivened this subject and will surely bring smiles to the faces even of security engineers.)

The arrival of this very substantial book convinces me that iris recognition is here to stay. This has some personal meaning for me because it was just 20 years ago that I submitted the first paper proposing and demonstrating a method for iris recognition, to *IEEE Transactions on Pattern Analysis and Machine Intelligence* (PAMI), titled "High confidence visual recognition of persons by a test of statistical independence." The core theoretical idea was that the *failure* of a test of independence could be a very strong basis for pattern recognition, if there is sufficiently high entropy (enough degrees-of-freedom of random variation) among samples from different classes, as I was able to demonstrate with a set of 592 iris images. But the idea that iris patterns might serve in the same way as fingerprints has older and deeper roots, notably in the writings of the British ophthalmologists Adler and Doggart around 1950 and of the French police officer Alphonse Bertillon in 1892. Indeed divination of all sorts of things based on iris patterns goes back to ancient Egypt, to Chaldea in Babylonia, and to ancient Greece as documented in ceramic artefacts and in the writings of Hippocrates. Iris divination persists today, as "iridology."

The explosive impact and scale of serious mathematical analysis of iris patterns is perhaps best seen in the fact that today on a daily basis more than 400 trillion, or 4×10^{14}, iris comparisons are performed. This juggernaut (a Hindi word, appropriately) was unleashed by the Indian Government to check for duplicate identities as the Unique IDentification Authority of India, or UIDAI, enrolls the iris patterns of all its 1.2 billion citizens within 3 years. This vastly ambitious programme requires enrolling about 1 million persons every day, across 36,000 stations operated by 83 agencies. Its purpose is to issue to each citizen a biometrically provable unique entitlement number (Aadhaar) by which benefits may be claimed, and social inclusion enhanced; thus the slogan of UIDAI is: "To give the poor an identity." With about 200 million persons enrolled so far, against whom the daily intake of another million must be compared for de-duplication, the daily workflow of iris cross-comparisons is 400 million–million, and growing. Similar national projects are also under way in Indonesia and in several smaller countries.

It is obvious that both matching speed and resistance to False Matches are vital for any such national-scale biometric deployment. I am reminded that during the first ten years after my 1993 PAMI paper, it was always very difficult to persuade leaders of the established biometrics community to take an interest in the claim that the iris algorithm had extraordinary resistance against False Matches, as well as enormous matching speed. The encoding of an iris pattern into a sign bit sequence enables not only extremely fast XOR matching (e.g., on a 32-bit machine, 32 parallel bits from each of two IrisCodes can be simultaneously compared in a single machine instruction, in almost a single clock cycle, at say 3 GHz). But even more importantly, the Bernoulli nature of random bit pair comparisons generates binomial distributions for the (dis)similarity scores between different eyes. The binomial distribution (for "imposter" comparisons) is dominated by combinatorial terms with geometric tails that attenuate extremely rapidly. For example, if you accept as a match any IrisCode pair for which no more than 32 % of the bits disagree, then the False Match likelihood is about 1 in a million; but if your criterion is just slightly stricter, say that no more than 28 % of the bits may disagree, then the False Match likelihood is about 1 in a billion (i.e., reduced by a further 1,000-fold as a result of a mere 4-percentile point [0.04] reduction in threshold). These claims became contentious in the year 2000 when the Director of the US "National Biometric Test Center" (NBTC) in San Jose wrote that in their testing of an iris recognition prototype at NBTC, many False Matches had been observed. I received copies of all the images, ran all-against-all cross-comparisons, and sure enough, there were many apparent False Matches. But when I inspected these putative False Match images visually, it became clear that they were all in fact True Matches but with changed identities. The Director of the NBTC later confirmed this and acknowledged that: *Clearly we were getting scammed by some of our volunteers (at $25 a head, they were changing names and coming through multiple times).*

Another obstacle to confirmation of the extreme resistance of this biometric to False Matches was the decision in the first large-scale test (ICE 2006: *Iris Challenge Evaluation*) to evaluate at a False Match Rate of 1 in a thousand (FMR = 0.001). In this very nondemanding region of an ROC plot, most biometrics will appear equally powerful. Indeed since ROC curves converge into the corners at either extreme, if one tested at say FMR = 0.01 then probably the length of one's big toe would seem as discriminating as the iris. The long tradition of face recognition tests had typically used the FMR = 0.001 benchmark for obvious reasons: face recognition cannot perform at more demanding FMR levels. Thus the ICE 2006 Report drew the extraordinary conclusion that face and iris were equally powerful biometrics.

Imagine how face recognition would perform in 200 trillion cross-comparisons, as done daily by UIDAI. And if iris were operating at the trivial FMR = 0.001 level, then every day in UIDAI, among 4×10^{14} comparisons there would be 400 billion False Matches.

A critical feature of iris recognition is that it produces very flat ROC or DET curves. By threshold adjustment the FMR can be shifted over four or five orders of magnitude while the FNMR hardly changes. Thus at FMR = 0.001 the performance of iris recognition may appear unremarkable, as in ICE 2006, and so Newton and Phillips (2007) disputed "the conventional wisdom" that iris was a very powerful biometric. But hardly any price is paid in iris FNMR when its FMR is shifted by several log units, to 0.0000001 or smaller, as required for deployments on national scales. Fortunately, subsequent tests by NIST have understood this point about the likelihood ratio (the slope of the ROC curve) and have pushed iris testing into the billions of cross-comparisons (IREX-I) and then 1,200 billion cross-comparisons (IREX-III). IREX-I confirmed (7.3.2) that "there is little variation in FNMR across the five decades of FMR," and also confirmed exactly the exponential decline in FMR with minuscule (percentile point) reductions in threshold as I had tabulated. IREX-III included a comparison of iris and face performance using the best face algorithms from 2010 on a database of 1.6 million police mugshot face images and also 1.6 million DoD detainee iris images. These NIST tests concluded that for any plausible FNMR target, iris recognition makes 100,000 times fewer False Matches than face. The value of iris is becoming established, as this book makes clear.

The research programme in some laboratories aims at finding all possible ways to make iris recognition fail and then rushing to a sensationalist press. Undoubtedly that has value, for the same reason that research in security engineering tries to launch all possible attacks. The work of the Salzburg group distinguishes itself by being positive and constructive, seeking ways to enhance robustness at all levels from early processing to template security, even when using images (as in Chap. 9) that are poorly acquired or are otherwise challenging. This monograph assembles and presents a very impressive body of research in the field of iris recognition. It is a major contribution, and I unreservedly commend it.

Cambridge, UK   John Daugman

Preface

Biometric recognition refers to the authentication of humans by their physiological or behavioral characteristics or traits. In this sense, biometrics may be as old as mankind itself. The possibility to automatize the recognition process and let computers perform this task has led to the successful development and deployment of numerous biometric technologies. The human iris has been discovered as one of the most reliable biometric characteristics. First experimental evaluations revealed impressive performance in terms of recognition accuracy holding tremendous promise for applying iris recognition in diverse application scenarios. In the past years, numerous studies have been conducted in this field of research and many essential improvements have been proposed. Iris recognition, which has now been used for several years at diverse nationwide deployments, is field-proven.

In addition to the growing public acceptance of biometric technologies, iris recognition sensors are constantly dropping in price, and usability has greatly improved. Ongoing research in the field of iris biometrics is focused on advanced issues, such as performing recognition under unconstrained conditions, liveness detection, indexing of biometric databases, and secure storage of iris biometric reference data, to mention just a few. Experts agree that in the foreseeable future, iris recognition technology will be deployed in commonplace access control systems, e.g., ATMs and car locks. This book reflects the progress made in iris recognition within this exciting period for biometric technologies.

In this book we attempt to describe the current state of the art in iris biometric recognition. In addition, we intend to provide students, scientists, and engineers with a detailed insight into diverse advanced topics in the field of iris biometrics, based on years of research experience, gathered by members of the Multimedia Signal Processing and Security Lab (WaveLab) at the Department of Computer Sciences, University of Salzburg, Austria. In-depth investigations, accompanied by comprehensive experimental evaluations, provide the reader with theoretical and empirical explanations of fundamental and current research topics. Furthermore, research directions and issues still to be solved are pointed out.

Objectives

Selected topics cover a wide spectrum of research on iris recognition; however, the book is intended to complement existing literature. As a major property compared to existing literature, this book represents a homogeneous work, i.e. the reader is provided with consistent notations, unified experimental test sets, and meaningful cross-references throughout the entire work. Key objectives, which this book is focused on, are:

- An introduction to (all components/ modules of) iris biometric recognition and an overview of current state-of-the-art technologies
- Detailed investigations of advanced topics including segmentation, image compression, improved comparators, template protection, and watermarking
- Guidance and support for researchers in the design and implementation of iris biometric technologies including reference software
- A comprehensive collection of references on iris biometric recognition

Audience

The book is divided into three different parts comprising a total of 16 chapters. Parts, as well as distinct groups of chapters, are meant to be fairly independent and the reader is encouraged to study only relevant parts or chapters.

This book appeals to a broad readership. Early chapters provide a comprehensive introduction to the topic, which address readers wishing to gain an overview of iris biometric recognition. Subsequent parts which delve deeper into the topic are oriented towards advanced readers, in particular, graduate students. The book provides a good starting point for young researchers as it is accompanied by open source software. In addition, the second and third part of the book may serve as a manual of instruction appealing to biometric system developers as well as a reference guide pointing at further literature.

Organization

Part I *Fundamentals in Iris Recognition*

The first part provides a general overview of iris biometric recognition. Chapter 1 gives a brief introduction to iris biometrics covering anatomy and history. Different tasks within an iris biometric system, from image acquisition to recognition, are summarized in Chap. 2. The state-of-the-art and current challenges in iris biometrics are discussed in Chap. 3, comprising an introduction to open biometric databases, contests, software, surveying reports, deployments, and open issues.

Part II *Iris Image Processing and Biometric Comparators*

Within this part improvements to traditional iris processing from preprocessing over compression methods to new biometric comparators are covered. Chapter 4 introduces eye detection and presents a method to enhance results by combining face and face-part detectors. Iris segmentation being conducted after pre-localization of the eye is surveyed in Chap. 5. Chapter 6 presents a robust multistage real-time segmentation technique in detail. Experiments with respect to presented eye detection and iris segmentation methods are discussed in Chap. 7, highlighting the critical role of segmentation: Mislocation of irides causes significant and irrecoverable mapping distortions, which cannot be overcome with simple matching based on Hamming distance. Also Chap. 8 discussing the effects of compression at several different stages in the iris biometric processing chain highlights a strong impact on segmentation. Insufficient normalization at preprocessing may be targeted by more sophisticated comparison techniques. Chapter 9 introduces new iris biometric comparators, which are evaluated in Chap. 10, yielding a trade-off between speed and accuracy.

Part III *Privacy and Security in Iris Recognition*

The third part provides an overview of security issues regarding iris biometric recognition, in particular, biometric template protection and watermarking. In Chap. 11 biometric cryptosystems are introduced and basic schemes are summarized. Subsequently, approaches to cancelable biometrics are reviewed in Chap. 12. Potential attacks against biometric template protection systems are discussed in Chap. 13. In Chap. 14 experiments on iris biometric template protection systems are presented. Open issues, challenges, advances, and applications related to security and privacy in biometrics are discussed in Chap. 15. Chapter 16 examines watermarking and PNRU sensor fingerprints in biometrics in general and in iris recognition in particular.

Acknowledgements

We would like to express our gratitude to all people who gave us the opportunity to write this book. First, we would like to thank all those, who were directly involved in underlying research projects and development of software, especially, H. Hofbauer, Y. Höller, K. Horvath, R. Huber, S. Jenisch, C. Koidl, M. Konrad, P. Meerwald, E. Pschernig, and K. Raab. All people who were a source of inspiration during the writing of this book deserve our thanks as well. We gratefully acknowledge the support, interest, and valuable hints of our colleagues and former colleagues of the Multimedia Signal Processing and Security Lab (WaveLab) at the local Department of Computer Sciences, University of Salzburg.

Research work reported in this book was funded by grants from the Austrian Federal Ministry for Transport, Innovation and Technology in cooperation with the Austrian Research Promotion Agency FFG (as part of the FIT-IT Trust in IT Systems *BioSurveillane* project 819382) and from the Austrian Science Fund (as part of the Translational Research Project TRP L554-N15).

We would like to thank Springer Verlag for the support and expedient publishing of this book. Additionally, the publishers ACM, GI, IARIA, IEEE, IET, InTech, and SciTePress deserve our acknowledgement for the permission to include parts of our published research work in this book.

This book would not have been possible without the fruitful input and academic exchange of ideas from our international colleagues during conferences, within review processes and in discussions. In particular, we would like to thank J. Daugman for his valuable comments and his disposition to writing the foreword to this book.

Finally, we would like to express our special thanks to our families and friends for their support and patience while we worked on this book.

Salzburg, Austria   Christian Rathgeb
                                                                                       Andreas Uhl
                                                                                       Peter Wild

Contents

Acronyms

AC	Active contours
AES	Advanced Encryption Standard
ANSI	American National Standards Institute
ASM	Active shape models
AUC	Area under curve
BER	Bit error rate
CRC	Cyclic redundancy check
CPU	Central processing unit
CMC	Cumulative match characteristic
DCT	Discrete cosine transform
DTW	Dynamic time warping
DET	Detection error trade-off
DFT	Discrete Fourier transform
DOF	Degrees of freedom
DRM	Digital rights management
EER	Equal error rate
FAR	False acceptance rate
FBI	Federal Bureau of Investigation
FMR	False match rate
FNMR	False non-match rate
FRR	False rejection rate
FTE	Failure to enroll rate
GA	Genetic algorithm
GAR	Genuine acceptance rate
GMM	Gaussian mixture model
HD	Hamming distance
HT	Hough transform
ICA	Independent component analysis
ICE	Iris Challenge Evaluation
ID	Identifier
IEC	International Electrotechnical Commission

IR	Infrared
IREX	The Iris Exchange
IRIS06	Iris Recognition Study 2006
ISO	International Organization for Standardization
ITIRT	Independent Testing of Iris Recognition Technology
JPEG	Joint Photographic Experts Group
JPEG-LS	JPEG Lossless
JPG	DCT-based JPEG
JXR	JPEG XR
J2K	JPEG 2000
LD	Levenshtein distance
LDA	Linear discriminant analysis
MBGC	Multiple Biometric Grand Challenge
MRP	Multistage random projection
NCC	Normalized cross correlation
NICE	Noisy Iris Challenge Evaluation
NIR	Near infrared
NIST	National Institute of Standards and Technology
NN	Neural network
PCA	Principal component analysis
PIN	Personal identification number
POT	Photo overlay transform
PNG	Portable Network Graphics
PRNU	Photo response non uniformity
PSNR	Peak signal-to-noise ratio
RANSAC	Random sample consensus
RB	Reliable bit rearrangement
ROI	Region of interest
ROC	Receiver operating characteristic
RP	Random permutation
RR-1	Rank-1 recognition rate
SIFT	Scale-invariant feature transform
SURF	Speeded Up Robust Feature
SVM	Support vector machine
USIT	University of Salzburg Iris Toolkit
VW	Visible wavelength
WM	Watermarking
WSQ	Wavelet Scalar Quantization

Part I
Fundamentals in Iris Recognition

Part I

Fundamentals in Iris Recognition

Chapter 1
The Human Iris as a Biometric Identifier

In 1984, a photographer named Steve McCurry traveled to Pakistan in order to document the ordeal of Afghanistan's refugees, orphaned during the Soviet Union's bombing of Afghanistan. In the refugee camp Nasir Bagh, which was a sea of tents, he took a photograph of a young girl approximately at the age of 13. McCurry's portrait turned out to capture emotion quite well and in June 1985 it ran on the cover of National Geographic. The girl's sea green eyes have captivated the world since then and because no one knew her name she became known as the "Afghan girl" [368].

In 2002, 17 year later, McCurry and National Geographic Television went back to Pakistan to search for the green-eyed girl. However, in the still standing Nasir Bagh refugee camp there were a number of women who came forward and identified themselves erroneously as the famous Afghan girl when they were shown her 1985 picture. In addition, a handful of young men falsely claimed the Afghan girl as their wife. The team was able to finally confirm her identity with the help of Prof. John Daugman's iris recognition software, which matched her iris patterns to those of the photograph with almost full certainty [48, 114]. Her name was Sharbat Gula, an estimated 30-year-old woman, and she had not been photographed since then. The revealing of Sharbat Gula's identity manifested the strength of iris recognition technologies.

The term biometrics refers to "automated recognition of individuals based on their behavioral and biological characteristics" (ISO/IEC JTC1 SC37). Several physiological as well as behavioral biometric characteristics have been used [227] such as fingerprints, iris, face, hand, voice, and gait, depending on types of applications. Biometric traits are acquired applying adequate sensors and distinctive features are extracted to form a biometric template in the enrollment process. During verification (authentication process) or identification (processible as a sequence of verifications and screenings) the system processes another biometric measurement which is compared against the stored template(s) yielding acceptance or rejection. Iris biometrics refers to high confidence recognition of a person's identity by mathematical analysis of the random patterns that are visible within the iris of an eye from some distance [116], see Fig. 1.1.

C. Rathgeb et al., *Iris Biometrics: From Segmentation to Template Security,*
Advances in Information Security 59, DOI 10.1007/978-1-4614-5571-4_1,
© Springer Science+Business Media, LLC 2013

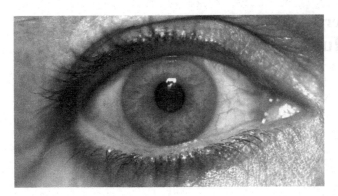

Fig. 1.1 An example of a light pigmented human iris captured under visible light

1.1 Iris Anatomy

The iris is an annular structure of elastic connective tissue forming a rich pattern of random texture, visible in the eye. It is located between the darker pupil and brighter sclera. The corresponding anatomical details are illustrated in Fig. 1.2 depicting frontal and side views of the human eye. The pupil is the hole centered in the middle of the iris, where light can enter the eye. There are dilator and sphincter muscles which control the amount of entering light into the eye by changing the size of the iris. As an organ of photoreception, changes in nerve cells in the retina (rods and cones) result in nerve action potentials which are transmitted to the brain through the optical nerve. While the pupil typically appears black, because most light is absorbed by tissues inside the eye, the surrounding sclera region of approximately 11.5 mm in radius riddled with blood vessels appears white. The transparent frontal 0.52–0.67 mm thick covering of the iris is called cornea and has a radius of approximately 7.8 mm. Prior to entering the internal retina, light passes through the lens, a biconvex structure, which is responsible for sharp images focusing the object of interest by changing shape and, thus, refracting entering light. The collarette boundary divides the iris in pupillary and limbic zones. The iris surface consists of several layers and is characterized by radial and contraction furrows (ridges resulting from dilation), as well as crypts (openings that allow the stroma and deeper iris tissues to be bathed in aqueous humor) [155].

The iris has also been used by an alternative medicine technique referred to as "iridology" (iris diagnosis), which hypothesizes that genetic diseases may lead to specific inheritable patterns in irides [317]. Distinct sectors within irides are believed to indicate specific body parts, a technique historically introduced by Dr. Ignatz von Peczely. However, sophisticated scientific studies of iridology have denounced it as "medical fraud." Controlled clinical trials and experiments have shown that iridology has no ability to detect disorders in other parts of the body [32].

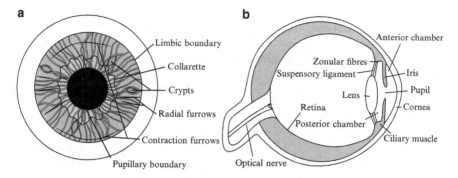

Fig. 1.2 Schematical anatomy of the human eye: (**a**) frontal view and (**b**) side view

1.2 History of Iris Recognition

The history of iris recognition dates back to the nineteenth century. In 1882, Alphonse Bertillon started to conduct body measurements on police record cards for arrestee identification purposes. He was also the first to propose properties of the human eye (color) for biometric recognition in 1886 [33]. The idea of using iris patterns for identification was born in 1936 with Frank Burch [112].

The origins of modern automated iris recognition were founded in 1986, when Leonard Flom and Aran Safir filed in a patent for the first iris recognition system, but without any algorithm [152]. Among all biometric characteristics the pattern of an iris texture is believed to be the most distinguishable among different persons [44]. In contrast to other biometric characteristics, such as fingerprints, the iris is a protected internal organ whose random texture is complex, unique, and believed to be very stable throughout life. More precisely, the iris pattern of an eye develops from the third month of gestation while the structure persists from approximately the eighth month [276]. Recently, it was found that iris patterns do slightly alter over time, i.e. aging does affect recognition accuracy in a way that dissimilarities between iris pattern of a single subject increase [149]. However, compared to faces or other physiological biometric characteristics changing more drastically, the iris remains relatively stable and is rarely affected by external elements. As an internal organ the iris is well protected and cannot easily be altered [452]. The structure of the iris is substantially different between different persons, even in case of monozygotic twins [120].

Less than 10 years after the introduction of the idea by Flom and Safir, John Daugman patented the first modern automated iris recognition system in 1994 [110]. It was based on doubly dimensionless coordinates for normalization, 2D Gabor filters as features, and Hamming distance (HD) scores as comparator. Since the randomness of iris patterns has very high dimensionality, recognition decisions are made with confidence levels, high enough to support rapid, and reliable exhaustive searches through national-sized databases. From a technical point of view, iris biometrics differs from other biometrics in being based on a test of statistical independence, founded by Daugman's work [109], with fails of this test (i.e., comparison against all other irides) indicating a genuine comparison [116]. As of 2012, almost all commercial iris recognition solutions are based on Daugman's algorithms.

Chapter 2
Iris Biometric Processing

In past years, the ever-increasing demand on biometric systems entailed continuous proposals of new iris recognition techniques [44]. Still, the processing chain of traditional iris recognition (and other biometric) systems has remained almost unaltered. In particular, generic iris recognition systems consist of four major stages:

1. Iris image acquisition
2. Image preprocessing
3. Feature extraction
4. Comparison (feature matching)

In Fig. 2.1 a flowchart of a generic iris recognition system is shown. With respect to image acquisition, good-quality images are necessary to provide a robust iris recognition system. Still, most current implementations of iris recognition systems require users to fully cooperate with the system. At preprocessing, the pupil and the outer boundary of the iris are detected. Subsequently, the vast majority of iris recognition algorithms unwraps the iris ring to a normalized rectangular iris texture. To complete the preprocessing, the contrast of the resulting iris texture is enhanced applying histogram stretching methods. Based on the preprocessed iris texture, feature extraction is applied. Most iris recognition algorithms follow the approach of Daugman [116] by extracting a binary feature vector, which is commonly referred to as "iris-code." While Daugman suggests to apply 2D Gabor filters in the feature extraction stage, plenty of different methods have been proposed. Most comparison techniques apply the bit-wise XOR-operator to decide whether two iris-codes have the same biometric source (match) or not (non-match). The decision is based on a comparison score by counting the number of miss-matching bits: the (fractional) HD, the minimum number of substitutions required to change one bit-string into the other (divided by the string length), indicates the grade of dissimilarity. Small fractional HD values indicate high similarity. In order to compensate against head tilts, template alignment is achieved by applying circular shifts in both directions. The minimum HD between two iris-codes refers to an optimal alignment. Hence,

C. Rathgeb et al., *Iris Biometrics: From Segmentation to Template Security*,
Advances in Information Security 59, DOI 10.1007/978-1-4614-5571-4_2,
© Springer Science+Business Media, LLC 2013

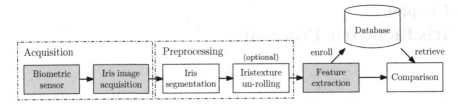

Fig. 2.1 Iris biometrics: the processing chain of a generic iris recognition system comprising image acquisition, image preprocessing, iris texture feature extraction, and recognition

the comparison of iris-codes can be performed in an efficient process, which can be parallelized easily. In contrast to other biometric systems based on different modalities requiring a more complex matching procedure, millions of comparisons can be done within one second. With respect to biometric recognition systems operating in identification mode, iris recognition algorithms are capable of handling large-scale databases. In addition, potential occlusions originating from eyelids or eyelashes are masked out during comparison by storing a bit-mask generated in the preprocessing step.

In the following sections the different tasks in iris recognition systems are described in more detail.

2.1   Image Acquisition

Image acquisition plays a critical role in iris recognition. The certification of inferior cameras has led to unpractical results in the past. Poor imaging conditions have been shown to affect the genuine score distribution, i.e. similarity score values typically decrease when comparing iris templates from the same subject under bad quality conditions. Impostor scores are largely independent of image quality [117]. However, it has to be mentioned that not only the camera itself, but also the entire environmental recording conditions have an important impact on the quality of the obtained biometric samples and the resulting recognition accuracy. Traditional systems have been quite restrictive and require active participation in the image capturing process, especially for cameras with small focal volumes (on-axis zones, where the iris can be captured in focus). Even in case of larger volumes, motion blur, occlusions, illumination, and other noise factors may be present when iris images are captured on-the-move and at-a-distance. Most commercial solutions therefore employ quality checks including feedback to the user (visual and/or acoustic) to assist the user in providing well-aligned (on-axis) noise-free biometric samples.

According to the Mitre report [574], there are four different camera types for iris acquisition, see Fig. 2.2:

1. *Access control*: Typically wall-mounted cameras capturing both eyes simultaneously with a moderate focal volume and requiring active user cooperation.

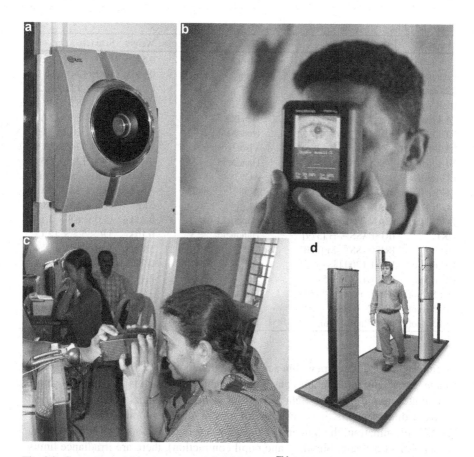

Fig. 2.2 Camera types: (**a**) access control (LG IrisAccess™ 3,000 system, photo by C. Delaere), (**b**) handheld (L1-Identity Pier™ 2.4 system, photo by S. Murphy, US Marine), (**c**) visor (Cogent 3M CIS 202 system, photo by K. Shanmugam), (**d**) portal (SRI Sarnoff IOM Passport™ system, photo by SRI International)

2. *Handheld*: Typically portable cameras with small focal volumes for single-eye capture and requiring attended capture.
3. *Dual-eye visor*: Cameras shielding both eyes from direct sunlight, requiring active cooperation and attended capture of both eyes simultaneously.
4. *Stand-off portal*: Next-generation portal devices with large focal volume, full portrait capture and requiring less active user cooperation (but users are required to look towards the camera).

All these camera models have a common operation scheme: Light is emitted from a near infrared (NIR) illumination source (emitting light with wavelengths between 700 and 900 nm), for example LEDs, reflected off the iris surface, and collected by the camera sensor. Even stand-off systems depend on controlled illumination. During exposure time, the iris must be within a sensor-dependent 3D volume and

Table 2.1 List of common commercial iris image acquisition devices

Manuf.	Product	Type	Dist. (cm)	Weight	Size (cm×cm×cm)
Crossmatch	I Scan™ 2 [106]	Visor	< 10	0.5 kg	15.3 × 15.7 × 5.0
Cogent 3M	CIS 202 [101]	Visor	12–14	0.56 kg	14.2×12.0×6.4
IrisGuard	IG-AD100® [219]	AC	21–37	0.7 kg	19.2 × 12.0×12.2
IrisKing	IKEMB-100 [220]	AC	22–40	–	33.5×18.5×7.9
L1-Identity	Pier™ 2.4 [287]	Handheld	10–15	0.5 kg	15.3 × 8.9 × 4.6
L1-Identity	HIIDE™ Ser. 4 [286]	Handheld	20–26	1.36 kg	12.7 × 20.3 × 7.6
L1-Identity	Mobile-eyes™ [285]	Visor	5.8	1 kg	17.5 × 7.1 × 20.6
L1-Identity	Pier-T™ [288]	Handheld	≈ 15	0.34 kg	9.0 × 12.5 × 6.5
LG/IrisID	IrisAccess™ 2200 [301]	AC	8–25	–	17.8 × 25.4 × 12.7
LG/IrisID	IrisAccess™ 3000 [302]	AC	8–25	3.64 kg	18.2 × 33.5 × 20.3
LG/IrisID	iCAM 4000 [216]	AC	26–36	2 kg	21.8 × 16.4 × 8.0
LG/IrisID	iCAM TD100 [217]	Handheld	36	0.23 kg	15.0 × 8.3 × 3.1
OKI	IRISPASS®-H [379]	Handheld	≈ 3	0.16 kg	5.9 × 5.2 × 12.1
OKI	IRISPASS®-M [380]	AC	30–60	5 kg	32.8 × 19.7 × 8.4
Panasonic	BM-ET200 [384]	AC	30–40	0.9 kg	20.3 × 19.0 × 7.7
Panasonic	BM-ET330 [385]	AC	30–40	2.4 kg	21.2 × 21.6 × 5.5
SRI Sarnoff	IOM Passport™ [494]	Portal	≈ 300	–	22.0 × 12.2 × 12.5
SRI Sarnoff	IOM N-Glance™ [493]	AC	53–80	0.9 kg	22 × 18 × 19
SRI Sarnoff	IOM RapID-Cam™ II [495]	Handheld	30–45	2 kg	24.1 × 28.9 × 15.2

oriented toward the camera within a narrow angular cone to produce a sharp in-focus image. Especially motion blur constitutes a challenge, which is targeted by using a fast shutter, requiring more light [337]. But also for maximizing the iris area and to avoid dilated pupils, it is desirable to have a certain illumination level. Since for NIR illumination, the human eye does not respond to its natural light avoiding mechanisms (aversion, blinking, and pupil contraction), there are irradiance limits [14, 102] of approximately 10 mw per centimeter for NIR illumination [407]. Therefore, light sources have to be quite close to the subject to be captured in order to produce high-quality input. According to Kalka et al. [242] the quality factors with highest impact on recognition accuracy are: Defocus blur, motion blur, and off-axis image acquisition (optical axes of eye and camera are not coaxial).

Table 2.1 lists well-known commercial enrollment systems by manufacturer, type, acquisition distance, weight, and size. Iris recognition has been shown to be practically applicable with respect to acquisition at distances of up to 10 m [142]; however, most devices operate at a much closer range (0.2–0.4 m).

The vast majority of commercial iris acquisition cameras captures iris images in the NIR band. In contrast to visible wavelength (VW) light, NIR rays are able to penetrate the surface of the iris and reveal structural patterns merely visible for heavily pigmented (dark-colored) irides [452]. The iris surface under VW appears smooth with hardly perceivable patterns for brown irides, because melanocytesin in the stroma are heavily pigmented. In contrast, blue irides exhibit a more irregular pattern under VW light, since they have a less pigmented stroma, see Fig. 2.3. The apparent absorbance spectrum of melanin in human skin is illustrated in

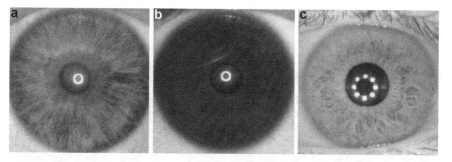

Fig. 2.3 The iris under visible wavelength light for (**a**) blue sample and (**b**) brown sample (taken from UPOL [383]) versus (**c**) under near infrared (taken from CASIA.v3-Interval [89])

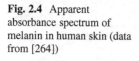

Fig. 2.4 Apparent absorbance spectrum of melanin in human skin (data from [264])

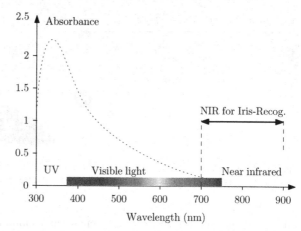

Fig. 2.4. Irides with only moderate levels of pigmentation can be captured rather well under visible light also [44], which is supported by several open VW iris databases. Typical iris cameras provide a 640×480 pixels sized image of the eye with an iris diameter of approximately 140–320 pixels [574].

2.2   Image Preprocessing

Iris image preprocessing comprises segmentation and normalization steps and is a crucial step for successful recognition. The goal of iris segmentation is to accurately and robustly locate the iris in images of the human eye regardless of the presence of noise (e.g., eyelids, eyelashes, reflections, or occlusions) for different people, sensors, and image properties like size, compression, or format. Figure 2.5a,b illustrate this process identifying pupillary and limbic boundaries. Usually, also occlusions are detected at this stage (e.g., by identifying specular

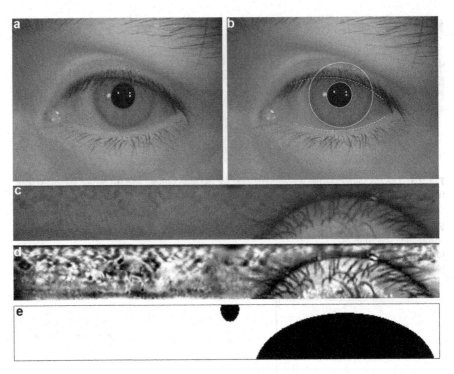

Fig. 2.5 Preprocessing steps: (**a**) original (taken from CASIA.v3-Lamp), (**b**) segmentation result, (**c**) iris texture before enhancement, (**d**) normalization result after enhancement, (**e**) noise mask

reflections and eyelid boundaries) and inpainting techniques are applied to remove specular reflections. Normalization uses the found pupillary and limbic boundaries of the iris to map the annular texture in the rectilinear iris image into a doubly dimensionless polar format, originally proposed by Daugman [116], see Fig. 2.5c,d. Noise masks as in Fig. 2.5e are used to mask areas of the iris texture, which should not be used for comparison, e.g. because the iris is occluded or areas have been inpainted due to reflections.

Typically, errors at the segmentation stage cannot be corrected at later stages in the processing chain, i.e. incorrect segmentation leads to false rejections. For both, rectilinear iris images and normalized iris textures, there are standardized (ISO/IEC 19794-6:2005) image formats permitting raw or compressed storage. For the storage of segmented iris images without normalization into doubly dimensionless coordinates, Daugman uses an ROI-encoded version with masked-out eyelids yielding a more compact representation [121]. Despite the more compact storage, rectilinear images are often preferred over normalized iris textures for iris image interchange, because of sampling and segmentation consistency problems [574].

There are several different approaches for iris segmentation, Chap. 5 presents major methodologies in more detail. Still, most methods are only minor refinements of two approaches [44]:

1. *Integro-differential operator*: Daugman's original approach [116] applies an exhaustive search for center and radius using an operator looking for the maximum in the blurred derivative with respect to increasing radius, of normalized contour integrals along circular trajectories. Both search procedures are performed simultaneously, with interdependency.
2. *Hough transform (HT)*: Wildes' [579] approach is similar, but uses binary edge maps and circular HT to localize pupillary and limbic boundaries. Votes in Hough space are accumulated to estimate the parameters (origin and radius) of the boundary circles. Again, this procedure is applied twice, for the inner and outer boundaries.

Other segmentation methods, like active contours (AC), active shape models (ASM), model-fitting and polar techniques, typically build upon and extend these two approaches. Still, iris segmentation is one of the most active research topics in iris biometrics, since many recognition errors result from insufficient segmentation capabilities. Apart from more accurate segmentation, coarse localization of the pupil has also attracted researchers, in order to speed up the segmentation process.

Before an iris image is subjected to feature extraction, it is important to guarantee a certain quality level. Quality of iris images is typically evaluated by assessing the sharpness of the pupil/iris boundary [44], for which a patent by Zhang and Salganicoff [610] and several research papers exist. Common techniques employed for iris quality assessment are: Fourier spectral analysis (high frequencies are typically missing in blurred images) and kernels for focus assessment [113, 246], Neural networks (NN) [405], Gaussian mixture models (GMM) [274] as a probabilistic model for representing the presence of subpopulations within an overall population using Gaussians, maximization of the integro-differential operator value as a measure of iris circularity after affine transform for off-axis estimation [242, 476], and fusion of quality factors by using Dempster–Shafer theory [242].

2.3 Feature Extraction

The purpose of the feature extraction module is to generate a compact representation of the biometric characteristic in order to alleviate the comparison (matching) process. For each biometric sample (normalized iris image) s within a universe of samples S, an (iris) *feature extractor* is a function $E : S \to F$, which maps each sample $s \in S$ to its feature vector representation $f \in F$ in feature space. At enrollment, these features are stored in a so-called *system database*: Let M denote the database of n enrolled members, $M := \{m_1, m_2, \dots m_n\}$, then each member $m_i \in M$ is characterized as a tuple $m_i := (i, f_i)$ for $i = 1, \dots, n$ where i is the member's label (user ID) and f_i is the corresponding stored template (feature vector).

Many different feature extraction methods have been proposed for iris recognition, see [44, 553] for comparisons. Table 2.2 lists a selection of feature extraction techniques distinguished by the type of generated feature vectors: Binary and

Table 2.2 Selection of various different iris biometric feature extraction algorithms

Authors	Ref.	Description	Type
Boles and Boashash	[37]	Zero-crossing representation of 1D wavelet transform	Real
Chen and Yuan	[84]	Local fractal dimension	Binary
Chen et al.	[83]	Gradient direction coding with Gray code versus delta modulation coding	Binary
Chou et al.	[95]	Convolution with Laplacian-of-Gaussian filter	Binary
Chu et al.	[96]	Linear prediction cepstral coefficients and linear discriminant analysis (LDA)	Real
Daugman	[116]	2D Gabor wavelet representation and quantizing the phase information with 2 bits	Binary
de Martin–Roche et al.	[334]	Zero-crossing discrete dyadic wavelet transform	Real
Dorairaj et al.	[134]	Principal component analysis (PCA) and independent component analysis (ICA) on entire iris region	Real
Hosseini et al.	[204]	Shape analysis techniques applied to adaptive filter result	Real
Huang et al.	[207]	Independent component analysis (ICA) on small windows	Real
Ives et al.	[224]	Normalized histogram of pixel values	Real
Ko et al.	[261]	Cumulative-sum-based change analysis	Binary
Liam et al.	[313]	Self organizing map networks	Real
Ma et al.	[322]	Gabor filters (2 scales) and Fisher's LDA	Real
Ma et al.	[323]	1D dyadic wavelet transform around the inner part of the iris.	Binary
Miyazawa et al.	[347]	Phase only correlation (2D DFT)	Real
Monro et al.	[348]	1D discrete cosine transform (DCT) on diamond-shaped overlapping image patches	Binary
Noh et al.	[376]	Thresholded (1 bit) wavelet frame decomposition with 1D Haar wavelets as local feature (results are combined with a geometric moment as global feature).	Binary
Rydgren et al.	[461]	Wavelet packet approach	Binary
Sun et al.	[499]	Convolution of the gradient vector field with a Gaussian filter and quantizing the phase information in 6 bins	Binary
Tisse et al.	[525]	Instantaneous phase and emergent frequency (Hilbert transform) for iris texture demodulation	Binary
Thoonsaengngam et al.	[524]	Local histogram equalization and quotient thresholding	Binary
Vatsa et al.	[555]	1D Log–Gabor and Euler number	Binary
Wildes	[579]	Isotropic band-pass decomposition from Laplacian-of-Gaussian (LoG) filters	Real
Xu et al.	[590]	Intersecting cortical model network	Binary

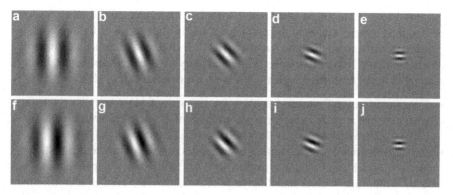

Fig. 2.6 Examples of (**a**)–(**e**) odd and (**f**)–(**j**) even Gabor filters at different rotations and frequencies

real-valued methods. Compared to real-valued techniques, binary feature vectors follow Daugman's iris-code approach [116] supporting the matching process by quantizing intermediate features to get a more stable and compact template that can be effectively compared. Despite the variety of available techniques, all main commercial systems apply Daugman's iris-code algorithm based on 2D Gabor wavelets. The 2D Gabor function is a product of an axis-stretched Gaussian and a complex plane wave, generalized by Daugman [108, 123] as follows:

$$G(x,y) = e^{-\pi\left((x-x_0)^2\alpha^2+(y-y_0)^2\beta^2\right)}e^{-2\pi i\left(u_0(x-x_0)+v_0(y-y_0)\right)} \qquad (2.1)$$

where β/α is the aspect ratio of the Gaussians, (x_0,y_0) is the center in the spatial domain and (u_0,v_0) specify harmonic modulation with spatial frequency $\sqrt{u_0^2+v_0^2}$ and orientation $\arctan(v_0/u_0)$ [123]. Examples of real (even symmetric) and imaginary (odd symmetric) Gabor filters are given in Fig. 2.6. From the output of the convolution result, phase information only is used and quantized with two bits (four states) encoding the phase quadrant. By this operation, illumination, camera gain and other noise factors, which typically affect magnitude information only, are suppressed [116].

2.4 Comparison

Recognition by biometric characteristics involves a comparison of feature vectors. Two feature vectors are compared by executing a biometric *comparator*, which is a function $C : F \times F \to \mathbb{R}$ returning a similarity (or dissimilarity) score $C(f_1,f_2)$ indicating the degree how much two feature vectors $f_1, f_2 \in F$ resemble each other. Note that the term *matching* as a synonym for *comparison* has been deprecated in the ISO SC37 Harmonized Biometric Vocabulary. Adequate comparators have to be designed depending on biometric features and modalities, in order to provide a proper comparison of biometric templates [227]. As mentioned earlier, the majority of iris-biometric feature extractors generate binary biometric templates. A binary representation of biometric features offers two major advantages [115]:

- *Compact storage*: Compared to the vast majority of biometric characteristics which require a more complex representation of extracted reference data, iris-codes usually consist of a few thousand bits (e.g., 2,048 bits in [116]).
- *Rapid authentication*: comparisons of iris-codes can be performed in an efficient process (which can be parallelized easily), i.e. millions of comparisons can be done within one second handling large-scale databases, even in identification mode.

Comparisons between binary iris-biometric feature vectors are commonly implemented by the simple Boolean exclusive-OR operator (XOR) applied to a pair of binary biometric feature vectors, masked (AND'ed) by both of their corresponding mask templates to prevent occlusions caused by eyelids or eyelashes from influencing comparisons. The XOR operator $\oplus$ detects disagreement between any corresponding pair of bits, while the AND operator $\cap$ ensures that the compared bits are both deemed to have been uncorrupted by noise. The norms ($|| \cdot ||$) of the resulting bit vector and of the AND'ed mask templates are then measured in order to compute a fractional HD as a measure of the (dis-)similarity between pairs of binary feature vectors {codeA, codeB} and the according mask bit vectors {maskA, maskB} [115]:

$$HD = \frac{||(\text{codeA} \oplus \text{codeB}) \cap \text{maskA} \cap \text{maskB}||}{||\text{maskA} \cap \text{maskB}||}. \tag{2.2}$$

Template alignment is performed within a single dimension, applying a circular shift of iris-codes. The main reason for shifting one of the two paired iris-codes is to obtain a perfect alignment, i.e. to tolerate a certain amount of relative rotation between the two iris textures. Since iris-codes are composed of localized features, bit shifts in an iris-code correspond to angular shifts of the underlying iris texture. It is a very natural approach to preserve the best match only, i.e. the minimum HD value over different shifts, because this value most likely corresponds to the best alignment of two codes. The impact of bit shifts on interclass comparisons has been shown to just skew the distribution to the left and reduce its mean [116]. In Fig. 2.7 the procedure of aligning two iris-codes during comparison is illustrated.

While for most biometric modalities, e.g. fingerprints, comparisons represent an essential task and require complex procedures, within iris biometrics trivial comparisons based on HD calculations have been established. It is generally conceded that more sophisticated comparison techniques which may require additional computational effort improve the recognition accuracy or iris biometric recognition systems (see Chap. 9).

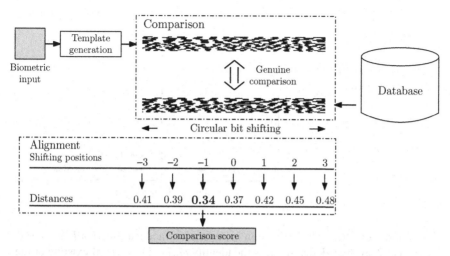

Fig. 2.7 Iris-biometric comparator: Iris-codes are circularly shifted in order to obtain an optimal alignment (minimal dissimilarity score)

Once subjects are enrolled to a biometric system and according reference data (templates) are stored in databases, biometric authentication can be performed in two different operation modes:

1. *Verification*, which involves a 1 : 1 comparison. In verification mode the subject is required to raise an identity claim, i.e. the subject claims to be a distinct person which has previously registered with the system. This can be done by employing IDs, cards, or external knowledge- or token-based unique identifiers. Subsequently, the according template is looked up in the database and compared to the given one. With respect to an adequate threshold the biometric comparator yields acceptance or rejection [451]:

   Given a biometric sample s and a claimed identity $i \in \{1, \ldots, n\}$, in verification mode a function $V : S \times M \to \{genuine, impostor\}$ is evaluated, determining whether the claim is true (belonging to the class *genuine*) or false (belonging to the class *impostor*), based on a threshold η:

$$V(s, m_i) := \begin{cases} genuine, & if \ C(E(s), f_i) \geq \eta \\ impostor, & else. \end{cases} \quad (2.3)$$

2. *Identification*, which involves a 1 : n comparison, where n is the number of subjects registered with the system. In identification mode the subject is not required to raise an identity claim, i.e. the extracted biometric template is compared to every single template in the reference database. Once a rank-1 candidate (the template which exhibits the highest degree of similarity to the given one) is discovered, acceptance or rejection is yielded based on an adequate threshold [451].

Fig. 2.8 Performance of an (iris) biometric system: Interrelation between false rejection rate (FRR), false acceptance rate (FAR) and equal error rate (EER)

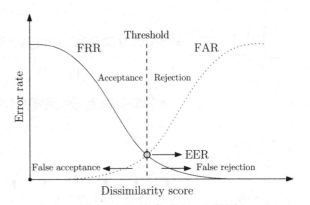

For a biometric sample $s \in S$, in identification mode, a function $I : S \to M \cup \{reject\}$ is evaluated, determining the identity $m_i, i \in \{1, \ldots, n\}$ if existing or the state *reject* in case of no suitable identity can be determined:

$$I(s) := \begin{cases} m_i, & if \ i = \underset{j}{\arg\max}\{C(E(s), f_j)\} \wedge C(E(s), f_i) \geq \eta \\ reject, \ else. \end{cases} \tag{2.4}$$

In case of large-scale data sets biometric database indexing can be applied to reduce computational effort. Regarding iris biometrics, different approaches to database indexing have been proposed [175, 428].

Several metrics exist when measuring the performance of biometric systems. Most important factors include false rejection rate (FRR), false acceptance rate (FAR), and equal error rate (EER) [229]. While the FRR defines the "proportion of verification transactions with truthful claims of identity that are incorrectly rejected", the FAR defines the "proportion of verification transactions with wrongful claims of identity that are incorrectly confirmed" (ISO/IEC FDIS 19795-1). The genuine acceptance rate (GAR) is defined as $GAR = 1 - FRR$. As score distributions overlap, FAR and FRR intersect at a certain point (FRR=FAR), defining the EER of the system. According to intra- and interclass accumulations generated by biometric algorithms, FRRs and FARs are adjusted by varying system thresholds. In general, decreasing the FRR (corresponds to increasing the GAR) increases the FAR and vice versa. The interrelation between FRRs and FARs and resulting EERs is illustrated in Fig. 2.8. Sometimes, instead of FAR and FRR, rates called false match rate (FMR) and false non-match rate (FNMR) are reported. These rates refer to similar errors, but do not include errors specific to biometrics [38], such as the failure-to-enroll rate (FTE), the proportion of people failing to enroll successfully.

For visualizing biometric system errors, often receiver operating characteristic (ROC) curves are used, these are curves of GAR and FAR (or, 1-FNMR and FMR) pairs for varying thresholds describing a biometric system. Detection error trade-off (DET) represents a variant of ROC with FRR and FAR (or FNMR and FMR) pairs, often using logarithmic scales.

In identification mode, the situation is slightly different with the corresponding hypotheses for false accepts and false rejects referring to the existence of an enrolled template in the system database with the same identity. In this context, a false accept occurs, if the template under test is found to be matched with a template of an enrolled member, but indeed they do not share the same identity. False rejects denote falsely rejected genuine authentication attempts. Since the size of the gallery may influence results, usually systems are evaluated in verification mode. However, there are situations, e.g. for testing prescreening techniques, where such an evaluation is not useful. In this case, the rank-1 recognition rate (RR-1), the rate of the correct identity being ranked at first position in identification mode, is reported. By analogy, rank-n recognition rates can be given additionally in cumulative match characteristic (CMC) representations.

Chapter 3
State-of-the-Art in Iris Biometrics

Iris biometrics has received remarkable attention in the biometric community due to its unrivaled properties. Possessing epigenetic (not genetically determined) pattern information apart from color, the iris is widely employed as a biometric identifier because of its high *universality* (almost every person has the characteristic), *distinctiveness* (high discriminative power due to its entropy), *permanence* (stability except for pigmentation change over time), and *performance* (accuracy and speed). While according to the classification by Jain et al. in 2004 [229] there are other modalities with better *collectability* (the characteristic can well be measured), *acceptability* (people are willing to provide the characteristic), and *circumvention* (how easy the system can be fooled) properties, a lot of research effort has been invested to improve iris recognition with respect to these biometric properties. Typically, a good way to find a suitable biometric modality for a target application is to formulate conditions according to the characteristics. Wayman [575] classifies applications in a binary manner according to *cooperativity* (users are required to cooperate with the system), *user-awareness* (ouvert vs. covert acquisition), *habituation* (usability of the system), *attendance* (presence of operators), *standard environment* (indoors vs. outdoors), *publicity* (whether the system is open to public users), and *biometric data exchange* (being open or closed to exchange with other systems). Apart from the mainstream of cooperative, habituated, attended, indoor, private and closed applications, iris research has focused on noncooperative, covert, unattended, and outdoor applications, as well as approaches to facilitate iris biometric data exchange by conducting several challenges in the past, which are discussed in detail in Sect. 3.2. like the Noisy Iris Challenge Evaluation (NICE) [483], Multiple Biometric Grand Challenge (MBGC) [374], or Iris Challenge Evaluation (ICE) [372].

The world's largest biometric deployment, the Aadhaar project [548] by the Unique Identification Authority of India employs iris and fingerprints in a multi-biometric configuration to issue a unique identification number to each Indian resident launched in 2009. It has affirmed that iris biometrics exhibits excellent performance with its rapidly attenuating tails of the impostor score distribution: in a recent report [549] failure-to-enroll rates as low as 0.14%, false positive

C. Rathgeb et al., *Iris Biometrics: From Segmentation to Template Security*,
Advances in Information Security 59, DOI 10.1007/978-1-4614-5571-4_3,
© Springer Science+Business Media, LLC 2013

identification rates as low as 0.057%, and false negative identification rates of 0.035% were reported for the entire multibiometric system using a database of 84 million gallery samples. Performance studies of iris recognition technology have been performed since the early days of iris recognition [574]. Among the most visible reports are the Independent Testing of Iris Recognition Technology by IBG in 2005 [552], Daugman's report from the analysis of 200 billion iris comparisons in UAE's border control programme in 2006 [117], AuthentiCorps' Iris Recognition Study 2006 [19], the Technology Assessment for the State-of-the-Art Biometrics Excellence Roadmap by Mitre in 2009 [574], the recent Iris Recognition Exchange reports IREX I in 2009 [173], IREX II in 2011 [506], and IREX III in 2012 [172], as well as the open iris challenges introduced before. A common property revealed among all studies are remarkably flat ROC curves, i.e. iris recognition is suitable to be applied in scenarios where low FARs are requested. Nonetheless, it is difficult to compare reported error rates, since the FNMR is largely influenced by the number of low quality images [506].

3.1   Databases

The advance in the state-of-the-art in iris recognition is probably best perceived by investigating the type of open iris datasets, being part of challenges or published as donations for public research. Claims of biometric systems to demonstrate excellent performance based on closed or proprietary datasets are difficult to reproduce, making public datasets a valuable means to compare existing approaches. According to Flynn [153], biometric databases should be *relevant* (large number of intra-class samples, i.e. of the same person, in identification mode), *large* (size should exceed the required lower bound needed to support the claimed accuracy), *representative* (vary in gender, age, and other demographic properties), *targeted* (with respect to specific sensor types, models, etc.), *tagged* (provide meta information), *time-variant* (characteristics are captured over large time spans), and *un-edited* (without post-processing).

There are several different biometric databases available to iris recognition, see Fig. 3.1 for corresponding iris samples. Table 3.1 lists common open sets with detailed characteristics, which are freely disposable for research purposes. Lists of available biometrics databases for other modalities may be found in [153]. Further comments on comparing some of the listed iris databases are given by Proença et al. [409]. The *Bath* dataset [550] provides extraordinary high resolution (1,280 × 960 pixels) and is JPEG2000 encoded. One of the most well-known iris datasets is provided by the Institute of Automation, Chinese Academy of Sciences (CASIA): the Biometrics ideal test datasets [89]. Being one of the first available public datasets, *CASIA.v1* concentrated on feature extraction and (to preserve intellectual rights on their illumination system) comes with an edited pupillary area [393] allowing for rather simple segmentation methods. *CASIA.v2* consists of images captured by two sensors and is, like the previous database,

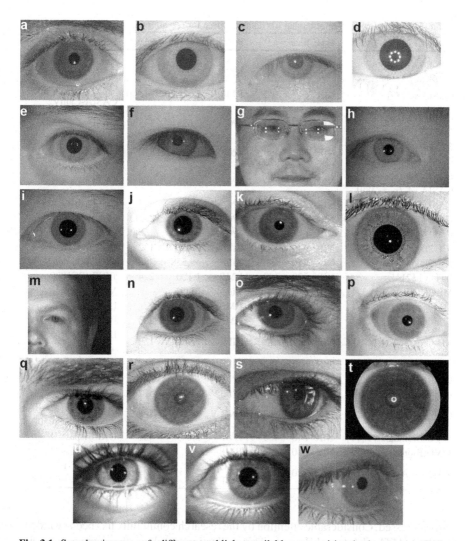

Fig. 3.1 Sample images of different publicly available open iris databases: (**a**) Bath, (**b**) CASIA.v1, (**c**) CASIA.v2, (**d**) CASIA.v3-Interval, (**e**) CASIA.v3-Lamp, (**f**) CASIA.v3-Twins, (**g**) CASIA.v4-Distance, (**h**) CASIA.v3-Thousand, (**i**) CASIA.v4-Syn, (**j**) ICE 2005, (**k**) ICE 2006, (**l**) IIT-D, (**m**) MBGC-NIRVideo, (**n**) MMU.1, (**o**) MMU.2, (**p**) ND-CrossSensor, (**q**) ND-Iris-0405, (**r**) UBIRIS.v1, (**s**) UBIRIS.v2, (**t**) UPOL (**u**) WVU-Biomdata.v1, (**v**) WVU-Biomdata.v2, (**w**) WVU-OffAxis

Table 3.1 Overview of common open iris databases free for research purposes

Dataset	Type	Size	Format	Images	Classes	Sensor
Bath [550]	NIR	1,280 × 960	J2K	1,600	800	ISG LW-1.3S-1394
CASIA.v1 [89]	NIR	320 × 280	BMP	756	108	CASIA-Cam
CASIA.v2 [89]	NIR	640 × 480	BMP	2 × 1,200	2 × 60	OKI Irispass-H CASIA-CamV2
CASIA.v3-Interval [89] CASIA.v4-Interval [89]	NIR	320 × 280	JPG	2,639	395	CASIA-Cam
CASIA.v3-Lamp [89] CASIA.v4-Lamp [89]	NIR	640 × 480	JPG	16,212	819	OKI Irispass-H
CASIA.v3-Twins [89] CASIA.v4-Twins [89]	NIR	640 × 480	JPG	3,183	400	OKI Irispass-H
CASIA.v4-Distance [89]	NIR	2,352 × 1,728	JPG	2,639	395	CASIA-LR-Cam
CASIA.v4-Thousand [89]	NIR	640 × 480	JPG	20,000	2,000	Irisking IKEMB-100
CASIA.v4-Syn [89]	NIR	640 × 480	JPG	10,000	1,000	N/A (Synthetic)
ICE 2005 [372]	NIR	640 × 480	TIFF	2,953	132	LG 2200
ICE 2006 [372]	NIR	640 × 480	TIFF	59,558	480	LG 2200
IITD.v1 [214]	NIR	320 × 240	BMP	1,120	224	JIRIS JPC1000
MBGC-NIRVideo [374]	NIR	2,000 × 2,000	Video	571	–	MBGC-Portal
MMU.1 [357]	NIR	320 × 240	BMP	450	92	LG 2200
MMU.2 [357]	NIR	320 × 238	BMP	995	200	Panas. BM-ET100
ND-CrossSensor [103]	NIR	640×480	TIFF	264,945	1,352	LG 2200 + LG 4000
ND-Iris-0405 [103]	NIR	640 × 480	TIFF	64,980	712	LG 2200
UBIRIS.v1 [485]	VW	200 × 150	JPEG	1,877	246	Nikon E5700
UBIRIS.v2 [486]	VW	400 × 300	TIFF	11,102	522	Canon 5D
UPOL [383]	VW	576 × 768	PNG	384	128	TOPCON TRC50IA + Sony DXC-950P
WVU-Biomdata.v1 [71]	NIR	640 × 480	BMP	3,043	462	OKI Irispass-H
WVU-Biomdata.v2 [71]	NIR	640 × 480	BMP	763	144	OKI Irispass-H
WVU-OffAxis [71]	NIR	720 × 480	JPG,TIF	268	38	Sony DSC-F717
			BMP	597	146	EverFocus EQ100A

uncompressed. Considerable attention by the research community has been awarded to the *CASIA.v3-Interval* dataset. This collection employs the same sensor as *CASIA.v1*, but without darkened pupils. Like the next two sets, it is also available as part of the 4th version of the CASIA database. The *CASIA.v3-Lamp* dataset consists of less cropped eye images. *CASIA.v3-Twins* is dedicated to the analysis of iris images from monozygotic twins. Recently, the *CASIA.v4-Distance* dataset has been released, which—in contrast to most other iris databases—consists of full portrait NIR samples supporting the smooth transition from iris to ocular biometrics and pushing iris segmentation techniques towards extraction of iris images at-a-distance and on-the-move. The use of traditional face databases for iris biometrics research is typically difficult, because of the necessary minimum resolution of at least 150 pixels iris diameter for medium-quality iris images as per ISO 19794-6:2005(E). *CASIA.v4-Thousand* is a special dataset for methods like indexing techniques requiring a large number of subjects (1,000) and *CASIA.v4-Syn* is one of the few synthetic datasets including effects like blurring and rotation. The two *ICE* datasets 2005 and 2006 [372] mainly differ in the amount of provided sample images with the latter being targeted for a large-scale experiment, both datasets contain off-axis iris images. The iris database *IITD.v1* [214] resembles the characteristics of *CASIA.v3-Interval*, but employs a different sensor. MBGC [374] is a completely different dataset targeting at-a-distance capture, like *CASIA.v4-Distance*, and provides high-resolution (2,000×2,000 pixels) NIR video sequences from a portal challenge. MMU datasets [357] version 1 and version 2 represent low-resolution datasets. *ND-CrossSensor* and *ND-Iris-0405* are large datasets available from the University of Notre Dame [103] with the prior being dedicated to iris recognition algorithms for application across different iris sensors (LG 2200 and LG 4000 iris cameras are employed). The majority of available datasets are captured in NIR light due to reasons outlined in Sect. 2.1, only very few VW light databases exist, most notably the *UBIRIS* datasets [485, 486] provided by the University of Beira Interior with the latter *UBIRIS.v2* dataset being released as part of the NICE.I challenge for iris segmentation. The *UPOL* iris database [383] consists of color VW iris images acquired with an optometric framework under laboratory conditions. The Center for Identification Technology Research at West Virginia University (WVU) [71] offers multibiometric databases (*WVU-Biomdata.v1* and *WVU-Biomdata.v2*) providing iris data acquired using the mobile OKI IRISPASS-H device. Also available from WVU is a dataset with off-axis iris images (*WVU-OffAxis*) targeting better segmentation techniques being able to tolerate off-gaze.

With respect to the selection of a particular database, sample size and target image characteristics of the employed dataset is an important factor influencing recognition accuracy. Also the selection of the right database with respect to present noise factors, e.g. to illustrate the robustness of a particular segmentation algorithm, is a critical task, since bad quality images may degrade performance significantly [506]. Within this context, Table 3.2 lists subjectively perceived noise factors in different open iris datasets. Furthermore, detailed investigations by the research community have identified labelling errors in biometric datasets, requiring researchers to check for updates before employing a particular dataset. For example, in the ICE 2005 dataset image 246260.tiff of subject 289824 is erroneously classified as left eye [391]. Also in CASIA.v3-Interval labeling errors have been identified [90], which are corrected in the latest available versions.

3.2 Performance Challenges

There have been several free of charge open contests in iris recognition. One of the first open challenges to be conducted was the Iris Challenge Evaluation (ICE) 2005 [372] organized by NIST. The goal of this challenge was to promote the state-of-the-art in iris biometrics and to advocate this biometric modality in the

Table 3.2 Noise factors in common open iris databases

Dataset	Noise/quality degrading factor					
	Reflections	Off-gaze	Occlusions	Blur	Illumination	Size
Bath	★	★	★★	★★		
CASIA.v1			★			★
CASIA.v2	★		★		★★	★
CASIA.v3-Interval CASIA.v4-Interval	★★		★		★	
CASIA.v3-Lamp CASIA.v4-Lamp	★		★★		★★	★
CASIA.v3-Twins CASIA.v4-Twins	★		★★		★	★★
CASIA.v4-Distance	★★		★★		★	★★
CASIA.v4-Thousand	★		★★		★★	★
CASIA.v4-Syn	★		★			★
ICE 2005	★	★	★★	★		★
ICE 2006	★	★	★★	★		★
IITD.v1	★		★	★		
MBGC-NIRVideo	★★		★★	★		★★
MMU.1	★		★			★★
MMU.2	★	★	★			★★
ND-CrossSensor	★		★★	★	★★	★
ND-Iris-0405	★	★	★★	★		★
UBIRIS.v1	★★		★		★★	★★
UBIRIS.v2	★★	★★	★★	★	★★	★
UPOL	★					
WVU-Biomdata.v1	★	★	★	★		★
WVU-Biomdata.v2	★	★	★	★		★
WVU-OffAxis	★	★★	★			★

★: present, ★★: frequently/problematic

U.S. Government: 12 algorithms from 9 submitters were evaluated between August 2005 and March 2006. Experimental results on left and right irides reported in [391] yielded, that (1) 70 %–99 % GAR could be achieved at 0.1 % FAR with the top 5 algorithms exhibiting GARs higher than 99.5 % for the right eye (GARs for left eye were up to 1 % lower) and (2) correlation was found to be present between left and right irides' match scores for all algorithms and non-match scores for all algorithms except the ones submitted by WVU and CASIA.

Soon after ICE 2005, NIST initiated a second Iris Challenge Evaluation, the ICE 2006 [372] to be conducted combined with the Face Recognition Vendor Test (FRVT) 2006 from June 2006 until March 2007. The goal of this second challenge was an independent evaluation with sequestered data instead of a technology evaluation and to alleviate comparison between face and iris biometrics by employing a common testing protocol. Experiments outlined in [394] involve verification mode tests with an upper limit given on processing time (three weeks for all tests on a 3.6 GHz CPU). Algorithms from 3 groups are evaluated: Sagem–Iridian (SG-2), Iritech

(Irtch-2), and Cambridge (Cam-2). Results indicate interquartile range overlaps between all tested algorithms. For Cam-2 an average FRR as low as 0.01 at 0.001 FAR is reported, Irtch-2 and SG-2 have slightly higher mean FRRs at around 0.02. In contrast to ICE 2005, this time left eye results are slightly better than for right eyes. A large variation in processing time (6 h versus 300 h) is reported.

Building on the latter two challenges, from 2007 to 2009 NIST conducted the Multiple Biometrics Grand Challenge (MBGC) [374, 392]. Consisting of several subchallenges (still face, video and portal), the main goal of this project was to evaluate face and iris recognition technology on both still images and video towards more real-world-like scenarios: (1) exploring more realistic low resolution with 90–120 pixels across the eye, (2) evaluation of capturing conditions, (3) development of multimodal algorithms, (4) comparing video with still iris images, (5) assess controlled versus uncontrolled capture, and (6) evaluate across sensors (NIR vs. HD video) comparing different type of data. For iris, the portal challenge is of special interest as it has pushed development towards ocular biometrics. As sensor for high-quality iris images, an LG 2200 camera was employed. All contestants had to locate irides, segment and normalize iris texture, generate an iris template and combine results. Experiments of the portal challenge yielded [374] (1) still iris versus NIR video results of 20–95 % verification rate (VR) at 1 % FAR, but up to 98 % VR at 1 % FAR with missing and partial irides removed, (2) video iris versus NIR video accuracy of 20–95 % VR at 1 % FAR, (3) still face versus HD video results of 15–100 % VR at 1 % FAR, (4) still iris and still face versus NIR video and HD video VRs of 80–100 % at 0.1 % FAR. In summary, results were almost perfect for face, iris accuracy was promising, but raising the need for larger datasets and future experiments. Unconstrained video turned out to be the most difficult challenge.

The Noisy Iris Challenge Evaluation (NICE) organized in 2007–2009 by University of Beira Interior's SOCIA Lab was the first initiative towards iris recognition from unconstrained data. It was conducted in two separate parts (NICE.I [483] and NICE.II [484]) and employed VW instead of NIR iris images (in contrast to e.g., ICE). The UBIRIS.v2 dataset of largely Latin Caucasian irides (90 %) was employed in experiments with 15 eye images per session. The goal of NICE.I was to enhance the state of the art in iris segmentation and noise detection and was organized as a segmentation-only evaluation focusing on less-constrained image acquisition conditions and robustness to noise. Given an iris image, the challenge consisted in generating an iris mask image deciding on iris membership for each pixel. All participants were reported the classification error rate (proportion of disagreeing pixels with respect to ground truth based on 500 manually constructed binary segmentation masks), as well as type-I and type-II error rates (average between false positive rate and false negative rate). The best participants were invited to publish their results. From the 97 submitters, the algorithm by Tan et al. [510] with an error of 0.0131 % was selected as winner with the top 6 algorithms exhibiting errors less than 0.03 % [407]. Generally, clustering-based iris localization yielded best results, details of other approaches are discussed as part of the segmentation survey and may be briefly looked up in [407]. Most of the errors were caused by inaccurate pupillar boundary segmentation—in contrast to NIR data, where the pupillary boundary is easier to detect.

The subsequent NICE.II challenge in the 2009–2011 time frame has attracted 67 participants. In the second phase of NICE focus was put on encoding and comparison techniques. Given 2 iris images with corresponding binary segmentation masks, the challenge consisted in generating a dissimilarity score (i.e., extract template and perform comparison) following the conditions of a metric. Results of the challenge are briefly outlined in [43]. Based on decidability index [111] the best algorithm by Tan et al. [511] considers multibiometric combination (sum rule) of iris and periocular data based on global color-based features and local ordinal measures. Following the best decidability measure of 2.57, the top 4 algorithms exceeded a decidability of 1.5. Approaches are quite different employing, e.g. adaptive boosting of Gabor-based features, features based on Scale-invariant feature transform (SIFT, a rather scale-independent algorithm to detect and describe local features), local binary patterns and discriminable textons, and co-occurrence phase histograms. For verification experiments at 0.01 % FAR, two algorithms (CASIA and NU) correctly recognized more than half of the subjects. For identification experiments (using rank and cumulative rank histograms) relative performance differences compared to the verification contest are reported. For fusion experiments only little improvement was observed when combining approaches, with the product rule on the top 4 algorithms delivering best results. Finally, the impact of segmentation on recognition was evaluated (using less accurately segmented data) yielding a significant degradation in performance. Two algorithms [306, 505] were found to be most robust to less accurately segmented data.

3.3   Resource in Literature

Apart from literature of the early 1990s based on the works of Daugman [109] and Wildes [580], numerous proposals of diverse authors have been published. Until now there has been tremendous growth in the literature in the area of iris biometric recognition. In order to provide the reader with references and further reading, a short list of major works regarding iris recognition is presented:

- *General reference works*:
  - [227] Handbook of Biometrics, A. K. Jain, P. J. Flynn and A. A. Ross (Eds.), *Springer-Verlag*, 2008;
  - [312] Encyclopedia of Biometrics, S. Z. Li (Ed.), *Springer-Verlag*, 2009;
  - [63] Handbook of Iris Recognition, M. J. Burge and K. W. Bowyer (Eds.), *Springer-Verlag*, 2012.

  In order to get acquainted with biometrics in general, references [227] and [312] give an overview of biometric authentication systems including iris recognition as well as definition entries regarding concepts, modalities, algorithms, devices, systems, security, performance testing, applications, and standardization. The Handbook of Iris Recognition [63] represents a collection of diverse topics regarding iris biometrics, i.e. this book provides the reader with a more detailed overview of iris recognition.

- *Articles and Chapters*:

  - [116] J. Daugman: How iris recognition works, *IEEE Transactions on Circuits and Systems for Video Technology*, 14:1, 21–30, 2004;
  - [44] K. W. Bowyer, K. P. Hollingsworth and P. J. Flynn: Image understanding for iris biometrics: A survey, *Computer Vision and Image Understanding*, 110:2, 281–307, 2007;
  - [45] K. W. Bowyer, K. P. Hollingsworth and P. J. Flynn: A Survey of Iris Biometrics Research: 2008–2010, in *Handbook of Iris Recognition*, M. J. Burge and K. W. Bowyer (Eds.), *Springer-Verlag*, 2012.

Nowadays the vast majority of new proposals to iris recognition as well as public deployments are based on the work of Daugman. In [116] a detailed description of the concepts of Daugman's work, which most iris recognition systems build upon, is given. Bowyer et al. [44] presented a comprehensive survey on iris biometrics. This review article covers historical development and the state of the art up to 2007. More recently the authors proposed a detailed complementing book chapter which surveys iris biometric research form 2008 up to 2010.

This list of suggested literature is not intended to be exhaustive, but to quickly grasp the big picture of iris biometrics for researchers which are new to this field.

3.4 Reference Software

Until the expiration of the broad iris recognition patent by Flom and Safir (U.S. Patent 4641349) [152] in 2005, access to the market for companies with own iris algorithms has been limited. The expiration of U.S. Patent number 5291560 by Daugman [110] in 2011 protecting the iris-code approach now opens opportunities for even more competition in the iris recognition market. Nevertheless, there are not many open source iris recognition algorithms available:

- *Masek*: The probably most widespread publicly available iris recognition algorithm is provided by Masek and Kovesi [336], developed as part of Masek's thesis [335] and being an open-source re-implementation of Daugman's iris-code [116] approach. The MATLAB source code is provided for research and testing purposes and includes functions for segmentation, feature extraction, and comparison. Segmentation routines are based on circular HT, restricted to an interval of interest for pupil and iris radii, employing gamma correction, detecting eyelids with line HT and Canny edge detection, and eliminating eyelashes by thresholding. Feature extraction is based on convolving each row of an image with 1D Log–Gabor filters, using the polar iris representation with noise masks generating the iris template and according bit mask. Finally, the provided comparison functions take two biometric templates and bit masks as input to generate the fractional HD as output.

- *OSIRIS*: The Open Source for Iris (OSIRIS) [273, 275] reference system is—like Masek's software—based on Daugman's work. The software has been developed as a baseline algorithm for iris recognition within the BioSecure framework and provides executables for normalization, feature extraction, and matching. It is reported to outperform Masek's solution [273]. At the time of writing this book, the most recent available version is 2.01 as of 2009. Code is based on C++ and the OpenCV [215] framework. While the first version simply employed circular HT for segmentation, an AC approach is applied in version 2, initialized by the outcome of rough HT-based pre-localization refining the resulting mask. As feature extraction method, the normalized image is convolved with Gabor filters at pre-fixed points, mapping the resulting coefficients to a binary code. The matching module employs HD.

- *VASIR*: The Video-based Automatic System for Iris Recognition (VASIR) [297, 298, 375] is an iris recognition algorithm implemented by NIST for less-constrained distant video captures. It has been employed as a baseline reference for the MBGC challenge and consists of several components for image acquisition, eye region detection and extraction, quality-based selection, segmentation, normalization, feature extraction, and comparison. Segmentation employs fast morphological-based preselection on the Gaussian blurred binarized input. Classical circular HT is used for boundary fitting and line HT for eyelid detection. The normalization and feature extraction stages are based on Masek's algorithm. VASIR supports cross-scenario comparison (e.g., distant-video to classical-still) and utilizes OpenCV.

Together with this book, open source iris recognition software is made available under http://www.wavelab.at/sources/. This "University of Salzburg Iris Toolbox" (USIT) software package provides many reference implementations for image preprocessing, feature extraction, and recognition algorithms. From the available algorithms, the following image preprocessing techniques have been used for experiments in this book:

- *Weighted Adaptive Hough and Ellipsopolar Transforms [541] (WAHET)*, the iris segmentation algorithm based on a weighted adaptive Hough transform, iteratively refining an ROI to find an initial center point, which is used to polar transform the image and extract polar and limbic boundary curves one after another from an (ellipso-)polar representation discussed in Chap. 6;
- *Iterative Fourier-based Pulling and Pushing [540] (IFPP)*, an iris segmentation algorithm based on the iterative Hough transform proposed in Chap. 6 and successive refinement applications of Fourier-based trigonometry as well as pulling and pushing methods;
- *Contrast-adjusted Hough Transform [178] (CAHT)*, is a Masek-like [335] custom implementation of an HT approach using (database-specific) contrast

adjustment to enhance pupillary and limbic boundaries, Canny edge detection to detect boundary curves, and enhancement techniques to remove unlikely edges.

Furthermore, the following re-implementations of feature extraction techniques are employed in experiments and are available with USIT:

- *Ma* [323]: In this approach the normalized iris texture is divided into stripes to obtain 10 one-dimensional signals, each one averaged from the pixels of 5 adjacent rows (the upper 512×50 rows are analyzed only). Subsequently, a 1-D wavelet transform is applied to each of the ten 1-D intensity signals. Detected minima and maxima from two specific subbands serve as features where sequences of 1s and 0s are assigned to the iris-code until new maxima or minima are found. This whole process is applied to two subbands extracting a total number of $2 \times 512 \times 10 = 10,240$ bits.

- *Masek* [335]: This feature extraction algorithm resembles Daugman's feature extraction method and analyzes the same ten 1-D intensity signals as above using Log–Gabor filters on rows of the iris texture (as opposed to the 2D filters used by Daugman). Here, a row-wise convolution with a complex Log–Gabor filter is performed on the texture pixels. The phase angle of the resulting complex value for each pixel is discretized into 2 bits leading to a binary code consisting of $512 \times 20 = 10,240$ bits.

- *Ko* [261]: This feature extraction technique performs cumulative-sum-based change analysis. It is suggested to discard parts of the iris texture, from the right side [45°–315°] and the left side [135°–225°], since the top and bottom of the iris are often hidden by eyelashes or eyelids. The resulting texture is divided into basic cell regions (sized 8×3 pixels). For each basic cell region an average grayscale value is calculated. Then basic cell regions are grouped horizontally and vertically. It is recommended that one group should consist of five basic cell regions. Finally, cumulative sums over each group are calculated to generate an iris-code. If cumulative sums are on an upward slope or on a downward slope, these are encoded with 1s and 2s, respectively, otherwise 0s are assigned to the code. In order to obtain a binary feature vector the resulting iris-code is rearranged such that the first half contains all upward slopes and the second half contains all downward slopes. With respect to the above settings the final iris-code consists of 2,400 bits.

- *Rathgeb* [430]: In this algorithm, similar to the approach in [261], parts of the iris are discarded, [45°–315°] and [135°–225°]. By tracing light and dark intensity variations of grayscale values in horizontal stripes of distinct height, pixel-paths are extracted. For a height of 3 pixels each position within pixel-paths is encoded using 2 bits. For a total number of 21 stripes and a texture length of 256 pixels the resulting iris-code consists of 10,752 bits.

3.5 Recognition Performance: The State-of-the-Art

The state-of-the-art in iris recognition performance clearly depends on the quality of iris images [506]. Nevertheless, in case sufficient quality is retained, the iris is one of the best performing biometric modalities, as verified by a range of studies.

The first large-scale independent iris recognition evaluation with more than 100 thousand samples is the Independent Testing of Iris Recognition Technology (ITIRT) by the International Biometric Group in 2005 [552]. ITIRT was organized by the U.S. Department of Homeland Security (DHS) and Intelligence Technology Innovation Center in order to estimate state-of-the-art match rates, enrollment and acquisition rates, as well as level of effort (like transaction duration or FTA rates), in both intra-device and cross-device constellation. The study has been conducted using commercial hardware (LG IrisAccess 3000, OKI IRISPASS-WG, Panasonic BM-ET300) with a gallery of 24,627 and probe set of 87,004 iris-codes. With respect to failures, results [574] of ITIRT indicated 1.6–7.1 % FTE (no irides were enrolled) and 0.3–0.7 % FTA (none of three attempts per eye could be acquired). Mean enrollment duration was 32–35 s, mean transaction duration yielded 1.9–5 s for successful and 12.3–32.3 s for failed acquisition. Regarding accuracy, very flat ROC curves were observed with 0.58–1.57 % FNMR at 0.0004–0.0088 % FMR (at HD threshold $t = 0.334$), or 0.26–0.81 % EER for intra-device comparisons. Error rates for cross-device comparison were clearly higher: FNMR increases to 2.297–3.240 % (0.50–1.29 % EER) at comparable FMR. Presumably, Daugman's algorithm was found to ideally suite high security demands in identification mode with low requested FMR.

One of the first large-scale studies was presented by Daugman analyzing 200 billion iris comparisons from the United Arab Emirates' border control programme in 2006 [117]. In this study of 632,500 iris images, FMR was found to be less than 1 in 200 billion. Theoretical calculations yield HD thresholds to be set to 0.25 to obtain less than 1 false match in 10^{12} comparisons, and a threshold of 0.225 for less than 1 false match in 10^{15} comparisons. This exceptional property of iris recognition makes it an ideal candidate for large-scale identification systems: fractional HD values were found to be in the interval $[0.265, 0.750]$ and the impostor score distribution is reported to well fit a binomial probability density function. According to Daugman's study, a reasonable choice for the HD threshold is 0.33 for 1:1 matching and 0.22 for 1:n matching. The recommendation to use HD threshold of 0.33 for 1:1 matching is to achieve an FMR of 1 in a million and the HD = 0.22 threshold is in order to perform all-against-all cross-comparisons in a database like the UK of 60 million persons (single eye), i.e. 10^{15} comparisons without getting any false matches.

Another assessment of the state of the art has been conducted in AuthentiCorp's Iris Recognition Study 2006 (IRIS06) [19]. This study targets especially trade-offs between speed, image quality, capture volume, and accuracy. Again very low failure rates (three attempts per eye) could be verified: 0.35–3.39 % FTE and 1.5–6.9 %

FTA. Reported transaction duration is 7.9–21.4 s (including failures) and the total accuracy is 0.0–1.8 % FNMR using camera-specific algorithms (at HD threshold $t = 0.32$). Further findings comprise a flat ROC curve, similar performance for left and right eyes, and that a recording timespan of several minutes until weeks does not degrade performance.

Starting in 2007, NIST has conducted a program called The Iris Exchange (IREX) in several instances with specific goals. IREX I [173] evaluates the effect of compression on iris matching performance of commercial algorithms (Cambridge University, Cogent Systems, Crossmatch Technologies, Honeywell, Iritech, L1 Identity Solutions, LG, Neurotechnology, Retica Systems, Sagem) and the interoperability of formats (ROI encoded, polar). IREX II [506] targets large-scale iris quality calibration and evaluation. IREX III [172] is a large-scale (6.1 million images) performance evaluation of iris identification algorithms. The following insights were obtained by the study:

1. *Compression results*: IREX I suggests cropped images, if pre-localization is available (storage reduced to 50–80 KB in lossless mode), cropped and masked images as the primary exchange format (suitable for smartcard storage) and discourages the unsegmented polar format. JPEG and JPEG2000 negatively affected FNMRs and, for some algorithms, also FMRs.
2. *Speed results*: IREX I reports high variation with respect to computational efficiency (fastest implementations are more than twice as fast as the slowest). IREX III reports 0.02–0.8 s for template generation and 10^5–10^7 iris-code comparisons per second per core (factor 2 in accuracy between extremes). IREX III also found high variation in processing time (factor 400 between slowest and faster algorithm of same accuracy).
3. *Quality results*: IREX II concludes that differences in FNMRs between high- and low-quality images are as large as two orders of magnitude. The rejection of the 10 % lowest quality images reduces FNMR from 0.1 % to 0.07 %. Greatest impact on recognition accuracy in the order of effect have: usable iris area, iris pupil contrast, pupil shape, iris-sclera contrast, gaze angle, and sharpness (results on motion blur and signal-to-nose-ratio were inconclusive). In IREX III, the most accurate quality measure failed to provide low scores for 76.4 % of the poorest 2 % of false negative outcomes.
4. *Large-scale accuracy*: IREX III verification mode assessments yield FRRs of 1.5 % (single eye) and 0.7 % (both eyes) and 98.5 % RR-1 in identification mode. FAR can be arbitrarily low with reported 2.5 % FRR at 25 false matches in 10^{13} comparisons. Failures of left eye comparison are found to be correlated with right eyes (simultaneous off-gaze, occlusion by long eyelashes, etc.). Compared to face, iris exhibits 10^5 times fewer false positives than face (equal false negative identification rate). Some algorithms exhibit false positive rates independent of population size at a fixed operating threshold. FRR and FAR are found to be related to pupil and iris radii ratios (e.g., different dilations, large dilations).

3.6 Deployments of Iris Recognition

For the crossing of international borders, execution of financial transactions, signing treaties and other applications, reliable personal identification is inevitable. Traditional token-based methods and knowledge-based identification exhibit the drawback of not necessarily implying legal ownership, e.g. via theft or fraudulently passed tokens or knowledge [38]. There are even applications like negative recognition (i.e., screening subjects against a watchlist) working only in case a person cannot deny of having a certain identity, a condition which is supported by using biometrics. This property and further ways how biometrics facilitate our daily lives in several ways are given in [332]:

- *Permanence*: Biometric characteristics are bound to an identity and may neither be lost without intention nor forgotten like passwords.
- *Singularity*: For characteristics like the human *iris*, there is evidence for uniqueness.
- *Efficiency and user convenience*: Biometric systems enable high throughput and accuracy at low cost.

Since no biometric is considered optimal in a sense that it meets requirements of all applications [332], today many applications target multiple biometrics at the same time. There is a clear trend towards portal-based, at-a-distance, on-the-move and unattended acquisition. Especially for iris recognition, which is likely to be employed for large-scale applications because of its excellent uniqueness properties, there is a growing demand for these properties.

Until now iris recognition has been successfully applied in diverse access control systems managing large-scale databases. Especially at airports and border crossings, iris recognition represents a widely adopted technique. Examples of iris recognition deployments are described by Daugman [119], Wayman et al. [574], and Iris ID Inc. [218].

For instance, the UK project IRIS (Iris Recognition Immigration System) has identified over a million frequent travelers on different UK airports including London Heathrow and Gatwick, Manchester and Birmingham for automated border-crossing using iris recognition [542]. After quick registration (usually between 5 and 10 min), enrolled passengers do not even need to assert their identity. They just look at the camera in the automated lanes crossing an IRIS barrier in about 20 s. In 2009, the Unique Identification Authority of India (UIDAI) started issuing a 12-digit so-called Aadhaar number to each Indian resident [548]. This number is linked to biometric information including a photograph, ten fingerprints and iris, making it the most widely deployed biometric system. De-duplication procedures checking for similarities with respect to the recorded biometric information guarantee that nobody is enrolled twice in the system. Aadhaar's primary goal is to provide a form of identity to identity-less persons and thus to provide the basis for better delivery of services like the entry for poor residents into the formal banking system, availability of financial aids, and effective governance. As of February 2012, more than 200

Table 3.3 High-visibility implementations of iris biometric systems

Name	Country	Enrollments	Purpose
UIDAI Aadhaar	India	>200 million (2012)	National identity number for financial aids, governance, etc. [548]
UNHCR Repatriation	Afghanistan	>2 million (2008)	Refugee registration for aid (assistance package, food, etc.) [547]
UAE Border Control	UAE	>1.5 million (2008)	Expellees tracking and border control in the United Arab Emirates [122]
TSA CLEAR	US	>175 thousand (2008)	Frequent traveler border crossing at major US airports [9]
National Airport Sec.	Canada	>150 thousand (2010)	Security solution at 29 Canadian airports [218]
IRIS	UK	>100 thousand (2009)	Heathrow, Manchester, Birmingham and Gatwick airports border control [542]
NEXUS	US, Canada	>100 thousand (2006)	Frequent traveler border-crossing [66]
York County Prison	US	>35 thousand (2012)	Inmates registration [218]
Privium	Netherlands	>30 thousand (2009)	Frequent traveler border control at Schiphol airport using smartcard [474]

million people have been issued a number, while the designated goal of UIDAI is to enroll all 1.2 billion citizens of India. Many more high-visibility implementations of iris biometric systems are listed in Table 3.3.

3.7 Open Issues

While widespread deployments have shown that iris recognition works well under constrained environmental conditions, there are still many yet insufficiently addressed questions regarding unattended or uncooperative capture. As raised in [8] not only accuracy is important for applications, but also other influencing factors, like the ability to circumvent biometric detection systems, cost of biometric sensors, or enrollment and transaction times. As part of the State-of-the-Art Biometrics Excellence Roadmap (SABER) study in 2007–2008, the MITRE Corporation as the executing body has worked with governmental agencies mandated to survey biometric methods and has identified the following open issues in their report [574]:

1. Long-term (10 years) multispectral data collection to determine stability.
2. Investigation of VW images in low- and high-resolution for surveillance-based biometrics.
3. Exploration of human-aided recognition to be admissible at court.
4. Development of at-a-distance on-the-move systems.

With respect to multispectral recognition, research work by Boyce et al. [46] and Ross [454] show promising results and raise new questions regarding segmentation. Among the several tasks in iris biometrics, image preprocessing is one of the most critical steps, which has attracted many researchers in recent years [44, 407] to develop more accurate segmentation techniques of less intrusively captured iris images. Since iris biometrics uses patterns of the iris of an individual's eye for human recognition, it is necessary to employ a robust method to identify the region within an image, which represents the "iris pattern," and regions, which contain "non-iris" data, e.g., skin, eyebrows, sclera, or eyelashes. Without a proper segmentation and normalization, recognition rates typically significantly decrease. This is due to non-overlapping iris parts unlikely producing similar features [116], and the inclusion of non-iris or exclusion of iris pixels likely leading to mapping errors, deforming the normalized template and thus yielding a bad alignment [541].

Despite significant improvement in verification capabilities for face recognition with 1 % False Reject Rate (FRR) at 0.1 % False Accept Rate (FAR) reported at [371] required accuracy for authentication (0.1 % FRR at 0.1 % FAR) and large-scale identification (0.001 % FRR at 0.0001 % FAR) as quantified in [229] is yet to be achieved for this modality. With the addition of iris biometrics and multibiometric techniques (combining face and iris techniques as well as different iris algorithms in multiple-matcher configurations) not only recognition rates are expected to increase drastically (see [159, 568, 572, 614]), but also a relaxation of typically restrictive recording conditions in the domain of iris recognition may be feasible. There is also a patent for iris and face fusion [129].

Using surveillance-type imagery for biometric recognition purposes is a promising idea. In particular, applying face and iris biometrics to semi-constrained face imagery is a prospective application. Initially, face and iris biometric fusion has been proposed by Wang et al. [572] for Eigenfaces and dyadic wavelet-transform-based iris recognition (see [323]). They report perfect separation on randomly paired datasets (450 face and 450 iris images of 90 subjects). However, still these two technologies are rather different in both image recording conditions (e.g., face images are typically acquired in VW, while iris images in NIR) and biometric properties, requiring some effort to build high-accuracy single-sensor multibiometric systems composed of these two modalities.

The impact of visual (non-NIR) imagery (e.g., surveillance video or high-quality digital passport images as templates) on iris recognition and cross-sensor comparisons are active research topics. Less restrictive capture devices and image enhancement techniques for semi-constrained surveillance scenarios are being developed and researched.

Part II
Iris Image Processing and Biometric Comparators

Chapter 4
Eye Detection

Biometric systems without active participation of users by means of which people can be identified in surveillance scenarios represent an active research topic. Unconstrained iris recognition is a relatively new branch in iris biometrics. It is driven by the demands to push biometric image acquisition towards an extraction of biometric signals with the subject of interest moving or being at-a-distance from biometric sensors. Advantages of such systems comprise better usability, higher throughput, and the ability to acquire biometric measurements without required cooperation. While iris recognition in reasonably constrained environments provides high confidence authentication with EERs of less than 1% [44], a reduction of constraints is quite challenging. First-generation prototype iris identification systems, designed for stand-off video-based iris recognition, e.g. Sarnoff's Iris-on-the-move [337], or General Electric's Stand-off Iris Recognition system [578], have proven the feasibility of iris recognition from surveillance-type imagery. In addition, the need for better segmentation techniques than usually applied in still-image iris recognition to account for distortions like motion blur, de-focusing, or off-axis gaze direction have been identified as main issues. Challenges like the Multiple Biometric Grand Challenge (MBGC) [374] have provided standardized datasets to aid in finding solutions to these problems. This new generation of portal-based iris-and-face recognition devices [337,578] operates on full portrait images and is about to replace traditional *stop and stare* iris recognition cameras with low throughput and narrow depth of field. Whereas initially not targeted as *iris segmentation* issues, they also raise the need for reliable eye detection techniques. This task is different from iris segmentation in being a *detection* instead of a *localization* task, i.e. the assumption, that a single iris is present in the input image is not generally valid. While a variety of general purpose object detectors exist, especially for iris biometrics it is desirable to exploit multiple existing techniques; therefore, an approach combining multiple single detectors to form a more robust face and face-part classifier [539] is presented and discussed in this chapter.

The recognition of people from facial or more generic images employing iris as biometric modality requires the tasks of *face detection* and *eye localization* to be

C. Rathgeb et al., *Iris Biometrics: From Segmentation to Template Security*,
Advances in Information Security 59, DOI 10.1007/978-1-4614-5571-4_4,
© Springer Science+Business Media, LLC 2013

a

b

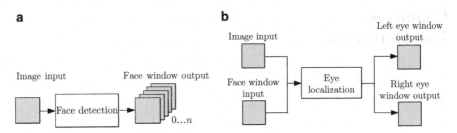

Fig. 4.1 Typically nested tasks of face detection and eye localization. (**a**) Face detection task, (**b**) Eye localization task

solved. A face (object) detector is a function $F : s \mapsto \{r_1, \ldots, r_{k(s)}\}$ assigning each sample image s the set of $k(s)$ regions $r_i = (x_i, y_i, w_i, h_i)$ with origin x_i, y_i and size $w_i \times h_i$ containing a face (object) within the image. The task of eye (object-part) localization is usually much simpler, i.e. a function $P : (r, s) \mapsto (r_1, \ldots, r_l)$ assigning a sample image s and region of interest (ROI, e.g., a face) r the l (fixed, e.g. $l = 2$ for left and right eye) locations of instances of eyes (object-parts) within r in s [277]. These two tasks are illustrated in Fig. 4.1 and are the subjects of interest within this chapter. A lot of highly accurate specialized object detectors exist [608]: (1) knowledge-based; (2) feature invariant; (3) template matching and, most notably; (4) appearance-based methods, learning face models from training images widely adapting the Viola–Jones [563] approach.

Whereas traditional iris cameras expect an iris or eyepair image as input and therefore have to solve *eye detection* or *eye localization* tasks only, considering full portrait images has a number of advantages:

- *Higher throughput*: Less constrained recording conditions can significantly raise throughput of biometric systems. While in first iris biometric systems [116, 579] localization required exact placement of the eyes within predefined localization areas and within a rather narrow depth-of-field, sometimes assisted by visually displaying the current position of the captured iris, new portal-based vision systems [337, 578] support iris capture *on-the-move* tolerating motion blur to a large extent.
- *Unattended acquisition*: Higher tolerance with respect to initial recording conditions alleviates the unattended capture of biometric signals and makes the system more applicable for inexperienced users. New active vision systems [337, 578] typically have an increased capture distance permitting higher degrees of freedom during acquisition and usually require much less cooperation of the subject.
- *Biometric fusion*: The combination of face and iris biometric modalities seems to be a very natural choice exploiting biometric properties in the head region at different resolutions (while face recognition does not demand high-resolution input images, iris biometric systems typically operate at higher resolutions). A prototype system can be found in [572]. Fisher linear discriminant analysis is employed in [159] on good-quality face and iris matching scores gained from also randomly paired samples (280 face and 280 iris images of 40 subjects) and

is shown to improve accuracy. The first single-sensor face and iris multibiometric system based on Eigenfaces and iris-code-based iris recognition is proposed in [614] using a high-resolution 10 megapixel NIR camera equipped with active 850 nm LED lights for frontal illumination at 0.6–0.8 m distance. Score-combinations of left-eye, right-eye and face yielded 0.25 % FRR at 0.1 % FAR on a dataset of 380 images (76 subjects), which is significantly better than face (2.65 % FRR) and iris (4.58 % FRR) as single features utilizing not only still images but also video datasets, as proposed in [374].

Full-portrait iris recognition systems depend on efficient and robust detection of eyes in face images before iris segmentation is able to extract the highly unique texture. Coarse segmentation errors in early steps make subsequent finer normalization impossible. While various different approaches for detecting faces, as well as face-parts, e.g., eye, nose, mouth or eyepairs, do exist (see [608] for a survey), the high variability in recording conditions of surveillance-type imagery suggests to combine successful approaches to achieve even higher recognition accuracy, e.g. [30, 105, 367, 467, 588]. While face recognition typically operates on very low resolution VW input [563], it is iris recognition with its demands for high resolution focused NIR images of human eyes which challenges current state-of-the art systems, often solved by employing separate cameras for face and eye extraction [578]. However, recent challenges like MBGC [374] and NICE [483] emphasize both, face recognition in NIR and iris recognition under VW to merge both technologies. The approach presented in this chapter [539] aims at combining object detection approaches to solve the heterogeneous face detection and eye localization problem prior to iris segmentation.

4.1 Categorization

In applications not only the face, but multiple face-part objects with spatial relationships need to be detected in order to increase recognition accuracy by biometric fusion (e.g., in [614]), or benefit from more accurate face alignment (e.g., in [277, 570]). Depending on the amount of information available, detector fusion approaches may be grouped into feature-level fusion (having access to individual features exploited by function F of the face detection task introduced before), score-level fusion (in architectures, where F evaluates candidate regions r by means of score-based metrics) and decision-level fusion (where the only information available is $F(s)$, i.e. the result).

Belaroussi et al. [26, 27] propose examples of the first feature-level fusion type. Their face detection scheme is a weighted sum of different location maps based on an appearance-based associative multilayer perceptron (Diabolo) map, an ellipse general HT map, and a skin map, with a product-combination of eye detectors. Jin et al. [238] present a hybrid eye detection approach integrating characteristics of single-eye and eyepair-detectors. In a first stage, eye candidates are determined by a cascade projecting normalized eye images onto a weighted eigenspace and further filtered by eyepair templates. The authors employ Gaussians to model the probability distribution of left-eye classes within the eigenspace as well.

Most fusion methods are score-based: Ma et al. [323] examine a novel approach for finding eyes in faces using a probabilistic framework. After face detection an appearance-based eye detector is applied to derive detection scores for various locations, which are then fused by pairwise assessment of candidates. Xiao [588] employs weighted sum-rule fusion on the detection scores to combine multiple detection algorithms on the same face image for the target application of face detection in dark environments (illumination by monitor light source). Weights are estimated depending on image quality (contrast, sharpness, color bit depth) by applying fuzzy adaptive fusion. Belhumeur et al. [30] train a global model of part-locations as hidden variables of a Bayesian objective function and combine the outcome of local detectors with a non-parametric set of prior models of face shape. Each local detector returns a score at each evaluation point used as likelihood that the desired part is located at this position. The authors keep track of the best global models and adopt a generate-and-test approach similar to Random sample consensus (RANSAC), an iterative parameter estimation method from noisy data containing outliers, to find a list of models that maximize the conditional probability. This approach refers to Burl et al. [64], which also detects multiple candidate facial features and selects the most face-like constellation using a statistical model, also able to deal with incomplete constellations. Aarabi et al. [1] present a fusion scheme of different frontal face detectors for live web-based face detection. They combine computationally inefficient, but reliable template-based techniques, popular neural networks, and subspace methods by moving a window of varying size over the image and optimizing for a fusion of face detection metrics. While these methods show good performance, they require access to detection scores, which are not always available. It is therefore desirable to target the latter decision-level fusion scenario.

Decision-level fusion techniques in face detection are typically nested approaches reducing false negatives of face detectors by applying face-part detection on the found face objects. Wang et al. [570] study a hierarchical system detecting a face prior to locating eyes within the face boundary. Cristinacce et al. [105] propose a nested variant of locating facial features after face detection and combine individual locator results using a novel algorithm they call Pairwise Reinforcement of Feature Responses (PRFR) learning the pairwise distribution of all true feature locations relative to the best match of each individual feature detector. Face detection is used to predict approximate locations for each facial feature and local detectors are constrained to these locations. Nanni and Lumini [367] combine multiple face and eye detection systems using a serial scheme. In the first stage they employ two face detectors. In the second stage they eliminate false-positive detections, applying a novel eye detector yielding 99.3 % detection rate on BioID (faces detected with errors less than 25 % offset with respect to the inter-eye distance) instead of 67–97.8 % for partial combinations. In case no eyes are found in the second stage, the window is rejected as false positive. Micilotta et al. [345] present a coarse-to-fine approach for combining AdaBoost-based single body part

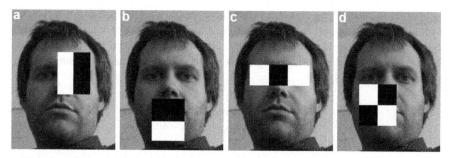

Fig. 4.2 Different Haar features used by Viola and Jones [563] for a sample face image. (**a**) Type A, (**b**) Type B, (**c**) Type C, (**d**) Type D

detectors (face, torso, legs, and hand-based classifier) using a GMM and RANSAC for assembly (selection of random body configurations), heuristics to eliminate outliers, a comparison of configurations with a trained a priori mixture model of upper-body configurations, and selection of the configuration maximizing the likelihood.

Hierarchical methods are ideally suited for the combination of fast methods with a low false negative rate but possibly higher false positive rate and more accurate but possibly costly methods to eliminate false positives in the second stage. The presented *Gaussian model-driven face with face-part classifier fusion* method [539] is different in being able to account for false negatives as well, in contrast to e.g. [367]. While Cristinacce et al. [105] make only use of position, this method takes also detection size (w_i, h_i) into consideration.

4.2 The Viola–Jones Approach

The so-called *Viola–Jones approach* is a widely employed and adapted technique for object detection. In 2001, Viola and Jones [563] developed a very robust, accurate and real-time capable technique to the object detection problem by employing rectangular Haar-features computed from the integral image for fast calculation. Four different types of features illustrated in Fig. 4.2 were considered, which can be calculated efficiently with simple index operations in the integral image (4 operations suffice to estimate a single rectangular area, where white rectangular areas refer to the addition of intensity values, while black areas refer to the subtraction of intensity values). Each feature computed for fixed-sized windows w within s corresponds to a weak classifier H_j together with parity p_j (sign) and threshold θ_j (obtained by calculating means for the feature on both class sets and averaging) [563]:

$$H_j(w) = \begin{cases} 1 & \text{if } p_j F_j(w) < p_j \theta_j \\ 0 & \text{otherwise.} \end{cases} \tag{4.1}$$

In order to build strong classifiers from these simple weak ones, *AdaBoost* selects a small number of important features (at the drawback of long exhaustive classifier training and feature selection). This way, classifiers are trained by selecting one feature at a time and updating weights to produce a strong classifier using single features for t rounds [563]:

$$H(w) = \begin{cases} 1 & \text{if } \sum_{j=1}^{t} \alpha_j H_j(w) \geq \frac{1}{2} \sum_{j=1}^{t} \alpha_j \\ 0 & \text{otherwise.} \end{cases} \tag{4.2}$$

Finally, a cascaded combination of classifiers is established, letting only windows pass on, which likely represent positive matches. This way, focus is put to promising regions, while retaining low false negative rates to speed up recognition (each node is trained with the false positives of the prior to quickly reject more likely non-face windows), i.e. iterative checks and rejection as soon as one classifier classifies the window as "non-face."

4.3   Nested Face and Face-Part Detection

Unfortunately, the obvious approach to employ eye instead of face detection using the Viola–Jones approach has several disadvantages: (1) the size of the input image is typically quite large compared to the size of the sought object type, i.e. eyes; (2) there is high risk of contradicting information with respect to the position of eyes, e.g. whenever an eye is found there should be another left or right eye in the neighborhood; (3) especially for low-angle-shots nares are likely to produce false positive eye detections, which can be avoided taking into account spatial relationships between detection responses. One obvious improvement is the application of both eye and face detection in parallel and additional topological property checks. At the cost of additional processing time, this approach may be used to increase accuracy; however, a more practical solution accounts for the inclusion property (eyes are detected within face regions) applying a nested face and face-part detection. In this configuration, a face cascade is performed to estimate multiple face candidates. For each detected face, a face-part (eye) detection is performed. Compared to the first approach, this method can be expected to consume less computational resources, since face-parts operate on subwindows only, and typical input images can be assumed to contain only a few facial regions. When used as a preprocessing step to face biometrics only, this approach may be used to reduce the number of false positive face detections by checking for the presence of eyes in faces. However, detection accuracy largely depends on the accuracy of both, eye and face detectors. Accuracy may degrade in case accurate face detectors are followed by inaccurate eye detectors, and even the best eye detectors may fail completely in case face detectors do not provide reasonable input. This may even likely be the case if training data for both detectors are different in type, e.g. the application of NIR images for eye detector training and VW images for face detector training. Figure 4.3 lists the processing chain of nested face and face-part detectors.

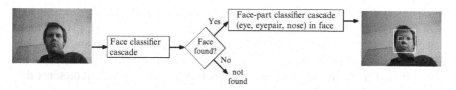

Fig. 4.3 Eye detection applying nested face with face-part classifier combination

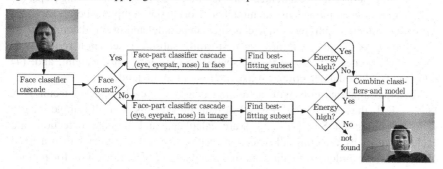

Fig. 4.4 Gaussian model-driven face with face-part classifier fusion

A simple way to improve nested detection is to eliminate false positive face-parts by assessing a face–facepart energy function for each face-part detection or pairwise facepart–facepart functions estimating the likeliness of a co-occurrence of two detections taking into account their spatial relationship. This way, speed advantages of the nested approach can be maintained, since face parts operate on subwindows only, but still, false negatives cannot be corrected. An extension of this idea evaluating not only pairwise detections but also all possible subsets of detections leads to model-driven *face with face-part classifier fusion* as proposed in the next section.

4.4 Face with Face-Part Classifier Fusion

Model-driven face with face-part classifier fusion assesses each combination of detected face parts with the corresponding face to determine the combination that maximizes a fitting function with respect to the model. Missed parts are reconstructed from the best-matching model. While this procedure requires checks of all subsets of classifier results, practical evaluations show that this method is quite practicable in case of reliable individual detectors with few false positive detections. Its major advantage compared to prior presented techniques is an improvement with respect to false negatives and false positives.

Uhl and Wild [539] proposed a fusion framework for object detectors $F_i : s \mapsto \{r_{i1}, \ldots r_{ik(s)}\}$ detecting faces and face-part objects, see Fig. 4.4. While this fusion method is generic in accepting arbitrary detectors, for experiments Viola–Jones

[563] based detectors are employed for faces, eyes, eyepairs, and noses, shipped with OpenCV [215] following the implementation by Lienhart et al. [314]. These detectors perform (1) *feature extraction*, calculating properties of image regions; (2) *evaluation*, selecting discriminative features with respect to the object to be detected, and; (3) *classification*, judging whether a given window represents the object or not.

The combination of face and face-part classifiers requires the following steps: (1) *model estimation* builds a Gaussian model of priors and is computed beforehand; (2) *individual detection* employs single classifiers in parallel and/or serial combination; (3) *grouping* of results identifies the best-fitting subset of detection results with respect to an energy function taking spatial relationships into account, and; (4) *refitting* of individual detection results with respect to the model.

Model estimation starts with a training phase. For each object detector $F_i \in \{F_1, \ldots, F_m\}$, the sets $C_i = \cup_{j=1}^{n} F_i(s_j)$ of detection results over all sample images s_j in a training set $S = \{s_1, \ldots, s_n\}$ are calculated and all false detections are excluded (e.g., by rejecting all detection results with offsets greater than a fixed offset limit). In order to obtain scale-independent comparable results for regions $r \in F_i(s_j)$, position coordinates and size triples $r = (x, y, s)$ are given with respect to a coordinate system employing the midpoint O between left and right eye as origin, and the inter-eye distance u as unit value, see Fig. 4.5. A single size parameter s is employed instead of width and height, since typically classifiers employ a fixed w/h size ratio. Gaussian distributions N_x, N_y, N_s are fitted to the parameters of each detector F_i using its output on the sample set S, i.e. the mean of parameters μ_x, μ_y, μ_s and standard deviations $\sigma_x, \sigma_y, \sigma_s$ for each F_i are estimated. Instead of predicting the position of the classifier, given the ground truth face position, the output of F_i given an image s_j can be used to estimate the approximate localization O of the face according to the trained model. While for detectors in case of single localizations ($l = 1$, e.g. nose, mouth, eyepair) this procedure applies straightforward, detectors with multiple expected detections ($l > 1$, e.g. eyes) need multiple prediction models (for left and right eyes two reverse predictions are estimated, from which one is rejected during grouping). For training, μ_x, μ_y also consider the flipped classifier output for left and right eyes as well as the nose classifier. For eyes, σ_y is corrected (by factor 3) to account for more variation with respect to head tilt. For face and eyepairs, location parameters μ_x and μ_y, respectively, are set to zero, to avoid overfitting with respect to the dataset. Finally, Z-normalization is applied to the Gaussians.

After individual face(part) detection, the best-fitting subset of detection results has to be identified with respect to the trained model. First, for m single classifiers, all combinations that can be formed for a subset containing i classifiers, $i \in \{1, \ldots, m\}$, are selected. By iterating from $c = 1$ to $c = 2^m$ and selecting the t-th classifier to be part of the subset, if the t-th bit in c is set, $c[t] = 1$, all possible combinations of detection results for these detectors are considered. There may be no combinations for a selected subset, if the classifier finds no objects of its type. Second, the location (reference position O) and size (inter-eye distance u) of the

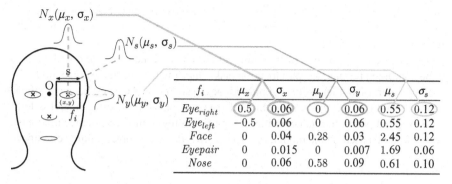

Fig. 4.5 Reference model under Gaussian assumption with trained parameters

f_i	μ_x	σ_x	μ_y	σ_y	μ_s	σ_s
Eye_{right}	0.5	0.06	0	0.06	0.55	0.12
Eye_{left}	−0.5	0.06	0	0.06	0.55	0.12
$Face$	0	0.04	0.28	0.03	2.45	0.12
$Eyepair$	0	0.015	0	0.007	1.69	0.06
$Nose$	0	0.06	0.58	0.09	0.61	0.10

face with respect to a detection result (x,y,s) of the t-th detector is predicted using the trained classifier models N_x, N_y, N_s for detector type t. Origin $O = (a,b)$ and inter-eye distance u are predicted as follows:

$$a := x - \mu_x s; \qquad b := y - \mu_y s; \qquad u := \frac{s}{\mu_s}. \tag{4.3}$$

Each of the three model parameters is assumed to exhibit the following scatterings:

$$\alpha := \sigma_x u; \qquad \beta := \sigma_y u, \qquad \gamma := \sigma_s u. \tag{4.4}$$

For a set $L := \{L_1, \ldots, L_m\}$, $L_i = (a_i, b_i, u_i, \alpha_i, \beta_i, \gamma_i)$, of model locations the average model location $\bar{L} = (\bar{a}, \bar{y}, \bar{u})$ is defined as follows:

$$\bar{a} := \left(\sum_{i=1}^{m} \frac{1}{\alpha_i} \right) \cdot \left(\sum_{i=1}^{m} a_i \cdot \frac{1}{\alpha_i} \right); \qquad \bar{b} := \left(\sum_{i=1}^{m} \frac{1}{\beta_i} \right) \cdot \left(\sum_{i=1}^{m} b_i \cdot \frac{1}{\beta_i} \right);$$

$$\bar{u} := \left(\sum_{i=1}^{m} \frac{1}{\gamma_i} \right) \cdot \left(\sum_{i=1}^{m} u_i \cdot \frac{1}{\gamma_i} \right). \tag{4.5}$$

Location and size are weighted with the inverse deviation of each individual model prediction. Finally, it is desirable to estimate to which certainty a subset represents a face. For L and a corresponding average model location $\bar{L} = (\bar{a}, \bar{b}, \bar{u})$ the location energy is defined as,

$$E(L) := \frac{1}{m} \sqrt{1 + \sum_{i=1}^{m} \max\left(\frac{|a_i - \bar{a}|}{\alpha_i}, \frac{|b_i - \bar{b}|}{\beta_i}, \frac{|u_i - \bar{u}|}{\gamma_i} \right)}. \tag{4.6}$$

This energy function turned out to be an adequate compromise between few well-fitting classifiers and many worse-fitting classifiers. Small values (less than 1) represent suitable model fits.

Finally, detection results of individual classifiers and the best-fitted model have to be combined for the face-part location task. Once the best-fitting average model $\bar{L}$ has been identified, the position of individual classifiers can be reset. Each classifier (left eye, right eye, eyepair, nose, face) that is part of the best-fitting model is left at its original position. Each classifier not participating in the best average model is reconstructed based on the model, i.e. from μ_x, μ_y, μ_s of the corresponding classifier type.

Chapter 5
Iris Segmentation Methodologies

Traditional iris processing following Daugman's approach [116] extracts binary features after mapping the textural area between inner pupillary and outer limbic boundary into a doubly dimensionless representation. In this model, pixels are identified by their angular position and shift from pupillary to limbic boundary. This way, variations in the dilation of the pupil caused by different illumination conditions can largely be tolerated. Figure 5.1 depicts two left iris samples of the same user in the CASIA.v4-Lamp dataset with large and small pupil dilation before and after normalization. Early approaches to iris segmentation employ Daugman's integro-differential operator [116] or Wildes' circular HT [579] to find a parameterization of the boundaries required for the mapping process. However, iris images captured under more realistic, unsurveilled conditions induce diverse problems. Noisy artifacts caused by blur, reflections, occlusions, and most notably oblique viewing angles may lead to severe segmentation errors. Most publications regarding iris recognition in unconstrained environments aim at more sophisticated preprocessing techniques to successfully localize and segment images of the human eye, see Table 5.1 for a selection of recently published multi-step iris segmentation techniques. Proença et al. [408] identify the critical role of segmentation and observe a strong relationship between translational segmentation inaccuracies and recognition error rates. Matey et al. [338] assess the effect of resolution, wavelength, occlusion, and gaze as the most important factors for incorrect segmentation and give a survey of segmentation algorithms. If such errors occur, subsequent recognition is almost impossible. Since iris segmentation is susceptible to poor image quality, efficient and fast segmentation of iris images is still an open research question [408]. While iris boundaries have been modeled as circles, ellipses and more complex shapes still despite the applied model variety the processing chain of the vast majority of iris recognition algorithms resembles Daugman's and Wildes' standard approaches closely: after successful determination of the inner and outer boundaries, the iris-ring texture of a person's eye is unwrapped and further processed by feature extraction modules. Refinements of this model usually refer to more sophisticated generation of noise-masks determining pixels containing

C. Rathgeb et al., *Iris Biometrics: From Segmentation to Template Security*,
Advances in Information Security 59, DOI 10.1007/978-1-4614-5571-4_5,
© Springer Science+Business Media, LLC 2013

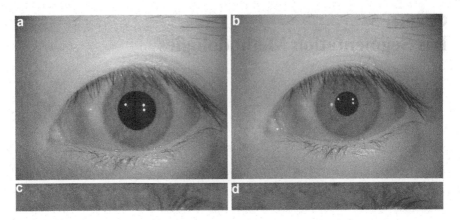

Fig. 5.1 Varying pupil dilation under different illumination in CASIA.v4-Lamp dataset. (**a**) Iris image #2002L01, (**b**) Iris image #2002L03, (**c**) #2002L01 after normalization, (**d**) #2002L03 after normalization

Table 5.1 Experimental results of recently proposed multi-step iris segmentation algorithms

Ref.	Algorithm	Database	Accuracy	Time (s)
[290]	(1) Agent-based method for center localization (2) multiple views boundary refinement	CASIA.v3, UBIRIS.v2	90–97 %	0.68
[189]	(1) Reflection removal (2) AdaBoost-cascade for approximate center detection (3) Pulling-and pushing model	CASIA.v3, ICE	0.5–1.3 % EER	0.01–0.02
[86]	(1) Sclera location (2) fast HT for limbic boundary, (3) eyelid detection (4) correction of limbic boundary by another HT (5) eyelash detection and reliability	UBIRIS.v2	97–98 %	0.83
[320]	(1) Color component selection (2) reflection extraction (3) limbic polar morphologic boundary extraction (4) center reestimation (5) pupillary boundary estimation	UBIRIS.v2	97 %	3.00
[403]	(1) Sclera detection (2) iris detection by machine learning (3) parameterization of iris shape	UBIRIS.v2, ICE, FRGV, FERET	1.9–4.6 % EER	0.70–0.78

eyelashes, eyelids, or other types of distortions. The fact that efficient and robust segmentation of iris images represents one of the most challenging problems in the field [403], especially for biometric systems without active participation of users, has led to a variety of public iris segmentation challenges in the last decade, e.g. the Iris Challenge Evaluation (ICE) [372], or the Noisy Iris Challenge Evaluation (NICE) [483]. Computational demands, as a very important factor in real-world applications, and the trade-off between accuracy and speed, have largely been neglected in evaluations so far. Furthermore, it has become common practice to enable participants to optimize their segmentation algorithm based on available training sets, which may lead to non-reproducible results when changing underlying datasets. This situation is even more critical since the majority of segmentation algorithms is not publicly available for independent evaluations. Indeed, segmentation accuracy is not the only quality factor of "good" iris segmentation systems, but iris segmentation is driven by three different quality factors:

- *Accuracy*: Robust segmentation of less intrusively or noncooperatively captured iris images is still a challenging task in iris biometrics.
- *Usability*: Experiments in e.g. [541] highlight the problem of database-specific optimizations in existing solutions. Also independence of sensors is a critical property of iris segmentation software.
- *Speed*: There is a growing demand for real-time capable solutions.

Within the scope of iris image processing this chapter surveys the main approaches to iris segmentation found in literature. Augmenting this survey, Chap. 6 discusses two new approaches [540, 541] towards real-time sensor- and database-independent iris processing in more detail. While most proposed iris segmentation techniques follow holistic approaches [44], optimizing the parameters for a more-or-less simple (circular, elliptic) model of the iris, multistage iris segmentation frameworks decoupling the tasks of initial center detection and boundary have certain advantages: instead of employing some sort of exhaustive searching or single error-prone strategies to derive pupillary and limbic boundary curves, it is possible to employ multistage iris segmentation for heterogeneous processing of VW and NIR imagery using the same processing technique. Especially for combinations of face and iris biometric modalities, there is a growing demand for iris segmentation techniques without strong assumptions on source image characteristics. Iris segmentation in VW frequently employs sclera search for approximate location [402], but this preprocessing raises problems in NIR due to lower contrast between sclera and iris. On contrary, NIR iris processing often relies on the pupil being easy localizable as a homogeneous dark region with high pupillary contrast, often violated in VW for dark irides. Commercial solutions typically operate under NIR light to be able to extract iris features including heavily pigmented iris images [116]. Challenges like NICE [483] now focus on VW images in order to push attention towards iris recognition from surveillance-type images. However, recent research has also focused on exploiting information from multiple spectra [46, 454] to even improve recognition accuracy.

Whereas commonly subsumed as *iris segmentation* tasks, there are many different preprocessing steps required to obtain a normalized representation of an iris texture. Current iris segmentation algorithms are mainly influenced by Daugman's normalization model identifying the inner and outer boundaries of the iris and mapping the enclosed area onto a rectangular stripe [116]. It should be noted that there are also iris feature extraction algorithms operating directly on unnormalized iris data, e.g., SIFT-based features [12], which therefore do not require this form of preprocessing.

Consequently, there is no a universal formulation of the iris segmentation problem: iris segmentation is needed to assist feature extraction and template alignment—if feature extraction could provide features, which are invariant under environmental effects (distance to subject, pupillary dilation, gaze, etc.) and still provide enough discrimination between classes, indeed segmentation would be unnecessary. But this is not the case in practice. Challenges like NICE [483] or ICE [372] have put special attention on the segmentation problem. Until then, segmentation has largely been evaluated as part of the total iris recognition system. Nevertheless, segmentation is likely to be responsible for many false rejections in experiments, caused by segmentation failures and the resulting misalignment between pairs of genuine iris templates. Finally, the lack of publicly available baseline software with respect to iris segmentation is a major problem making evaluations sometimes difficult to compare even if public databases are employed for testing. Except the implementations by Masek [335], OSIRIS [275], and USIT (see Sect. 3.4), there are hardly any public open source reference algorithms available for iris segmentation. Furthermore, available solutions largely depend on the type of iris data. Typically, segmentation approaches for NIR and VW images are quite different—or at least require training on datasets exhibiting the same image characteristics like the dataset employed for testing. Besides the absence of a universal notion of the segmentation task, there are also no universally applied measures assessing the accuracy of the segmentation stage. While challenges like NICE considered the inclusion or exclusion of pixels in the input image to the set of iris pixels in order to derive a classification error rate, ICE evaluated entire systems, including feature extraction and recognition with respect to FRR at a specific FAR. With the introduction of the aforementioned iris challenges and with the raised demand for iris recognition systems to be applied in less-controlled environments, a more narrow definition of the iris segmentation task is being created by the scientific community. In order to avoid any confusion, we distinguish between "iris normalization" and "iris segmentation" to emphasize the fact that segmentation algorithms considered in this work all refer to Daugman's normalization model [116], see Figs. 5.2 and 5.3. That is, we restrict iris segmentation to the task of determining iris boundaries as well as noise masks concentrating on the selection of inner (pupillary) and outer (limbic) boundary curves in the original eye image. In contrast, normalization refers to mapping iris pixels into Daugman's doubly dimensionless coordinate system using the found boundaries, noise mask, and original input image by applying the rubbersheet transform.

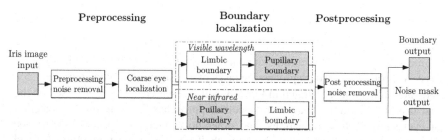

Fig. 5.2 Iris segmentation processing chain: Preprocessing, boundary localization, postprocessing

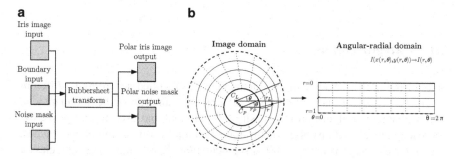

Fig. 5.3 The iris normalization task and its according rubbersheet transform model. (**a**) Normalization, (**b**) Rubbersheet transform

Following a more formal description, the main task of iris normalization is to map the iris texture of an $m \times n$ sized eye image I into Daugman's homogeneous rubbersheet model [116]. More precisely, a rendering map R is sought, which assigns each pair (θ, r) of angle θ and pupil-to-limbic radial distance r to the corresponding originating location $R(\theta, r)$ within I, regardless of pupillary dilation and iris size:

$$R : [0, 2\pi) \times [0, 1] \to [0, m] \times [0, n]. \tag{5.1}$$

In Daugman's representation, R is established as a linear combination from closed pupillary and limbic polar boundary curves $P, L : [0, 2\pi) \to [0, m] \times [0, n]$, parameterizable with a single parameter:

$$R(\theta, r) := (1 - r) \cdot P(\theta) + r \cdot L(\theta). \tag{5.2}$$

While originally modeled as circles with not necessarily coinciding centers, P and L may be modeled as arbitrary polar sampled curves. The requirement of the pupillary boundary being contained within the limbic boundary has given this new coordinate system its name: "Faberge coordinates" [116]. In case an iris texture is occluded by eyelids, the model assumes that P and L mark the true possibly occluded pupillary and limbic iris boundaries, respectively. Within the resulting iris texture, areas occluded by eyelids, eyelashes, or reflections should be masked out using binary noise masks N of the same size:

$$N : [0, 2\pi) \times [0, 1] \to \{0, 1\}. \tag{5.3}$$

Finally, R, P, L, and N are typically discretized in implementations. The task of iris segmentation is to find accurate boundary curves P, L as well as the binary noise mask N. From these two preprocessing tasks of "segmentation" depicted in Fig. 5.2 and "normalization" illustrated in Fig. 5.3, active research is mainly focused on the first task. Furthermore, apart from specific approaches focusing on the detection of eyelashes, eyelids, reflections, and other noise factors, especially the robust detection of P and L constitutes a major challenge for unconstrained images and therefore deserves special attention.

5.1   Categorization

State-of-the-art iris segmentation systems may be classified according to different criteria. Whereas for many of the early segmentation algorithms the dominant idea of a segmentation algorithm may easily be identified and used to categorize the approach, new algorithms often incorporate techniques from different approaches, which makes categorization of an iris segmentation algorithm into a single class a difficult task. In this survey of iris segmentation approaches, each iris segmentation technique will be classified with respect to the dominant innovative aspect, grouped into three stages (1) *preprocessing*, for approaches innovating initial noise removal (inpainting) or coarse localization of pupil or iris centers; (2) *boundary localization*, as the mainstream task of reliably detecting P and L; (3) *post-processing*, typically focusing on noise removal techniques, as illustrated in Fig. 5.2.

The majority of iris recognition systems employ NIR imaging, capturing images at 700–900 nm wavelength, sacrificing pigment melanin information at the benefit of less reflections and even clearer texture information for heavily pigmented dark irides. In contrast, recent challenges like NICE focus on the processing of VW iris images. While images of the first type typically exhibit a very clear pupillary boundary, for the latter VW iris images, reflections, more heavily pigmented irides, and typically smaller pupillary areas cause a much clearer limbic boundary. As a consequence, segmentation approaches are entirely different. Regarding preprocessing, VW approaches frequently employ an additional *sclera detection* phase [403], while early NIR segmentation methods often coarsely localize the pupil based on its intensity. Note, however, that intensity or threshold-based methods are prone to errors, since the pupil may sometimes be even brighter than the iris due to reflections. There may be also other low-intensity areas in the face, like eyebrows or frames of eyeglasses. The distinction between VW and NIR approaches is also reflected in boundary localization, since NIR approaches typically employ pupillary before limbic boundary detection, while VW approaches change this order [403] to avoid a propagation of errors.

According to the survey of Bowyer et al. [44], existing iris segmentation software in the field is largely based on two classical approaches with minor refinements only. Daugman's approach [116] applies an exhaustive search for center and radius using an *integro-differential operator* to approximate P and L as circles. Wildes' [579] approach is similar, but uses binary edge maps and *circular HT*. The vast majority of known segmentation algorithms in literature builds upon these ideas. So far, the following improvements to these two main approaches have been proposed: (1) better models, such as ellipses or view-angle transformations to account for off-gaze [476]; (2) better occlusion detection [621]; (3) post-fitting refinements permitting more complex shapes including AC, ASM [2] and Fourier series expansions [118]. Especially the introduction of the aforementioned AC as models for iris segmentation has influenced many of today's applied iris segmentation algorithms towards more generic pupillary and limbic boundary shapes. In this survey AC are therefore grouped in an own class of segmentation approaches. Finally, there are also more custom techniques fitting parameters of an iris boundary model onto the original or transformed eye image. Once iris center coordinates have been found, a common employed transform (e.g., in [189, 290, 320]) for this group of *model-fitting* techniques is the polar transform.

While many of these boundary localization techniques fit a parameterized shape by some exhaustive searching method to derive P and L, there are also *multi-stage* methods, where not a single but multiple different models are applied to solve subproblems of the segmentation task. Frequently, these techniques also employ a combination of methods, e.g. separate stages for sclera detection, center-detection, pupillary and limbic boundary detection. High computational demand represents the major disadvantage of most single-strategy techniques. Each stage within a multistage method employs a simpler model, thus, the amount of parameters is reduced permitting simpler—and often more effective—techniques. The result after each stage serves as a subsequent transformation input to simplify the next stage.

With respect to postprocessing, we survey different approaches to *noise models*, which are mainly employed to determine the binary noise mask, selecting iris pixels, which should not be considered during the comparison stage. This is necessary in order to avoid a comparison of corresponding iris-code bits which result from occlusions caused by, e.g., eyelids, eyelashes, or reflections. Some recently published approaches in the NICE.I contest [235, 305, 464, 510] combine several sophisticated noise detection approaches to achieve high accuracy on the challenging UBIRIS.v2 dataset. Proença and Alexandre [407] survey the best iris segmentation algorithms in the NICE contest being composed of two challenges, NICE.I for iris segmentation identifying noise-free iris parts, and NICE.II for encoding features and matching. Results indicated that iris segmentation under VW is still very challenging. According to [406], *noncooperative iris recognition* refers to automatically recognizing humans by their iris patters at-a-distance without requiring specific actions supporting the acquisition process. This acquisition mode requires dealing with several factors degrading the quality of an iris image (off-gaze, motion blur, etc.).

5.2 Performance Measurement

There are two different methods to assess the performance of the segmentation stage:

- *Impact on recognition accuracy*: In order to compare different iris segmentation algorithms, one possible solution is to compare the total recognition accuracy of the entire biometric system using two instances of the same system (unchanged comparison and feature extraction modules) replacing the segmentation module with the current algorithm under test. While both verification and identification mode assessment (e.g., in [316, 337]) could be performed, typically verification mode experiments with its performance indicators like EER, FRR at a specified FAR, or Area under the ROC-Curve (AUC) are preferred. Examples of segmentation algorithms employing this type of assessment are: [81, 126, 136, 171, 189, 241, 459, 478, 541, 556, 609, 617, 621, 622].
- *Iris-pixel classification accuracy*: If ground truth regarding the segmentation of iris images is available, i.e. for an image set $I = \{I_1, \ldots, I_k\}$ of $m \times n$ input images there are ground-truth masks $G = \{G_1, \ldots G_k\}$ of the same size, such that for all indices i and positions (a, b) we get $G_i[a, b] = 1$ for "in-iris" pixels and $G_i[a, b] = 0$ for non-iris pixels, the accuracy (or E^1 classification error rate) is given by [483]:

$$E = \frac{1}{k} \sum_{i=1}^{k} \frac{1}{m \cdot n} \sum_{a=0}^{m-1} \sum_{b=0}^{n-1} G_i[a, b] \oplus S(I_i)[a, b] \qquad (5.4)$$

where $\oplus$ refers to the exclusive-or operator and S refers to a segmentation function assigning an input image I_i the segmentation mask $S(I_i)$ where $S(I_i)[a, b] = 1$ for "in-iris" pixels and $S(I_i)[a, b] = 0$ for non-iris pixels with respect to the segmentation result. Apart from this measure, also weighted versions and measures exist, explicitly referring to both types of errors, "iris pixel" is classified as "non-iris pixel" and "non-iris pixel" is classified as "iris pixel." The NICE contest explicitly employs an evaluation protocol using these measures [483]. Examples for methods employing iris-pixel classification accuracy are: [11, 57, 86, 88, 235, 263, 290, 369, 403, 404, 464, 509, 510].

Compared to iris-pixel classification accuracy-based evaluations, the obvious advantages of segmentation assessment based on recognition impact are:

- *Ground truth*: no manual segmentation of the underlying dataset is necessary, which makes this method of comparison easily applicable in case this information is not readily available.
- *Neutrality*: recognition assessment is neutral with respect to the system module to be tested (i.e., this method is not limited to segmentation, but may also be used for assessing other system modules, e.g. feature extraction).

- *Impact*: recognition assessment highlights the impact of segmentation on recognition accuracy, which is the most necessary performance indicator of an iris biometric system.

However, there are also a series of disadvantages:

- *Dependency*: reported segmentation accuracy depends on other employed modules (e.g., feature extraction and comparison), and therefore segmentation algorithms cannot easily be compared based on the obtained rates.
- *Systematic errors*: some segmentation errors (e.g., consequently detecting outer boundaries as inner boundaries) may even lead to higher accuracy, although the segmentation result is not accurate [540]. These side effects may be avoided when employing iris-pixel classification accuracy-based evaluations.
- *Genuine samples*: segmentation assessment with respect to recognition accuracy needs multiple samples per user, whereas for accuracy estimation no genuine comparison pairs are needed.

5.3 Preprocessing

For reliable iris boundary localization, typically a preprocessing phase is executed. First, this is useful for removal of negative effects resulting from noise, like hair or reflection, which could otherwise affect the subsequent search for optimal parameters fitting a model to the input image or constitute local optima of the applied operators. Second, a rough localization of the pupillary center is a useful information for heuristic checks assessing the quality of the segmentation stage. Third, preprocessing is able to provide suitable restrictions to the parameter space (e.g., a window of interest with respect to the circular center of the pupillary boundary) saving processing time. Depending on the type of iris data (VW versus NIR) sclera and pupil localization are common approaches.

5.3.1 Sclera Localization

Proença [403] identifies the sclera as the most easily distinguishable part of the eye. He surveys the most important recently published iris segmentation algorithms and found most algorithms to employ pupillary boundary detection before scleric boundary detection (e.g., [25, 186, 188, 253, 316, 355, 456, 476, 556, 592, 616, 621]), and only few techniques performing scleric before pupillary curve estimation (e.g., [404, 602]) or even in parallel (e.g., [57, 510]). The method proposed in [403] first performs sclera localization using neural networks (NN) on Viola–Jones-based Haar features and later, at the second stage, use color-space average and standard deviation features and NN to create an iris mask, which is refined using polynomial fitting. Experiments yield high accuracy on VW images (1.87 % segmentation errors versus 6.2 % for [118] on UBIRIS.v2).

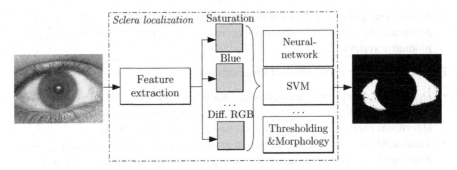

Fig. 5.4 Typical processing chain of sclera detection methods on a UBIRIS.v1 image

Tan and Kumar [509] investigate pixel-based iris segmentation for VW images. For these types of images sclera detection is an efficient means of localization due to less pronounced pupillary boundaries. Their approach comprises two stages, a classification stage with sclera feature extraction and detection as well as iris classification, and a post-classification stage with boundary refinement after polar transform and introduction of noise masks. Their approach uses discriminative color features and localized Zernike moments as well as a feed-forward network classifier and, alternatively, a classifier based on support vector machines (SVM).

Chen et al. [85, 86] present yet another sclera detection-based approach and build upon an accelerated (20 times faster) HT for boundary fitting. The processing chain is as follows: (1) sclera detection by adaptively thresholding the saturation channel in the hue-saturation-intensity space (the sclera is less saturated), classification of the binary map result into single or double sclera areas, and definition of an ROI for approximate eye localization; (2) outer iris boundary detection by horizontal edge detection and circular HT; (3) eyelid detection using line HT; (4) multi-arc and multi-line outer iris boundary correction using a second HT within a defined area and computing the disk intersections; (5) pupil and eyelash detection using hard thresholding.

From the above-listed approaches, we can see that especially for VW images, the sclera may easily be segmented using rather simple methods. The saturation, blue channel or differences between the red, green, and blue color channels may be used with standard classification approaches: thresholding, SVMs or NNs [403] may be applied and refined using morphology operations to accurately find the sclera image region, see Fig. 5.4.

The sclera may even be used as a biometric feature. Zhou et al. [618] focus on sclera detection and propose a Gabor-filter based multi-angle sclera recognition method. They also give details on their employed sclera segmentation steps using Otsu thresholding. Eyelid and iris boundaries are refined using the Fourier AC approach by Daugman [118].

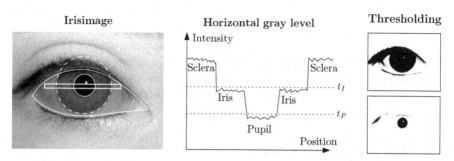

Fig. 5.5 Pupil detection exploiting the typical horizontal gray level profile of cooperatively captured NIR iris images

5.3.2 Pupil Localization

Pupil detection typically exploits the ideally three-valued horizontal gray-level profile through the pupil, see Fig. 5.5. Because of the hollow structure of the eye, the gray-level of the pupil is very frequently at the lowest level (except for eyelids and eyebrows, where this condition may be violated). While this condition is not always true, for some cooperatively captured databases, techniques have been reported employing pupillary localization by binarization [91]. However, especially for uncooperatively captured images of the human eye, or even images captured in less controlled environments this assumption does not hold. Furthermore, region-based filtering testing for circularity or checking for the existence of corneal reflection hot spots inside or near the candidate region [91, 136] is usually necessary to distinguish the pupil from other dark regions.

Du et al. [136] employ k-means clustering to determine different regions in the iris image and coarsely localize the pupil close to the darkest region with a specular reflection near the region. Rakshit and Monro [417] search for a large dark area close to the image center and employ histogram analysis to approximate 16 edge points of the pupillary boundary, which is then modeled by Fourier-based shape descriptions. Matey et al. [337] present one of the first less-constrained portal-based iris recognition systems focusing on high-resolution cameras and targeting an extraction while subjects are moving, i.e. Iris on the Move (IOM) devices. Their system is Iridian-based employing Daugman's proposed algorithm [116]. For coarse segmentation they look for special reflections of illumination light sources within the corneal surface; however, there are reported problems with jewelry, eyeglass frames, and other reflective objects. Regarding failures, interestingly, they report 50% of failures to be caused by less than 20% of users.

Especially for real-time applications coarse pupil localization approaches are frequently applied, since clustering or thresholding can be executed fast and provide valuable information for finer, more time consuming segmentation steps. Even without sophisticated boundary localization steps, quite accurate segmentation results can be achieved for the first publicly available iris databases. Especially

CASIA.v1 can easily be segmented, because the pupillary area in images has been manually replaced by circular regions of uniform intensity [393] in order to protect intellectual property rights of the employed NIR illumination scheme [89]. Still, also for CASIA.v3-Interval and other NIR-based images captured under controlled conditions, the pupil is usually the darkest area within iris images, unless hair, eyebrows or nonuniform illumination violate this condition.

5.4   Boundary Localization

The boundary localization task is at the heart of the iris segmentation problem, as it determines accurate boundary curves P and L. Besides the classical *integro-differential operator* and *HT*-based approaches targeting circular (and in extension of the original operators also elliptical) shapes, approaches discussed as part of the groups of *AC* and *model-fitting and polar techniques* employ more generic boundaries permitting higher degrees of freedom in modeling pupillary and limbic boundaries.

5.4.1   Integro-Differential Operator

Classical iris segmentation is based on Daugman's algorithms [109]. It is the well-known baseline algorithm employing an integro-differential operator for finding boundaries of the iris and the pupil within an iris image $I(x,y)$:

$$\max_{(r,x_o,y_0)} \left| G_\sigma(r) * \frac{\partial}{\partial r} \oint_{r,x_0,y_0} \frac{I(x,y)}{2\pi r} \, ds \right|. \tag{5.5}$$

The boundary is circular, described by center (x_0,y_0) and radius r. The operator applies a Gaussian smoothing function G_σ searching for the optimal circular boundary yielding a maximum difference in intensity values. When discretized in implementations, the change in pixel values is estimated and smoothing is progressively reduced by iterative application of the operator [335], see Fig. 5.6. This operator has good robustness to various noisy artifacts; however, it suffers from local optima, especially reflections cause problems. Therefore more recent variants employ reflection removal and image inpainting techniques [476] as preprocessing steps, or restrict evaluations to two opposite cones (usually 90 degrees) centered on the horizontal axis through (x_0,y_0) to suppress the effect of eyelids and eyelashes on the detection [507]. Another drawback is rather slow performance due to the exhaustive search.

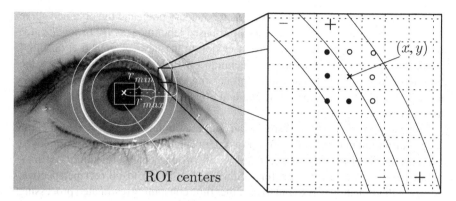

Fig. 5.6 Implementation of Daugman's integro-differential operator: Parameter search of (x_0, y_0) within ROI and r within interval $[r_{\min}, r_{\max}]$ assessing smoothed sum of pixel intensity differences

For the outlined reasons, several refinements to the initial approach by Daugman have been proposed in literature and still the majority of iris segmentation algorithms builds upon this model: Zheng et al. [616] investigate color image segmentation in HSV space and employ an integro-differential operator-based approach for pupil detection, as well as an iterative shrink and expand process minimizing average intensity for limbic boundary extraction. Zuo et al. [621] employ the integro-differential operator for iris segmentation taking shape, intensity, and location information into account, in contrast to pupil segmentation which first finds candidates using HT on the median filtered image, and assesses location information (weighted distance from iris center) to exclude unlikely candidates. They also apply specular reflection compensation by hard thresholding and partial differential equation-based inpaiting. Kennell et al. [253] combine the integro-differential operator approach with morphological operators for pupillary boundary fitting and variance-based image binarization on pixels for limbic boundary form fitting. Also, Nishino and Nayar [370], Camus and Wildes [65], and Martin–Roche et al. [334] present minor refinements to the integro-differential operator approach, again maximizing a function for three circumference parameters (center and radius), keeping the high computational bound. Whereas processing time is frequently targeted by database-specific assumptions restricting parameter space, an obvious way to speed up implementations is to implement approaches in hardware: Grabowski and Napieralski [171] present a hardware-accelerated architecture using the integro-differential operator for iris segmentation. Wang and Xiang [569] extend the integro-differential operator by RANSAC, a method estimating parameters of the boundary model from a set of observed data containing outliers. After coarse center detection, an integro-differential operator is applied and coarse iris boundary curves are refined using the RANSAC algorithm in 3 steps: (1) application of a linear basis function able to deal with outliers by controlling the number of basis functions;

(2) calculation of the distance between each boundary point and the obtained curve (by the linear basis function) and threshold-based labeling as *valid* or *invalid*; (3) iterative application of the linear basis function to the new set. Labati et al. [289] present an integro-differential-based technique with boundary refinement in the polar domain for image linearization (processing radial gradients). Iris boundaries are regularized using low-pass filtering and effects from eyelashes and reflections are suppressed.

Schuckers et al. [476] investigate an angle compensation method using the integro-differential operator for off-axis iris segmentation. The operator is employed to measure the circularity of the pupil as an off-gaze measure finding optimal parameters of a projective transformation (angles ϕ', ψ') to correct perspective. However, their method was found to be rather time consuming (estimated processing time exceeding 10 s per image on a 3.06 GHz CPU) requiring an exhaustive search and an initial rough estimate of the rotation angle. They propose a maximization of the integro-differential operator function using perspectively corrected versions $I(x', y' : \psi, \phi)$ of the image $I(x', y')$ utilizing angles ϕ', ψ':

$$(\phi', \psi') = \arg\max_{\psi, \phi} \max_{(r, x_0, y_0)} \left| G_\sigma(r) * \frac{\partial}{\partial r} \oint_{r, x_0, y_0} \frac{I(x', y' : \psi, \phi)}{2\pi r} ds \right|. \qquad (5.6)$$

With respect to the NICE.I contest [483], optimized versions of the integro-differential operator are found among the best-ranked approaches: Tan et al. [510] describe their NICE.I-winning algorithm, which is based on an accelerated version of an integro-differential operator inspired by gradient descent evaluating a fraction of candidate points only instead of an exhaustive search. They propose a so-called integro-differential ring instead of the original operator to determine a direction for the next iteration with respect to the gradient-descent-like method. The algorithm includes steps for reflection removal, clustering-based coarse iris localization (classifying pixels as hair, eyebrow, eyelashes, iris-region, skin, etc.), as well as noise (eyelashes and eyebrows) detection using a curvature and prediction model. Sankowski et al. [464] present an algorithm, which is ranked 2nd in the NICE.I contest and specially dedicated to both NIR and VW processing. It consists of the following stages: (1) reflection localization using thresholding and morphologic operators; (2) reflection removal using inpainting [65]; (3) iris boundary localization using the integro-differential operator first on the outer, then on the inner boundary (noise caused by eyelids is avoided by restricting the search to 105 degrees left and right sectors); (4) lower eyelid detection using a circular arc [579]; (5) upper eyelid detection using a line model [622]. In order to operate under NIR, modifications need to be applied to this method, in particular an inverse processing of boundaries. Iris segmentation by Li et al. [305] combines the ideas of the HT with k-means clustering based on the gray level co-occurrence histogram for boundary detection and the integro-differential operator with RANSAC for upper eyelid detection. It is ranked 4th place in the NICE.I contest.

5.4.2 Hough Transform

Whereas from an implementation perspective, the integro-differential operator may be seen as a variation of the HT [335], it is the pioneering work of Wildes [579] using a binary edge map followed by a circular HT for circle detection, which made HT one of the two standard approaches to iris segmentation. The idea of the HT initially proposed and patented by Paul Hough [205] is to find imperfect instances of parameterized objects of a given type using a voting procedure executed in parameter space. By assessing edge information in the original image and increasing values in parameter space corresponding to shapes supporting the position of the current edge pixel, object candidates can be obtained as local maxima in the so-called *accumulator* space. In iris segmentation, pupillary and limbic boundaries are traditionally detected using a circular HT. Whereas also elliptical as well as more general HT variants exist, an increased number of parameters for more generic shapes typically constitutes problems in practical solutions. For the purpose of eyelid detection, the line HT is a frequently employed technique (e.g., in [88]). The circular HT detects circles in images. A circle with center (a, b) and radius r is the set of points (x, y) satisfying the circle equation:

$$r^2 = (x - a)^2 + (y - b)^2. \tag{5.7}$$

Circular Hough space is a three-dimensional space of parameters (a, b, r) describing circles in 2D space. The corresponding accumulator assigns each discretized triple (a, b, r) a numerical value indicating the support of this circle by edge data. In order to reduce search space to 2D, not a 3D accumulator, but an array of 2D accumulators tracking parameters (a, b) for a fixed discretized radius value $r \in [r_{min}, r_{max}]$ is employed, where r_{min} and r_{max} refer to minimum and maximum considered circle radii. Given an edge point (x, y), i.e. the neighborhood of the pixel indicates an edge, the circular HT algorithm increases for each discrete $r \in [r_{min}, r_{max}]$ the numerical value of all accumulator cells of parameters describing circles through this point. Such cells in Hough space lie on circles through (x, y) with an according radius r, see Fig. 5.7.

Many existing approaches adopt the HT approach, frequently accompanied by coarse pupil localization to reduce the search space. For example, Chen et al. [88] investigate NIR video-based iris image acquisition and propose an acquisition method employing: (1) video frame selection and eye extraction checking for the presence of 4 pairs of reflections (by hard thresholding) generated by the illumination light sources; (2) segmentation using adaptive thresholding for pupil localization and a circular HT on the Sobel edge detection image for defining the outer boundary. Specific assumptions on the ratio between pupil and iris radii, and assumptions on the position of the center using ROIs alleviate segmentation. Upper and lower eyelids are detected using a line HT after removing unlikely edges. By searching for arcs in angular sectors and employing lines connection, over- and undersegmentation errors are corrected. Zuo and Schmid [625] present a method for segmenting nonideal iris images using HT to localize the pupillary boundary

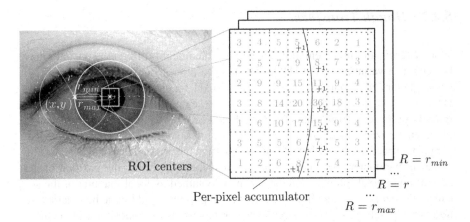

Fig. 5.7 Illustration of the voting step within the circular HT

after image inpainting and de-noising with a Wiener filter, contrast enhancement, and rough localization assuming the pupil has the smallest intensity values in the image. Further refinement is achieved using ellipse fitting and evaluation of the pupil segmentation. But limbic boundary detection uses image translation and inpainting, as well as directional edge detection similar to Daugman's integro-differential operator, introducing an off-center penalty and contrast compensation to account for close distances between iris and pupillary centers or uneven illumination. Cui et al. [107] propose a slightly modified version of the circular HT based on texture segmentation selecting randomly three edge points in the edge map to compute the centroid and radius. Xu and Shi [592] employ integral projection functions, median filtering, and circumference shifting for pupil localization, as well as a weighted HT for precise pupil center detection and radius refinement. Dobes et al. [131] propose an angular constrained HT after Canny edge detection for scleric boundary detection. Iris images are preprocessed using histogram equalization and Gaussian blurring. He and Shi [186] implement an HT-based algorithm using Canny edge detection to determine boundary candidates for limbic contour extraction. For pupillary boundary determination a form-fitting approach is applied using geometrical projection methods. Often, segmentation approaches combine the ideas of the HT and integro-differential operator: Zuo et al.'s approach [621] is based on both the integro-differential operator for limbic boundary detection as well as a randomized elliptical HT to fit the pupil. Proença and Alexandre [404] survey iris segmentation methodologies capable of noncooperative recognition using the UBIRIS database and compare results with their proposed method. The employed method in their paper relies on Tuceryan's moment-based texture segmentation [530]. This approach first employs a feature extraction using moments in small windows, and k-means clustering to segment the image. Finally, Canny edge detection is employed and used as input to a circular HT. Liu et al. [316] optimize Masek's segmentation algorithm (see Sect. 3.4) employing Canny edge detection and circular HT with a restricted voting area as well as a hypothesize and verify strategy to suppress false Hough maxima: (1) the order of detection is changed to pupillary before limbic boundary localization to benefit of strong pupil-to-iris contrast in NIR images; (2) edge points are reduced by filtering out all pixels with high intensity values, which most likely represent reflection edges; (3) a modified HT is applied by restricting the accumulated vote to an area of 30 degrees on each side of the local normal direction and testing three radius values only; (4) a hypothesize and verify strategy suppresses false Hough maxima by checking whether the iris is darker than the sclera and the pupil is darker than the iris and tests check, whether centers are within a reasonable image region and their distance does not exceed half the difference between iris and pupil radii; (5) eyelids are detected in each of four iris parts instead of global modeling as horizontal lines in Masek's implementation.

While the majority of iris segmentation approaches uses the grayscale intensity image as input only, Filho and Costa [150] investigate iris segmentation in hue-saturation-intensity and red–green–blue color space. Both boundaries are first approximated using k-means clustering on selected color components, then subjected to morphological processing, and finally refined using HT. For the inner boundary, the hue component is reported to deliver best results, for the outer boundary a combination of red and green components of the color space.

5.4.3 Active Contours

A significant modification to circular segmentation methods was introduced with AC and ASM. AC, also called snakes, is a family of methods for delineating object outlines. ASMs are an extension of this concept to shapes. Ritter [447, 448] proposed the first AC approach, finding the equilibrium of an internal force favoring circularity of a boundary curve and an external force pushing the iris/pupil boundary towards the maximum gradient. Abhyankar et al. [2] proposed ASMs to account for inaccurate circular iris segmentation, especially for off-gaze iris images. ASMs use an idea similar to ACs, seeking for a contour minimizing an energy function composed of shape and image energy. While the image energy is defined in terms of the intensity difference on two sides of the contour, shape energy tracks the difference between the current and average trained shape. Figure 5.8 illustrates these two driving forces of AC based techniques.

Arvacheh and Tizhoosh [18] present an AC-based approach to iris segmentation. Following the work of Ritter [447], this approach uses two forces, an internal continuity criterion force applied in radial direction towards the contour vertex mean, and an external force pulling the contour towards the maximum boundary gradient employing Daugman's integro-differential operator (using the distance between the maximum circular gradient and the contour vertex for a particular angular position). Furthermore, an iterative algorithm excluding eyelids by fitting with elliptic curves, and finding the limbus is proposed, based again on the integro-differential operator.

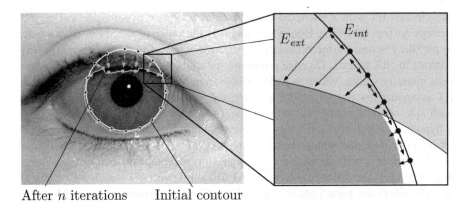

After n iterations   Initial contour

Fig. 5.8 AC find the equilibrium between inner and outer energy functions

In 2007, Daugman [118] proposed an AC-based approach describing inner and outer boundaries in terms of Fourier series expansions. The series of k polar boundary gradient values $(r_\theta)_{\theta=0}^{k-1}$ is modeled and smoothed using the first l Fourier coefficients $(f_t)_{t=0}^{l-1}$ to form a new boundary $(r'_\theta)_{\theta=0}^{k-1}$:

$$f_t := \sum_{\theta=0}^{k-1} r_\theta e^{-2\pi i t\theta/k}, \quad r'_\theta := \frac{1}{k}\sum_{t=0}^{l-1} f_t e^{2\pi i t\theta/k}. \tag{5.8}$$

Off-axis detection and correction is executed by assuming the orthographic image of the iris to reveal a circular pupil, i.e. gaze direction θ and magnitude γ are computed from the boundary as an oriented ellipse:

$$X(t) = a\cos(t) + b\sin(t), \ Y(t) = c\cos(t) + d\sin(t) \tag{5.9}$$

where $a = A\cos^2(\theta) + B\sin^2(\theta)$, $b = c = (B-A)\cos(\theta)\sin(\theta)$, and $d = B\cos^2(\theta) + A\sin^2(\theta)$, i.e. parameters a, b, c, d are real and imaginary parts of the complex Fourier coefficients of the empirical contour function. The off-gaze iris image is transformed into a frontal image using an affine transform specified by θ, γ. Still, a problem of this approach is the need for an initial center, as well as the existence of boundary outliers and eyelashes.

Shah and Ross [478] introduce an iris segmentation scheme, initially proposed in [456], using geodesic AC (GAC), free of shape constraints and iteratively refined guided by local and global properties. For pupil segmentation, the image is smoothed using a 2D median filter, thresholded using a fixed threshold, region-filtered (median-filter), boundary-traced, and circle-fitted. Reflection's impact is avoided by thresholding and inpainting. For iris segmentation, a level sets representation [331] of GAC is employed, combining an energy minimization of classical snakes with curve evolution, i.e. the embedding function being initially a circle with a radius just beyond the pupillary boundary itself starts to grow until it satisfies the stopping criterion. In contrast to Daugman's work [118], this method is not approximated using the first important Fourier coefficients, but relies on the order of the Fourier series. Thin plate splines are used to minimize the energy of the contour and avoid nonuniform evolution. An advantage of GACs is the property to handle splitting and merging of boundaries. Details of the level set approach can be found in [331,478]. Final normalization is achieved by employing Perona–Malik anisotropic diffusion [390].

In [81], Chen et al. employ adaptive mean shift for rough iris center location, followed by an AC model in terms of level set theory incorporating the local probabilistic prior, as well as boundary and region information using Markov random fields. The proposed mean shift variant adapts shape, scale, and orientation of the kernel to the local structure of iris textures and is an iterative non-parametric procedure using orientational gradient features. Eyelids, eyelashes, reflections, and shadows in iris regions are excluded by minimizing this energy function. Experiments show even better accuracy than current state-of-the-art techniques [478,556] and the method is reported to be real-time capable.

Zhang et al. [613] present another level set-based AC technique based on an initial approximation using HT, which is refined using a semantic iris-contour map combining spatial and gradient information in order to remove the gradient local extrema before applying the AC technique.

Koh et al. [263] present an AC model based on a circular HT. After rough eye localization in an ROI using binarization (the pupil is assumed to have lowest intensities), noise is removed using Gaussian blurring and morphology-based region filling and HT is applied to the edge detected image using the Canny operator. Pupil and iris boundaries are detected one after another. As AC approach, a Chan–Vese [75] model is applied solving a subcase of the Mumford and Shah [358] segmentation problem.

Nguyen et al. [369] employ a shrinking and expanding AC model for iris segmentation after initial rough estimation based on histogram thresholding and morphology operators. While for the pupillary boundary localization a shrinking curve is chosen, the curve is expanded to fit the outer iris boundary. Since typically for NIR images the outer boundary is less pronounced and considerable noise due to occlusions by eyelids and eyelashes may be present, shrinking contours are reported to perform worse. The internal energy is used to control the deformability of the snake, while the external energy tracks intensity and gradient values, representing the image structure.

5.4.4 Model-Fitting and Polar Techniques

Apart from AC-based approaches, there are also other techniques fitting parameterized models with pupillary and limbic contours. Especially the polar transform T (with its inverse T^{-1}) is frequently applied by such techniques, since it simplifies

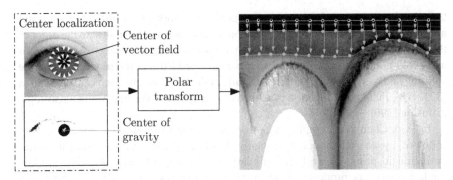

Fig. 5.9 Polar-based model fitting uses an initially found pupillary center to assist boundary detection

the fitting task by orienting boundary edges in approximately the same direction using an accurate iris center as origin of the transform, see also Fig. 5.9:

$$T : [0, 2\pi) \times \mathbb{R}_0^+ \to \mathbb{R}^2, \quad T \begin{pmatrix} \theta \\ r \end{pmatrix} := \begin{pmatrix} x + r\cos\theta \\ y + r\sin\theta \end{pmatrix}. \tag{5.10}$$

He et al. [189] use polar transform as an intermediate step to get gradient values for their pulling-and-pushing model. Labati et al. [290] present an agent-based method for center localization with multiple views boundary refinement after polar transform using the located center. Their method is shown to be fast (0.68 s) and still highly accurate. Du et al. [137] identify the pupil by adaptive thresholding first, employ a polar transform, and look for the maximum horizontal Sobel edge to determine the outer iris boundary. Vatsa et al. [556] introduce a new two-level hierarchical iris segmentation algorithm with special focus on quality enhancement. The first stage uses intensity thresholding to detect an elliptical initial boundary, while the second level more accurately models the boundary by a Mumford–Shah functional (used to evolve curves for nonideal iris image segmentation). SVM-based learning builds a globally enhanced image from locally enhanced parts. They confirm that in nonideal images (off-axis, motion blurred) the assumption of circular boundaries is not valid. Furthermore, they propose a new match score fusion technique combining textural Log-Polar Gabor transform and topoligical Euler features (invariant under translation, rotation, scaling, and polar transform), as well as indexing to improve speed. They report of certain unconstrained images, where the pupil appears lighter than the surrounding iris, e.g. because of reflections. In this case intensity-based initialization of AC finds the outer iris boundary as pupillary boundary. The proposed approach exhaustively seeks for the best parameters modeling the boundary as an elliptical region, and the resulting curve is evolved using a modified Mumford–Shah functional in a narrow band (5 pixels for the inner, 10 pixels for outer bands). Eyelids are masked using parabola fitting. For feature extraction, only the left and right iris parts are used.

Oroz et al. [320] apply mathematical morphology for polar/radial-invariant image filtering in a multistage iris segmentation approach: (1) color component selection; (2) reflection extraction; (3) limbic polar morphologic boundary extraction; (4) center reestimation; (5) pupillary boundary estimation. In contrast to several iris detection approaches, center detection does not rely on circularity but on a close-holes operator based on the assumption that pupil is darker than iris, iris is darker than sclera, and sclera is lighter than skin.

Examples for model-fitting-based techniques have been implemented by the following authors: Ryan et al. [460] propose an adaptive Starburst algorithm for elliptical fitting of iris boundaries, common for the purpose of eye tracking. Starburst identifies feature points on the limbus for the localization of pupil centers and fits an ellipse to the boundary pixels. Liam et al. [313] employ contrast enhancement, binarization and disk parameter search to find the outer iris boundary first, and then the inner pupillary boundary. Du et al. [136] present a direct least-squares fitting of ellipses method following a coarse-to-fine segmentation scheme with quality filter for video-based iris recognition. The quality filter simply involves a high-pass filter to check, whether reflections are present indicating opened eyes, rejecting frames with no reflections. In case reflections are found, coarse pupil localization and validation is performed, followed by pupil and limbic boundary modeling employing least squares fitting of ellipses [151]. Rough pupil detection is performed via k-means clustering based on intensities and PCA, and selecting an ROI close to the darkest clustered region (for consecutive frames the search space is reduced in case pupils were found). Least squares fitting of ellipses is first applied to the pupillary, and then to the limbic boundary. In order to account for the weaker boundary, an angular derivative replaces the gradient image. Eyelids and eyelashes are detected by a window-based variance and intensity adaptive thresholding algorithm excluding windows with strongest edges taking the boundary gradient magnitude into account. Eyelids are fitted with a second-order polynomial and excluded from the iris pattern. Roy et al. [459] suggest to apply game theory decision making using the modified Chakraborty and Duncan's algorithm [74], which combines region-based and gradient-based boundary finding methods. Preprocessing includes reflection removal, Gaussian smoothing, and morphological opening. Direct least square elliptical fitting approximates the pupillary boundary, before the game theory algorithm exactly matches the boundary by finding the nash equilibrium of the system. De Marsico et al. [126] propose an iris segmentation technique using a direct fast circle detection technique initially proposed by Taubin [513] using homogenity (histogram-based) and separability (integro-differential-based) as ranking criteria. Morimoto et al. [355] employ elliptical form fitting after Sobel edge detection and involving a multi-scale image cascade. Pulling and pushing proposed in [188] is based on Hooke's law and iteratively calculates a composition force of identical massless springs between the current center and all edge points on the contour.

5.5 Postprocessing

Apart from the localization of limbic and pupillary boundaries, fitting eyelids with lines or—more accurately—parabolas is an essential task to derive noise masks. Other types of noise typically present in iris images comprise reflections and eyelashes. Despite different noise detection models, also methods targeting segmentation quality may be employed as postprocessing tasks.

5.5.1 Noise Models

While common noise detection methods are part of almost any iris segmentation technique, some segmentation methods have put special emphasis on this postprocessing technique. Kong and Zhang [267] refine the eyelids and eyelashes model in Daugman's approach [116]. They focus on noise detection models for iris segmentation introducing a separable eyelash condition, non-informative condition and connectivity criterion for eyelash detection. Eyelashes can be divided into separable and multiple eyelashes. While the eyelid may well be described with parabolas [116], eyelashes are not considered in the original Daugman model. The separable eyelash condition captures single eyelashes by a spatial 1D Gabor filter and thresholded convolution. The second non-informative condition tracks multiple eyelashes in a region being of lower intensity than the surrounding area. Finally, a connectivity criterion takes results from both criteria into consideration requiring each eyelash point to be connected to another eyelid or eyelash point. For reflection detection, a simple thresholding is conducted, and Kolmogorov–Smirnov godness tests are proposed to test if intensity values are close to normal distribution. In order to detect weak reflection points, an iteratively executed statistical test is formulated. Huang et al. [206] combine edge and region information for iris segmentation by fusion with a special focus on noise removal. They find all noise to exhibit visible edge and region information (e.g., intensity). In contrast to the work in [267] noise is not detected before, but after normalization (segmentation), i.e. segmentation comprises three steps: (1) localization and normalization by edge detection, HT, and Daugman's rubber sheet model; (2) edge extraction based on phase congruency following Kovesi [272] by a bank of Log–Gabor filters comprising radial and angular components; (3) infusion of edge and region information for overcoming the illumination problem determining pupil and eyelashes by simple thresholding. After removing the pupil, reflections and eyelashes by using this method, eyelids are determined by employing the HT on a specific ROI window. Santos and Proença [466] investigate the role of the employed interpolation method in the Daugman rubbersheet transform process [109] on recognition accuracy (using also Daugman's recognition algorithm). From the tested interpolation methods *bilinear, bicubic,* and *nearest neighbor,* the choice had an impact on recognition accuracy with bicubic interpolation performing best; however, the impact is rather low (98.8% vs. 96.7% iris pixel usage on UBIRIS.v2 for *bicubic* vs. *nearest neighbor*). In Zuo and Schmid [625], occlusions are estimated in form of occlusion masks and merged with specular reflection masks to form an unwrapped iris noise mask.

5.5.2 Segmentation Quality

Methods testing for segmentation quality may be employed to either retry segmentation using different parameters and algorithms, or to reject input images requiring a recapture of the biometric signal.

Zuo and Schmid [624] present an algorithm evaluating the precision of iris segmentation analyzing the effect of noise (low sclera contrast, occluded iris images, strong specular reflections, low contrast iris images, unevenly illuminated images, and out-of-focus) on iris segmentation. The presented algorithm employs threshold-based pupil size tests, cumulative-gradient boundary checks, and pupil-to-iris intensity ratio tests. A similar segmentation algorithm integrating quality checks is presented in [622].

Kalka et al. [241] introduce another method for assessing segmentation quality based on probabilistic intensity and geometric features. The pupil segmentation measure assumes that the pupil is a flat homogeneous region of dark intensities compared to the iris. As geometric iris measure the eccentricity and concentricity of the pupil and iris boundaries is employed. Experiments yielded better performance for iris segmentation than pupil segmentation; however, a fusion of both measurement provided best results.

Zhou et al. [617] investigate methods to enhance current systems without changing core parts, in order to operate under unideal conditions. They report that most quality-based assessments [3, 28, 87, 187] require segmentation, which itself is quality dependent. Among the proposed modules to add are: (1) a quality filter unit eliminating iris images of insufficient quality, e.g. interlacing frames or blurred frames by assessing focus or model-based glare detection; (2) a segmentation evaluation unit assessing the intensity histograms of pupil, iris, and boundaries by checking for homogeneity, as well as segmentation scores fusion; (3) a quality measure unit, combining scores for the amount of feature information present, selecting portions of the iris with most distinguishable patterns, an occlusion measure estimating the amount of occluding noise, e.g. eyelids, eyelashes, and a dilation measure calculating the pupillary and limbic radii ratio; (4) a score fusion unit combining segmentation with quality scores. The proposed quality filter is shown to work well on the MBGC dataset.

5.6 Alternative Techniques

A classification of all segmentation approaches based on the dominant idea is not always unique. Besides refinements of the well-known integro-differential operator, HT, AC and (polar) model-fitting approaches, there are rather unique segmentation techniques: Puhan and Jiang [410] employ local Fourier Spectral Density for iris image binarization and construct a set of 1D signals and gradient analysis for limbic boundary detection. Poursaberi and Araabi [398] employ morphological operators after inpainting for iterative boundary-fitting. Zaim [602] proposed a split-and-merge approach for pupillary region determination and normalize the iris image based on the pupillary boundary. Morphologic operators are employed for eyelash removal. Basit and Javed [25] employ a segmentation method using iterative bijections and maximize the radial difference of intensities for limbic boundary detection.

Broussard and Ives [56, 57] propose artificial neural networks (ANNs) as multidimensional statistical classifiers for iris segmentation, classifying each pixel as either iris or non-iris pixel. In their refined version [56], they use feature saliency to identify 8 from 22 critical measures used as input to the ANN: Radius from pupil center, presence of eyelids, 5×1 mean, 1×15 horizontal gradients (with and without histogram equalization), 15×15 standard deviation, 5×5 vertical gradient, and 15×1 kurtosis. The feed-forward multilayer perceptron NN with 10 hidden nodes was trained using 500 images from the Bath database. Experiments illustrated ANN-created masks to be more accurate than circular boundary segmentation techniques.

There are also AdaBoost-based techniques: Jeong [235] uses AdaBoost eye detection and a color segmentation technique, ranked 5th in NICE.I. He et al. [189] describe a fast iris segmentation method trying to avoid conventional exhaustive search approaches. The proposed processing chain comprises reflection removal and iris detection by AdaBoost for rough center localization (using an approach initially proposed in [188]). Pupillary and limbic boundaries are localized by detecting edge points, employing a pulling and pushing approach (using restoring forces for refined center detection), and spline-refitting to smooth the outcome. Eyelids are localized using a rank filter for noise suppression and a histogram filter for shape irregularity, as well as eyelash and shadow detection employing a learned model and thresholding. For specular reflection removal they simply employ an adaptive thresholding for reflection mask computation and simple inpainting techniques. AdaBoost-based iris detection simply employs a trained cascade (10,000 positive and 18,939 negative examples) being able to identify irides (sized 24×24 pixels) after reflection removal. For eyelid localization an ROI is filtered with a 1D horizontal nonlinear filter, whose response is based on ranking pixels contained in the image area encompassed by the filter, noise edge points are excluded employing histograms, and finally a parabolic curve is fitted. Eyelashes and shadows are identified by their property of being darker than the surrounding region employing a statistic on histograms.

Proença and Alexandre [406] investigate noncooperative iris recognition proposing a segmentation method by classifying the iris into 6 parts with independent feature extraction (and comparison) for each region. Since iris recognition is found to substantially degrade under bad quality, noise can better be handled if it is divided into these 6 regions (regions 1–4 correspond to successive quadrants starting at $-45°$, regions 5 and 6 correspond to inner and outer iris rings). While reflections are predominant in left and right (1,3) sectors, occlusions by eyelids or eyelashes occur in the upper and lower (2,4) sectors. This approach somewhat follows the idea of best bits [196] and is reflected within the incremental iris recognition approach [438] presented in Sect. 9.2.2.

There are also techniques based on SIFT and Speeded Up Robust Features (SURF) completely avoiding rubbersheet-based segmentation and normalization: Belcher and Du [29] extract SIFT-based features directly from a left, right and bottom rectangular iris region. Alonso–Fernandez et al. [12] also investigate SIFT-based iris features: characteristic SIFT feature points in scale space (in the original eye image) are extracted and matching is executed using information around the feature points. They analyze different SIFT parameters and propose fusion with common techniques. Yang and Du [595] apply the segmentation in [189] and propose the use of SURF for noncooperative iris recognition.

Almeida [11] applies a knowledge-based approach to iris segmentation resulting in the 3rd rank at the NICE.I competition for this expert system. The algorithm is based on iterative improvement using rules, e.g., *"The pupil should be a very dark small circle, located in the central region of the image,"* based on which likely candidate position of pupils and irides are calculated . Results are combined by testing each possible combination. Pupil and iris segmentation is based on evaluating several seed points. While pupil location is based on rules exploiting intensity assumptions on the grayscale image (e.g., seeking for dark squares at multiple scales), red component images are employed for iris segmentation.

Chapter 6
Multi-stage Real-Time Iris Preprocessing

Motivated by the growing demand for real-time capable solutions, this chapter presents in detail a multistage approach to iris segmentation [540, 541]. As noted in the previous chapter, segmentation consumes high amounts of processing time, especially for less constraint and highly resolved input images, but it is a crucial and error-prone step in the processing chain. Furthermore, most techniques highly depend on database specific assumptions like pupil intensity, iris ratios, rough center position and—most notably—wavelength. The presented approach targets all three quality criteria of segmentation: efficiency, usability in terms of sensor independence, and speed by proposing the following 4 different ideas:

- *Two-stage algorithms*: Coarse center detection and fine boundary localization usually combined in traditional approaches are decoupled. Therefore, search space at each stage is reduced without having to stick to simpler models.
- *Fast HT*: An adaptive multi-resolution HT is presented to estimate the approximate position of the iris center assessing not only gradient magnitude but also direction.
- *Polar and ellipsopolar transforms*: Subsequent polar and ellipsopolar transforms detect elliptic limbic or pupillary boundaries one after another. While a polar transform detects the first elliptic limbic or pupillary boundary, an ellipsopolar transform finds the second boundary based on the outcome of the first. This way, both iris images with clear limbic (typical for VW) and with clear pupillary boundaries (typical for NIR) can be processed in a uniform manner.
- *Gaussian weighting*: While typically, less-constrained image acquisition needs higher degrees of freedom with respect to the employed models in order to accurately fit the observed data, simpler models with strong assumptions on the average underlying data (e.g., assuming circularity of pupils) may even deliver better results, since they incorporate prior knowledge. The presented approach proposes the application of Gaussian weighting functions to incorporate model-specific prior knowledge without sacrificing high degrees of freedom of the employed models.

C. Rathgeb et al., *Iris Biometrics: From Segmentation to Template Security*,
Advances in Information Security 59, DOI 10.1007/978-1-4614-5571-4_6,
© Springer Science+Business Media, LLC 2013

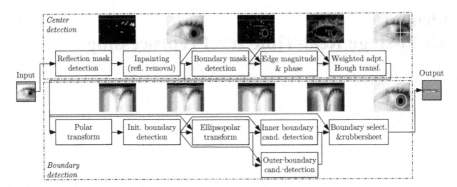

Fig. 6.1 Architecture of the proposed two-stage iris segmentation framework (WAHET)

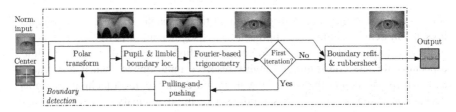

Fig. 6.2 Alternative boundary detection module (IFPP) for the proposed framework

The proposed approach may be seen as an iris segmentation *framework* with reference implementations, concentrating on efficient and robust ways to obtain pupillary and limbic boundaries. The segmentation software is written in C++, uses the OpenCV [215] image library, and is made publicly available with this book (USIT, see Sect. 3.4). Two reference implementations [540, 541] have been published so far. The first implementation, *Weighted Adaptive Hough and Ellipsopolar Transforms* (WAHET), is proposed in [541] and illustrated in Fig. 6.1. It differs from the alternative *Iterative Fourier-based Pulling and Pushing* (IFPP) method proposed in [540] and illustrated in Fig. 6.2 in a completely different (refined) boundary detection procedure. WAHET proposes an ellipsopolar transform and Gaussian weighting functions instead of a twofold pulling and pushing with Fourier-based trigonometry [118] approach used in the IFPP algorithm.

The first task consists of finding a center point C within the input image I completely inside the limbic and pupillary boundary. The key operation to derive C is an adaptive HT, which determines the center of multiple approximately concentric rings at iteratively refined resolution. It accumulates lines in direction of the gradient at boundary edge candidate points. The WAHET implementation gives a higher weight to locations in the center of the accumulator, refining the original implementation in IFPP. While C is not unique, ideally it will be close to the centers of circles approximating the limbic boundary L and pupillary boundary P. The idea is to exploit orientation and magnitude of both pupillary and limbic edges to find C, instead of sequential boundary extraction. As noted in [403], until now, almost all state-of-the-art segmentation systems employ a fixed order, in which pupillary and limbic boundaries are fitted, usually influenced by the type of training data. The reason for this behavior can be explained by the different nature of NIR images, with high contrast pupillary boundaries, and VW images, with clearly visible limbic edges. The advantage of the presented approach is a uniform processing of different image types emphasizing database-independence.

The second task consists of extracting P and L from a polar representation using C as origin. Within this representation all boundary edges have approximately the same orientation, which reduces the cost of edge detection. Like in the stage before, no strict order for the detection of limbic and pupillary boundaries is given. Instead, in the WAHET implementation an initial boundary B is detected from the polar transformed input by (1) determining the maximum-energy horizontal line (modeling a circle in Cartesian coordinates); (2) maximizing the vertical polar gradient for each column (discrete angle); (3) smoothing the resulting curve; (4) remapping candidates to Cartesian coordinates; (5) fitting the edge points with an oriented ellipse. Since the detected boundary B is either the limbic or pupillary boundary, the algorithm continues to find the second boundary based on the two hypotheses $H_0 : B = P$ and $H_1 : B = L$ using an Ellipsopolar transform. This transform maps ellipses concentric with elliptic boundary B to horizontal lines, which is helpful since P and L should be approximately concentric. Again, steps (1)–(5) are executed to derive an inner candidate P' and outer candidate L'. Based on the outcome of the gradient energy GE of these contours, one hypothesis is rejected. In case $GE(P') > GE(L')$ hypothesis H_0 is rejected and $P = P'$, otherwise $L = L'$. Finally, the rubbersheet transform is applied. In the IFPP implementation, P and L are detected from the polar representation by (1) convolution with a set of oriented Gabor kernels; (2) estimating the three best vertical filter responses for clustering radius-values using the k-means clustering algorithm; (3) exclusion of unlikely contour points using the 0.2 and 0.8 quantiles; (4) fitting with a Fourier series as in [118]; (5) center restoration using pulling and pushing [188] and re-execution of steps (1)–(4).

The proposed framework supports generic iris segmentation techniques under hard constraints:

1. Segmentation in the order of deciseconds.
2. No strong assumptions on image type and conditions.

While most segmentation algorithms employ some sort of exhaustive searching or single error-prone strategies to detect pupillary and limbic boundaries [44, 403], the framework supports two-stage iris segmentation techniques. Compared to traditional approaches it has three major advantages: First, modules may easily be extended to incorporate more sophisticated techniques for individual tasks, yielding a trade-off between computation time and segmentation accuracy. Second, in the presented configuration the incremental technique is faster and more scalable with respect to resolution. Third, failures can be detected and corrected in early stages leading to more robustness.

An intended goal of the proposed framework is the uniform processing of pupillary and limbic boundaries for VW and NIR images, the latter exhibiting a sharper pupillary boundary, especially for dark irides. Also noise masks, using, e.g., methods in [189], are not yet computed. While they may certainly improve recognition rates when employing the HD comparator, they are not critical for the rubbersheet mapping, fast and well-working methods already exist, and there are even new comparators available as alternatives to the storage of noise masks [427, 438], see Sect. 9.2.

6.1 Reflection Removal

The first task in the proposed processing chain enhances the input image by reducing the amount of noise able to degrade segmentation accuracy. Reflections inside the pupil may significantly affect iterative center search. While generally, determining a proper segmentation input resolution and reducing effects from defocus or motion blur may be implemented at this stage of processing, the current implementation concentrates on reflection removal. Hot spots caused by the use of flash, pupillary reflections of windows, or other objects emitting light can be suppressed by looking for small objects with high luminance values. While the sclera in eye images typically represents the area with highest luminance in VW, in NIR the sclera is typically much darker. Still, reflections can be accurately identified by size filtering.

The reflection mask $M : [0,m] \times [0,n] \to \{0,1\}$ is computed by the WAHET algorithm in three steps:

1. *Adaptive thresholding*: This procedure selects all pixels (x,y) with intensities exceeding the local mean $A(x,y)$ in the 23×23 neighborhood plus a constant $c = 60$:

$$M_A \begin{pmatrix} x \\ y \end{pmatrix} := \begin{cases} 1 & \text{if } I(x,y) > A(x,y) + c \\ 0 & \text{otherwise.} \end{cases} \tag{6.1}$$

2. *Region size filtering*: All connected one-components in M_A, which are less than 10 and greater than 1,000 pixels, are set to zero.
3. *Morphological dilation*: A circular 11×11 structuring element is applied to the image.

The approach deriving a reflection mask in IFPP is similar. In order to remove reflections, the original image I is inpainted using M, i.e. all selected regions are reconstructed from their boundary using the *Navier–Stokes* method natively provided by the OpenCV library, resulting in inpainted image I'.

6.2 Approximate Localization of Pupil and Iris

Edge phase $P_E : [0,m] \times [0,n] \to [0,2\pi)$ and magnitude $M_E : [0,m] \times [0,n] \to \mathbb{R}_0^+$ are estimated from the inpainted image I' using horizontal and vertical Sobel kernels (7×7 for WAHET, 3×3 for IFPP). A boundary edge mask $E : [0,m] \times [0,n] \to \{0,1\}$ detects initial candidate points for center estimation in the next step: From

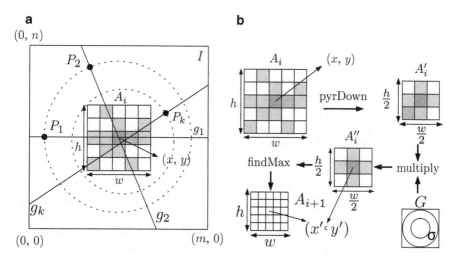

Fig. 6.3 Weighted adaptive HT: Illustration of (**a**) voting and (**b**) weighting steps

the top 20% of edge points with respect to edge magnitude all candidates within cells of a 30×30 grid with a dominant mean orientation (i.e., the magnitude of the mean orientation exceeds $m = 0.5$) are selected. The idea of this filtering is to remove candidate points in eyelashes with an almost equal amount of high edges with opposite directions.

6.3 Iterative Hough Transform

The center of an eye is not unique, but ideally, a center point should be close to the centers of circles approximating the boundaries L and P. In order to speed up traditional HT, an iterative approach to finding the center point C proposed by Cauchie et al. [68] is adopted. Instead of estimating center and radius of the most dominant circle, this method tries to find the center of the most distinctive concentric circles in the image, using not only gradient magnitude but also gradient orientation. Compared to the basic version of this algorithm in [68], a number of modifications have been applied: (1) Bresenham's [50] fast line algorithm is used to fill accumulator cells; (2) voting accounts for magnitude information; (3) a new weighting step employs a Gaussian function to account for prior knowledge; (4) the ROI refinement step has been simplified to select a highest energy cell only.

Starting with $i = 0$ the modified version of this algorithm consists of three iteratively executed steps at each stage i, see also Fig. 6.3:

1. *Initialization*: For a rectangular ROI R_i of size $m_i \times n_i$ (initially $R_0 = I'$), an accumulator A_i consisting of a fixed $w \times h$ grid of cells covering R_i is initialized

with zero. From the set of candidate edge points E_{i-1} (initially $E_{-1} = \{(x,y) : E(x,y) = 1\}$), all points $P_j \in E_{i-1}$, whose gradient lines g_j do not intersect with R_i, are rejected in E_i.

2. *Voting*: All cells in A_i crossed by a gradient line g_j of a candidate point in E_i are incremented using the absolute gradient value.
3. *Weighting*: The accumulator A_i is downscaled, multiplied with a centered Gaussian kernel G, the cell of maximum value is found and R_{i+1} is centered in the cell's center (x', y'). As long as R_{i+1} (with $m_{i+1} = \frac{m_i}{2}, n_{i+1} = \frac{n_i}{2}$) is larger than a predefined threshold, the algorithm repeats with step (1), following a coarse to fine strategy, otherwise $C = (x', y')$.

By adding a weighting step, modeled by Gaussian G, it is possible to incorporate the heuristic that at each stage the maximum cell near the center of the accumulator is likely to be found. Especially for early stages this is a valuable prior knowledge to suppress eyelid gradients. In contrast to WAHET the IFPP implementation does not include the weighting step (with Gaussian sigma set to one third of the downscaled accumulator size), but downscaling and maximum selection only. While both approaches employ 0.5 pixel as the accumulator precision threshold, the accumulator size is smaller (10×10 instead of a 101×101 accumulator grid) for IFPP.

6.4   Pupil and Iris Boundary Models in Polar Coordinates

In the polar transform stage, the found center C is used to polar unwrap the iris image I' using a discretized version of Eq. (5.10), restricted to a maximum mapped radius, resulting in a $k \times g$ polar image I_p. The angular dimension typically depends on the desired output resolution, and is set to $k = 512$ per default, the radial dimension is set to $g = 512 * \frac{n}{m}$, the maximum mapped radius corresponds to the maximum distance from C to each image corner. Depending on the implementation, either polar and ellipsopolar boundary detection (WAHET) or k-means and Fourier-based boundary detection (IFPP) is performed.

6.4.1   Polar and Ellipsopolar Boundary Detection

Initial boundary detection operates on the polar transformed I_p to derive a boundary contour. Therefore, in WAHET I_p is convolved with an oriented 21×21 Gabor kernel:

$$G(x,y) := \frac{\gamma}{2\pi\sigma^2} \exp\left(-\frac{x'^2 + \gamma^2 y'^2}{2\sigma^2}\right) \cos\left(2\pi\frac{x'}{\lambda} + \psi\right)$$

$$\text{where } x' = x\cos(\theta) + y\sin(\theta), \quad y' = y\cos(\theta) - x\sin(\theta). \tag{6.2}$$

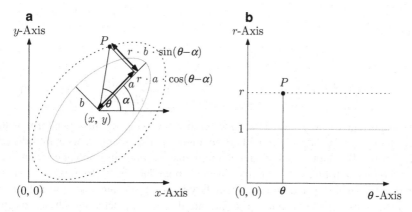

Fig. 6.4 Ellipsopolar transform: (**a**) Cartesian domain and (**b**) ellipsopolar domain

All candidate edges have the same orientation; therefore, a suitable choice is $\lambda = 8\pi, \psi = \frac{\pi}{2}, \sigma = 6, \gamma = 0.5, \theta = -\frac{\pi}{2}$. The resulting gradient image is denoted by G_p. The initial boundary B is determined as follows:

1. Starting at an offset $o = 12$ (to avoid image border effects), for each radial value $r \in [o, g-1] \cap \mathbb{N}$ (corresponding to a line in G_p) the sum of gradient values at each discrete polar angle $\theta \in [0, k-1] \cap \mathbb{N}$ is computed and the polar contour series $(b_\theta)_{\theta=0}^{k-1}$ is initialized by the radius r_{max} with maximum gradient sum, i.e.:

$$\forall \theta : b_\theta = r_{max}. \tag{6.3}$$

2. Using gradient fitting within a local radial window W (we use $W = [-15, 15] \cap \mathbb{N}$), the contour gradient is maximized yielding a refined contour $(b'_\theta)_{\theta=0}^{k-1}$:

$$\forall \theta : b'_\theta = b_\theta + \max_{i \in W} \arg \left(G_p(\theta, b_\theta + i) \right). \tag{6.4}$$

3. The resulting contour is smoothed using 1D Fourier series expansions (see Eq. (5.8)) keeping the DC and 1 coefficient, followed by another gradient fitting with reduced window size 5 and again a Fourier fitting keeping the DC plus 3 coefficients, resulting in $(b''_\theta)_{\theta=0}^{k-1}$. Finally, the polar contour $(b''_\theta)_{\theta=0}^{k-1}$ is transformed to Cartesian coordinates (using the inverse polar transform) and fitted with an oriented ellipse in a least-squares sense using the *Fitzgibbon* algorithm natively provided by OpenCV. Boundary curve B is sampled from this best-fitted ellipse.

Typically, after the first iteration of polar boundary detection, the detected curve B can be used to derive a more accurate center than C. An even better idea is to take the shape of B into consideration: we propose the application of an ellipsopolar transform, which is essentially a polar transform after translation, rotation and stretching, mapping concentric ellipses to axis-parallel lines, see Fig. 6.4. Let B be the polar sampled representation of a general oriented ellipse with center (x, y), half axes a, b and angle of inclination α, then the general ellipsopolar transform is defined as:

$$T_E : [0, 2\pi) \times \mathbb{R}_0^+ \rightarrow \mathbb{R}^2$$

$$T_E \begin{pmatrix} \theta \\ r \end{pmatrix} := \begin{pmatrix} x \\ y \end{pmatrix} + \begin{pmatrix} \cos\alpha & -\sin\alpha \\ \sin\alpha & \cos\alpha \end{pmatrix} * \begin{pmatrix} ra\cos(\theta - \alpha) \\ rb\sin(\theta - \alpha) \end{pmatrix}. \qquad (6.5)$$

It is important to note that again a discretized version of this transform with maximum mapping radius of is applied, analogous to the polar transform introduced in Eq. (5.10). By mapping the inpainted input image I' into ellipsopolar coordinates, again boundary fitting (i.e., seeking an inner boundary by restricting our search to radial values $r < 1$ and an outer boundary with $r > 1$) can be performed using the same steps (1)–(4) introduced in the initial boundary detection phase, except that now the initialization phase favors an elliptic boundary concentric to B, which is a very good first approximation. In order to further incorporate model-specific prior knowledge in step (1), a Gaussian weighting function is applied to the sum. The actual weight depends on the radial distance r of the current radial distance to the reference contour B (we use Gaussian parameters $\mu_i = 0.66, \sigma_i = 0.44$ for the inner search and $\mu_o = 2.5, \sigma_o = 1$ for the outer boundary search). The result of inner and outer boundary detection are elliptic boundary candidates P' and L'.

Having computed P' and L' based on the hypotheses $H_0 : B = P$ and $H_1 : B = L$, respectively, the task of boundary (hypothesis) selection involves the computation of the following gradient energy function GE for an ellipsopolar sampled boundary curve X with respect to ellipse B (defining the ellipsopolar mapping):

$$GE(X) := \sum_{\theta=0}^{k-1} M_E\big(X(\theta)\big) W(\mu, \sigma, V(X, \theta, B)), \qquad (6.6)$$

i.e., the gradient values in M_E at discrete sample points of X are summed and weighted using a Gaussian weighting function W using the ellipsopolar radial value $V(X, \theta, B)$ of X with respect to transform ellipse B at angle θ and fixed Gaussian parameters. Depending on whether the inner or outer boundaries are evaluated, μ_i, σ_i or μ_o, σ_o are used. If $GE(P') > GE(L')$, the pupillary boundary is set to $P = P'$, otherwise the limbic boundary is set to $L = L'$.

Finally, the resulting boundary curves P and L are subjected to Daugman's rubbersheet model (see Eq. (5.2)), and the resulting iris texture is enhanced using contrast-limited adaptive histogram equalization [446].

6.4.2   K-Means and Fourier-Based Boundary Detection

IFPP executes the following steps to derive boundary curves:

1. In IFPP not a single, but several different Gabor kernels G are employed ($\lambda = 8\pi, \psi = \frac{\pi}{2}, \sigma = 2, \gamma = 0.1$ and $\theta \in \{-\frac{9\pi}{16}, -\frac{\pi}{2}, -\frac{7\pi}{16}\}$, see Eq. (6.2)) taking the

maximum response for the first iteration. The second iteration uses a single kernel $\left(\theta = -\frac{\pi}{2}, \sigma = 6, \gamma = 1\right)$ after the determined center C has been used to polar unwrap the iris image I.

2. For a set of equidistant polar angles (i.e., corresponding to the polar image width), the three best vertical filter responses are used for clustering r-values using the k-means clustering algorithm implemented in OpenCV. The next step determines the best candidate for each polar angle within each cluster K in the set evaluating a clustering energy function CE, using the distance to the cluster center c and the convolution result $I_p * G$:

$$CE(r, \theta) := 1 - \frac{|r - c|}{\max_{(r_K, \theta_K) \in K} |r_K - c|} + \frac{I_p * G(r, \theta)}{\max_{(r_K, \theta_K) \in K} I_p * G(r_K, \theta_K)}. \qquad (6.7)$$

3. The 0.2 and 0.8 quantiles with respect to distance from center are evaluated and all contour points outside the interval are excluded. Finally, missing values are linearly interpolated in polar coordinates from their immediate neighbors.
4. The contour is fitted with a Fourier series and the result is restricted to the 3 best complex Fourier coefficients using Fourier-based trigonometry [118].
5. Typically, after the first iteration of polar boundary detection, detected boundary curves can be used to derive a better center point C to target clustering errors. Therefore, pulling and pushing [188] is applied to restore the center point C to its equilibrium within the most pronounced boundary and the polar detection procedure is restarted a second time. A problem with this technique is the less pronounced boundary being largely affected by noise or eyelids. Therefore, the less expressive boundary is reconstructed from the more stable one, exploiting that both contours exhibit an almost constant distance.

Again, the resulting boundary curves P and L are subjected to Daugman's rubbersheet model, and contrast-limited adaptive histogram equalization [446].

Chapter 7
Experiments on Iris Image Processing

This chapter presents an experimental evaluation of eye detection and iris segmentation techniques discussed in Chaps. 4 and 6. Evaluation targets all three different quality factors of segmentation software listed in Chap. 5, namely accuracy, speed, and usability.

With respect to eye detection, accuracy refers to a low number of false negative and false positive detections of eyes in full portrait images, as well as small eye-offsets with respect to ground truth positions. Regarding iris segmentation, segmentation errors of pupillary and limbic boundaries should be avoided. Especially robustness to moderate noise factors is desirable, e.g., defocus, motion blur, varying illumination, off-axis gaze direction, high variance in iris size, or nonlinear distortions by the application of imperfect iris models. Accuracy is evaluated by assessing the impact of segmentation on verification recognition accuracy, i.e. ROC curves, in case of multistage real-time iris processing. For eye detection, left and right eye offsets as well as detection rates with respect to the employed datasets are given.

Speed, i.e. adherence to near real-time constraints (at least less than 1 s processing time per image) is a quality factor often neglected in comparison studies, but this factor is most critical in applications. Average segmentation time is evaluated for each of the employed databases and tested algorithms.

Usability is the quality factor most difficult to quantify, but possibly the most important of all three factors. Usability refers to which extent a segmentation algorithm can be used with effectiveness, efficiency, and satisfaction. This includes reproducibility of segmentation performance under different sensors and environmental conditions (i.e., the algorithm avoids database-specific tuning), the ability to exchange and improve single submodules of the algorithm (i.e., ideally availability as open source software), easy parameterless configuration, and intuitive use of the segmentation tool. Usability is evaluated by setting results on different databases into context and analyzing segmentation errors.

C. Rathgeb et al., *Iris Biometrics: From Segmentation to Template Security*,
Advances in Information Security 59, DOI 10.1007/978-1-4614-5571-4_7,
© Springer Science+Business Media, LLC 2013

7.1   Experimental Setup

Experiments for eye detection target the extraction of eye windows from portrait images. We have compared:

1. *FFF*: Results of the model-driven face with face-part classifier fusion presented in all details in Sect. 4.4.
2. *Eye-only*: A single Haar classifier trained to detect eyes (using an implementation provided by the OpenCV framework).
3. *Nested*: A classifier performing a nested cascade, i.e. eyes are detected in the most prominent face detection result (using again configurations provided by OpenCV).

In order to judge the accuracy of detection results, left-eye and right-eye offset (LO, RO) in percent of the inter-eye distance are employed and detection rate (DR) results with respect to successful eye detections (detections with less than 20% LO and RO, respectively) are given. Furthermore, detection processing time (DT) in seconds is evaluated. Eye detection tests are carried out using two different datasets:

1. *Casia-D* is a subset of 2 images per user (282 images in total) from the first publicly available long-range (3 m) and high-quality NIR iris and face dataset with $2,352 \times 1,728$ pixel resolution, CASIA.v4-Distance, with manually selected eye and nose positions for ground truth. Since it employs NIR images, this datasets covers the scenario of extracting eye images for iris recognition on-the-move and at-a-distance [337]. As an interesting, yet challenging, aspect of this dataset, it should be noticed that images do not cover full portrait images, instead large parts of the lower face, e.g. mouth, chin, are sometimes missing, making a successful application of face detectors difficult.
2. *Yale-B* is a manually labeled subset of 252 images from challenging (varying illumination, different pose) VW 640×480 pixel resolution full-portrait face images (90 pixels eye distance) in *Yale Face Database B* [162]. This dataset represents an input test for classical face detection operating in the VW spectrum. Extracted eye images typically do not satisfy the required lower bound of 100 pixels iris diameter (ISO/IEC 19794-6 quality criteria for level "low"), 140 pixels [115, 116] or even 200 pixels, respectively [578].

For iris segmentation tests, the following algorithms have been used, see also Sect. 3.4:

1. *WAHET*, the Weighted Adaptive Hough and Ellipsopolar Transforms iris segmentation algorithm introduced in Chap. 6 and available as part of USIT.
2. *IFPP*, the USIT implementation of the Iterative Fourier-based Pulling and Pushing iris segmentation algorithm discussed in Chap. 6.
3. *OSIRIS* [275], an open source reference system for iris recognition using a two-stage approach for segmentation: First, the pupil region in the image is

Table 7.1 Experimental results for eye detection: Offset (in percent of inter-eye distance u), detection rate (eye offset less than 20 % of u) and detection time (in seconds) per image

Algorithm	Left-eye offset		Right-eye offset		Detection rate (%)		Detection time (s)	
	Casia-D	Yale-B	Casia-D	Yale-B	Casia-D	Yale-B	Casia-D	Yale-B
Eye-only	19.48	14.06	32.73	17.13	65.8	87.3	0.60	0.61
Nested	81.6	3.78	139.9	5.26	14.6	97.6	0.65	0.28
FFF	5.95	4.30	5.74	3.91	96.4	99.2	1.28	0.28

roughly searched using a binarization and exploiting the circularity of the pupil. Subsequently, limbic and pupillary contours are determined using HT and AC for refinement.

4. *CAHT*, the USIT implementation of Contrast-adjusted Hough Transform.

For all tested iris segmentation algorithms, evaluations use the 512×64 pixel iris texture in doubly-dimensionless coordinates only. Neither noise masks nor other enhancement methods on the original textures are considered. All obtained textures are enhanced using contrast-limited adaptive histogram equalization [446]. To assess the impact on recognition accuracy, the feature extraction technique by Ma et al. [323] is applied, using the USIT implementation optimized for the CASIA.v3-Interval database (see Sect. 3.4). Fractional HD is applied as dissimilarity measure and alignment is achieved applying up to 7-bit circular shifts in each direction. Note that higher error rates compared to evaluations where noise masks are considered or the feature extraction stage is optimized for the employed dataset are expected and do not necessarily reflect segmentation errors (especially for the more challenging datasets).

Experiments for iris segmentation are carried out using different datasets from open biometric databases:

1. *Casia-I* consists of the left-eye subset (1,332 images) of CASIA.v4-Interval, good quality NIR illuminated indoor images with 320×280 pixel resolution.
2. *Casia-L* is composed of the first 10 left-eye samples of the first 100 users (1,000 images) in the CASIA.v4-Lamp iris database, a more challenging 640×480 pixel resolution indoor NIR images dataset.
3. *ND* is a subset of 42 classes with 10 samples per class (420 images) in the ND-IRIS-0405 dataset, nonideal 640×480 pixel resolution indoor NIR images.
4. *UBIRIS* presents the first 100 classes (817 images) in UBIRIS.v1, highly challenging VW images (200×150 pixel resolution).

7.2 Eye Detection

From the detection rates in Table 7.1 we can see that the proposed FFF method delivers clearly the best results for the NIR dataset Casia-D with 5.95 % left-eye offset (LO) and 5.74 % right-eye offset (RO) and a total of 96.4 % detection

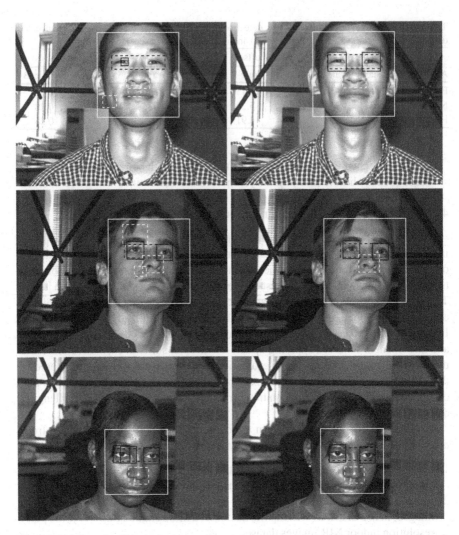

Fig. 7.1 YaleB results: Detector responses (Face, eye, eyepair, and nose) for the algorithms *Nested* (*left*) versus *FFF* (*right*)

rate (DR). Since in addition to performing a nested cascade for face detection FFF tests each combination of detected face parts with the corresponding face to determine the combination that best matches a trained model, it is much more stable to single false detections. This is very likely the case if the tested dataset differs in nature and/or recording conditions from the dataset used for feature training. Both eye-only detectors, with 19.48 % LO, 32.73 % RO, and 65.8 % DR and nested with 81.6 % LO, 139.9 % RO (these high rates occur, since frequently no eye can be detected), and 14.6 % DR do not deliver satisfactory results. For YaleB, results

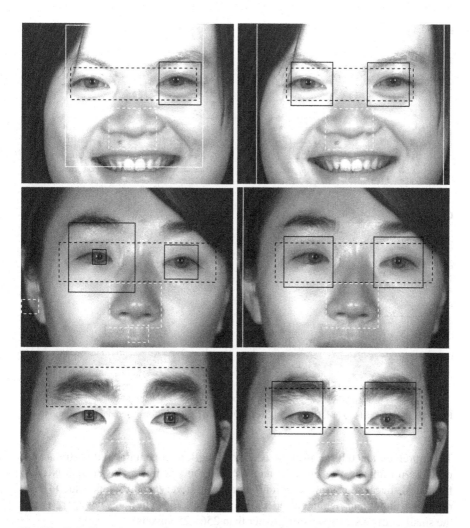

Fig. 7.2 Casia-D results: Detector responses (Face, eye, eyepair and nose) for the algorithms *Nested* (*left*) versus *FFF* (*right*)

are much closer, still the proposed variant delivers highest 99.2 % DR (4.3 % LO, 3.91 % RO), before nested with 97.6 % DR (3.78 % LO, 5.26 % RO) and eye-only with 87.3 % DR (14.06 % LO, 17.13 % RO).

Regarding speed, the proposed FFF method requires twice as much time for Casia-D than the other approaches with 1.28 s DT per image, because of many false-detections of faces and the conducted rerun on the entire image. Since this rerun is not performed by the nested variant, it is significantly faster with 0.65 s DT (eye-only is only slightly faster with 0.6 s DT). However, the additional time needed by grouping and refitting is negligible, as can be seen from the low difference in YaleB detection times between Nested and Proposed (both 0.28 s per image).

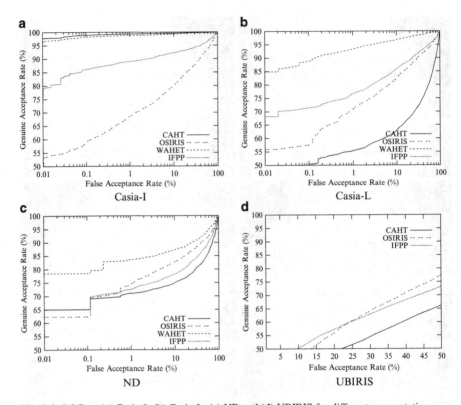

Fig. 7.3 ROC on (**a**) Casia-I, (**b**) Casia-L, (**c**) ND and (**d**) UBIRIS for different segmentation

The aforementioned rerun is not needed for YaleB, as it contains full portraits and no close-up images, see Figs. 7.1 and 7.2. Eye-only is much slower than Nested for YaleB, because nested detection operates on a very small image (due to low resolution input and pyramidal operation mode, i.e. detection always operates on the smallest downscaled version greater than 256×256 pixels).

Recapitulatory, while the idea of grouping and refitting needs a check of all subsets of classifier results, and thus exponential complexity in the number of returned detection results, practical evaluations show that given a sufficient accuracy of individual responses the average case can be executed quite fast.

7.3 Iris Segmentation

Experimental results for iris segmentation in form of ROC curves for verification assessments are illustrated in Fig. 7.3. Performance rates are summarized in Table 7.2. Furthermore, speed evaluations comparing results with eye detection processing time are given in Fig. 7.4.

Table 7.2 Iris segmentation results: EER and segmentation time (in seconds per image)

	Equal error rate (EER) (%)				Segmentation time (s)			
Algorithm	Casia-I	Casia-L	ND	Ubiris	Casia-I	Casia-L	ND	Ubiris
CAHT	0.74	28.77	22.01	39.65	0.49	1.96	2.29	0.18
OSIRIS	16.40	14.89	15.45	33.51	3.46	6.21	6.27	2.03
IFPP	8.07	12.90	19.04	34.56	0.18	0.46	0.48	0.11
WAHET	1.20	4.36	12.90	–	0.21	0.26	0.25	–

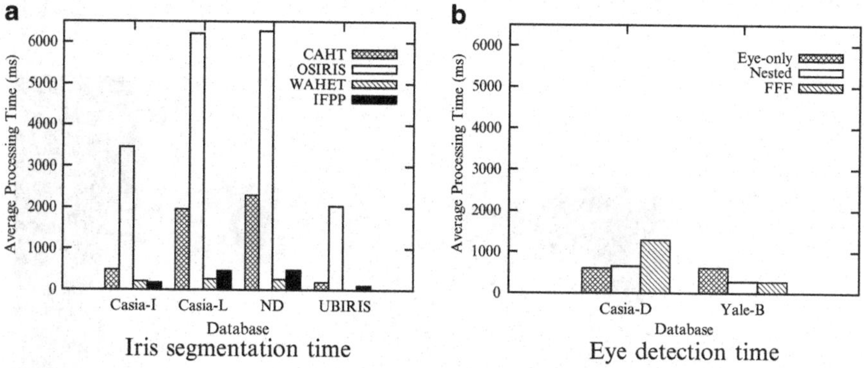

Iris segmentation time

Eye detection time

Fig. 7.4 Speed: (**a**) iris segmentation performance versus (**b**) eye detection performance

For the *Casia-I* dataset, experiments resulted in the best EER of 0.74 % at on average 0.49 s segmentation time per image (ST) for the CAHT implementation. This result is not too surprising, as this method is explicitly tuned to deliver good results for this database, boundaries can well be represented with circles and usually strong models provide good results in case of weak data (such as soft limbic boundaries). However, a strong model becomes useless if the data cannot well be represented, see Fig. 7.5. The proposed WAHET method follows closely with only slightly higher 1.20 % EER at 0.21 s ST. The third best accuracy on this set provides the proposed IFPP method with 8.07 % EER at 0.18 s ST. Finally, OSIRIS with 16.4 % EER at 3.46 s ST delivered worst accurate results and also the highest ST. When looking at the type of segmentation errors made by the algorithms, it is interesting to see that OSIRIS frequently leads to over-segmentation errors (due to less pronounced limbic boundaries) while WAHET reveals a few over-segmentation errors due to sharp collarettes.

In *Casia-L* the WAHET method provides the best results (4.36 % EER at 0.26 s ST) clearly outperforming IFPP (12.9 % EER at 0.46 s ST), OSIRIS (14.89 % EER at 6.21 s ST), and CAHT (28.77 % EER at 1.96 s ST). It is interesting to see that a quite well-working segmentation system (CAHT) may fail completely, if assumptions do not hold. CAHT segmentation errors include many complete failures and some under-segmentation errors due to eyelids. OSIRIS exhibits many

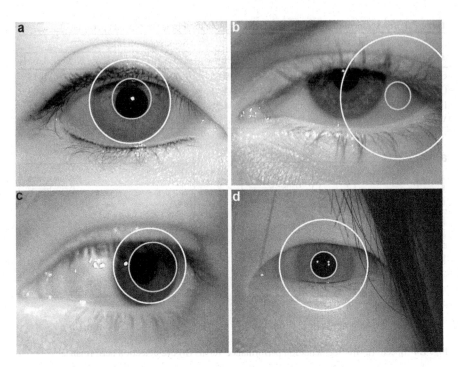

Fig. 7.5 Typical CAHT segmentation failure types: (**a**) eyelid matches circular model, (**b**) squeezed eyes, (**c**) inaccurate model for off-gaze, and (**d**) oversegmentation due to hair

over- and under-segmentation errors. For this dataset segmentation of the proposed algorithm works quite well, except in case of very strong eyelids, which affect ellipse fitting.

Even though the OSIRIS algorithm is tuned to deliver good results for ICE-2005 the WAHET implementation delivers the best results for *ND* (the parent database is a superset of ICE-2005) with 12.90 % EER at 0.25 s ST, followed by OSIRIS (15.45 % EER at 6.27 s ST), IFPP (19.04 % EER at 0.48 s ST), and CAHT (22.01 % EER at 2.29 s ST). The types of segmentation errors made by all three algorithms are comparable to Casia-L, with slightly more stable results provided by OSIRIS. Still a severe problem in OSIRIS is the fact that the computation of snakes is not reflected in the rubbersheet mapping, yielding mapping distortions, see Fig. 7.6.

Finally, in *UBIRIS*, the three tested techniques IFPP, OSIRIS, and CAHT provide unsatisfactory results (OSIRIS with 33.51 % EER at 2.03 s ST, IFPP with 34.56 % EER at 0.11 s ST, and CAHT with 39.65 % EER at 0.18 s ST). Interestingly, OSIRIS provides slightly better results, even though it exhibits a systematic error: Typically, the outer iris boundary is identified as pupillary boundary, so not irides are used for biometric identification, but sclera and surrounding eyelids and eyelashes, which works better than expected, probably due to the short capturing timespan within

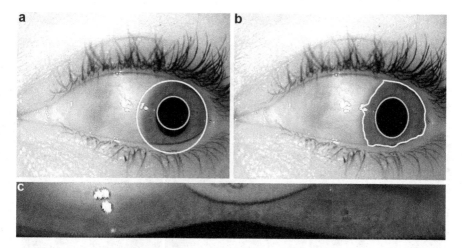

Fig. 7.6 Osiris ND #0428d197 segmentation failure: (**a**) rubbersheet mapping, (**b**) according accurate snakes, and (**c**) resulting distortions

each session. While CAHT, again, exhibits many complete segmentation failures, the IFPP algorithm estimates the center quite robust, but again boundary refitting causes some problems.

In summary, from the tested algorithms the proposed WAHET technique clearly provided fastest and most stable results across databases. Furthermore, compared to IFPP, it is even less affected by the size of the original image, since most time-consuming processing steps are executed after the polar transform, which depends on the required output angular resolution. This is also supported by the choice of a much denser accumulator grid in WAHET (101×101 instead of 10×10), thus alleviating a more effective approximate center search requiring less iterations to achieve the required accuracy. However, for very small input images, there is a slight overhead in processing time, compared to IFPP. Examples of accurate segmentation results using WAHET are illustrated in Fig. 7.7. From the examples we can see that WAHET is highly tolerant with respect to hot spot pupillary reflections (e.g., present in Casia-I), expressive eyelids (e.g., present in Casia-L and ND), and even off-gaze examples (although this case largely depends on the ability of the iteratively executed HT to find an arbitrary center). From an implementation perspective, the presented two-stage layout is a compromise for a rather quick reduction of search space without having to sacrifice accuracy, since the risk of selecting an unsuitable center point is rather low. Still, in case eyebrows or hair mislead the first detection stage (i.e., a point outside the boundaries is selected), a correction of the center within the second stage is hardly possible.

Typically, iris segmentation algorithms are optimized with respect to a given database, neglecting the need for high usability of segmentation algorithms. WA-HET and IFPP are implementations of a two-stage iris segmentation framework, which aims to account for all three quality factors of segmentation: accuracy, speed,

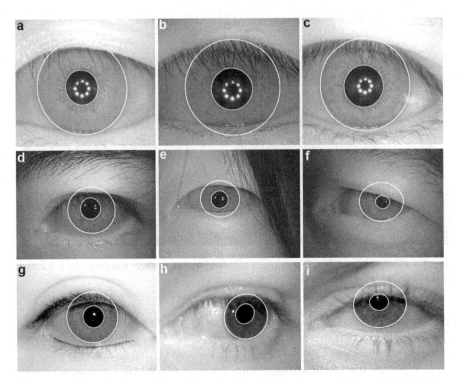

Fig. 7.7 Good segmentation results of the WAHET algorithm for challenging examples: (**a**)–(**c**) Casia-I, (**d**)–(**f**) Casia-L, (**g**)–(**i**) ND

and usability. They are shown to require less processing time and to exhibit more robustness than tested open iris segmentation software. Experiments confirm that existing segmentation software in the field is highly affected by the type of iris data, i.e. the used iris database. The proposed methods try to avoid this over-fitting with respect to input data and do not use database-specific segmentation parameters or assumptions.

7.4 Discussion

Being the first task in an automated iris recognition system based on full portrait data (e.g., [337, 578]), an approach to face and face-part classifier fusion has been presented and evaluated. In order to overcome limited capabilities of detection techniques with respect to database-independent face and eye detection, information of single classifiers can be combined taking into account spatial relationships between detection responses [539]. Experimental results indicate that face and face-part classifier fusion works relatively robust and does not consume significantly more time than nested approaches. By exploiting spatial relationships between single detectors, heterogeneous detection of faces and face-parts (eyes, nose, eyepairs, etc.) in NIR and WV images can be achieved, benefiting of the best currently available detectors for each type of imagery without suffering from a high individual false-detection rate because of high variability between training and testing datasets. While there are several approaches reducing false positive detections by incorporating multiple (face-part) detectors, e.g. [105, 367], the proposed *Face with Face-part Classifier Fusion* technique is one of very few fusion techniques able to reduce false negatives restaurating missing information (e.g., caused by occlusions). Simple integration into existing detectors is alleviated, and access to detection scores is not needed.

Having obtained a detection response ROI containing an eye image, further iris processing typically involves the subtasks of *iris segmentation* finding iris boundaries and according noise mask output, as well as *iris normalization* employing Daugman's Rubbersheet model. For the former task, this chapter has evaluated a *multistage real-time iris processing* method and compared it to standard HT-based approaches. From experiments we can see that iris segmentation—at least for less constrained iris images—still represents an active research problem, with a strong focus on real-time capable methods. Typically, iris segmentation algorithms are optimized with respect to a given database, neglecting the need for high usability of segmentation algorithms. Especially the focus on either VW or NIR images, in order to benefit from strong assumptions with respect to pupil or sclera contrast, makes current segmentation algorithms not universally applicable, at least not without training on the target dataset. However, the growing demand for integrated solutions extracting irides from facial images makes both iris recognition in VW, as well as face recognition in NIR, active research topics demanding for iris segmentation techniques able to process either type of data. The presented two-stage iris segmentation framework targets all three quality factors of segmentation: accuracy, speed, and usability and has been shown to require less processing time and to exhibit more robustness than tested open iris segmentation software OSIRIS and CAHT. Experiments confirmed that existing segmentation software in the field is highly affected by the type of iris data, i.e. the used iris database. The presented method tries to avoid this over-fitting with respect to input data, especially database-specific segmentation parameters.

Chapter 8
Image Compression Impact on Iris Recognition

The International Organization for Standardization (ISO) specifies iris biometric data to be recorded and stored in (raw) image form (ISO/IEC 19794-6), rather than in extracted templates (e.g., iris-codes). On the one hand, such deployments benefit from future improvements (e.g., in feature extraction stage) which can be easily incorporated (except sensor improvements), without reenrollment of registered users. On the other hand, since biometric templates may depend on patent-registered algorithms, databases of raw images enable more interoperability and vendor neutrality [121]. Furthermore, the application of low-powered mobile sensors for image acquisition, e.g., mobile phones, raises the need for reducing the amount of transmitted data. These facts motivate detailed investigations of the effect of image compression on iris biometrics in order to provide an efficient storage and rapid transmission of biometric records.

Previous evaluations (e.g., [121, 223, 416]) confirm the applicability of lossy image compression in iris biometric systems; however, there is a need for more comprehensive analysis distinguishing between different application scenarios, i.e., the point in the iris processing chain, where compression is applied. This chapter provides a comprehensive study of the effects of lossy image compression on iris biometrics. We present an exhaustive evaluation targeting different operating points of compression, i.e., applied to the original image, after segmentation using a ROI-encoded image, and after normalization compressing the unrolled iris texture with a special focus on the impact of segmentation. Furthermore it is demonstrated that the optimization of certain parameters in lossy image compression standards with respect to the target imagery can lead to significantly improved iris recognition accuracy. Finally, we assess the applicability and performance of lossless (image) compression algorithms when applied to iris image data.

C. Rathgeb et al., *Iris Biometrics: From Segmentation to Template Security*,
Advances in Information Security 59, DOI 10.1007/978-1-4614-5571-4_8,
© Springer Science+Business Media, LLC 2013

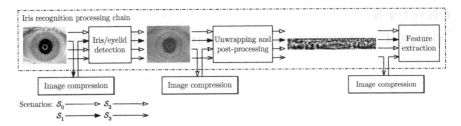

Fig. 8.1 Application scenarios: No compression (S_0), compression of the original image after acquisition (S_1), compression of the ROI-encoded image after segmentation (S_2), compression of iris texture after normalization (S_3)

8.1   Application Scenarios

Compression's impact on accuracy largely depends on the type of application scenario, as will be shown in the next few sections. Results are different whether templates extracted from compressed images are compared to ones generated from uncompressed or compressed images. For this purpose image compression is applied at various positions within a common iris biometric processing chain yielding three different scenarios on a common data set.

1. *Scenario S_1*: Image compression is applied to the original image of the eye, i.e., no preprocessing is applied prior to image compression (e.g., in [222, 268]).
2. *Scenario S_2*: After detecting the inner and outer boundaries of the iris, non-iris regions are substituted using different gray levels, i.e., segmentation is alleviated or even lead in a certain direction (e.g., in [121]).
3. *Scenario S_3*: Image compression is applied to preprocessed iris textures, i.e., normalized iris textures resulting from an unrolling process and subsequent illumination enhancement are compressed (e.g., in [223, 416]).

All three scenarios (and iris recognition without compression), which are illustrated in Fig. 8.1, are evaluated for different feature extraction algorithms in both modes, compressed vs. compressed as well as compressed vs. uncompressed.

8.2   Existing Studies

Several researchers have investigated effects of lossy image compression on iris recognition. Table 8.1 summarizes proposed approaches according to applied compression standards, considered scenarios, and obtained results. In [416] normalized iris textures of size 512×80 pixel are compressed using JPEG2000 (J2K). Subsequently, diverse feature extraction methods are applied in order to compare pairs of compressed textures. The authors observe improvement in recognition accuracy for low compression levels. A more comprehensive study based on

Table 8.1 Summarized results for diverse studies of compression algorithm's impact on iris recognition in literature

Ref.	Compression	Scenarios	Results
[416]	J2K	S_3	0 % EER until 0.3 bpp
[340]	JPG, J2K, SPIHT, PRVQ, FRAC	S_1	~50 % FRR at 0.01 % FAR
[121]	JPG, J2K	S_1, S_2	0.24 % EER (vs. 0.11 %) for J2K 1:150
[173]	JPG, J2K	S_1	~1.6 % (vs. 1.45 %) FRR at 0.1 % FAR J2K
[268]	JPG	S_1, S_3	~4 % EER (vs. ~3 %) for 1:15
[222]	J2K	S_1	4.45 % EER (vs. 1.35 %) for J2K 1:100
[200]	JXR, J2K	S_1	~1.9 % EER (vs. ~1.3 %) for 0.4 bpp

different compression standards, including DCT-based lossy JPEG (JPG) as well as J2K, which are utilized to compress original iris images, is presented in [340]. Increased accuracy was achieved when comparing pairs of iris-codes, both resulting from compressed iris textures. Focusing on original iris images the authors conclude that iris segmentation tends to fail at high compression rates. Besides, in general original iris images exhibit greater filesize compared to preprocessed texture stripes. Similar results are obtained in [222, 223], where severe compression of original iris images causes EERs as high as 4 %, compared to a compression of normalized iris textures, which does not significantly decrease accuracy [416]. In order to overcome these drawbacks an ROI isolation was proposed in [121], i.e., non-iris regions (eyelids and sclera) are substituted using two different gray levels. Applying J2K it is found that ROI isolation leads to a twofold reduction in filesize while enabling an easy localization of eyelid boundaries in later stages. For a filesize of 2,000 bytes only 2–3 % of bits in extracted templates change, while recognition accuracy is maintained. In [177] a similar approach applying J2K ROI-coding to the iris region is proposed.

Regarding standardization of image compression in biometrics, the ISO/IEC 19794 standard on "Biometric Data Interchange Formats" represents the most relevant one. With respect to iris biometrics (ISO/IEC 19794-6), in the most recent version only J2K is included for lossy compression and recommended for standardized iris images (IREX records) by NIST [373]. The study in [173] gave quantitative support to the revision of the ISO/IEC 19794-6 standard. For lossless compression, the PNG format is defined (as opposed to an earlier version of the standard, in which JPEG-LS was suggested). By analogy, the ANSI/NIST ITL 1-2011 standard specifies iris images to be compressed with J2K in the lossy case, for lossless compression both J2K and PNG are supported.

While it is generally conceded that the JPG compression standard is not suitable at high compression rates, in [268, 271] it is shown that custom-designed quantization tables in JPG significantly improve recognition performance. In [200] effects of JPEG-XR (JXR) compression on iris recognition are examined. JXR is found to be competitive to the current standard J2K while exhibiting significantly lower computational demands.

8.3   Lossy Iris Biometric Image Compression

Experimental evaluations are carried out on the CASIA.v3-Interval and IITD.v1 iris databases (see Sect. 3.1), more specifically we evaluate all left-eye images. While the IITD database consists of uncompressed images a slight JPG compression is applied to the entire CASIA.v3-Interval dataset. However, it will be shown that slight compression has no negative impact on recognition accuracy. In the following subsections the impact of different compression standards on image quality is analyzed according to various compression rates, which are defined by the ratio of resulting average filesize compared to the average filesize of uncompressed images. We measure the impact on recognition accuracy in terms of FRR at a certain FAR. At all authentication attempts 7 circular texture-shifts (and according bit-shifts) in each direction are performed and the minimum HD is returned to achieve rotation-invariance.

8.3.1   Compression Standards

In this study three different types of lossy image compression standards are applied:

- *DCT-based lossy JPEG (JPG)*: This is the well-established (ISO/IEC 10918) DCT-based method of compressing images by the Joint Photographic Experts Group. Compression ratios can be varied by using more or less aggressive divisors in the quantization phase.
- *JPEG2000 (J2K)*: This refers to the wavelet-based image compression standard (ISO/IEC 15444), which can operate at higher compression ratios without generating the characteristic artifacts of the original DCT-based JPG standard.
- *JPEG XR (JXR)*: JXR generally provides better quality than JPG and is more efficient than J2K, with respect to computational effort. In the default configuration the Photo overlay/overlap transformation is only applied to high pass coefficients prior to the Photo core transformation (ISO/IEC 29199-2).

Iris cameras capture digital photos of the iris patterns in human eyes. Imaging does not involve lasers or flash, instead today's commercially available solutions use infrared light to illuminate the iris to be able to process also heavily pigmented iris images. Whereas specialized iris acquisition systems exist, ranging from simple handheld iris cameras, like the OKI IRISPASS-H, to completely integrated systems like the LG4000 IrisAccess system featuring two-factor and two-eye authentication, active research aims at providing sensor-independent segmentation algorithms [541]. By observing compression in various different scenarios, we assess the impact on different applications taking different types of iris sensors into account.

With respect to image quality J2K and JXR reveal superior performance compared to the JPG compression standard. In Fig. 8.2 peak signal-to-noise ratio (PSNR) values are plotted for compressing original iris images and normalized

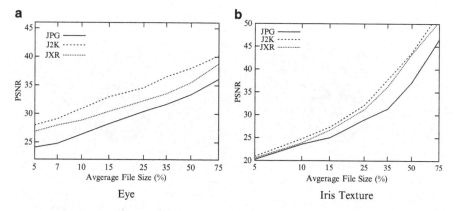

Fig. 8.2 Filesize vs. PSNR trade-off: quality degradation for compression of (**a**) original eye (S_1), and (**b**) segmented texture (S_3) images

iris textures for various average filesizes. In terms of PSNR a compression of preprocessed iris textures does not affect image quality as drastic as a compression of original iris images at low compression levels. Obtained results justify the deprecation of the JPG standard in ISO/IEC 19794-6.

8.3.2   Compression Rates

In order to investigate how various scenarios affect an optimal choice of compression several different filesizes are considered for each compression standard within different scenarios. Compression rates are defined according to specific average filesize of resulting images, estimated in percent of the filesize of original images (which vary among scenarios), e.g., JPG-25 indicates a 1:4 filesize ratio between the JPG compressed and the corresponding reference image. Figure 8.3a shows a sample image of the applied database, obtained segmentation results and the extracted iris texture are shown in Fig. 8.3b,c.

Figure 8.4 illustrates the effects of JPG-5 according to different scenarios. Obviously, a compression of preprocessed iris textures (S_3) retains significantly more information than a compression of the original iris image (S_1) at the same rate. For the applied dataset correctly detected "iris rings" cover on average 30.86 % of the entire (non-cropped) image. In case ROI-encoding is performed (S_2), compression of non-iris regions requires negligible additional information [121], i.e., obtained image quality of the iris is equated with three times higher compression rates related to the original image (e.g., JPG-5 in S_1 is equal to JPG-15 in S_2). Still the scenario S_2 appears controversial. On the one hand it is motivated by the fact that, compared to S_3, deployed systems may benefit from future improvements in the segmentation stage. On the other hand it requires some kind of preprocessing (eyelid detection, sclera detection, etc.) which is expected to force any segmentation

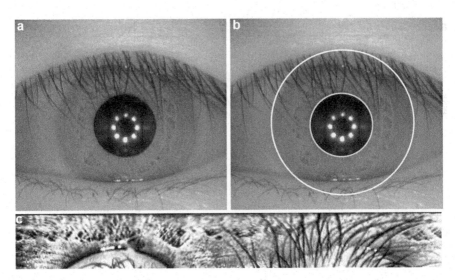

Fig. 8.3 Iris recognition processing chain intermediate results for uncompressed sample #S1041L01 of CASIA.v3-Interval database. (**a**) Iris image, (**b**) Segmentation, (**c**) Iris texture

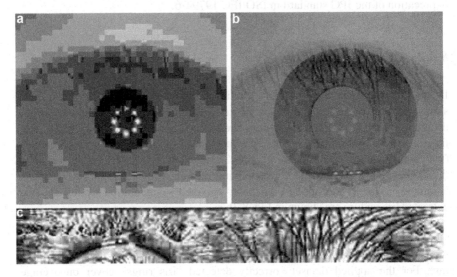

Fig. 8.4 JPG compression for sample #S1041L01 of CASIA.v3-Interval database for various scenarios (S_1-S_3) obtaining relative filesize of 0.05. (**a**) S_1: Iris image compression, (**b**) S_2: "ROI-encoded" compression, (**c**) S_3: Iris texture compression

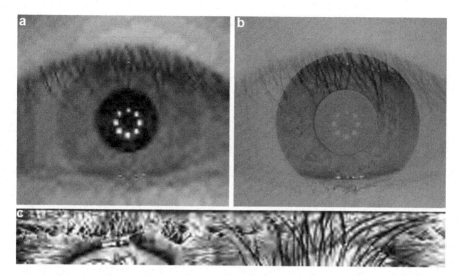

Fig. 8.5 J2K compression for sample #S1041L01 of CASIA.v3-Interval database for various scenarios (S_1-S_3) obtaining relative filesize of 0.05. (**a**) S_1: Iris image compression, (**b**) S_2: "ROI-encoded" compression, (**c**) S_3: Iris texture compression

algorithm to detect distinct regions. In addition, the required ROI-encoding may not be available in different application scenarios, e.g., immediate transmission of image data after acquisition. Figure 8.5 shows the impact of J2K compression according to different scenarios obtaining significantly improved image quality compared to the JPG compression.

8.4 Image Compression Impact on Accuracy

In order to provide a comprehensive analysis of the effect of image compression on recognition accuracy the impact of applied feature extraction methods as well as segmentation issues resulting from severe compression are examined with respect to the predefined scenarios.

8.4.1 Choice of Iris Database

Left-eye images of the CASIA.v3-Interval database exhibit an average filesize of 11.51 kB for image sizes of 320×280 pixel. Uncompressed images (converted with lossless JPG) of the IITD.v1 database with smaller images of 320×240 pixel are on average 15.22 kilobyte in size. In order to show that an initial slight JPG compression does not degrade accuracy, images of the IITD.v1 database are JPG compressed obtaining an average filesize of less than 9.86 kilobyte (11.51 kilobyte

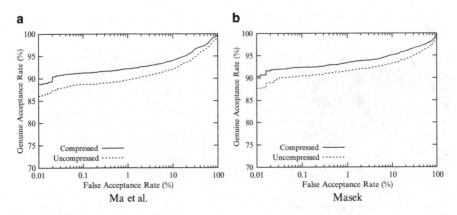

Fig. 8.6 Effect of slight compression on the IITD.v1 database for the feature extraction of (**a**) Ma et al. and (**b**) Masek

times the 240/280 ratio). In Fig. 8.6 ROC curves are plotted for uncompressed as well as compressed images of the IITD.v1 database applying different feature extractors. As observed by other authors [121, 222], a slight compression is equal to de-noising, thus even slightly improved recognition rates are obtained. From an application side of view, the more challenging CASIA.v3-Interval database, which is slightly JPEG compressed (comparable to native JPEG compression commonly implemented in iris image acquisition devices) represents a more realistic basis for experimental evaluations than using uncompressed images as performance reference. In subsequent experiments original images of the CASIA.v3-Interval dataset are interpreted as "uncompressed" reference instances.

8.4.2 Impact on Feature Extraction Algorithms

In order to investigate the impact of image compression on recognition accuracy of diverse feature extraction methods, the USIT implementations of the algorithms of Ma et al. [323], Masek [335], Ko et al. [261], and Rathgeb et al. [430], as described in Sect. 3.4 are applied (and in the following will be referred to as *Ma, Masek, Ko,* and *Rathgeb* features).

Figure 8.7 illustrates the impact of image compression on EERs obtained by all feature extraction algorithms. Despite the fact that some feature extraction methods require the same row-wise processing of texture stripes (which is common for iris recognition algorithms [44]) the relative effects of image compression exhibit the same characteristics (e.g., the superior accuracy of J2K compression in general and of JPG compared to JXR until an average filesize of 10 %). Without loss of generality obtained results indicate an algorithm-independent effect of image compression on iris recognition.

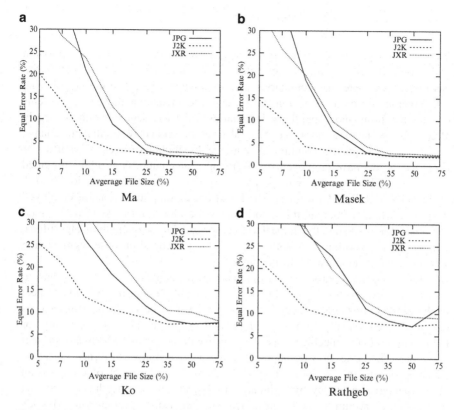

Fig. 8.7 Effect of compression on EERs: Comparing compressed (S_1 with S_1) images for the feature extraction algorithms (**a**) Ma, (**b**) Masek, (**c**) Ko, and (**d**) Rathgeb

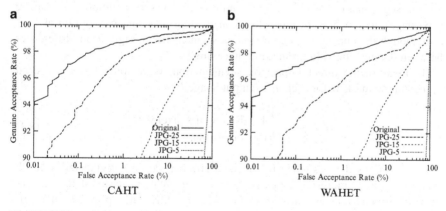

Fig. 8.8 Effect of image compression on different segmentation algorithms (**a**) CAHT (**b**) WAHET

8.4.3   Impact on Iris Segmentation

From the iris processing chain in Fig. 8.1 it should be clear that compression within scenario S_1 may affect segmentation accuracy. While for NIR-illuminated iris images, the outer iris-boundary typically has low contrast to the neighboring sclera regions, even for visible range iris images, segmentation may cause problems due to less pronounced pupillary boundaries. Like iris segmentation is largely affected by the database employed [541], also compression may significantly change initial image set-specific assumptions, e.g., the distribution of intensity values. For experiments, we have employed two different segmentation algorithms provided as part of USIT to investigate the impact of compression on segmentation: CAHT [178] and WAHET [541], see Sect. 3.4. The strong assumptions about the employed dataset (CASIA.v3-Interval) this algorithm was developed for make CAHT a good candidate for assessing the impact on sensor-specific segmentation algorithms. The WAHET algorithm represents a more generic general-purpose segmentation algorithm, without database-specific tuning.

While the general purpose algorithm has the advantage of being more robust to changes in image recording conditions, it is generally less restrictive with respect to the pre-assumed shape (boundaries do not need to be circular). However, as can be derived visually from the compressed images in Fig. 8.4, especially for high compression at specific sectors there is even no clear outer boundary present any more. Therefore, holistic approaches like Hough transform turned out to be advantageous in this scenario. Figure 8.8 compares the effect of compression on segmentation accuracy by estimating ROCs, i.e., measuring the total impact on recognition accuracy, for each segmentation algorithm by employing Masek's feature extraction. Nevertheless, for the remainder of comparisons we employ WAHET as segmentation algorithm, since (a) still, general-purpose algorithms are the segmentation of choice for vendor-neutral iris recognition (b) adaptive (two-stage) approaches are much faster alleviating real-time recognition and (c) even though the impact of compression on segmentation is significant, differences between segmentation algorithms are rather small.

To measure the direct impact on segmentation, we employ an $m \times n$ sized segmentation mask M for each $m \times n$ input image I:

$$M(x,y) := \begin{cases} 1 & \text{if } (x,y) \text{ iris pixel wrt. } I \\ 0 & \text{otherwise.} \end{cases} \tag{8.1}$$

This mask is used to estimate the average HD between the segmentation result (masks) of the compressed input versus the segmentation masks of the uncompressed, original images. As seen in Fig. 8.9a, for J2K only up to 2 % of pixels are incorrectly classified. This amount increases drastically for JPG and JXR with resulting filesizes of 25 % and above until 11 % for JPG and 7 % for JXR for resulting filesizes of 5 %. When considering a segmentation of being tolerable if its falsely classified pixels do not exceed 5 %, we get a plot of average filesize

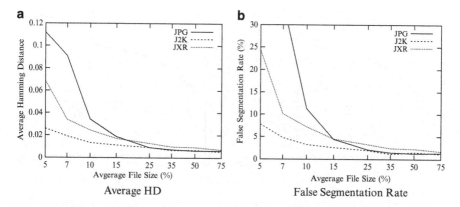

Fig. 8.9 Effect of image compression on segmentation masks: (**a**) Average HD of S_0 vs. S_1, and (**b**) rate of false segmentations per filesize

Table 8.2 EERs for various scenarios using different compression standards and filesizes

File size (%)	S_0S_1			S_0S_2			S_0S_3		
	JPG	J2K	JXR	JPG	J2K	JXR	JPG	J2K	JJXR
75	1.93	1.86	2.17	1.78	1.76	1.81	1.77	1.76	1.77
50	1.98	2.09	2.33	1.79	1.88	1.95	1.77	1.76	1.76
35	1.90	2.04	2.24	1.83	1.81	2.05	1.77	1.79	1.78
25	2.23	2.17	2.60	2.00	1.88	2.37	1.77	1.78	1.81
15	4.86	2.59	5.02	3.38	2.14	4.26	1.77	1.76	1.80
10	10.94	2.92	10.00	7.30	2.42	7.90	1.81	1.78	1.78
7	28.55	5.82	14.67	16.73	4.35	11.29	–	–	–
5	30.95	8.57	24.85	17.11	5.67	17.31	1.79	1.77	1.86
3	–	–	–	–	–	–	1.80	1.81	1.84

File size (%)	S_1S_1			S_2S_2			S_3S_3		
	JPG	J2K	JXR	JPG	J2K	JXR	JPG	J2K	JJXR
75	2.13	1.87	2.37	1.84	1.75	1.88	1.77	1.77	1.77
50	2.14	2.02	2.65	1.80	1.87	2.15	1.77	1.77	1.76
35	2.26	2.21	2.74	1.99	1.96	2.62	1.77	1.79	1.79
25	2.88	2.69	4.23	2.30	2.07	3.95	1.77	1.81	1.80
15	7.82	3.24	9.79	5.70	2.57	8.81	1.73	1.80	1.81
10	18.96	4.14	20.04	14.21	3.59	17.44	1.79	1.78	1.83
7	36.08	10.47	25.89	22.20	8.05	22.27	–	–	–
5	37.66	14.56	34.82	22.55	11.29	27.99	1.83	1.74	1.90
3	–	–	–	–	–	–	1.81	1.84	1.94

versus false segmentation rate for each algorithm, illustrated in Fig. 8.9b. With respect to recognition performance a direct comparison of scenario S_1 and S_2 (see Table 8.2) reveals that the impact of segmentation errors on the overall accuracy is quite significant at distinct filesizes.

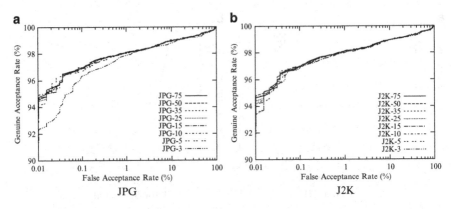

Fig. 8.10 Effect of iris texture compression (S_3) on ROCs for Masek's feature extraction algorithm using (**a**) JPG, and (**b**) J2K with different filesizes

8.4.4 Segmentation Error Analysis

For low-power sensors or continuous sensing, e.g., by remote cameras, scenario S_1 is probably the only practicable solution, i.e., after image acquisition the full eye image needs to be compressed to reduce the amount of submitted data. But there are better solutions in case the remote sensing device offers computation resources to employ segmentation remotely, in order to avoid large impact on segmentation.

Scenario S_3 avoids segmentation errors by employing compression after normalization. Results depicted in form of ROC curves, plotted in Fig. 8.10 for different resulting filesizes for the standards JPG and J2K, illustrate that in this scenario compression has much lower impact on recognition accuracy. For JPG and J2K, recognition rates stay rather low at approximately 1.77–1.84 % EER, only very high compression, e.g., JPG-3, show a slightly worse recognition rate for high security applications with requested low FAR.

Another alternative to compression before segmentation is scenario S_2 employing some sort of ROI compression after segmentation. In our experiments segmentation is conducted on the original input and the segmentation result is used to compress only parts of the input image which correspond to the iris texture. This way, segmentation is artificially simplified, but compression artifacts are yet to be mapped into Daugman's doubly dimensionless coordinate system. From the results illustrated in Fig. 8.11 one can see that, in contrast to scenario S_3, this type has much more impact on recognition accuracy. However, it has to be taken into account that compression rates refer to the original image size in S_2, whereas the normalized iris textures compressed in S_3 are typically much smaller in size. When considering an average iris image containing 30.86 % of iris texture pixels, filesizes of 5 % in S_2 correspond to approximately 15 % in scenario S_3 when ignoring the size impact of the artificial uniform eyelid, sclera and pupil segmentation areas illustrated in Fig. 8.1.

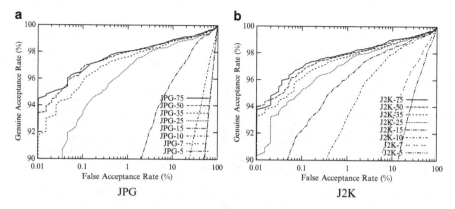

Fig. 8.11 Effect of ROI compression (S_2) on ROCs for Masek's feature extraction algorithm using (**a**) JPG, and (**b**) J2K with different filesizes

8.5   Gallery vs. Probe Compression

Since authentication attempts involve an execution of the processing chain for both, probe and gallery images, compression scenarios S_0 to S_3 may be applied at enrollment (for the gallery image) and/or at authentication (for the probe image). Considering the reported effect of JPG to even increase recognition accuracy as long as no severe compression artifacts occur [340] it is interesting to see, whether the compression of both images results in better or worse performance than comparing compressed with uncompressed samples, given the potential high impact on segmentation errors. Tested combinations of scenarios reflect the following applications:

- *Low-power sensor*: The sensor is capable of acquiring input images only, but does not have the ability to conduct iris segmentation. The compressed image is transferred to some computing device, which may have access to the full-sized original gallery image or feature vector extracted from this image ($S_0 S_1$), or compressed gallery images and templates extracted from these images, respectively ($S_1 S_1$).
- *Intelligent sensor*: Within this application scenario, the sensor is specifically designed to the application domain of iris image acquisition (e.g., specialized iris cameras) and is capable of iris preprocessing, but comparison is still centralized for security issues. Still, in order to minimize the amount of transmitted information and encryption efforts, iris images should be compressed (encryption is executed after compression). This application is reflected with scenario combination $S_0 S_2$ in case the gallery is composed of templates extracted from original uncompressed images and $S_2 S_2$, if the same sensor is employed for enrollment.

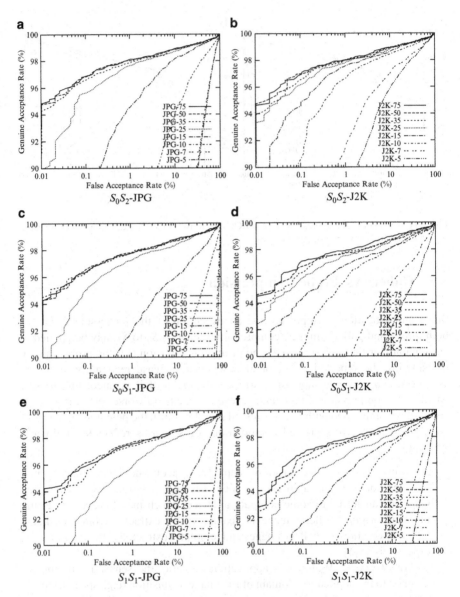

Fig. 8.12 Gallery vs. probe compression's effect on ROCs: (**a**)–(**b**) uncompressed vs. compressed ROI, (**c**)–(**d**) uncompressed vs. compressed originals, (**e**)–(**f**) compressed vs. compressed originals

- *Integrated sensor*: This scenario reflects typical smartcard solutions, where both the user template and acquired probe image do not leave the integrated system and are compared on-card. Since typically resources are strictly limited on such devices, it is desirable to store relevant information only, e.g., the normalized compressed iris texture. Considering this application we are interested in, whether an additional compression of the probe image (S_3S_3) increases or decreases recognition accuracy, compared to scenario combination S_0S_3.

ROC curves comparing resulting filesizes for the most prominent application scenarios S_0S_1, S_0S_2, and S_1S_1 are plotted for each compression standard in Fig. 8.12, while Table 8.2 lists the obtained EERs for all of the introduced combinations of scenarios for various average filesizes.

Regarding the low-power sensor application, one can see that for each employed compression standard (JPG, J2K and JXR), superior performance is obtained by employing gallery templates from uncompressed instead of compressed images. For both JPG and J2K, EERs are on average 1.31 times higher in the compressed vs. uncompressed scenario, and 1.52 times higher for JXR. Interestingly, the improvement for J2K almost increases with compression rate and is very pronounced for filesizes less than 10 %, whereas for JPG and JXR the improvement is most pronounced for medium filesizes (10 %, 15 %).

The intelligent sensor application reveals a similar result: again compressed versus uncompressed comparison yielded better recognition accuracy for almost every compression algorithm over the entire range of tested rates (solely J2K for very low compression turned out to exhibit no perceivable difference). On average, EERs are 1.3 times higher for JPG, 1.34 times higher for J2K, and 1.62 times higher for JXR, with again most pronounced improvement for medium filesizes for JXR and JPG, whereas J2K exhibits the highest improvement for filesizes less than 10 %.

Finally, in case of the integrated sensor application it is evident that compression has very little impact in general. EERs are in the range of 1.76–1.86 % for all algorithms in scenario S_0S_3 and in the range of 1.76–1.94 % for S_3S_3. Considering these recognition results, it is advisable to stick to the fastest available implementations in this scenario and neglect the impact on recognition accuracy.

Finally, comparing the overall recognition rates, we notice that (1) J2K delivers throughout better performance than JPG, followed by JXR, (2) compressed versus uncompressed comparison (S_0S_1, S_0S_2) delivers better results than the corresponding compressed versus compressed application (S_1S_1, S_2S_2), and (3) recognition accuracy is better in scenarios, where compression is applied late in the processing chain (S_3 is better than S_2, followed by S_1).

8.6 Customization of Lossy Compression Algorithms

There are two reasons which suggest to use lossy compression algorithms in different mode as the default configuration when to be used in iris recognition systems: First, iris imagery might have different properties as compared to common arbitrary images (for which default configurations are designed for), and second, a pleasant viewing experience as being the aim in designing the lossy algorithms' default settings might not deliver optimal comparison results in the context of biometric recognition (e.g., sharp edges required for exact matching could appear appealing to human observers).

8.6.1   Custom JPG Quantization Matrices

Although J2K has been shown to deliver superior results in terms of compression and respective iris-code comparison results, JPG is still attractive, especially for low-power environments, due to its low computational demand and the widespread availability of JPG hardware. Therefore, we investigate if a customization to the specific target application scenario can improve the result in terms of recognition accuracy. The JPG still image compression standard [389] allows to use custom quantization tables (Q-tables) in case image material with special properties is subject to compression. These tables are signaled in the header information. Contrasting to the optimization of the JPG quantization matrix with respect to human perception as done for the development of the standard matrix, rate/distortion criteria have also been used successfully for the design of this matrix (see, e.g., [154]). Chen et al. [80] propose compression algorithms tuned for pattern recognition applications, which are based on a modification of the standard compression algorithms. Such modification is achieved by emphasizing middle and high frequencies and discarding low frequencies (the standard JPG quantization matrix is rotated by 180°). JPG quantization matrix optimization has already been considered in biometrics—Jeong et al. [236] employ a rate/distortion criterion in the context of face recognition and achieve superior recognition performance as compared to the standard matrix.

To investigate the properties of iris images in the context of JPG compression, 8×8 pixel blocks have been subjected to DCT transform and the resulting coefficients are averaged for a large number of blocks. Block counts of 2,000 blocks, 525 blocks, and 44,160 blocks have been used for different image types:

- *Arbitrary*: As a first class of blocks, we have used arbitrary images with randomly extracted blocks.
- *Horizontal*: The second class of blocks is extracted iris texture taken left and right of the pupil.
- *Normalized*: The third class is taken from normalized iris texture images generated by the employed comparison algorithm.

Figure 8.13 displays the result of all three classes where the DC and the largest AC coefficient are set to white, zero is set to black and the remaining values are scaled in between (note that the logarithm is applied to the magnitude of all coefficients before this scaling operation).

The arbitrary blocks (Fig. 8.13a) show the typical expected behavior with decreasing coefficient magnitude for increasing frequency and symmetry with respect to the coordinate axes. Figure 8.13b reveals that in normalized iris texture images there is more energy in the higher frequencies in horizontal direction as

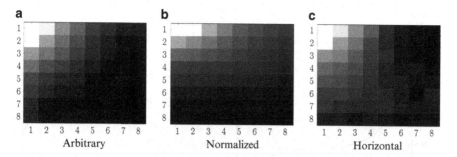

Fig. 8.13 Different types of applied averaged 8×8 DCT (iris) blocks used in experiments. (**a**) Arbitrary, (**b**) Normalized, (**c**) Horizontal

Table 8.3 Different JPG quantization tables: Q-table 12, Q-table 13, Q-table 15, and Q-table 16

Q-table 12								Q-table 13							
16	11	10	16	24	40	255	255	16	11	10	16	24	255	255	255
12	12	14	19	26	255	255	255	12	12	14	19	255	255	255	255
14	13	16	24	255	255	255	255	14	13	16	255	255	255	255	255
14	17	22	255	255	255	255	255	14	17	255	255	255	255	255	255
18	22	255	255	255	255	255	255	18	255	255	255	255	255	255	255
24	255	255	255	255	255	255	255	255	255	255	255	255	255	255	255
255	255	255	255	255	255	255	255	255	255	255	255	255	255	255	255
255	255	255	255	255	255	255	255	255	255	255	255	255	255	255	255

Q-table 15								Q-table 16							
16	11	10	16	255	255	255	255	16	11	10	255	255	255	255	255
12	12	14	255	255	255	255	255	12	12	255	255	255	255	255	255
14	13	255	255	255	255	255	255	14	255	255	255	255	255	255	255
14	255	255	255	255	255	255	255	255	255	255	255	255	255	255	255
255	255	255	255	255	255	255	255	255	255	255	255	255	255	255	255
255	255	255	255	255	255	255	255	255	255	255	255	255	255	255	255
255	255	255	255	255	255	255	255	255	255	255	255	255	255	255	255

compared to vertical direction. This is to be expected since luminance fluctuations in iris texture are more pronounced in radial direction as compared to perpendicular direction. Finally, Fig. 8.13c confirms this expectation showing more energy in the higher frequencies in vertical direction.

While we cannot exploit the direction bias of iris texture in compression since we are dealing with rectilinear iris images in scenario S_1, we conjecture that the highest and medium frequencies might not be required for the comparison stage due to the coarse quantization used for template generation while at least medium frequencies are required for pleasant viewing. Table 8.3 displays the Q-tables used in experiments.

From left to right, an increasing amount of high frequencies is suppressed following the zig-zag scan known from JPG bitstream generation (by dividing

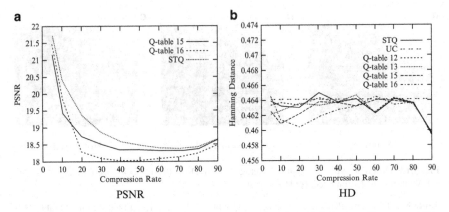

Fig. 8.14 Impact of varying compression rate in terms of PSNR and impostor HD scores. (**a**) PSNR, (**b**) HD

the coefficients by 255), coefficients not affected are quantized as defined in the default Q-table. For the rightmost Q-table 16, only the 6 leading coefficients are quantized in the regular manner, the rest is severely quantized. The rationale behind the selection of these matrices is to investigate the importance of medium frequency information in iris recognition (high frequency information is assumed to be not useful in any case).

In the following experiments, we use Libor Masek's Matlab implementation of a 1-D version of the Daugman iris recognition algorithm (see Sect. 3.4). Rectilinear iris images of 100 persons using 3 images for each eye (i.e., 600 images) from the CASIA.v1 database are used for computing error rates and HD values.

For investigating intra-class matches (matches from legitimate users enrolled in the database), experiments rely on 12,000 generated images. For each of the 100 persons, we use 3 images for each eye, resulting in 3 possible genuine authentication attempts per eye. For 200 eyes, this totals in 1,200 images for each of the 10 employed compression rates. While this is the case for the scenario with only 1 compressed image, for 2 compressed images the number is halved due to symmetry reasons. For investigating inter-class matches (impostor matches), far more data is available of course and all possibilities are used.

Figure 8.14a shows the averaged rate distortion comparison of the different compression algorithms applied to all iris images considered for three Q-tables. Clearly one can see that employment of the default Q-table results in the best PSNR across the entire range of bitrates considered. Therefore, a corresponding comparison behavior (best results for the default Q-table) could be expected in the context of iris recognition.

In the following, we investigate the impact of compression on the comparison score (i.e., obtained HD). The interval of $0.26 \le t \le 0.35$ for HD threshold t is discussed as the border between match and mismatch in iris recognition [116]—based on recommendations for the specific technique [221] used and results shown subsequently we suggest to choose $t = 0.34$ as decision criterion between match and

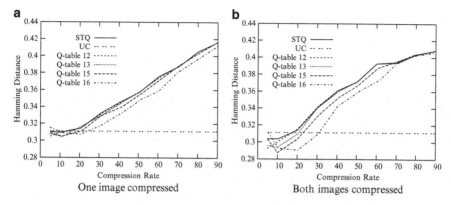

Fig. 8.15 Impact of varying compression rate on HD of genuine users' comparisons. (**a**) One image compressed, (**b**) both images compressed

mismatch. Figure 8.14b shows the plot of the HD after applying the iris recognition algorithm to both JPG compressed iris images in the case of impostor matches (i.e., irises of different persons/eyes are matched against each other). For reference, we have included the average HD for the case of uncompressed images (labeled UC).

For the case of impostors JPG compression does not introduce any false positive matches on average no matter how severe compression is applied—HD remains above 0.46 across the whole range of compression rates. Of course, this does not exclude the possibility of the existence of statistical outliers. There are no significant differences among the different Q-tables since the fluctuations occur in a negligible range. The same behavior is observed in case only one image is compressed (not shown).

In the case of genuine user comparisons (see Fig. 8.15), the mean value of the HD in the uncompressed case is approximately 0.31. First, we consider the standard Q-table (labeled STQ). For increasing compression rate the HD stays constant at approximately 0.305 until the compression rate exceeds 10 and increases subsequently. A further increase of the compression rate leads to a steady increase of HD and crosses the suggested comparison threshold of 0.34 between compression rates 30 and 40. Note that the reported numbers refers to averaged HD values which implies the occurrence of a significant number of false negative matches at this compression rate. In the case of both images being compressed, HD is lower on average up to a compression rate of 20.

When comparing these results to those obtained with different Q-tables, we notice that Q-tables 15 and 16 clearly improve on the results of STQ from compression rate 20 upwards where Q-table 16 does so in a more pronounced manner. For compression rate 10 all other Q-tables improve slightly on STQ and for compression rate 5, Q-tables 12 and 13 are superior to STQ in terms of average HD. In the case of two images being compressed, the observed behavior is more significant but similar in principle. These results indicate that PSNR is indeed *not* a good predictor for comparison performance with compressed iris images in terms of average HD. The claim that compression up to a rate of 16 even improves the

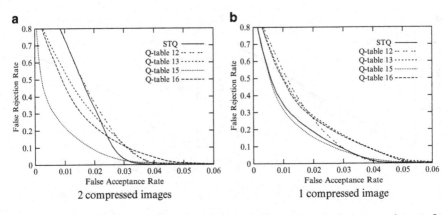

Fig. 8.16 Receiver operation characteristic curves for different Q-tables for compression rate 5. (**a**) 2 compressed images, (**b**) 1 compressed image

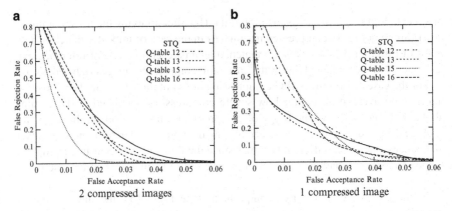

Fig. 8.17 Receiver operation characteristic curves for different Q-tables for compression rate 10. (**a**) 2 compressed images, (**b**) 1 compressed image

comparison scores of not compressed images [415] can be supported at least for the 2 compressed images case and the STQ, for "better" Q-tables this is correct even up to compression rate 20 and higher.

In order to consider the hidden statistical outliers in the comparisons we focus on ROC for different compression rates. Figures 8.16, 8.17, and 8.18 compare the ROC of different Q-tables for compression rates 5, 10, and 20, since it is not realistic to operate an iris recognition system at a higher compression rate. Again, the two compressed image scenario is compared to the case where only one image is compressed. For compression rate 5, our proposed Q-tables are not really able to substantially improve ROC. While for one compressed image (Fig. 8.16b) only Q-table 15 improves STQ slightly (and only within a specific ROC range), significant improvements are seen for Q-tables 15, 16, and 13 in case of two compressed images (Fig. 8.16a). However, only Q-table 15 improves STQ for reasonable low

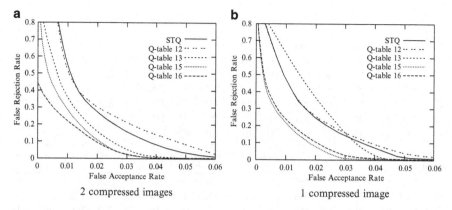

Fig. 8.18 Receiver operation characteristic curves for different Q-tables for compression rate 20. (**a**) 2 compressed images, (**b**) 1 compressed image

FRRs (starting at 0.04). In the case of compression rate 10, the situation changes drastically. Again, Q-table 15 shows the most significant improvements. For two compressed images (Fig. 8.17a) at FAR 0.028, Q-table delivers an FRR of almost zero whereas STQ exhibits an FRR of 0.15. Also the other proposed Q-tables improve on STQ in the interesting lower FRR range.

In the case of only one compressed image we still find improvements, but far less pronounced (Fig. 8.17b). For an FAR of 0.041, again Q-table 15 returns an FRR of almost zero whereas STQ is almost at 0.9 FRR. Again, also Q-tables 13 and 16 improve STQ. Finally, when turning to compression rate 20 in Fig. 8.18 the situation is different. Here, Q-table 16 shows the most significant improvements in the two compressed images case and shows behavior similar to Q-table 15 also for one compressed image. The most noticeable improvement is found in the latter case at an FAR of 0.035 where Q-table 15 exhibits an FRR close to zero and STQ has 0.2 FRR.

There is one more interesting thing to note: at least for compression rate 20 it is entirely clear that it is *not* advantageous to compress both images involved in comparison—in terms of ROC, clearly the case of one compressed image is superior here. For compression rates 5 and 10 the better choice highly depends on the target FAR/FRR and the Q-table in use.

When working with normalized iris texture images, i.e., scenario S_3 instead of scenario S_1, we may exploit the direction bias of iris texture in compression directly. The selected Q-tables shown in Table 8.4 partially reflect this asymmetry and are used in the following experiments. The first matrix shows the standard case (STQ) where the entries exhibit a steady increase from low frequencies to high frequencies following the well-known zig–zag pattern [389] (which results in more severe quantization applied to middle and high frequencies).

Q-table 22 and Q-table 24 have been obtained by large-scale trial-and-error experimentation, setting a large amount of entries to 255 (which causes the

Table 8.4 JPG Quantization tables: STQ, Q-table 22, Q-table 24, Q-table Ok05, and Q-table Ok10

STQ									Q-table 22							
16	11	10	16	24	40	51	61		10	10	76	255	255	255	255	255
12	12	14	19	26	58	60	55		85	112	255	255	255	255	255	255
14	13	16	24	40	57	69	56		151	255	255	255	255	255	255	255
14	17	22	29	51	87	80	62		255	255	255	255	255	255	255	255
18	22	37	56	68	109	103	77		255	255	255	255	255	255	255	255
24	35	55	64	81	104	113	92		255	255	255	255	255	255	255	255
49	64	78	87	103	121	120	101		255	255	255	255	255	255	255	255
72	92	95	98	112	100	103	99		255	255	255	255	255	255	255	255

Q-table 24									Q-table Ok05							
16	11	10	16	255	255	255	255		16	11	10	16	24	246	255	255
12	12	14	255	255	255	255	255		12	12	14	29	26	255	255	250
255	255	255	255	255	255	255	255		14	13	16	24	255	255	255	224
255	255	255	255	255	255	255	255		14	17	22	255	255	255	242	255
255	255	255	255	255	255	255	255		18	255	255	255	255	255	255	255
255	255	255	255	255	255	255	255		24	247	255	255	255	255	255	255
255	255	255	255	255	255	255	255		255	255	255	255	255	255	255	255
255	255	255	255	255	255	255	255		255	255	255	241	255	241	255	244

Q-table Ok10							
15	6	17	19	255	255	255	255
5	15	13	255	255	255	250	255
255	255	247	255	248	255	255	255
255	250	248	255	255	250	255	255
255	222	237	255	251	255	255	250
255	252	251	250	220	249	229	232
254	246	255	251	255	255	255	248
255	255	247	252	255	255	248	255

corresponding coefficients to be divided by 255 and results in most of them being quantized to zero). Both matrices are asymmetric in the sense that they "protect" more coefficients in horizontal direction (which have been shown to carry more energy as their vertical counterparts, see Fig. 8.13b). Q-table 24 is more pronounced in this respect and retains the values of STQ at the positions not set to 255. The rationale behind the selection of these matrices is to investigate the importance of medium frequency information in the iris recognition process (high frequency information is assumed to be not useful in any case) and to reflect the specific properties of normalized iris texture images. Q-table Ok05 and Q-table Ok10 have been found using the Genetic optimization approach as described below in its first version [268] using Q-table 22 and Q-table 24 as individuals of the initial population in addition to randomly generated tables. These tables have been specifically optimized for application with compression rates 5 and 10, respectively.

For the experiments, again sample data from the CASIA.v1 database is used, here the images of 50 persons using 3–4 images for each eye are employed (i.e., 334 images with 826 genuine user and 110,304 impostor comparisons, respectively).

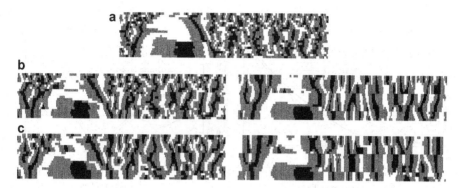

Fig. 8.19 Comparison of iris templates extracted from (**a**) uncompressed; (**b**) compressed normalized iris texture images with compression rate 10; and (**c**) compression rate 15

Note that the fact that the pupil area has been manipulated in these data [393] does not affect our results in the case of scenario S_3 (contrasting to scenario S_1), since we restrict compression to the iris texture area by compressing normalized iris images only.

Figure 8.19 shows examples of iris templates extracted from uncompressed and JPG compressed iris texture patches of one person. The two patches in Fig. 8.19b are compressed with rate 10 using STQ and Q-table Ok10, respectively. By analogy, patches in Fig. 8.19c are compressed with rate 15 using STQ and Q-table 22, respectively. Note that the images have been scaled in y-direction for proper display, the original dimension is 240×20 pixels.

In the iris texture data (not shown), compression artifacts are clearly visible for both rates displayed; however, the STQ compressed variants are visually more close to the original and seem to have conserved the texture details much better. However, when computing the HD between both variants having applied compression rate 15 with the uncompressed second image of the same eye in the database, we obtain 0.327 for STQ but only 0.317 for Q-table 22. Obviously, the HD between templates does not reflect the visual appearance at all. The smoothing achieved by compression seems to play an important role indeed. More fine grained differences seem to get introduced by the STQ quantization, while the other two matrices tend to produce rather smooth templates.

Again we use two settings in the experiments: either both images are compressed and matched against each other or only one image is compressed in the comparison stage. For investigating recognition accuracy, 15 different compression rates are applied (rates 2–16). We have employed a Genetic algorithm (GA) to generate customized Q-tables as follows (the MATLAB GA-Toolbox is used). The Q-table entries (we have restricted the values to be integers from the interval [0, 255]) constitute the genes of each individual, where an individual represents a distinct Q-table. The population size is set to a fixed number of individuals and we limit the number of computed generations to 40 due to reasons of computational demand. Additionally, the optimization is stopped if no improvement in terms of

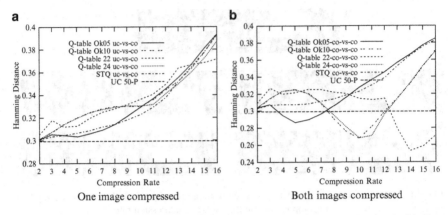

Fig. 8.20 Impact of varying compression rate on HD of genuine users' comparisons. (**a**) One image compressed, (**b**) Both images compressed

best individual fitness function is found for a certain number of generations. In each generation, the two best individuals are selected to be the "elite" and are kept for the subsequent generation. Six individuals are selected for crossover, while two individuals of the subsequent generation are created by mutation. As the cost function to be evaluated for determining which individuals are kept, we compute the sum of the following items for a fixed compression rate: average of FAR over a selected number of thresholds and average of FRR over the same set of thresholds. This cost function has to be minimized of course. For more parameters and specific settings of the GA used, see [269].

First, we investigate the impact of compression on the comparison score (i.e., obtained HD). Figure 8.20 shows the plots of the HD after applying the iris recognition algorithm if normalized iris texture images have been JPG compressed in the case of genuine user comparisons. The x-axis shows the compression rates, whereas the y-axis shows the averaged HD. For reference, we have included the average HD for the case of uncompressed images.

The mean value of the HD in the uncompressed case is approximately 0.3. First we consider the standard Q-table (labeled STQ). For increasing compression rate the average HD increases steadily and crosses the suggested comparison threshold of 0.34 at compression rates 12 for both cases (one or two images compressed, respectively). Note that the reported numbers refer to averaged HD values which implies the occurrence of a significant number of false negative matches at this compression rate.

Concerning the one compressed image scenario in Fig. 8.20a, STQ is beaten by Q-table Ok05 (rates around 6), Q-table 24, and Q-table 22 (rates 14 and higher), but only by a very small amount. The situation is different when regarding the two compressed images scenario (Fig. 8.20b). Q-table Ok05 is clearly better than STQ between rate 4 and 8 (and even beats the uncompressed case between rate 4 and 7). Q-table 24 and Q-table Ok10 are better than STQ for rates higher than 7 and also

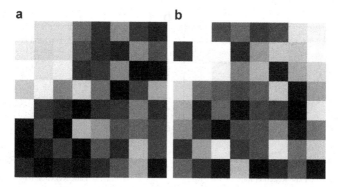

Fig. 8.21 Examples of evolved matrices in the scenario where one image is compressed. (**a**) Compression ratio 5, (**b**) Compression ratio 12

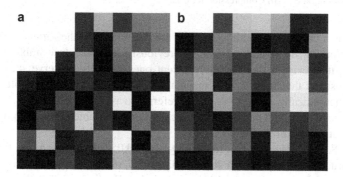

Fig. 8.22 Examples of evolved matrices in the scenario where two images are compressed. (**a**) Compression ratio 5, (**b**) Compression ratio 12

beat the uncompressed case between rate 8 and 11. Finally, Q-table 22 beats STQ for rates higher than 10 and is also superior to the uncompressed case for rates 13 and higher.

We have genetically optimized matrices for compression ratios reaching from 2 to 16 for both scenarios, one and two compressed images involved in comparison. Figures 8.21 and 8.22 display examples for evolved matrices, the optimized tables for compression ratios 5 and 12 and the scenario of one compressed image are illustrated in Fig. 8.21. The graphics below each table are for additional improved readability where the matrix elements are represented by grayscale areas. In Fig. 8.22, two evolved tables of the two compressed image scenario of the same compression ratios (5 and 12) are visualized. Although all four matrices are computed from initial tables with random items, a basic trend is clearly detectable. There are always low values for low frequencies while some higher frequency components are also preserved. If we compare the matrices for the two different scenarios, we also notice some similarities in the upper left corner while the rest of

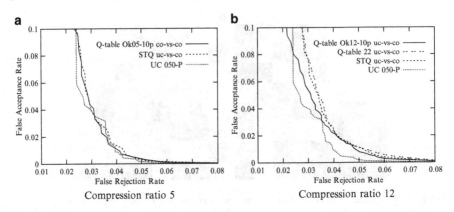

Fig. 8.23 Receiver operation characteristic curves for the scenario where 1 image is compressed. (**a**) Compression ratio 5, (**b**) Compression ratio 12

the table is highly varying, although they are optimized for the same compression rate. Comparing these tables to those previously designed (see Table 8.4, also in [268]), it is evident that the more recent ones partially preserve some higher frequencies and that they have a much more random structure. Q-table 22 was designed heuristically and Q-table Ok05 (referred to as "Ok05-old" in Fig. 8.24) was also genetically evolved but with heuristically designed tables as initial population and without an optimized parameter set.

Figure 8.23a shows the error rates of Q-table Ok05-10p uc-vs-co (see Fig. 8.21a for its structure) compared to the standard JPG matrix and the uncompressed reference in the one compressed image scenario. We discover that the optimized matrix shows only slightly better results compared to the standard table (between 0.03 and 0.045 FRR). The second diagram Fig. 8.23b illustrates the performance of Q-table Ok12-10p uc-vs-co (see Fig. 8.21b for the structure) and Q-table 22 compared to the reference cases. The optimized table provides significantly superior results compared to the standard matrix. The performance of uncompressed images cannot be reached (except around one single threshold value), Q-table 22 is clearly inferior, especially at low FRR values.

The ROC characteristics for the scenario of two compressed images are illustrated in Fig. 8.24. In Fig. 8.24a results for compression rate 5 are shown. The new evolved table (see Fig. 8.22a) clearly outperforms the standard table as well as even the uncompressed case. The "older" optimized table (see Table 8.4) is able to achieve the results of the uncompressed reference for higher FRR values and reaches the performance of the standard table for lower FRR values. It can be clearly seen that the optimization of the GA parameter set provides better performing tables [269]. Figure 8.24b illustrates ROC characteristics for compression ratio 12. In addition to Q-table Qk12-10p (see Fig. 8.22b) which clearly beats the standard table in terms of error rates, also Q-table Ok05-10p optimized for compression rate 5 shows very good results at this compression ratio. We have seen that JPG compression per-

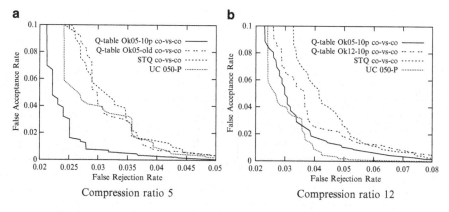

Fig. 8.24 Receiver operation characteristic curves for the scenario where 2 images are compressed. (**a**) Compression ratio 5, (**b**) Compression ratio 12

formance can significantly be improved by customizing quantization tables. These conclusions are at least valid for optimization within a set of users. If quantization tables optimized in the described manner also show superior performance on unseen datasets or different feature extraction schemes remains to be investigated.

8.6.2   J2K ROI Compression

J2K can be extended and optimized in various manners. For example, J2K Part 2 technology has been used in the transformation stage (i.e., wavelet packet decomposition structures are used [176]) instead of the dyadic decomposition of the Part 1 transform, which did not show impact on recognition performance in scenario S_3. Here, we consider a scenario similar to scenario S_2 discussed before. After detecting the iris region in the rectilinear image data, J2K ROI coding is applied to the iris texture area (which allocates higher quality to this ROI as compared to the rest of the image) in order to preserve more textural detail in this area of the images (see [177] for more details on J2K ROI coding). Contrasting to scenario S_2, we do not replace the remaining image data with constant gray but retain corresponding texture information, but with lower quality as compared to the iris texture area. For example, this still facilitates extraction of periocular features from compressed images while these features have disappeared in scenario S_2.

For the experiments, iris segmentation, feature extraction, and comparison are executed using Masek's software (see Sect. 3.4). For compression, the JAVA reference implementation JJ2000 [465], which also supports ROI coding, is employed. We use 40 users' image sets (3 images per user) from the CASIA.v1 database and 20 users' image sets (4 images per user) from the UBIRIS.v1 database. In these

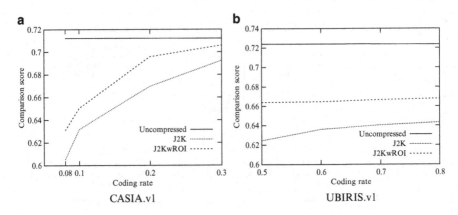

Fig. 8.25 Average comparison scores over all applied image sets (coding rate in bpp). (a) CASIA.v1, (b) UBIRIS.v1

experiments, we consider the case of one image out of two involved in comparison is employed in compressed manner.

For the CASIA.v1 images, on average 38 % of the image area belongs to the iris. For UBIRIS.v1, the average size of the iris is 20 %. We performed the tests for J2K coding with rates of 0.3, 0.2, 0.1, and 0.08 bits per pixel (bpp) on the CASIA.v1 image sets and coding rates of 0.8, 0.7, 0.6, and 0.5 bpp for the UBIRIS.v1 image sets. Note, that in the case of UBIRIS.v1 images, we apply a re-compression to JPG-compressed imagery where results are different as compared to compressing raw image data [233]. As comparison score in the subsequent figures $1 - HD$ is used.

Figure 8.25 shows the average comparison results over all image sets considered, we compare the application of J2K with default settings to the employment of the proposed ROI functionality (J2KwROI). For the CASIA.v1 image sets, the average comparison score for the uncompressed case (original) is slightly above 0.71, see Fig. 8.25a. For the four bitrates considered, we find the variant exploiting the ROI functionality being consistently superior to the default J2K case, the comparison score is constantly higher by approximately 0.02 and reaches almost uncompressed performance at 0.3 bpp.

For the UBIRIS.v1 image sets, average comparison score is slightly above 0.72 in the "uncompressed" case (recall that UBIRIS.v1 images already come as JPG files). Here, superiority of the ROI approach is even more pronounced, the observed comparison score gain is in the range 0.02–0.04 and decreases for increasing bitrate.

Having documented the gain in terms of average comparison score, it is not yet clear in how far this gain will impact on actual recognition performance. In order to investigate this in more depth, we provide averaged comparison score results for each image set separately. Figure 8.26 shows the corresponding results for the CASIA.v1 image sets compressed at 0.2 bpp. For reference, also a hypothetical decision threshold value is included in the plot at comparison score 0.6 (corresponding to $HD = 0.4$ accordingly).

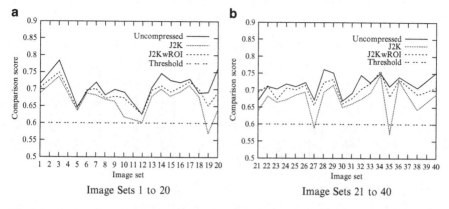

Fig. 8.26 CASIA.v1 dataset: obtained comparison scores at a coding rate of 0.2 bpp. (a) Image Sets 1 to 20, (b) Image Sets 21 to 40

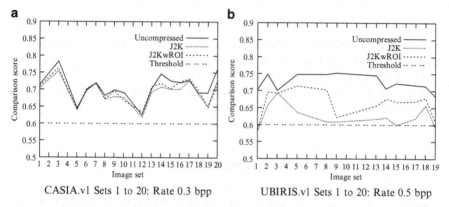

Fig. 8.27 Comparison scores at coding rates 0.3 bpp and 0.5 bpp for CASIA.v1 and UBIRIS.v1. (a) CASIA.v1 Sets 1 to 20: Rate 0.3 bpp, (b) UBIRIS.v1 Sets 1 to 20: Rate 0.5 bpp

We notice that for applying J2K with ROI functionality, comparison score values stay well above 0.6 (even above 0.65 for all but sets 5 and 12), while for the standard J2K case we find values below the threshold for sets 19, 27, and 35.

Figure 8.27 shows corresponding results for the CASIA.v1 sets 1–20 at 0.3 bpp and the UBIRIS.v1 sets at 0.5 bpp. For the CASIA.v1 sets, at the higher bitrate now no set is below the decision threshold, while the superior performance of J2KwROI is still visible. For the UBIRIS.v1 sets in Fig. 8.27b, again the superiority of J2KwROI is clearly visible. In addition to the better overall values, only 1 image set results in a comparison score below the threshold while 3 sets are affected in the default J2K case.

In order to get entirely rid of averaging effects in the comparisons (note that HD-results of each image set are still averaged in the latter results), we provide the number of false negative matches setting the decision threshold to 0.6 (which can

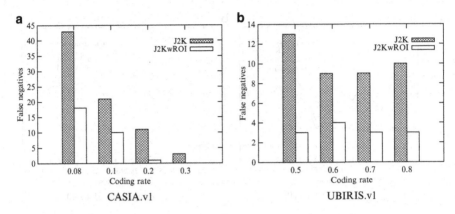

Fig. 8.28 False negatives ($T_{\text{Match}} = 0.6$) comparing J2K and J2K with ROI encoding. (**a**) CASIA.v1, (**b**) UBIRIS.v1

be used to compute the FNMR). Figure 8.28 shows corresponding results. For both types of images, the number of false negatives is significantly lower in case of using the ROI approach as compared to the default usage of J2K.

This means that obviously the ROC is improved by employing the proposed approach, especially in the area of improving user convenience by significantly reducing the number of false negative matches.

8.6.3   Custom JXR Subband Quantization

JXR has been shown to be an interesting alternative to J2K for medium-to-high bitrates [200] in scenario S_1. It has been again illustrative to observe that the higher PSNR results as obtained by J2K compression do not directly propagate to a better recognition performance. Only in low bitrate scenarios, J2K provides significantly better recognition rates for two of the considered feature extraction schemes. It has been shown that for no feature extraction algorithm there is a clear indication whether application of POT (in-loop block artifact reduction filter) would be beneficial or not in the transform stage [200].

The following configurations are considered:

- LBT=0: no POT application.
- LBT=1: application of POT at one stage.
- LBT=2: application of POT in both transform stages.

Figures 8.29–8.32 visualize corresponding extracted iris textures (CASIA.v3-Interval) as well as computed Masek iris-codes (see Sect. 3.4) for the three settings described and the uncompressed case. When computing the HD to the iris-code derived from the uncompressed image in Fig. 8.29, we obtain 0.35 for LBT=0, 0.403 for LBT=1, and 0.385 for LBT=2.

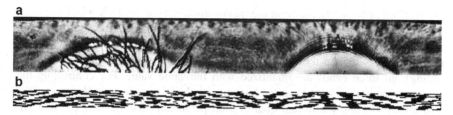

Fig. 8.29 Normalized iris texture and according iris-code with no compression applied. (**a**) Extracted texture, (**b**) Iris-code

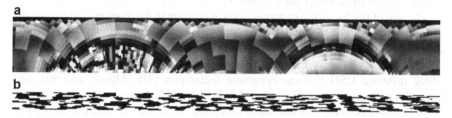

Fig. 8.30 Normalized iris texture and according iris-code with LBT=0, HD=0.35. (**a**) Extracted texture, (**b**) Iris-code

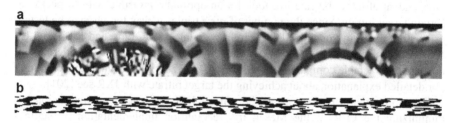

Fig. 8.31 Normalized iris texture and according iris-code with LBT=1, HD=0.403. (**a**) Extracted texture, (**b**) Iris-code

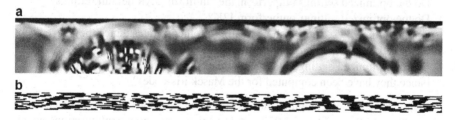

Fig. 8.32 Normalized iris texture and according iris-code with LBT=2, HD=0.385. (**a**) Extracted texture, (**b**) Iris-code

Here, we specifically focus on the quantization strategy in JXR which we want to customize to the iris recognition context (in scenario S_1). After the transform, the coefficients in the DC, LP, HP bands are quantized by an integer value q in the range 1–255. In the case of "uniform" quantization (which is the default setting), all three bands are quantized with the same value. For controlling the amount of compression, q is scaled but can only be of integer type. However, JXR also allows sto apply different quantization parameters for the DC, LP, and HP subbands besides the uniform strategy (in any case, the coefficients within one of these subbands are all quantized with an identical value). This corresponds to giving different emphasis to low frequency (DC band), mid frequency (LP band), and high frequency (HP band) information, respectively.

The aim of the following experiments is to customize the quantization parameter settings for the three DC, LP, HP bands in the context of iris recognition instead of applying the default uniform strategy. Results will also shed light on the question which frequency bands do carry the most discriminative information in iris imagery. Three different USIT feature extraction techniques (Ma, Masek, and Ko, see Sect. 3.4) are evaluated on the entire CASIA.v3-Interval dataset.

In JXR quantization customization, we aim at optimizing the *relation* among the quantization parameters for the three subbands DC, LP, and HP, i.e., we look for the triple q:r:s which provides the best solution in terms of recognition performance (measured in EER). Since it is not obvious that there exists a unique optimal solution independent of target bit rate, we look for an optimal q:r:s triple with respect to a certain target bitrate. Since the number of q:r:s triples is way too large to be tested exhaustively, we have quantized the search space into 18 DC bins, and 15 LP and 15 HP bins, respectively. Still 4,050 possible combinations need to be considered, but this is more tractable compared to $255^3 = 16,581,375$ triples without quantization. For detailed explanation about achieving the target bitrate with JXR see [201].

The optimization is done using the official JXR reference implementation by minimizing the EER of the Masek iris recognition implementation by setting LBT=0 since this is the fastest variant and there are no clear recognition advantages of using LBT=1,2 [200].

The questions we want to answer with our experiments are as follows:

1. Do the optimized settings outperform the "uniform" JXR default settings?
2. Do the optimized settings outperform J2K?
3. Do the optimized settings also generalize to other bitrates (since they have been computed for a single target bitrate)?
4. Do the optimized settings also generalize to other feature extraction schemes (since they have been computed for the Masek iris-code)?

Figure 8.33 shows computed tuples r:s, when all triples are normalized with $q = 1$. Out of all considered 4,050 r:s(:1) triples, dots show configurations when the obtained EER is at least 5 % better as compared to uniform q:r:s, and filled circles depict configurations with at least 15 % improvement. The target bitrate for the optimization has been set to 0.19 bytes/pixel (filesize is 17 kilobytes) for all experimental results shown. Note that experiments with different target bitrates lead

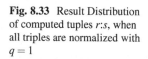

Fig. 8.33 Result Distribution of computed tuples $r{:}s$, when all triples are normalized with $q = 1$

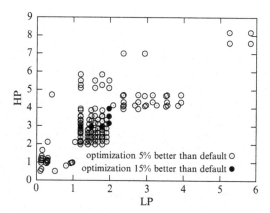

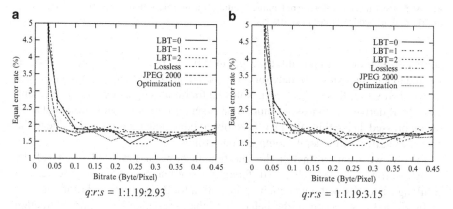

Fig. 8.34 Obtained equal error rates for the feature extraction algorithm of Masek. (**a**) $q{:}r{:}s = 1{:}1.19{:}2.93$, (**b**) $q{:}r{:}s = 1{:}1.97{:}3.15$

to highly similar results with respect to the answers to the four questions raised above, but of course not with respect to the actual triples $q{:}r{:}s$ computed.

We clearly note that the best triples are not close to the uniform setting $q{:}r{:}s = 1$ but $1 < r < 2$ and $2.9 < s < 4$. This means that the higher frequency gets, the more severe quantization should be applied.

Figure 8.34 shows the results of two good $q{:}r{:}s$ configurations for varying the bitrate in compression and performing iris recognition with the Masek iris-code. For comparison, we plot the curves for LBT=0,1,2 with uniform $q{:}r{:}s$ and a curve obtained from applying J2K. For both configurations we observe that for the optimization target bitrate, the optimized $q{:}r{:}s$ triple is clearly superior to the "uniform" JPEG XR variants and also superior to J2K.

However, this superiority does not at all extend to other bitrates. The bitrate range where these triples exhibit better performance is quite limited. This means that in an application, specific $q{:}r{:}s$ triples need to be optimized for different target bitrates. The behavior of those two configurations as shown in Figs. 8.34a and 8.34b is very

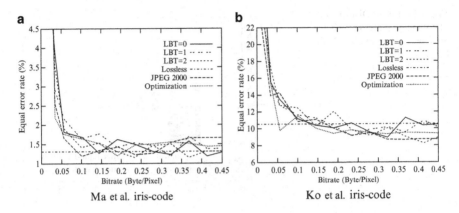

Fig. 8.35 Obtained EERs for the remaining feature extraction algorithms with $q{:}r{:}s = 1{:}1.97{:}3.15$. (a) Ma et al. iris-code, (b) Ko et al. iris-code

similar except for the range of bitrate less than 0.15. Here the better preservation of LP and to a lesser extent HP data for $q{:}r{:}s = 1{:}1.19{:}2.93$ leads to performance close or even better to J2K, see Fig. 8.34a. Note that for bitrates greater than 0.05, in many cases EER derived from lossy compression is superior to the values computed from uncompressed data—this effect has been observed in many studies and is due to the de-noising effect of moderate compression settings.

Finally, we want to answer the question in how far the good results of the computed triples do generalize to different types of feature extraction schemes and resulting iris-codes without explicit optimization for the respective algorithms.

In Fig. 8.35, we compare the behavior of the two remaining feature extraction techniques when applied to sample data which have been compressed using the triple $q{:}r{:}s = 1{:}1.97{:}3.15$—which has been optimized for the Masek iris-code at bitrate 0.19 bytes/pixel. We notice that for the target bitrate, the EER values are fairly good for both types of iris-codes. For both the Ma and Ko variants, the result is better compared to J2K and all three uniform variants. So it seems that this $q{:}r{:}s$ configuration is able to preserve texture information for the targeted bitrate very well, no matter which subsequent feature extraction technique is being applied.

On the other hand, we notice again that the bitrate range where this good behavior is observed is actually quite limited (except for the Ko et al. Iris Code, where we also see good results for lower bitrates). The specifically good results at bitrate 0.05 bytes/pixel for the Ko feature extraction scheme are probably due to optimal de-noising behavior at this compression ratio for this scheme.

To summarize, we have found that optimizing the JXR quantization strategy leads to improved iris recognition results for a wide range of different feature extraction types. The optimized strategy does not only outperform the default quantization strategy but also iris recognition relying on J2K compression. The observed behavior is only found in a small range of bitrates close to the target bitrate that has been used for optimization; however, the optimized parameters for a specific feature extraction technique do also provide good results for other types of iris-codes. The general trend with respect to the importance of different frequency bands is that as opposed to the JXR default configuration, middle LP frequencies and even more pronounced high HP frequencies should be quantized more severely compared to the low frequency DC information.

8.7 Lossless Iris Biometric Image Compression

While lossy compression techniques are mostly suggested in the context of biometric systems in order to maximize the benefit in terms of data reduction, the distortions introduced by compression artifacts potentially interfere with subsequent feature extraction and may degrade the comparison results depending on the application context. As an alternative, lossless compression techniques can be applied which avoid any impact on recognition performance but are generally known to deliver much lower compression rates. An additional advantage of lossless compression algorithms is that these are often less demanding in terms of required computations as compared to lossy compression technology.

There is not much work on applying lossless compression in biometrics. One of the few results exploits the strong directional features in fingerprint images caused by ridges and valleys. A scanning procedure following dominant ridge direction has shown to improve lossless coding results as compared to JPEG-LS and PNG [523]. In recent work [577] a set of lossless compression schemes has been compared when applied to image data from several biometric modalities like fingerprints, hand data, face imagery, retina, and iris. Extending the subsequent experiments, additional preprocessing has been applied in [496]; however, the general trends in the results have remained the same.

In the following, we apply an extended set of lossless compression algorithms to image data from different public iris image databases. Extensive results with respect to achieved compression ratio are shown. Again, we consider two different types of scenarios: Scenario S_1, where we compress rectilinear iris images (as commonly found in iris databases), and scenario S_3, where compression is applied to normalized iris texture images (as a result after iris detection, iris extraction, and mapping to polar coordinates).

We employ 4 dedicated lossless image compression algorithms (lossless JPEG, JPEG-LS, GIF, PNG), 3 lossy image compression algorithms with their respective lossless settings (J2K, SPIHT, JXR), and 5 general purpose lossless data compression algorithms (7Z, BZip2, Gzip, ZIP, UHA)—for details on the latter algorithms, see [498]:

- *Lossless JPEG*: Image Converter Plus [145] is used to apply lossless JPEG [566], the best performing predictor (compression strength 7) of the DPCM scheme is employed.

- *JPEG-LS*: IrfanView [482] is used to apply JPEG-LS which is based on using Median edge detection and subsequent predictive and Golumb encoding (in two modes: run and regular modes) [576].
- *GIF*: The Graphics Interchange Format is used from the XN-View software [170] employing LZW encoding.
- *PNG*: Is also used from the XN-View implementation using an LZSS encoding variant setting compression strength to 6.
- *JPEG2000*: Imagemagick [213] is used to apply J2K Part 1 in lossless mode [514].
- *SPIHT*: Lossy-to-lossless zerotree-based wavelet transform codec [463].
- *JPEG XR*: FuturixImager [157] is used to apply this most recent ISO still image coding standard, which is based on the Microsoft HD format [138].
- *7z*: Uses LZMA as compression procedure which includes an improved LZ77 and range encoder, we use the 7ZIP software [388].
- *BZip2*: Concatenates run-length encoding, Burrows-Wheeler transform and Huffman coding, also the 7ZIP software is used.
- *Gzip*: Uses a combination of LZ77 and Huffman encoding, also the 7ZIP software is used.
- *ZIP*: Uses the DEFLATE algorithm, similar to Gzip, also the 7ZIP software is used.
- *UHA*: Supports several algorithms out of which ALZ-2 (optimised LZ77 with an arithmetic entropy encoder) has been used, employing the WinUHA software [444].

We use iris sample data from the following data sets: CASIA.v1, CASIA.v3-Interval, MMU.1, MMU.2, UBIRIS.v1, Bath, and ND-Iris-0405 (see Sect. 3.1). For all our experiments we used the images in 8-bit grayscale information per pixel in .bmp format since all software can handle this format (except for SPIHT which requires a RAW format with removed .pgm headers). Database imagery has been converted into this format if not already given so, color images have been converted to the YUV format using the Y channel as grayscale image. We use the images in their respective original resolutions in case of scenario S_1 and the size of the resulting normalized iris texture images in scenario S_3 has been fixed to 240×20 pixels for all databases using the Masek segmentation and unwrapping (see Sect. 3.4). For further details on employed sample data and the way how normalized iris texture images are created for scenario S_3, please refer to [202] for scenario S_1 and [203] for scenario S_3.

8.7.1 Compression of Eye Images

In the subsequent plots, we display the achieved averaged compression ratio for different compression algorithms or databases. The small black "error" bars indicate result standard deviation in order to document result variability.

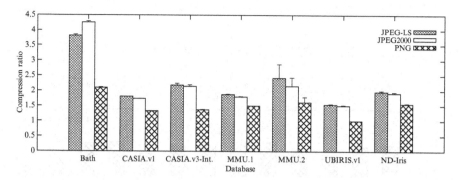

Fig. 8.36 Compression ratios achieved by JPEG-LS, JPEG 2000 and PNG (eye images)

Figure 8.36 lists results for the algorithms JPEG-LS, JPEG 2000, and PNG over the entire range of tested databases. When comparing all databases under the compression of a single algorithm, JPEG-LS provides a prototypical result, which is very similar to that of all other compression schemes with respect to the relative order of the compression ratios among the different datasets. For most images, we obtain a compression ratio of about 2. As it is to be expected, the only original data set with significantly higher resolution also gives higher compression ratio as compared to the others: The images from the Bath database achieve a ratio of more than 3.75. The UBIRIS.v2 dataset exhibiting the lowest resolution also results in the lowest compression ratio of 1.5. Also for J2K and dataset MMU, the compression ratio does not even reach 2.0. This significantly contradicts to the results provided in [577], where J2K excels in compressing iris images of the MMU database.

The most important algorithm with respect to standardization (according to ISO/IEC 19794-6 and ANSI/NIST-ITL 1-2011) is PNG. While the relative performance among the different databases is fairly similar to the results of JPEG-LS and J2K as seen before, the absolute compression ratios give the impression of being lower in most cases.

To investigate the relative ranking in more detail, we provide results comparing all compression techniques for each different database, visualized in Fig. 8.37.

The highest compression ratios obtained are 1.81 and 2.19 for CASIA.v1 and v3-Interval, respectively. For both datasets, we observe that JPEG-LS, J2K, and SPIHT result in the highest compression rates. With respect to the general purpose compression algorithms, UHA gives the best result similar to the JXR performance. It is particularly interesting to note that PNG delivers the second worst results, clearly inferior to the ratios obtained by the general purpose schemes. Only GIF is even inferior to PNG. The results for UBIRIS.v1 and MMU.2 are similar to the CASIA.v1 datasets.

Also results for MMU.1 and ND-Iris-0405 were similar. For both datasets, UHA provides the best results and, moreover, the other general purpose compressors achieve excellent compression ratios. Still GIF and PNG perform worst and J2K, SPIHT, and JPEG-LS are very close to UHA. The performance gap between PNG and the best performing techniques can be considered significant.

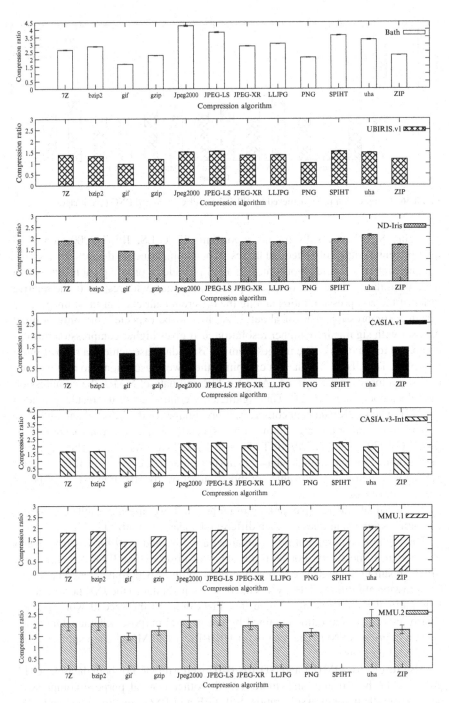

Fig. 8.37 Compression ratios achieved for different databases and algorithms (eye images)

For the Bath dataset, the results are somewhat different, both in terms of overall compression ratios (up to more than 4) and the top performing techniques—in this case, J2K is best, followed by JPEG-LS and SPIHT. As it is the case for all datasets, UHA is best for the "unspecific" techniques and GIF and PNG are worst performing overall.

The reason for the excellent performance of J2K in this case is probably due to the higher resolution, but also the original J2K file format (although converted to .bmp before compression) definitely contributes to this behavior. Still, the best non-J2K result (which is JPEG-LS) is almost a factor of 2 better compared to PNG.

Table 8.5 summarizes the results. It gets immediately clear that GIF is not an option for this kind of data, where for the UBIRIS.v1 database even data expansion is observed. The best performing technique overall is JPEG-LS which makes its inclusion in the former ISO/IEC 19794-6 standard a very plausible choice. Also J2K, as included in ANSI/NIST-ITL 1-2011 for lossless compression is among the top performing algorithms. It is surprising to find a general purpose compression scheme like UHA among the best performing techniques, image-specific compression schemes would have been expected to be best performing exclusively.

PNG turns out to be consistently the second worst compression scheme for all datasets considered, only superior to GIF. This fact makes the decision to replace JPEG-LS by PNG in the recent ISO/IEC 19794-6 standard and the inclusion of PNG in ANSI/NIST-ITL 1-2011 highly questionable. Moreover, as shown recently in [577], JPEG-LS turns out to be also significantly faster compared to PNG. The decision to replace JPEG-LS in ISO/IEC 19794-6, also motivated by the high danger of confusing it with classical JPEG formats, should be reconsidered in the light of our experimental results.

Compared to lossy compression like lossy J2K, the main advantages of lossless schemes are significantly lower computational demand [577] and the guarantee to avoid any impact on recognition performance. For corresponding lossy compression schemes high compression ratios (i.e., 20 and higher) with low impact on recognition performance have been reported (in some cases even improvements have been observed due to de-noising effects) [121,223,340]. Therefore, it is highly application context dependent, in which environment lossless schemes are actually better suited than their lossy counterparts.

8.7.2 Compression of Normalized Iris Textures

In this scenario, we consider the compression of normalized iris texture images, the compression ratio is given relative to the uncompressed normalized iris texture patch but *not* relative to the original rectilinear image data. In the subsequent plots, we display by analogy to the previous section the achieved averaged compression ratio for different databases or compression algorithms with small black "error" bars indicating result standard deviation. When comparing all databases under the

Table 8.5 Best and worst compression algorithm for each database (rectilinear iris images) with corresponding achieved compression ratio

Database	Best	Ratio	Worst	Ratio
CASIA.v1	JPEG-LS	1.81	GIF	1.15
CASIA.v3-Interval	JPEG-LS	2.19	GIF	1.20
MMU.1	UHA	1.99	GIF	1.36
MMU.2	JPEG-LS	2.42	GIF	1.47
UBIRIS.v1	JPEG-LS	1.54	GIF	0.96
Bath	J2K	4.25	GIF	1.66
ND-Iris-0405	UHA	2.09	GIF	1.40

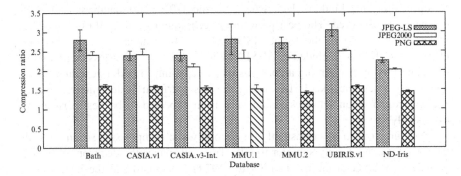

Fig. 8.38 Compression ratios achieved by JPEG-LS, JPEG 2000 and PNG (normalized textures)

compression of a single algorithm, JPEG-LS and PNG provide prototypical results shown in Fig. 8.38 which are very similar to that of most other compression schemes in that there are no significant differences among different databases. Please note that we cannot provide results for SPIHT since the software does not support the low resolution of the normalized iris texture images in y-direction.

For most databases, we obtain a compression ratio of about 2.5 or slightly above for JPEG-LS. PNG on the other hand exhibits even less result variability; however, compression ratio does not exceed 1.6 for all databases considered. In the light of the change from JPEG-LS to PNG in the recent ISO/IEC 19794-6 standard this is a surprising result.

In the following, we provide results for the different databases considered, see Fig. 8.39. We notice some interesting effect: (1) JPEG-LS is the best algorithm overall; (2) for CASIA.v1, ZIP is by far the best performing general purpose compressor while UHA is the best of its group for CASIA.v3-Interval; (3) we observe surprisingly good results for lossless JPEG; (4) the results for JXR are almost as poor as those for GIF and PNG.

For the MMU.1 (and MMU.2 which gives almost identical results) and the ND-Iris-0405 databases we obtain similar results as for CASIA.v1. ZIP is the best general purpose algorithm and JPEG-LS is the best algorithm overall. Also, lossless JPEG performs well. There is an interesting fact to notice. In [577], J2K has been applied to the MMU.1 dataset in lossless mode with surprisingly good results,

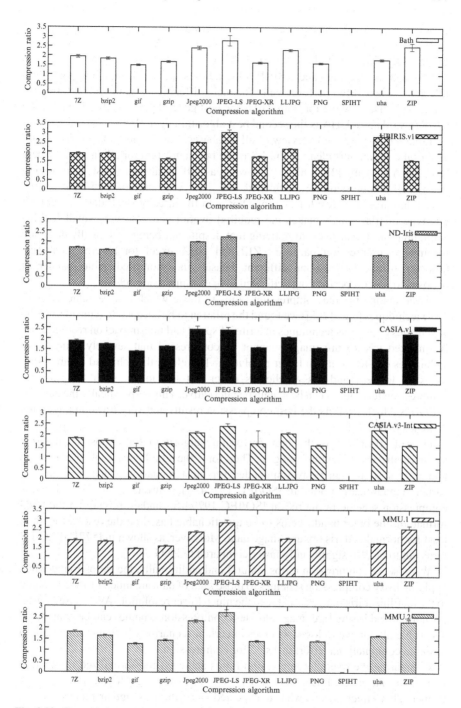

Fig. 8.39 Compression ratios achieved for different databases & algorithms (normalized textures)

however, in this work rectangular iris image data was considered. Here, we do not at all observe specific behavior of J2K when applied to the MMU.1 dataset, the results are perfectly in line with those for other datasets.

Similarly, for the Bath and UBIRIS.v1 databases JPEG-LS is the best algorithm, J2K and lossless JPEG perform well. The main difference is again the performance of ZIP and UHA—while for Bath ZIP is the best general purpose algorithm, for the UBIRIS.v1 dataset UHA is the second best algorithm overall.

Table 8.6 displays an overview of all databases. For the normalized iris texture images the situation is clear: JPEG-LS is the best algorithm for all datasets (except for CASIA.v1 with J2K ranked first) whereas GIF is always worst. Considering the overall compression ratio achieved, we observe a range of 2.25–3.04 for the best techniques. This result taken together with the already small data amount for this type of iris images makes the required overall data rate very small for this configuration. It is also worth noticing that despite not being specifically designed for image compression purposes, ZIP and UHA excel for several databases; however, results vary among different datasets in a non-predictable manner as opposed to the top-performing dedicated image compression schemes.

When comparing the compression ratios to those which can be achieved with lossy techniques (e.g., [268]) we found the relation to be acceptable (considering the advantages of lossless techniques in terms of speed and non-impact on recognition). Normalized iris texture images cannot be compressed that severely using lossy techniques due to the much lower resolution. Therefore, the achieved compression ratios of lossless and lossy schemes differ not too much, such that lossless compression techniques can be a realistic alternative. This is specifically the case for JPEG-LS which exhibits the best compression results and very low computational demands [576, 577].

Overall, JPEG-LS is the best performing algorithm for almost all datasets for normalized iris texture images. Therefore, the employment of JPEG-LS in biometric systems can be recommended for most scenarios which confirms the earlier standardization done in ISO/IEC 19794. The current choice for a lossless compression scheme in the recent ISO/IEC 19794-6 standard relying on the PNG format, on the other hand, seems to be questionable based on the results found, at least for normalized iris texture image data. Moreover, as shown in [577], JPEG-LS turns out to be also significantly faster compared to PNG.

We observe compression ratios about 3 and additionally, the ratios found when applying lossy compression schemes to those kind of data are much lower compared to the rectilinear iris image case due to the much lower resolution. As a consequence, for normalized iris texture images lossless compression schemes can be considered a sensible alternative to lossy schemes in certain scenarios where it is important to limit the computational effort invested for compression.

Comparing the overall compression ratios achieved for normalized iris texture images to that of rectilinear sample data, we surprisingly get higher ratios for the former. This effect is somewhat unexpected since the rectangular images exhibit much higher resolution. However, the texture in the rectangular images is quite inhomogeneous, ranging from background noise to eye lids and the various eye

Table 8.6 Best and worst compression algorithm for each database (normalized iris texture images) with corresponding achieved compression ratio

Database	Best	Ratio	Worst	Ratio
CASIA.v1	J2K	2.42	GIF	1.42
CASIA.v3-Interval	JPEG-LS	2.40	GIF	1.41
MMU.1	JPEG-LS	2.81	GIF	1.43
MMU.2	JPEG-LS	2.71	GIF	1.29
UBIRIS.v1	JPEG-LS	3.04	GIF	1.50
Bath	JPEG-LS	2.80	GIF	1.50
ND-Iris-0405	JPEG-LS	2.25	GIF	1.32

textures, whereas the texture of the normalized iris texture images can be considered as being more homogeneous across the entire image. Additionally, the effects of interpolation as used in the rubbersheet model [116] for polar coordinate conversion do lead to smoothed areas which can be compressed better as compared to unprocessed noisy data. These effects explain the (slightly) better results.

8.8 Discussion

In experimental evaluations various aspects and issues regarding lossy image compression in iris biometrics were pointed out. Three scenarios have been considered: (1) image compression of the original image; (2) "ROI-encoded" compression, and; (3) iris texture compression after normalization. Whereas compression is most effective in the first scenario in terms of data rate reduction it has the most severe impact on recognition accuracy among tested scenarios. Detailed analysis of the impact of compression on iris recognition accuracy in this scenario revealed that a loss of recognition accuracy is caused mostly by segmentation errors. In contrast, for the remaining scenarios compression impact is found to be much lower, since segmentation is performed prior to compression. It is found that comparing compressed with uncompressed images delivers superior results compared to matching compressed images only. The observed behavior was found to be independent of the choice of feature extraction or segmentation algorithms. Throughout all experiments J2K was confirmed to deliver the best results. Surprisingly, in most cases the recent JXR standard lead to even inferior results as compared to JPG. Despite all the negative effects of severe lossy compression, de-noising properties of low compression rates improve recognition accuracy throughout experiments.

Customization of lossy image compression algorithms to the iris recognition application scenario turned out to be fruitful. Improved recognition performance was achieved by optimizing JPG quantization tables, by applying J2K ROI coding to the iris texture area, and by optimizing JXR quantization which lead to more severe quantization the higher the considered frequency band was. However, most of these optimized parameters turned out to be quite specific for a considered target bitrate or application scenario, which means that the corresponding optimizations need to be conducted for a specific iris recognition deployment separately.

Lossless compression turned out to be an interesting alternative for the compression of normalized iris texture images only. Surprisingly, we have found that PNG as currently suggested in the corresponding ISO/IEC standard is not really competitive to other lossless compression techniques for both rectilinear and normalized iris texture images, respectively. It is unclear (at least from a purely technical viewpoint) why JPEG-LS has been replaced by PNG in the most recent version of this standard.

Chapter 9
Advanced Comparison Techniques for Challenging Iris Images

While better segmentation is certainly a highly effective approach to target iris processing for less constrained images, Daugman's rubbersheet transform model presents a rather simplified anatomical model of pupillary dilation. Therefore, it is likely that two normalized iris images are not perfectly aligned. The majority of feature extraction approaches extracts binary output (iris-codes) from the obtained normalized textures [44], and employs the fractional HD over different bit shifts between iris-codes in order to determine a degree of similarity at comparison stage. By shifting one of the two iris textures to be compared, or its corresponding iris-code, and calculating a comparison score employing the HD for each shift position, it is possible to account for the optimal alignment of both textures or iris-codes and to achieve so-called *rotational invariance*, i.e. likely present rotations of the head and consequently iris images are tolerated. However, the polar unwrapping with its simplifying assumptions may cause irrevocable mapping distortions even in case of generalizing from circular or elliptic shapes to AC-based approaches. In this case it is desirable to employ more sophisticated comparison techniques in order to exploit all the available information. Indeed, very few studies have proposed new or compared different binary similarity and distance measures, and it is a common agreement that HD-based comparison as proposed by Daugman [116] is the best method for this task. However, especially for unconstrained imagery more sophisticated comparison techniques are an efficient means to increase recognition accuracy without the necessity of re-enrollment. Another aspect to consider is speed-up of the recognition process. Traditional *identification mode* assessment involves a *1:n* comparison, where *n* is the number of registered *gallery* subjects, and consequently does not scale well with respect to the number of enrolled users. Especially the ongoing Aadhaar project in India employing fingerprint and iris biometrics to uniquely identify each Indian citizen, and the necessary de-duplication checks during enrollment to avoid the issue of multiple Aadhaar numbers to a single individual make efficient identification an ultimate goal. Indeed, by employing partial matching and indexing techniques, huge amounts of processing time can be saved [270]. While traditional approaches typically sacrifice recognition accuracy in favor of more efficient comparison, there are methods to increase both accuracy

C. Rathgeb et al., *Iris Biometrics: From Segmentation to Template Security*,
Advances in Information Security 59, DOI 10.1007/978-1-4614-5571-4_9,
© Springer Science+Business Media, LLC 2013

Table 9.1 Properties of several different proposed iris-biometric comparators

Ref.	Comparator	Comp. cost	Accuracy	Enroll. samples
[115]	*HD*	Low	Moderate	1
[124]	Majority decoding	Low	–	>1
[619]	Weighted *HD*	Medium	High	>1
[196]	"Best bits"	Medium	High	>1
[432]	Context-based	High	High	1
[538]	Levenshtein distance	Medium	High	1
[443]	Gauss.Fit+HD	Medium	High	1

and speed at the same time by effectively re-arranging iris-codes according to bit-reliability [440]. A similar technique may also be used to exploit single-instance multi-algorithm iris biometrics to increase accuracy without extending the total template size [439]. Therefore, the second part of this chapter targets the problem of iris recognition under unideal conditions from a different perspective, namely the application of sophisticated iris comparators and advanced serial iris identification techniques. Table 9.1 lists some of the techniques in a comparative manner accounting for computational cost, accuracy, and needed enrollment samples. Especially the latter is a typical restrictive condition in many application scenarios (e.g., forensics, high-throughput enrollment), where only a single enrollment sample is available.

Biometric recognition is essentially a pattern recognition problem, i.e., in *verification mode* the acquired biometric signal is used to classify authentication attempts (including the stored features of the claimed identity) into the classes *genuine* and *impostor*, and in *identification mode* the acquired biometric signal is used only for classifying the pattern into $n + 1$ classes representing n known (enrolled) subjects registered with the system plus an additional class representing unknown identities. Typically, for this task, features are extracted from biometric signals, to uniquely characterize the owner of the signal, i.e. the corresponding identity. Most iris biometric systems [44] have focused on the mapping of data into a feature space preserving useful information to describe the identity, while rejecting redundant information. The task of finding improved comparators employed to derive a measure of similarity (or dissimilarity) between two given feature vectors has attracted much less attention. Nevertheless, assuming that feature extraction itself is prone to errors and may itself contain not only discriminative but also redundant or noisy data, the task of "extracting features into feature space" leading to more robust or faster comparators is an interesting perspective leading to advanced comparison techniques. Like for the corresponding pattern recognition approaches, the boundary between feature extraction and comparators deriving the measure of similarity needed for classification is arbitrary [34]. Highly sophisticated comparators could accept raw biometric signals as input and be able to derive similarities on raw data, while "ideal" feature extraction techniques would make the task of finding comparators (testing for equality) trivial. For practical reasons however, it is difficult to find such strong feature extraction techniques, and even evaluation of current biometric systems is largely based on errors, which are likely to occur. For the storage of features, Daugman's proposed approach using a binary representation based on Gabor wavelet phase information [116] represents the state-of-the-art encoding method.

Apart from the fractional HD several other techniques of how to compare iris-codes have been proposed with different properties regarding comparison mode, computational cost, obtained accuracy, and the number of required enrollment samples. Within this chapter the following comparators will be discussed:

1. *Context-based comparison*: As concluded in Chap. 7, inaccurate iris segmentation may introduce distortions, which cannot be resolved by simple bit shifts during the alignment process. However, local mapping distortions are typically less severe, leading to the idea of applying an iris comparator locally and taking its immediate context, namely surrounding information, into consideration. Such a context-based comparator may be defined for iris-codes, as well as on quantified iris textures, see [432].

2. *Constrained Levenshtein comparator*: While the commonly applied HD on iris-codes shifted by discrete pixels (or bits with respect to iris-codes) may tolerate different head rotations in an ideal anatomical pupil dilation model, tilted shifts or nonlinear distortions can be more effectively suppressed if the Levenshtein distance is applied instead [538].

3. *Shifting score fusion*: Whereas the first two comparators require additional processing time, even rather simple optimizations may lead to an increased performance. The idea of shifting score fusion [442] is to take not only the minimum HD over several shifted iris-codes into account (in order to tolerate rotational variation) but also the maximum HD.

4. *Gaussian score fitting*: Refining the idea of shifting score fusion not only the worst alignment, but also the entire range of scores achieved during the alignment process may be used to assist recognition by fitting this distribution to a Gaussian and combining results with minimum HD [443].

5. *Bit reliability-based comparator*: Since reliabilities of bits in iris-codes are not uniformly distributed across entire templates [196], user-specific reliability masks can be stored in order to perform weighted comparisons [427].

6. *Incremental iris comparator*: In order to accelerate biometric identification an incremental approach to iris recognition, using early rejection of unlikely matches during comparison can be constructed [438]. Best-matching candidates in identification mode are incrementally determined, operating on reordered iris templates of a single algorithm, according to bit reliability (see [196]).

7. *Image metric-based comparators*: In contrast to common belief that original iris textures exhibit too much variation to be used directly for recognition, image quality metrics, interpreting iris textures as a noisy reproduction of the reference sample, provide quite reasonable accuracy when employed for iris recognition [194].

8. *Bit reliability score fusion*: When analyzing trade-off costs between the computational performance and recognition accuracy of iris-biometric comparators, a combination of bit reliability-based comparators [427] and shifting score fusion [442] provides a well-performing compromise [439].

9. *Selective bits fusion*: Extending the idea of incremental iris comparators to multi-algorithm multibiometric fusion [456], instead of storing multiple biometric templates for each algorithm, most discriminative bits can be extracted from multiple algorithms into a new template. This way, we can benefit of increased accuracy without the drawback of increased template size or additional processing requirements [440].

10. *Rotation-invariant pre-selection*: Serial reductive comparison techniques as employed in [537] may also be employed for iris recognition, e.g. combining fast but less accurate rotation-invariant techniques for initial screening and more but also time-consuming rotation-compensating techniques (due to the necessary alignment process) [270].

11. *Combining image metrics with iris-codes*: Finally, global features extracted by image metric-based comparators [194] tend to complement localized features encoded by traditional feature extraction methods.

The introduced operators are presented in more detail and grouped into four categories: *alignment-optimized comparison* for techniques targeting a more efficient matching of iris-codes (comparators 1–4), *reliability-based comparison* for methods exploiting bit reliability in single-algorithmic configuration (comparators 5 and 6), *comparators in the image domain* for approaches targeting not feature vectors (iris-codes) but original and normalized iris data (comparator 7), and *fusion-based approaches* targeting multi-algorithmic fusion (comparators 8–11).

9.1   Alignment-Optimized Comparison

Alignment-optimized comparison targets new iris biometric comparators for more accurate alignment of iris-codes, i.e. the ultimate goal is an easily calculable similarity or dissimilarity metric on binary data. Similarity measure selection is a problem encountered in various fields. Cha et al. [72] compare several binary vector similarity measures including a new variable credit similarity measure (altering credit for zero–zero and one–one matches) for iris biometric authentication. Their proposed metric improves and generalizes HD measures by introducing weights in order to give greater importance to error pixels in a neighborhood of error pixels. However, in order to determine parameters, a separate training stage is needed and the trained contributing factor was reported to vary considerably depending on the application data. A more exhaustive hierarchically clustered summary of binary similarity and distance measures can be found in Choi et al. [92].

9.1.1 Context-Based Comparison

Most iris recognition algorithms restrict their attention to the extraction of distinct features out of preprocessed iris images in order to create user-specific iris-codes, neglecting potential improvements in matching procedures. By exploiting local information of extracted iris-codes a context-based comparison is presented. This comparison technique can be applied to a trivial iris-code generation as well as binary feature vectors extracted by existing iris recognition systems. Focusing on a pair-wise comparison of iris biometric feature vectors, intuitively, large connected matching parts of features indicate a genuine comparison. On the other hand, large connected non-matching parts as well as rather small matching parts of feature vectors indicate non-genuine samples, tending to cause more randomized distortions. Based on these logically justifiable assumptions iris-codes are analyzed in a comparison strategy which is referred to as *context-based comparison* [432]. Emphasis is put on the comparison procedure, i.e. a rather trivial feature extraction method is introduced in order to clearly describe the comparator.

Preprocessing is adjusted to Daugman's approach [116]. After approximating the inner and outer boundary of the iris, the resulting iris ring is unwrapped in order to generate a normalized rectangular texture. Due to the fact that the top and bottom of the iris are often hidden by eyelashes or eyelids, these parts of the iris are discarded ($315°$ to $45°$ and $135°$ to $225°$). In order to obtain a smooth image a Gaussian blur is applied to the resulting iris texture. Subsequently, contrast is enhanced by applying contrast-limited adaptive histogram equalization [620]. The adapted preprocessing operates on local image regions where the image is subdivided into image tiles and the contrast is enhanced within each of these regions. In the feature extraction blocks of $x \times y$ pixels of a preprocessed iris texture are examined and each block is discretized by mapping according grayscale values of all included pixels p_i to a natural number less than a predefined parameter k such that,

$$p_i \mapsto \left\lfloor \frac{p_i}{\frac{n}{k}} \right\rfloor \tag{9.1}$$

where n is the number of possible grayscale values. In order to obtain feature vector elements the most frequent value of each block is assigned to the entire block, defining the codeword of the block. Iris-codes, which are interpreted as two-dimensional feature vectors (depending on the column and row of underlying pixel blocks), are generated by concatenating the resulting codewords of all discretized $x \times y$ blocks. Example parts of tertiary iris-codes ($k = 3$) are illustrated as part of Fig. 9.1.

The entire context-based comparison process consists of two steps: in the first step, a so-called matching-code is generated out of two given feature vectors, and in the second step, values of the matching-code are transformed in order to estimate a final comparison score.

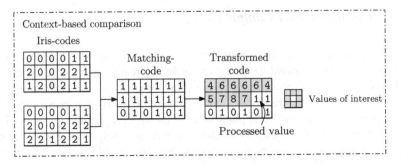

Fig. 9.1 Context-based comparison: Tertiary iris-codes are compared yielding a binary matching-code which forms the basis of the transformed matching-code for the defined values of interest

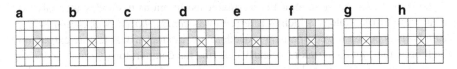

Fig. 9.2 Values of interest: Several different reasonable combinations of values of interest (*filled gray*), where the centered cell represents a processed value of a matching-code

1. *Matching-code generation*: The matching-code is generated by stapling one feature vector on top of another, where codewords of both feature vector are compared and 1s are assigned to matching feature elements and 0s to non-matching feature elements. Feature vectors need not necessarily be two-dimensional, however, within most iris recognition algorithms, distinct parts of feature vectors originate from distinct parts of preprocessed textures, i.e. most iris-codes can be adjusted in rows to generate two-dimensional matching-codes providing more local information. In Fig. 9.1 this process is shown for parts of two sample feature vectors.

2. *Matching-score estimation*: The two-dimensional matching-code, consisting of 1s and 0s is examined, in order to detect connected areas of matching as well as non-matching codewords (clusters of 1s and 0s), i.e. for each value of the matching-code, predefined neighboring *values of interest* are considered (these need not be identical). In Fig. 9.2 several examples of neighboring values of interest for matching and non-matching codewords (1s and 0s in the matching-code) are shown. Depending on the choice of values of interest, the initial values of the two-dimensional matching-code are transformed to decimal values, as shown in Fig. 9.1. If a processed value of the matching-code is 1, it is incremented for each value of interest which is 1 as well. By analogy, if a processed value is 0, it is decremented for each value of interest which is 0. By definition, the context-based comparator only increments a value of the matching-code resulting from matching codewords, while it only decrements a value of the matching-code resulting from non-matching codewords (1s and 0s, respectively). Figure 9.1 illustrates an example of this process, where the transformation is applied to

each value of a matching-code. The matching-score of two feature vectors a and b, denoted by $M(a,b)$, which declares the grade of similarity of these feature vectors, is calculated by summing up the signed powers of all values of the transformed code $a\overline{\oplus}b$ such that,

$$M(a,b) = \sum_{i=1}^{n} \text{sgn}(a\overline{\oplus}b\,[i]) \cdot 2^{|a\overline{\oplus}b\,[i]|} \qquad (9.2)$$

where n denotes the total number of values of the transformed code, $.[i]$ the i-th element of a sequence (element-wise access), and sgn(.) the signum function, respectively. By applying this procedure, large connected clusters become highly valuable. The larger the matching-score, the higher the grade of similarity. Minimum and maximum matching-scores depend on the predefined values of interest for matching as well as non-matching codewords and the dimension of the matching-code. An adequate threshold, which can be found by testing a certain set of iris images for the calculated matching-score, yields a successful authentication or rejection, respectively.

The context-based comparator generally improves recognition accuracy (at the cost of more computational effort) compared to traditional comparison techniques, due to the incorporation of local information which is analyzed in a context-based manner.

9.1.2 Constrained Levenshtein Comparator

While generic approaches to iris recognition focus on robust preprocessing, it is possible to account for distortions at the comparison stage as well. By the use of the Levenshtein distance (LD) [300], a binary biometric comparator can be constructed, referred to as *constrained Levenshtein comparator* [538], which is capable to tolerate segmentation inaccuracies and distortions caused by the linearity of Daugman's normalization model [116]. By introducing LD alignment constraints, the matching problem can be solved in $O(n \cdot s)$ time and $O(n+s)$ space with n and s being the number of bits and shifts, respectively. Furthermore, improvements to common implementations of LD computation, i.e. alignment constraints, can be established.

The LD dates back to the 1960s [300] and is a well-known classical distance measure in pattern recognition for sequences of possibly different length. The idea to use LD for biometrics is not new, e.g. Schimke et al. [473] employ an adapted version of LD based on event-string modeling and a nearest neighbor classifier for online signature verification. The application of LD within an iris recognition system is illustrated in Fig. 9.3.

The inherent idea of LD is to employ inexact matching allowing a sequence to exhibit additional or lacking parts of another similar sequence. Similarity is defined

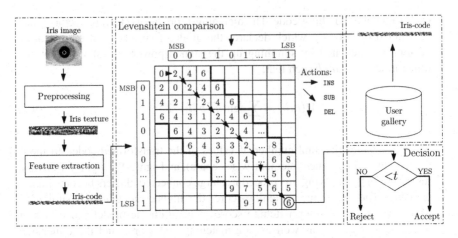

Fig. 9.3 Constrained Levenshtein comparator: The basic operation mode of the comparator as part of a generic iris recognition system

by an optimal transformation of one sequence into the other by three operations: *INS* (insert), *DEL* (delete), and *SUB* (substitute). Each operation is associated with a cost, c_{INS} and c_{DEL} are scalar values, $c_{SUB}(x,y)$ is a function depending on the symbols $x, y \in \{0,1\}$ at specific positions of the two sequences to be compared (in iris recognition we consider binary sequences only). Typically, $c_{SUB}(x,y) = 0 \Leftrightarrow x = y$ for symbol y replacing x. The LD is also called Edit Distance and can be calculated by Dynamic Time Warping (DTW) [359], a dynamic programming algorithm to align the sequences. Let $a \in \{0,1\}^m$ and $b \in \{0,1\}^n$ be binary sequences of length m and n (as LD is applied to iris-codes of fixed length, $m = n$ holds). DTW uses a matrix D of size $(m+1) \times (n+1)$, which is incrementally computed:

$$D[0,0] := 0 \tag{9.3}$$

$$\forall i > 0 : D[i,0] := D[i-1,0] + c_{DEL}, \tag{9.4}$$

$$\forall j > 0 : D[0,j] := D[0,j-1] + c_{INS}, \tag{9.5}$$

$$\forall i,j > 0 : D[i,j] := \min(D[i-1,j] + c_{DEL},$$

$$D[i,j-1] + c_{INS},$$

$$D[i-1,j-1] + c_{SUB}(a[i],b[j])). \tag{9.6}$$

The invariant maintained throughout the algorithm is that the subsequence $a[1..i]$ can be transformed into $b[1..j]$ using a minimum of $D[i,j]$ operations. The LD of a and b is:

$$LD(a,b) := D(m,n). \tag{9.7}$$

A traceback algorithm can be used to find the optimal alignment, i.e. an alignment path results from joining nodes and depending on the local direction an optimal (not necessary unique) sequence of transformation operations is derived, see Fig. 9.3. However, as the comparison stage needs the distance measure only, a storage of the entire matrix can be avoided in order to reduce space complexity from $O(n^2)$ (assuming $n = m$ in the application domain) to $O(n)$ with column-wise computation. Still, time complexity stays at $O(n^2)$ with this modification, which is not useful for commercial applications. The traditional HD dissimilarity measure needs $O(n \cdot s)$ time and $O(n + s)$ space with s being the number of bit shifts, which is usually a very small constant number.

In order to further reduce LD time requirements, additional constraints can be defined: computations are restricted to an evaluation region S on matrix D shaped as a stripe from top-left to bottom-right (see Fig. 9.3), i.e. technically $S := \{(x,y) : |x - y| \leq s\}$ is defined and set:

$$\forall (i,j) \notin S : D[i,j] = \infty. \tag{9.8}$$

By this modification, a maximum local deviation of the patterns by s shifts is enforced. The resulting final algorithm solves the matching problem in $O(n \cdot s)$ time and $O(n + s)$ space with n and s being the number of bits and shifts, respectively. It is worth to notice that the last optimization does no longer deliver the exact LD. However, it is a very natural constraint to give an upper limit on relative shifts, since it should not be too difficult to get estimators for eye tilt (e.g., localization of eye lids).

Finally, in order to obtain a normalized distance value, we note that for $m = n$ the condition $LD(a,b) \leq HD(a,b)$ holds, and we therefore divide the result by the code size n. Note that for LD the triangle inequality holds. The advantage of LD over traditional HD lies in its ability of nonlinear alignment. For this reason, it is widely accepted in computational biology, e.g. to estimate alignments of DNA.

A constrained Levenshtein comparator improves the recognition performance of traditional iris biometric systems based on binary feature vectors, especially if biometric systems operate in unconstrained environments where different types of distortions are most likely to appear.

9.1.3 Shifting Score Fusion

In case of having access to specific iris-codes only or black-boxed feature extraction, there may be situations where improved comparison, with respect to recognition accuracy (even at potentially higher processing cost), is desirable. One idea to improve iris biometric comparators is to utilize variations within comparison scores at different shift positions. It is demonstrated that by taking advantage of this information, which even comes at negligible cost, recognition performance can be improved. For genuine pairs of iris-codes a distinct shifting position reveals an optimal comparison score while iris-codes of different data subjects tend to exhibit

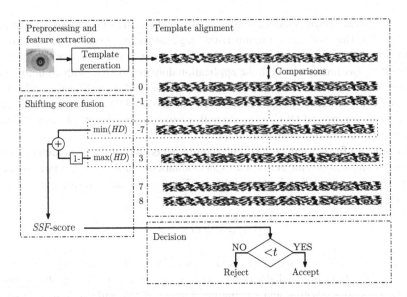

Fig. 9.4 Proposed comparison: the basic operation mode of the proposed comparison strategy

equally low similarity scores across different alignments. This claim is justified by the fact that iris-codes of different data subjects should appear random to each other per se, regardless of shifting positions, while unaligned iris codes of individual subjects might exhibit special effects (systematic error, improvement towards optimal alignment, etc.). This motivates the construction of an iris-biometric comparator, which exploits shifting variation in comparison scores.

As illustrated in Fig. 9.4, the main focus of our approach is put on a modification of the comparison stage. In traditional iris comparison [44], in order to obtain a comparison score indicating the (dis-)similarity between two iris-codes, the minimum fractional HD over different bit shifts is calculated. It is a very natural approach to preserve the best match only, i.e. the minimum HD value over different shifts. However, there is no evidence that the other computed HD scores of less perfect alignments might not be able to contribute to an even better recognition result. In an advanced iris-biometric comparator, which is referred to as *shifting score fusion* [442], the shifting variation, i.e. difference between maximum and minimum obtained HD scores, is tracked. Let $a \ll i$ denote an iris-code a shifted by $i \in \mathbb{Z}_n$ bits ($\mathbb{Z}_n := \{z \in \mathbb{Z} : |z| \leq n\}$) and $HD(a,b)$ be the HD of two iris-codes, then we define the shifting variation (SV) score for two iris-codes a, b as:

$$SV(a,b) = \max_{i \in \mathbb{Z}_n}\big(HD(a,b \ll i)\big) - \min_{i \in \mathbb{Z}_n}\big(HD(a,b \ll i)\big). \qquad (9.9)$$

Since multiplication and addition with constant values does not alter the ROC behavior of SV scores (denoted here with an equivalence relation $\approx$), the following modifications are performed to illustrate an interesting connection between *SV* and sum rule fusion:

$$SV(a,b) \approx \min_{i \in \mathbb{Z}_n}\big(HD\big(a,b \ll i\big)\big) - \max_{i \in \mathbb{Z}_n}\big(HD(a,b \ll i)\big)$$

$$\approx 1 - \max_{i \in \mathbb{Z}_n}\big(HD(a,b \ll i)\big) + \min_{i \in \mathbb{Z}_n}\big(HD(a,b \ll i)\big)$$

$$\approx \frac{1}{2}\bigg(\Big(1 - \max_{i \in \mathbb{Z}_n}\big(HD(a,b \ll i)\big)\Big) + \min_{i \in \mathbb{Z}_n}\Big(HD\big(a,b \ll i\big)\Big)\bigg). \quad (9.10)$$

Consequently, *SV* corresponds to a score level fusion of the minimum (i.e., best) HD and one minus the maximum (i.e. worst) HD using the sum rule [230]. By combining "best" and "worst" observed HD scores the variation between these scores is tracked, which represents a suitable indicator for genuine and impostor classes (SV scores tend to be higher for intra-class comparisons than for inter-class comparisons). In order to obtain distance scores comparable to minimum HD the latter term is reformulated using sum-rule fusion:

$$SSF(a,b) = \frac{1}{2}\bigg(\Big(1 - \max_{i \in \mathbb{Z}_n}\big(HD(a,b \ll i)\big)\Big) + \min_{i \in \mathbb{Z}_n}\Big(HD\big(a,b \ll i\big)\Big)\bigg). \quad (9.11)$$

The shifting score fusion (SSF) comparison technique improves the recognition performance of an existing system at negligible computational cost. Aligning pairs of iris-codes involves the calculation of comparison scores at diverse shifting positions, which is utilized within this comparator.

9.1.4 Gaussian Score Fitting

A common way to estimate the average entropy of biometric feature vectors is to measure the provided "degrees-of-freedom" which are defined by $d = p(1-p)/\sigma^2$, where p is the mean *HD* and σ^2 the corresponding variance between comparisons of different pairs of binary feature vectors, shown in Fig. 9.5. In case all bits of each binary feature vector of length n would be mutually independent, comparisons of pairs of different feature vectors would yield a binomial distribution,

$$B(n,k) = \binom{n}{k} p^k (1-p)^{n-k} = \binom{n}{k} 0.5^n \quad (9.12)$$

and the expectation of the HD would be $E(HD(a,b)) = 1/n \cdot E(X \oplus Y) = np \cdot 1/n = p = 0.5$, where X and Y are two independent random variables in $\{0,1\}$. In reality, parts of feature vectors are correlated. As a consequence, p decreases to $0.5 - \varepsilon$ while HD remains binomially distributed with a reduction in n.

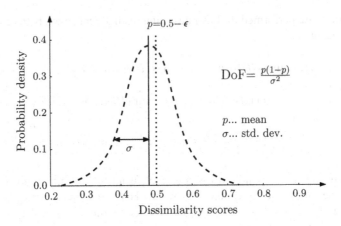

Fig. 9.5 Binomial distribution of HD between different pairs of binary biometric feature vectors

Based on the fact that not all bits in iris-codes are mutually independent (e.g., in [115] feature vectors of 2,048 bits exhibit 249 degrees of freedom) comparison scores are expected to improve until an optimal alignment is reached, which corresponds to a minimal obtained HD. In case two identical iris-codes are compared, the resulting scores constantly decrease until $0.5 - \varepsilon$ at a certain shifting position (in both directions). These observations motivate a tracking of progressions in all observed comparison scores by fitting comparison scores to an algorithm-dependent Gaussian function. The resulting comparator, which is referred to as *Gaussian score fitting* [443], comprises two main stages:

1. *Training stage*: In the training stage a set of iris-codes is applied to model an average algorithm-dependent distribution of comparison scores at a certain alignment. For this purpose all genuine comparisons within the training set are performed. Let again $a \ll i$ denote the shifting of an iris-code a by $i \in \mathbb{Z}_n$ bits, $\mathbb{Z}_n = \{z \in \mathbb{Z} : |z| \leq n\}$. Then the minimal HD of two iris-codes is defined as

$$MinHD(a,b) = \min_{i \in \mathbb{Z}_n}\big(HD(a,b \ll i)\big). \qquad (9.13)$$

Once an optimal alignment is detected for each pair of iris-codes (of a single subject), the progression of scores with respect to the optimal alignment is tracked in an histogram within an adequate range (e.g., ± 8 bit shifts in each direction). Based on all tracked comparison scores an average algorithm-dependent score is estimated at certain shifting positions with reference to an optimal alignment.

It is found that average distributions of comparison scores, in particular $1 - MinHD$, at certain shifting positions can be approximated by a Gaussian function,

$$G(k,i) = t + \frac{1}{\sigma\sqrt{2\pi}}e^{-(k-i)^2/(2\sigma^2)} \qquad (9.14)$$

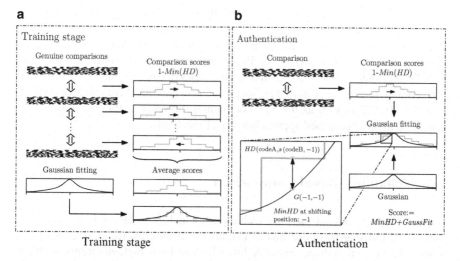

Fig. 9.6 Training stage and authentication: Scores obtained from comparisons within a training set are modeled applying a Gaussian. Scores at different shifting positions are fitted to a Gaussian. (**a**) Training stage, (**b**) Authentication

where t represents the decision threshold of the system and i refers to the optimal shifting position. An adequate Gaussian can be established by manual fitting or by applying any systematic approach, e.g. nonlinear least squares fitting. The proposed training stage is schematically illustrated in Fig. 9.6a.

2. *Comparison based on Gaussian fitting*: At the time of authentication the deviation of comparison scores to the corresponding Gaussian (estimated at training stage) is measured at different shifting positions. For this purpose the function *GaussFit* is defined, which calculates the quadratic error of the comparison score between two iris-codes a and b at a distinct shifting position k to a Gaussian G,

$$GaussFit(a,b,k) = \left(1 - HD(a,b \ll k) - G(k,i)\right)^2. \qquad (9.15)$$

The deviation is estimated for distinct shifting positions $k \in \mathbb{Z}_n$ based on the optimal shift i in order to calculate the final fitting score, denoted by $GaussFit(a,b)$. Subsequently, the final score is defined by $||\sum_{k=-n}^{n} GaussFit(a,b,k)||$, the sum of all quadratic errors which is normalized to the range $[0,1]$. Normalization is performed based on minimum and maximum values which are estimated from the applied training set (during experiments occurring outliers are set to 0 or 1, respectively). Subsequently, the resulting fitting score is combined with the *MinHD* comparator applying sum rule fusion. The proposed comparator, denoted by *MinHD+GaussFit*, is defined by

$$MinHD+GaussFit(a,b) = \left(MinHD(a,b) + GaussFit(a,b)\right)/2. \qquad (9.16)$$

Figure 9.6b illustrates the operation mode of the proposed comparison technique.

In contrast to the *MinHD* comparator the proposed comparator additionally tracks improvements of comparison scores towards the estimation of an optimal alignment, which is likely for genuine comparisons. On the other hand, the presented approach increases dissimilarity between pairs of iris-codes extracted from different subjects where Gaussian progressions in comparison scores are rather unlikely. Obviously, the proposed technique requires additional computational effort over the *MinHD* as well as the *SSF* comparator; however, extra cost is kept low compared to other proposed approaches (e.g., [538, 619]).

9.2 Reliability-Based Comparison

Besides conventional bit-masking techniques, which are designed to detect occlusions originating from eye lids or eye lashes, Hollingsworth et al. [196] have proposed a method to detect iris-code bits which underlie high variations. In other words, distinct parts of iris-codes turn out to be more consistent than others. This is because some areas within iris textures are more likely to be occluded by eyelids or eyelashes. By masking out these "fragile bits" during comparisons, recognition performance is increased. Additionally, parts of iris-codes which originate from analyzing the inner bands of iris textures are found to be more constant than parts which originate from analyzing the outer bands. To obtain representative user-specific iris templates during enrollment, Davida et al. [124] and Ziauddin and Dailey [619] analyze several iris-codes. While Davida et al. propose a majority decoding where the majority of bits is assigned to according bit positions, Ziauddin and Dailey suggest to assign weights to each bit position which are afterwards applied during comparison. Obviously, applying more than one enrollment sample yields better recognition performance [135]; however, commercial applications usually require single sample enrollment.

In [536] a more generic approach is presented for optimizing both, recognition and processing performance of multibiometric systems in identification mode. The proposed method exploits ranking capabilities of individual features by reducing the set of possible matching candidates at each iteration. When applied to hand-based modalities, the new system is as accurate as sum-rule-based fusion of individual classifiers, but twice as fast as the best single classifier on 86 classes.

Approaches closer related to the incremental comparator are quick screening or pre-classification techniques. Several authors have developed techniques to divide iris data into a certain number of categories in order to achieve a rough pre-classification before applying a more accurate matching technique. Qui et al. [413] use iris textons to generate five classes, and Yu et al. [601] use fractal dimension to generate four classes.

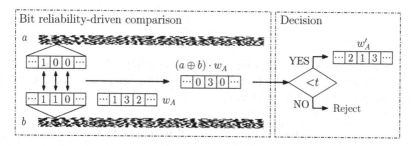

Fig. 9.7 Bit reliability-driven comparison: Weighted comparison of iris-codes is performed based on user-specific weights

9.2.1 Bit Reliability-Driven Comparator

Information of authentication procedures can be leveraged by maintaining so-called reliability masks for each subject, which indicate local consistency of enrollment templates. Based on user-specific reliability masks a weighted matching procedure can be performed in order to improve recognition performance, yielding a comparison technique which is referred to as *bit reliability-driven comparator* [427]. Hollingsworth et al. [196] have shown that masking out so-called "fragile" bits of iris-codes leads to a more accurate system. The bit reliability-based comparison strategy of iris-codes builds upon this observation. In contrast to existing approaches, which utilize weighted matching procedures (e.g., [597, 619]), this comparator does not require the acquisition of several enrollment samples. The basic operation mode of this comparator is illustrated in Fig. 9.7.

At the time of enrollment, an iris-code a of length n is obtained from subject A and stored as biometric template, $a \in \{0, 1\}^n$. Additionally, a user-specific reliability mask is stored, denoted by w_A and having n weights, which should indicate the reliability at each bit position of a. Initially, each value of w_A is set to 1, i.e. all bits of a exhibit the same reliability. Recall that the fractional HD (without considering noise masks) between two iris-codes a and b is calculated by,

$$HD(a,b) = \frac{\sum_{i=1}^{n} a[i] \oplus b[i]}{n} \qquad (9.17)$$

and if $HD(a,b)$ is below a predefined threshold t, $HD(a,b) < t$, successful authentication is yielded. Additionally, bit-masking can be applied to mask out bits of iris-codes which originate from parts of the iris which are occluded by eye lids or eye lashes (bit-masks need to be extracted at each feature extraction). In order to assign a degree of reliability to each bit position, a weighted HD is estimated, $WHD(a,b,w_A)$ is estimated. The mask w_A of the claimed identity A is applied to weight the comparison process by summing up weights at bit positions of mismatching bits where the result is divided by the sum of all weights,

$$WHD(a,b,w_A) = \frac{\sum_{i=1}^{n}(a[i] \oplus b[i]) \cdot w_A[i]}{\sum_{i=1}^{n} w_A[i]}. \tag{9.18}$$

Initially $\|w_A\|$ is n, since each bit of w_A is 1, i.e. $WHD(a,b,w_A)$ is equivalent to $HD(a,b)$. In case of successful authentication ($WHD(a,b,w_A) < t$), each bit of the stored mask w_A of user A is updated:

$$w_A'[i] = \begin{cases} w_A[i] + (a[i]\overline{\oplus}b[i]), & \text{if } WHD(a,b,w_A) < t; \\ w_A[i], & \text{otherwise.} \end{cases} \tag{9.19}$$

Upon each successful authentication weights of w_A are incremented at each position i where $a[i]$ is equal to $b[i]$, resulting in the updated mask w_A'. The pre-defined decision threshold t has to be set up according to the applied iris recognition algorithm. The threshold t remains unaltered for all users independent of the number of authentications. Since the weighted HD is calculated in relation to stored reliability masks, inter-class distances are not expected to decrease. In contrast, intra-class distances are expected to decrease due to the fact that unreliable bits are weighted less.

The proposed matching procedure exhibits several advantages: (1) The comparator does not require the acquisition of several enrollment samples in order to detect reliable bits in iris-codes; (2) since the weighted matching process is still kept simple, running the system in identification mode is not expected to cause a drastic performance decrease; (3) extracted weights are user-specific and after several successful authentications the mask of each user adapts to the iris-code extracted during enrollment. An example of this process is shown in Fig. 9.8. As can be seen, after a small number of successful authentications the mask adapts to the stored iris-code. Less reliable parts of the iris-code, which e.g., result from parts of the iris texture which suffer from occlusions, tend to reveal low weights while others exhibit high weights.

In addition, masking bits can be easily integrated into the stored mask. It is suggested to set the weights of stored masks to zero if bits of a bit-mask indicate that iris-code bits result form parts of the iris texture where some kind of distortions were detected. Still, generic bit-masking does not represent an alternative to the proposed technique since conventional "two-dome" patterns do not cover all unreliable bits (see Fig. 9.8) [196].

The bit reliability-based comparison technique develops a multi-level distribution of reliability as opposed to binary bit-masking. Initial user-specific weights are continuously refined after each successful authentication outperforming systems based on conventional comparison procedures. Furthermore, the technique is easily adapted to any existing iris recognition algorithm.

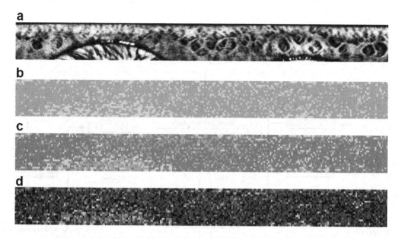

Fig. 9.8 Original texture and corresponding reliability mask (dark regions indicate reliable parts of the stored iris-code): (**a**) Original iris texture of an enrolled subject, (**b**) Reliability mask weights after one successful comparison, (**c**) Weights after two successful comparisons, (**d**) Weights after eight successful comparisons

9.2.2 Incremental Iris Comparator

In identification systems, single iris-codes (probes) have to be compared against a database of iris-codes (gallery) requiring linear effort. In case databases comprise millions of iris-codes, without choice, biometric identification will lead to long-lasting response times. Therefore, reducing the computational effort of iris-based identification systems represents a challenging issue [161].

It has been shown that the entropy of bits in iris-codes differs, depending on which parts of the iris texture these bits originate from [196]. The inter-relation of local origin and consistency of bits in iris-codes defines a global distribution of reliability. This fact can be exploited in order to accelerate iris biometric identification systems. From analyzing bit-error occurrences in a training set of iris-codes a global ranking of bit positions can be estimated, based on which given probes are rearranged, i.e. iris-codes are reordered. With most reliable bits being arranged in the first part of an iris-code, partial and incremental comparisons can be applied. This comparator, which is referred to as *incremental iris comparator* [438], represents a single-algorithm fusion technique and is illustrated in Fig. 9.9.

For a training set of n different classes U_i of iris images, where each class contains k iris images, $n \cdot k \cdot (k-1)/2$ intra-class matchings and $k \cdot n \cdot (n-1)/2$ inter-class matchings (for balancing reasons we only compare templates with equal indices within a class) are performed. Prior to estimating the error probability for each bit position, an optimal alignment is estimated by tolerating 7 bit-shifts.

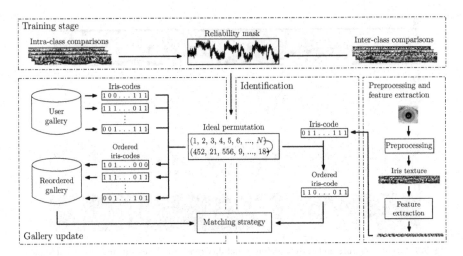

Fig. 9.9 Incremental iris comparator: the basic operation mode of this comparator involving a training stage, gallery update, and identification

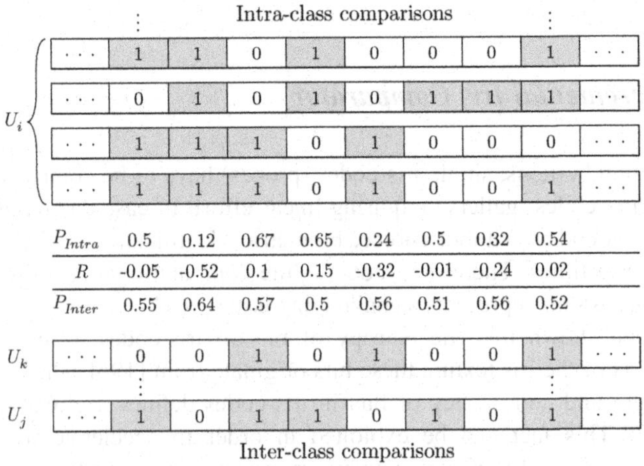

	Intra-class comparisons								
	...	1	1	0	1	0	0	0	1	...
U_i	...	0	1	0	1	0	1	1	1	...
	...	1	1	1	0	1	0	0	0	...
	...	1	1	1	0	1	0	0	1	...
P_{Intra}	0.5	0.12	0.67	0.65	0.24	0.5	0.32	0.54
R	-0.05	-0.52	0.1	0.15	-0.32	-0.01	-0.24	0.02
P_{Inter}	0.55	0.64	0.57	0.5	0.56	0.51	0.56	0.52
U_k	...	0	0	1	0	1	0	0	1	...
U_j	...	1	0	1	1	0	1	0	1	...

Inter-class comparisons

Fig. 9.10 Reliability mask construction: probabilities of intra-class and inter-class error occurrence are estimated to calculate the reliability at each bit position

Subsequently, for each bit position the probabilities of intra-class and inter-class error occurrence are estimated, denoted by P_{Intra} and P_{Inter}, respectively. The reliability at each bit position is defined by $R = P_{Intra} - P_{Inter}$. Reliability measures of all bit positions over all pairings define a global (user-independent) reliability distribution, which is used to rearrange given iris-codes in ascending order with respect to bit reliability (small values indicate high reliability). A schematical impression of this process is shown in Fig. 9.10.

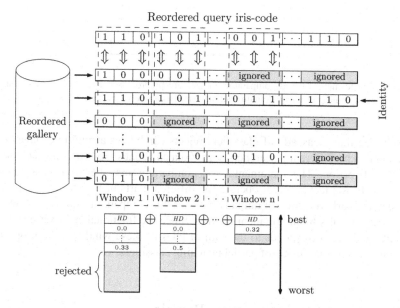

Fig. 9.11 Incremental iris comparator: HDs are incrementally calculated allowing early rejection of unlikely matches

Once the reliability mask is calculated, iris-codes of a given user gallery are updated. From the previously calculated reliability mask an ideal permutation of bit positions is derived and applied to reorder all enrollment samples such that the first bits represent the most reliable bits and the last bits represent the least reliable bits.

Biometric comparisons are performed in the transformed domain of reordered iris-codes. If galleries of original iris-codes are updated as outlined above, each probe needs to be permuted prior to comparison. Two different types of comparison strategies can be applied:

1. *Partial comparison*: This method involves a traditional determination of the fractional HD, but restricts codes to a certain length. By this means, the amount of bit comparisons—and therefore time complexity—can be controlled exactly at the cost of possible degradation of accuracy. In case the reliability mask can successfully identify "fragile" bits over different subjects, performance is expected to improve [196].

2. *Incremental comparison*: This technique (illustrated in Fig. 9.11) performs partial comparison of the probe with each gallery template for a given window size. After having obtained all partial HDs for a window, these are combined with the corresponding HDs from previous windows (incremental computation) and all gallery templates are ordered according to their HD. Only candidates with a high chance of being correct identities are kept, rejected candidates are excluded from further computations.

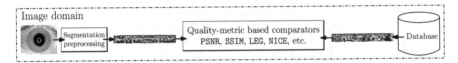

Fig. 9.12 Image metrics-based comparator: images are preprocessed and quality-metric-based comparators (operating in image domain) estimate similarities between pairs of images

The idea that a cascade of classifiers rejects candidates at multiple stages has been applied by different researchers, e.g. Viola and Jones [564] use this technique for face detection. The incremental iris comparator may be seen as a single-algorithm fusion technique. It operates on different parts of the iris texture [456]. By applying early rejection of unlikely matches this comparator improves accuracy and accelerates iris biometric identification. Since the fractional HD over a sum of adjoint windows corresponds to the sum of HDs of these windows, the proposed method is a sum-rule fusion of partial matching classifiers.

9.3   Comparators in the Image Domain

Image domain feature transforms, such as SIFT-based [12] or Phase-based [275] methods, can be utilized for iris recognition as well. Kekre et al. [248, 249] use the image feature set extracted from Haar Wavelets at various levels of decomposition and from walshlet pyramid for recognition. Subsequently, simple Euclidean distance on the feature set is applied as the similarity measure. Image quality metrics which tend to extract rather global features can be utilized for iris biometric recognition or can be combined with traditional more localized feature extraction methods.

9.3.1   Image Metrics-Based Comparator

In accordance with the ISO/IEC FDIS 19794-6 standard, biometric comparators can be constructed which are referred to as *image metric-based comparators*. ISO/IEC FDIS 19794-6 compliant databases, which (additionally) store raw iris biometric data, enable the incorporation of future improvements (e.g., in segmentation stage) without reenrollment of registered subjects. This motivates an application of comparators operating in the image domain, in particular image metrics.

In image domain iris processing, one full reference iris texture t is stored per subject. In order to score an authentication attempt given a claimed identity, the corresponding template image A is compared with the current sample image B. Both images of $w \times h$ pixels are compared by employing a quality metric $Q(A, B \ll m)$, where $B \ll m$ denotes a circular shifting of m pixels to the left or right in order to obtain a rotation invariant technique. For A and B the b bits per pixel are used with a maximum pixel value of $m = 2^b$.

In order to assess similarities between normalized iris textures, in the sense that a given sample is interpreted as the noisy reproduction of the stored reference sample, several image quality metrics can be employed:

- *Peak signal-to-noise ratio (PSNR):* A widely metric unrivaled in speed and ease of use and calculated as,

$$\text{PSNR} = 10\log_{10}\left(\frac{m^2}{\text{MSE}}\right), \quad \text{MSE} = \frac{1}{wh} * \sum_{i=1}^{w}\sum_{j=i}^{h}(A(i,j) - B(i,j))^2. \quad (9.20)$$

- *Structural similarity index measure (SSIM)* [573]: Uses the local luminance as well as global contrast and a structural feature after convolution with a 11×11 Gaussian filter.

$$\text{SSIM}(A,B) = \frac{(2\mu_A\mu_B + (0.01\,m)^2)(2\sigma_{AB} + (0.03\,m)^2)}{(\mu_A^2 + \mu_B^2 + (0.01\,m)^2)(\sigma_A^2 + \sigma_B^2 + (0.03\,m)^2)}, \quad (9.21)$$

where μ_A, σ_A^2 are the average pixel value and variance of pixel values in A, and σ_{AB} is the covariance of A and B.

- *Local edge gradients metric (LEG)* [195]: Uses luminance and localized edge information from different frequency domains.

$$\text{LEG}(A,B) = \text{LUM}(A,B) \cdot \text{ES}(A,B). \quad (9.22)$$

The LEG visual quality index is calculated by combining ES and LUM:

$$\text{LUM}(A,B) = 1 - \sqrt{\frac{|\mu(B) - \mu(A)|}{m}}, \quad (9.23)$$

where $\mu(X) = \frac{1}{wh}\sum_{x=1}^{w}\sum_{y=1}^{h}X(x,y)$ for an image X.

$$\text{ES}(A,B) = \frac{4}{wh}\sum_{x=1}^{\frac{w}{2}}\sum_{y=1}^{\frac{h}{2}}\left(\text{LE}(A_0,B_0,x,y) * \frac{1}{3}\sum_{i=1}^{3}\text{LED}(A_i,B_i,x,y)\right), \quad (9.24)$$

where wavelet decomposition with Haar wavelets is performed resulting in four subimages for each image X denoted as X_0 for the LL-subband, and X_1, X_2, X_3 for LH, HH, and HL subbands, respectively. The edge score is calculated by combining local edge conformity calculated using an edge map (LE) and local edge difference assessing the contrast changes in a neighborhood (LED).

- *Edge similarity score (ESS)* [333]: Uses localized edge information to compare two images after separating an image into n blocks of size 8×8, conducting Sobel edge detection on each block i to find the most prominent edge direction e^i

and quantization into one of eight directions. The ESS is based on the prominent edges of each block:

$$\text{ESS} = \frac{\sum_{i=1}^{n} w(e_A^i, e_B^i)}{\sum_{i=1}^{n} c(e_A^i, e_B^i)}, \tag{9.25}$$

where $w(e_1, e_2)$ is a weighting function. This function is defined as

$$w(e_1, e_2) = \begin{cases} 0 & \text{if } e_1 = 0 \text{ or } e_2 = 0 \\ |\cos(\phi(e_1) - \phi(e_2))| & \text{otherwise,} \end{cases} \tag{9.26}$$

where $\phi(e)$ is the representative edge angle for an index e, and $c(e_1, e_2)$ is an indicator function defined as $c(e_1, e_2) = 0$ if $e_1 = e_2 = 0$ and $c(e_1, e_2) = 1$ otherwise. In cases where $\sum_{i=1}^{N} c(e_A^i, e_B^i) = 0$ the ESS is set to 0.5.

* *Local feature-based visual security (LFBVS)* [527]: utilizes localized edge and luminance features which are combined and weighted according to error magnitude, i.e. error pooling.

$$\text{LFBVS}(A, B) = \sum_{i=1}^{n} \exp^{\frac{i}{n-0.5}} \text{OLVS}(A, B, i) / \sum_{i=1}^{n} \exp^{\frac{i}{n-0.5}}. \tag{9.27}$$

where *OLVS* refers to ordered local visual features $LVS(A, B, i)$ composed of a weighted sum of local luminance *LUM* and edge density *ED* features:

$$\text{LUM}(A, B, i) = (|\mu_B^i - \mu_A^i| + |\sigma_B^i - \sigma_A^i|) / 2l_{\max}. \tag{9.28}$$

where μ_X^i and σ_X^i refer to mean and standard deviations of 16×16 block i in image X and $l_{\max}$ is the maximum luminance.

$$\text{ED}(A, B, i) = \sum_{d=1}^{8} |H_i^B[d] - H_i^A[d]| / \sum_{d=1}^{8} \max(H_i^B[d], H_i^A[d]), \tag{9.29}$$

using histograms $H_i^X[d]$ of cumulative edge amplitude strength over edge directions d.

* *Visual information fidelity (VIF)* [479]: Modeling the reference image using natural scene statistics (NSS) based on GMMs and modelling distortion as signal gain and additive noise in the wavelet domain (this compensates for white noise and image blur in the image domain). The model is extended to include also information from the human visual system (HVS), i.e. optical point spread, contrast sensitivity, and internal neural noise, which is not covered by the NSS model. The amount of the original signal is calculated, taking into account different wavelet subbands, which can be reconstructed from the distorted signal given the NSS and the HVS model. This reconstructible fraction of the original signal is termed VIF.

- *Natural image contour evaluation (NICE)* [457, 458]: Uses gradient maps $\hat{I}$, generated from an image I for $i \in [1, \ldots, w]$ and $j \in [1, \ldots, h]$ as follows:

$$\hat{I}[i,j] := \sqrt{S_x(I,i,j)^2 + S_x(I,i,j)^2}, \qquad (9.30)$$

where $S_x(I,i,j)$ and $S_y(I,i,j)$ are the results of a Sobel filtering at position i, j in image I in direction x and y, respectively. This map is thresholded with the average gradient amplitude yielding a binary map $B_{\hat{I}}$ with $B_{\hat{I}}[i,j] := 1$ if $\hat{I}(i,j) > t_{\hat{I}}$ and $B_{\hat{I}}[i,j] := 0$ otherwise, where $t_{\hat{I}} = \frac{1}{wh} \sum_{i=1}^{w} \sum_{j=1}^{h} \hat{I}(i,j)$. Map $B_{\hat{I}}$ is transformed into $B_{\hat{I}}^+$ by applying a morphological dilation with a plus shaped structuring element. That is, each pixel $B_{\hat{I}}^+(i,j)$ is set to 1 if at least one of the 4-connected neighbors of $B_{\hat{I}}[i,j]$ or $B_{\hat{I}}[i,j]$ is 1, otherwise $B_{\hat{I}}^+[i,j] = 0$. The NICE score is calculated based on the normalized HD as

$$\text{NICE}(A,B) = \frac{\sum_{i=1}^{w} \sum_{j=1}^{h} (B_{\hat{B}}^+(i,j) - B_{\hat{A}}^+(i,j))^2}{\sum_{i=1}^{w} \sum_{j=1}^{h} B_{\hat{A}}^+(i,j)}. \qquad (9.31)$$

While this summary of quality metrics is intended to give an overview of employed techniques and present general ideas of such comparators, we refer to the original publications and [194] for a more detailed description.

Considering recognition accuracy metrics-based comparators do not outperform feature-based techniques [44]; however, image metrics are rather useful as additional features in fusion scenarios (see Sect. 9.4.4).

9.4 Fusion-Based Approaches

The human iris has been combined with different biometric modalities, in particular, the combination of iris and face data is a prospective application [614]. Still, the successful extraction of high-quality iris images from surveillance data in less constrained environments is a challenging issue. Regarding a combination of multiple iris algorithms operating on the same input instance, a couple of approaches have been published. Sun et al. [500] cascade two feature types employing global features in addition to a Daugman-like approach only if the result of the latter is in a questionable range. Zhang et al. [612] apply a similar strategy interchanging the role of global and local features. Vatsa et al. [555] compute the Euler number of connected components as global feature, while again using an iris-code as local texture feature. Park and Lee [386] decompose the iris data with a directional filterbank and extract two different feature types from this domain. Combining both results leads to an improvement compared to the single technique. Gentile et al. [161] suggested a two-stage iris recognition system, where so-called short length iris-codes (SLICs) pre-estimate a shortlist of candidates which are further processed. While SLICs exhibit only 8% of the original size of iris-codes the reduction of bits was limiting the true positive rate to about 93% for the overall system. All these techniques have in common that they aim at gaining recognition performance in biometric fusion scenarios at the cost of larger templates or more time-consuming comparison. In contrast, some of the following approaches try to improve both, resource requirements (storage and/or time) and recognition accuracy. Generally speaking, serial classifier combination aiming at a reduction of identification time is a relatively new research topic in biometrics, see [160, 536] for applications in hand biometrics and iris biometrics. Besides the aimed reduction in computational effort, it is of particular interest if the combination of two very different feature types can also lead to improved recognition results. Since features used in classifier combinations need to be as uncorrelated as possible to result in better results as compared to their single classifier counterparts [260], a recognition improvement might be expected in many of the presented cases, as long as features of the employed classifiers are of significantly different nature.

9.4.1   Bit Reliability Score Fusion

A composition of the bit reliability-driven comparator and the shifting score fusion comparator, which is referred to as *bit-reliability score fusion* [439], can be applied by fusing the minimum and one minus the maximum obtained weighted HD according to user-specific reliability masks. A composition of both comparators for two iris-codes a, b and weighting mask w_A is defined as:

$$BSF(a,b,w_A) = \frac{1}{2}\left(\left(1 - \max_{m \in \mathbb{Z}_n}\left(WHD(a,b \ll m, w_A)\right)\right)\right.$$
$$\left.+ \min_{m \in \mathbb{Z}_n}\left(WHD(a,b \ll m, w_A)\right)\right). \tag{9.32}$$

In case the estimated score is below a predefined threshold t the according reliability mask is updated where matching bits are obtained from the shifting position of the minimum obtained HD. Considering the bit reliability-driven comparator, additional computational cost is caused by calculating the weighted HD according to a distinct reliability mask. Furthermore, additional storage is required for reliability masks. Applying the shifting score fusion comparator improvement with respect to recognition accuracy comes at almost no additional computational cost. Furthermore, this comparator does not require the storage of any additional information. Table 9.2 summarizes additional computational costs and additional storage costs of the proposed comparators. Both techniques, as well as a fusion of these, can be applied in a single sample enrollment scenario.

Table 9.2 Bit reliability score fusion: computational cost, storage cost, and required enrollment samples single comparators and the fusion approach

Approach	Computational cost	Storage cost	Enrollment samples
BRD comparator	WHD	Mask W	1
SSF comparator	$\max(HD)$	–	1
BSF	$WHD + \max(HD)$	Mask W	1

9.4.2 Selective Bits Fusion

While a combination of different biometric traits leads to generally higher accuracy (e.g., combining face and iris [572] or iris and fingerprints [344]), such solutions typically require additional sensors leading to lower throughput and higher setup cost. Single-sensor biometric fusion, comparing multiple representations of a single biometric, does not significantly raise cost and has been shown to be still capable of improving recognition accuracy [386]. Generic fusion strategies at score level [260] require the storage of several biometric templates per subject according to the number of combined algorithms [456].

A generic fusion technique for iris recognition at bit-level, which is referred to as *selective bits fusion* [440], can be utilized in order to avoid a storage of multiple biometric templates, by extracting most discriminative bits from multiple algorithms into a new template being even smaller than templates for individual algorithms. Similar to the incremental iris comparator [438], a global ranking of bit positions for each applied algorithm is estimated within a training stage. Based on obtained rankings, enrollment samples are rearranged and merged by discarding the least reliable bits of extracted iris-codes. Selective bits fusion represents a generic fusion technique and integrates well in iris recognition systems, as illustrated in Figs. 9.13 and 9.14. These are the following three modules:

1. *Training stage and enrollment*: Following the idea in [438], a global reliability mask based on bit reliability [196] is computed in the training stage for each feature extraction method. Based on the reliability mask, an ideal permutation of bit positions is derived for each feature extraction method and applied to reorder given samples such that the first bits represent the most reliable ones and the last bits represent the least reliable ones, respectively. At the time of enrollment, preprocessing and feature extraction methods are applied to a given sample image. Subsequently, permutations derived from the previously calculated reliability masks are used to reorder iris-codes.

2. *Template fusion process*: The key idea of selective bits fusion is to concatenate and store the most important bits only. Furthermore, since bits in typically distorted regions (close to eyelids or eyelashes) are moved backwards in the iris-code, this approach makes a storage of noise masks obsolete, i.e. their effect is less pronounced because the least reliable bits are discarded. The result of the fusion process is a biometric template composed of the most reliable

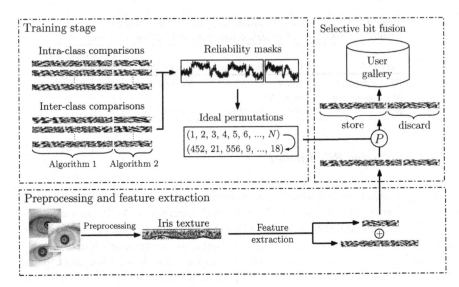

Fig. 9.13 Training stage and enrollment procedure of the selective bits fusion comparator

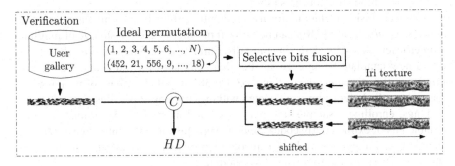

Fig. 9.14 Verification procedure of the selective bits fusion comparator

bits produced by diverse feature extraction algorithms. Focusing on recognition performance, a sensible composition of reliable bits has to be established.

3. *Verification*: In order to recognize subjects who have been registered with the system, in a first step feature extraction is executed for each algorithm in the combined template. Instead of comparing templates of all algorithms individually, this approach combines iris-codes of different feature extraction techniques based on the global ranking of bit reliability calculated in the training stage. However, since bits are reordered, local neighborhoods of bits are obscured resulting in a loss of the property tolerating angular displacement by simple circular shifts. Instead, in order to achieve template alignment, it is suggested to apply feature extraction methods at different shifting positions of the extracted iris texture. Subsequently, all reordered iris-codes are compared with the stored template. The minimal HD is returned as final comparison score. The verification process is illustrated in Fig. 9.14.

Templates generated by the selective bits fusion strategy can be designed to be at most as long as the average code size generated by the applied algorithms while recognition accuracy of traditional biometric fusion techniques is maintained or even increased.

9.4.3 Pre-selection Using Rotation-Invariant Operator

Rotation-invariant iris features represent an attractive alternative to approaches which apply circular shifts of feature vectors in order to compensate eye tilts. Spatial domain techniques working directly on the iris texture are therefore of special interest. Du et al. [135] employ first order moments of the iris texture line-histograms. While this technique is successful in providing rotation invariance and consequently fast matching procedures independent of eye positions, it does not deliver high recognition accuracy. However, spatially based rotation invariant iris recognition approaches can be combined with traditional local-feature-based schemes, yielding a serial classifier combination [270]. The aim is to decrease overall computational demand as compared to classical rotation compensating schemes while at least maintaining their recognition accuracy in identification mode. This is achieved by using the first scheme to determine a certain amount of the highest matching ranks of the entire database (this can be done quickly due to the high speed of the first scheme), while the second (and more accurate) scheme is applied to this predetermined subset for refinement of the comparison result. Such a comparator is different from techniques proposed in, e.g., [413, 601] in several ways. First, it is different compared to a single-sensor multibiometric approaches combining global and local features, since this approach: (1) focuses on a reduction of computational effort by limiting the required rotation compensation in the comparison stage instead of aiming at better recognition accuracy; (2) a serial classifier composition instead of parallel combination is applied. Second, it is different from the screening approaches since (1) templates are not partitioned into a certain number of classes limiting the actual comparison; (2) the "screening approach" is combined with a classical technique in serial manner.

The screening procedure results in a ranking of the enrolled database templates. This ranking is subsequently used to determine a set of templates the subsequent search is limited to. An important parameter of this approach is the amount of top ranked templates that is contained in the set. This parameter p expressed in percent of the database (e.g., if $p = 25$, the 25 % top ranked templates are subject to further processing by the following comparator) restricts the demands of the second computationally more expensive approach (which relies on local texture features and requires rotation compensation). Obviously, for increasing p the computational demand is increased.

Du et al. [135] have proposed a rotation invariant 1D signature approach, which is employed as the first screening stage. After generation of local texture patterns (LTPs) subtracting a localized mean value from the data, LTP values of entire rows of the polar iris image are averaged. The upper and lower three rows of the polar iris data are discarded, the remaining rows are used to create the final 1D signature. Two 1D signatures a, b are compared by using Du's measure [135] as follows:

$$Du(a,b) = \frac{1}{m} \cdot \|a - b\| \cdot D(A\|B) + D(B\|A) \cdot \tan\left[\cos^{-1}\left(\frac{\langle a,b \rangle}{\|a\| \cdot \|b\|}\right)\right]. \quad (9.33)$$

The inner product of the vectors a and b is determined by $\langle a,b \rangle$ and $\|a\|$ and $\|b\|$ describe the first norm of these vectors. The probability mass functions A and B are produced by the vectors a and b. $D(A\|B)$ denotes the relative entropy of A with respect to B. Parameter m is the total number of nonzero pairs of a and b. For the extension to 2D signatures, the "accumulated errors" approach [339] is applied (using 256 histogram bins). The Du measure is computed for each row and the resulting distances are accumulated for all rows. Moreover, a weighting factor greater than 1 is used for polar image rows close to the pupil and a factor of 1 is proposed for rows close to the sclera, weighting factors for the rows in between are obtained by linear interpolation.

In the second stage, localized feature extraction is applied where comparisons are performed at several shifting position seeking for an optimal alignment. Employing this serial combination of comparators, recognition accuracy can be maintained for decreasing p in an identification scenario while computational effort is significantly reduced.

9.4.4 Combining Image Metrics with Iris-Codes

While conventional extraction of rather short (a few hundred bytes) binary feature vectors provides a compact storage and rapid comparison of biometric templates, information loss is inevitable, thus motivating biometric comparators operating in image domain. Global features extracted by image metrics tend to complement localized features encoded by traditional feature extraction methods, i.e. a fusion scenario combining image metrics and traditional HD-based approaches improves recognition accuracy.

Such a fusion scenario is illustrated in Fig. 9.15. At the time of authentication, segmentation and pre-processing is performed on a given pair of iris images. Subsequently, the resulting iris textures are compared applying a distinct image metric. The image quality metric-based comparison score, S_M, is normalized and fused with the according HD-based score, S_{HD}, after feature extraction has been applied to both iris textures, in order to obtain the final score S_{MHD}. The biometric fusion is performed by applying sum-rule fusion [453]:

$$S_{MHD} = \frac{1}{2}(S_M + S_{HD}). \quad (9.34)$$

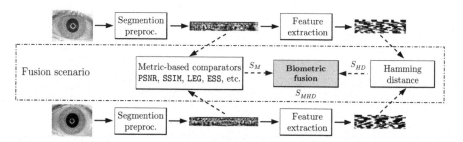

Fig. 9.15 Image metrics-based comparator: Images are preprocessed and quality-metric-based comparators (operating in image domain) estimate similarities between pairs of images

The incorporation of distinct image metrics (without an adaption of image metrics to biometric systems) in a fusion scenario is able to significantly improve recognition accuracy of iris biometric systems.

Chapter 10
Experiments on Biometric Comparators

Experiments with respect to advanced comparators discussed in Chap. 9 are conducted in this chapter, employing a common evaluation protocol and setup. Investigated issues comprise the accuracy of each comparator, computational requirements compared to the baseline technique using HD with applied bit-shifting to account for rotational alignment, as well as related questions. More specifically, the distribution of reliable bits or trade-offs between recognition accuracy and speed is evaluated. Whenever a comparator is applicable to binary feature vectors (for *context-based comparison*, the *constrained Levenshtein operator*, *shifting score fusion*, *Gaussian score fitting*, the *bit reliability-based comparator* and the fusion techniques *bit reliability score fusion* as well as *selective bits fusion*), the same two feature extraction algorithms are employed in experiments. Whereas most operators are examined in verification mode highlighting ROC curves, EERs and FRRs (or GARs, respectively) at specified FARs, two operators (the *incremental iris comparator* and *rotation invariant preselection*) explicitly target pre-screening techniques in identification mode and are therefore evaluated using rank-1 recognition rate (RR-1).

10.1 Experimental Setup

In order to obtain comparable recognition rates for evaluations, the CASIA.v3-Interval dataset comprising high-quality NIR iris images (sized 320×280 pixels) has been employed. Since for bit reliability-based techniques the employed (trained) reliability masks typically depend on the choice of left or right eyes, we generally refer to the left-eye subset (1,307 instances) when reporting recognition rates on this dataset in order to alleviate comparability between results. For identification experiments with respect to the *incremental iris comparator*, left-eye images in CASIA.v3-Interval have been partitioned into two sets:

C. Rathgeb et al., *Iris Biometrics: From Segmentation to Template Security*,
Advances in Information Security 59, DOI 10.1007/978-1-4614-5571-4_10,
© Springer Science+Business Media, LLC 2013

Table 10.1 Evaluations conducted for several different advanced comparators

Algorithm	Mode			Feature extraction		
	Verif.	Ident.	Database	Ma et al.	Masek	Ko et al.
Context-based comp.	✓	–	CASIA.v3	✓	✓	✓
Constrained Levenshtein comp.	✓	–	CASIA.v3, ICE	✓	✓	–
Shifting score fusion	✓	–	CASIA.v3	✓	✓	–
Gaussian score fitting	✓	–	CASIA.v3	✓	✓	–
Bit reliability-based comp.	✓	–	CASIA.v3	✓	✓	–
Incremental iris comp.	–	✓	CASIA.v3	✓	✓	–
Image metric-based comp.	✓	–	CASIA.v3	–	–	–
Bit-reliability score fusion	✓	–	CASIA.v3 +IITD.v1	✓	✓	–
Selective bits fusion	✓	–	CASIA.v3	✓	✓	✓
Rotation-invariant preselection	–	✓	CASIA.v3, v1,MMU	–	✓	–
Image metrics with iris-codes	✓	–	CASIA.v3	–	–	–

- *CASIA.v3-I-Training*: 87 images of the first 10 classes for parameter estimation purposes;
- *CASIA.v3-I-Testing*: 177 single-enrollment gallery images and 1,043 probe images of the remaining 177 classes for closed-set identification experiments.

In order to illustrate the effect of lower quality input, for the Levenshtein operator, also the right-eye subset (1,425 images) of the ICE 2005 dataset with 640×480 pixel resolution is applied.

The tested basic system (Table 10.1) comprises the following USIT preprocessing and feature extraction steps (see Sect. 3.4): CAHT preprocessing and feature extraction by Ma et al. [323], Masek [335], and Ko et al. [261], which are in the following abbreviated as *Ma*, *Masek*, and *Ko* algorithms. It is important to mention that the algorithms *Ma* and *Masek* are fundamentally different to the *Ko* iris-code version, as they process texture regions of different size, extract different features and produce iris-codes of different length.

Since experimental evaluations do not only depend on the selection of the dataset and feature extraction to be applied, but also further parameters, such as the employed number of genuine and impostor comparisons, selection of the bit-shift count, or number of enrollment images, it is difficult to make general statements about relative comparator performance from published reported error rates. Comparing all operators using common parameters does not completely solve this problem, since some operators are intended for specific applications and raise the need for, e.g., more than one enrollment image (*bit reliability-based comparator*), or a certain amount of bit shifts to benefit of better alignment (*constrained Levenshtein comparator*).

10.2 Alignment-Optimized Comparators

In order to alleviate comparability, experimental evaluations are re-conducted utilizing a common setup for all except one of the alignment-optimized comparators, resulting in slight variations to reported error rates in the original papers [432, 442, 443] due to the unified setup. For the *constrained Levenshtein comparator* it has been decided to refer to the original setup [538] executing 20 instead of 8 shifts. Applying the *MinHD* comparator with 8 shifts, EERs of 1.29% and 0.89% and FRRs of 6.59% and 2.54% at 0.01% FAR are achieved for the algorithms of Masek and Ma, respectively. In the evaluation in [539], *MinHD* with 20 shifts results in EERs of 0.89% and 0.58%, respectively, and FRRs of 6.33% and 1.34% at 0.01% FAR for Masek and Ma, i.e. more shifts yield improved recognition accuracy. Obtained error rates for each comparator are summarized in Table 10.2.

With respect to tested comparators executing 8 shifts, the highest improvement with respect to EER is reported by the *Gaussian score fitting*, with 7% relative improvement for Ma and 24% relative improvement for Masek. See Fig. 10.1 for obtained ROCs on both feature vectors. Considering *GaussFit* only, rather

Table 10.2 Alignment-optimized comparators: Summarized experimental results for CASIA.v3-Interval using both feature extraction methods of Masek and Ma

Comparator	Shifts	Masek FRR at FAR≤0.01%	EER	Ma FRR at FAR≤0.01%	EER
HD	8	6.59%	1.29%	2.54%	0.89%
	20	6.33%	0.89%	1.34%	0.58%
Context-based comparison	8	4.24%	1.23%	2.05%	0.88%
Shifting score fusion	8	6.12%	1.22%	1.89%	0.86%
Gaussian score fitting	8	4.44%	0.98%	1.89%	0.83%
Constrained Levenshtein comp.	20	4.87%	0.81%	0.72%	0.44%

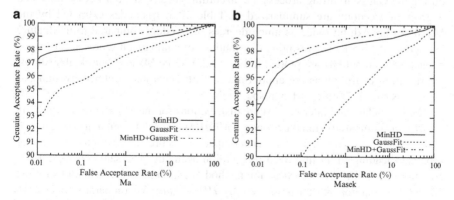

Fig. 10.1 ROC for (**a**) Ma and (**b**) Masek using Gaussian score fitting comparator

Table 10.3 Gaussian fitting benchmark values for Ma and Masek

Feature extraction	p	σ	DoF (bit)
Ma [323]	0.4965	0.0143	1,232
Masek [335]	0.4958	0.0202	612

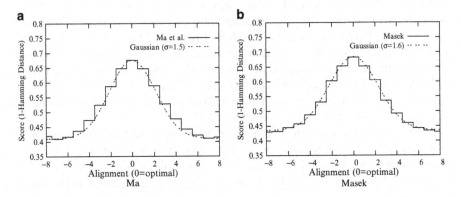

Fig. 10.2 Distributions of comparison scores according to a certain optimal alignment approximated by Gaussians for (**a**) Ma and (**b**) Masek

unpractical rates are delivered, e.g., for the feature extraction of Masek an EER of 4.11 % and FRR of 17.97 % at 0.01 % FAR, while for Ma an EER of 1.95 % and FRR of 8.21 % at 0.01 % FAR are obtained. But when combined with *MinHD*, the resulting *MinHD + GaussFit* comparator reveals an improved performance compared to the baseline technique: Experiments yield an EER of 0.98 % and FRR of 4.44 % at 0.01 % FAR for the Masek algorithm and an EER of 0.83 % and FRR of 1.89 % at 0.01 % FAR for the Ma algorithm, since in the fusion scenario additional information about score progressions towards an optimal alignment is added.

The *GaussFit* operator was trained on all genuine comparisons between pairs of iris-codes obtained from the first 10 subjects of the database. Obtained parameters during the Gaussian fitting process, i.e. according means, standard deviations, and degrees of freedom, are summarized in Table 10.3. Iris-codes extracted by the Ma algorithm exhibit twice as much degrees of freedom compared to the feature extraction of Masek. The resulting distributions of comparison scores according to a detected minimal HD are plotted in Fig. 10.2. For the Ma and Masek algorithms, the resulting distributions are approximated with Gaussians, defined by standard deviations $\sigma = 1.5$ and $\sigma = 1.6$, respectively.

The intra-class and inter-class score distributions for the Ma algorithm applying the *MinHD* comparator and the proposed *MinHD+GaussFit* comparator are plotted in Fig. 10.3. Applying the proposed comparator, score distributions are further separated leading to an improved recognition accuracy. The same characteristics are observed for the feature extraction method of Masek, score distributions for the *MinHD* comparator and the proposed *MinHD + GaussFit* comparator are shown in Fig. 10.4. Focusing on the *MinHD + GaussFit* comparator, for both feature

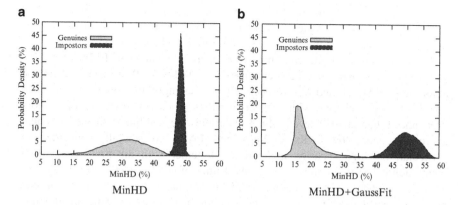

Fig. 10.3 Genuine and impostor score distribution applying (**a**) *MinHD* and (**b**) *MinHD+GaussFit* for the Ma algorithm

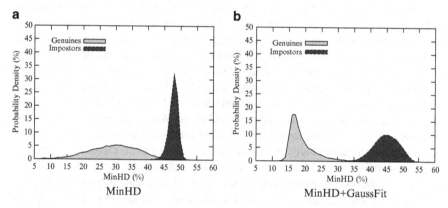

Fig. 10.4 Genuine and impostor score distribution applying (**a**) *MinHD* and (**b**) *MinHD+GaussFit* for Masek's algorithm

extraction techniques the vast majority of genuine comparison scores is further reduced while standard deviation of binomial distributions of impostor scores increases.

The second-best alignment-optimized comparator with respect to 8-shift experiments turned out to be *shifting score fusion* with 3 % relative lower EER for Ma and 5 % relative EER-improvement for Masek, i.e. again, for both feature extraction methods, the shifting score fusion comparator *SSF* reveals a slightly better performance over *MinHD* when evaluating EERs. While also in this case the individual *1−MaxHD* comparator shows rather unpractical rates (16.53 % EER and 82.06 % FRR at 0.01 % FAR for the Masek algorithm, 2.43 % EER and 7.72 % FRR at 0.01 % FAR for Ma), still the measured scores can well be combined with *MinHD* to even improve the final score. Even more surprisingly, *MaxHD* has an inverse similarity comparison property, i.e. if the maximum HD between two samples is very high, they are likely to be a genuine comparison pair—as opposed to *MinHD* where exactly the opposite is true. This suggests that for iris-codes originating from the same data subject, there are misalignments inducing some kind of systematic error—unseen for HD comparisons with iris-codes from different data subjects. This insight led to the development of Gaussian fitting-based comparison [443].

Obtained EERs for the combined *SSF* operator resulted in EERs of 1.22 % and 0.86 % and FRRs of 6.12 % and 1.89 % at 0.01 % FAR are achieved for the algorithms of Masek and Ma, respectively. Interestingly, for almost all evaluated operators, improvements with respect to FRRs at 0.01 % FAR are even more pronounced than at EER level, which underlines the worthiness of the presented approaches, since low FRRs at almost zero FARs are generally demanded, in particular, for high security applications. Together with the property of easy integration in existing comparators (only 4 lines of code needed to be changed in our implementation to switch from *MinHD* to *SSF*) and almost no additional time requirements (time differences were too small to be measured in experiments), this technique is an ideal enhancement of current *MinHD*-based implementations.

In Fig. 10.5 for both algorithms the inter-relation between *MinHD* and $1-MaxHD$ is shown. It is interesting to see that for Ma and Masek the intra-class variance is rather low, i.e. there is not much difference between minimum and (one minus) maximum HD. Furthermore, we can identify a much better separability of genuine and impostor score points by lines parallel to $y = -x$ than lines parallel to x-axis or y-axis. There is no strong correlation between both scores, indicating a promising fusion. ROCs for the employed *SSF* operator and $1-MaxHD$ are given in Fig. 10.6.

The smallest improvement was obtained when employing *context-based comparison*, see Fig. 10.7 for the corresponding ROC curve. When comparing performance with the baseline HD comparator, only a slight improvement in accuracy could be achieved, which additionally comes at the cost of complex calculation: relative improvements of 5 % (Masek) and 1 % (Ma) with respect to EERs could be achieved. In the original experiments [432], context-based matching fails to improve EER rates for the algorithm of Ko. In this algorithm, some sort of context-based matching is already applied, counting mismatching sequences of up- and downward slopes of cumulative sums, thus, further context-based matching does not pay off. Obviously, the proposed context-based matching procedure is more complex than measuring the HD between iris-codes. However, when applied to the introduced ternary context-codes matching time can even be saved. Time measurements are summarized in Table 10.4 (results refer to the execution on a single processor at 1.3 GHz). As can be seen, the context-code feature extraction is about twice as fast as those of Ma and Masek. For context-based matching all algorithms tend to require almost the same time, which depends on the number of values of interest and the size of iris-codes. If times of feature extraction and matching are summed up, as it is the case in verification mode, context-based comparison on context-codes is still about two times faster than those of Ma and Masek, exhibiting comparable performance results.

Since the *constrained Levenshtein comparator* benefits of higher degrees of freedom during the alignment process, it is useful to allow for a rather large number of bit shifts. For this reason, the conducted evaluation refers to a maximum number of 20 shifts and also considers the more challenging ICE dataset (Table 10.5).

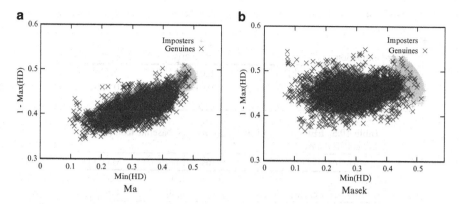

Fig. 10.5 1-Max(HD) scores vs. Min(HD) scores for 7 shifts using (**a**) Ma and (**b**) Masek

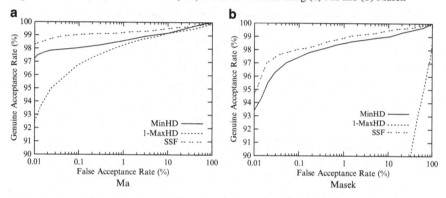

Fig. 10.6 ROC for (**a**) Ma and (**b**) Masek applying the shifting score fusion comparator

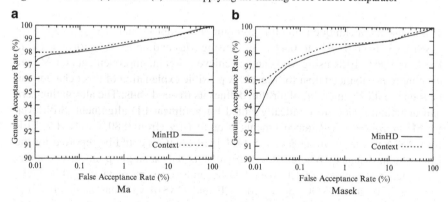

Fig. 10.7 ROC for (**a**) Ma and (**b**) Masek for context-based comparison

However, since a larger number of bit shifts typically results in higher accuracy (at the cost of additional processing time), rates have to be compared with the baseline techniques employing a maximum number of 20 bit shifts. With respect

Table 10.4 Time measurements (s) for context-based comparison vs. baseline techniques

Feature extraction	Time feature extr. (s)	Time HD-comparison (s)	Time context-comparison (s)
Ma [323]	0.135	0.014	0.026
Masek [335]	0.108	0.017	0.026
Context-code [432]	0.061	–	0.007

Table 10.5 EERs for Levenshtein distance vs. baseline techniques on the ICE dataset

Comparator	Shifts	Masek (%)	Ma (%)
HD	20	6.08	8.60
Constrained Levenshtein comp.	20	5.49	4.96

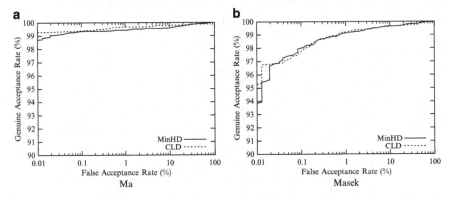

Fig. 10.8 ROC for (**a**) Ma and (**b**) Masek for Levenshtein-based comparison on CASIA.v3

to the baseline technique using this configuration, improvements of up to 24 % for CASIA.v3 (from 0.58 % to 0.44 % EER using Ma) and up to 42 % for ICE (from 8.6 % to 4.96 % EER using Ma) can be achieved. Again, improvements for Ma are even more pronounced than for Masek. A possible explanation of this behavior can be found in the manner this algorithm defines its iris-code bits: The alternating zero and one chains seem to be ideally suited for nonlinear LD alignment. Still, even for Masek relative EER improvements of up to 10 % (from 0.89 % to 0.81 % EER for CASIA.v3 and from 6.08 % to 5.49 % EER for ICE) could be reported for the Levenshtein distance. Whereas the EER reflects only a single point of operation, the better performance of LD over HD becomes even more visible, if we take a closer look at the ROC curves for ICE and CASIA.v3 datasets in Figs. 10.8 and 10.9. Almost all LD curves are clearly superior to HD, except the one for Ma on CASIA.v3, which also depends on the selected maximum shift count, as will be investigated in the next research question.

From Table 10.6 listing the time needed for comparison per image, it is evident that LD is on average 4–5 times slower than HD over different combinations of algorithms and datasets (results refer to the execution on a single processor at 2.8

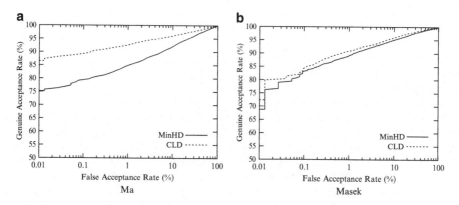

Fig. 10.9 ROC for (**a**) Ma and (**b**) Masek for Levenshtein-based comparison on ICE

Table 10.6 Time measurements for Levenshtein distance vs. baseline techniques

		Masek		Ma	
Comparator	Shifts	ICE (ms)	CASIA.v3(ms)	ICE (ms)	CASIA.v3(ms)
HD	20	0.73	0.97	0.73	0.99
Constrained Levenshtein comp.	20	3.71	3.66	4.07	4.04

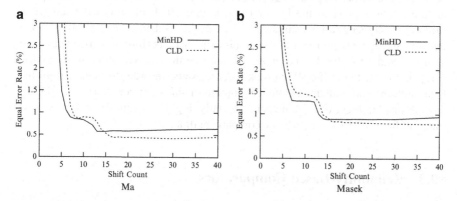

Fig. 10.10 Shifts-EER trade-off for HD and constrained LD on CASIA.v3 dataset. (**a**) Ma, (**b**) Masek

GHz). However, it is in the same complexity class as HD. While a single match using HD takes less than 1 ms, LD-based matching needs approximately 4 ms in case of 20 bit shifts. While assessing the performance of LD it was observed, that the number of shifts has an important impact on both recognition accuracy and certainly average matching time (due to additional comparisons). From the implementations it is easy to derive, that for both, HD and LD, in case of small bit shifts, doubling the number of shifts also results in approximately twice as long matching time.

The trade-off, which exists between the maximum number of shifts, time complexity, and recognition accuracy, is highlighted in Figs. 10.10 and 10.11. The number of shifts is essential in order to cope with angular displacement of two iris

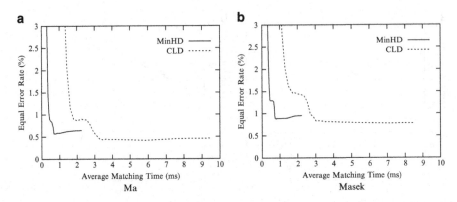

Fig. 10.11 Time-EER trade-off for HD and constrained LD on CASIA.v3 dataset. (**a**) Ma, (**b**) Masek

textures to be matched. Furthermore, as shifts should be executed on iris-codes and not on iris textures in order to avoid multiple extraction of features with resulting time overhead, it is important to consider the bit sampling rate with respect to texture pixels. For the tested algorithms, the number of bits per texture row is equal to the number of pixels per row. A one bit shift corresponds to shifting the texture a single pixel to the left or right. Figure 10.10 illustrates the impact of shift count on recognition accuracy for the CASIA.v3 dataset. It is worth noticing that for all algorithms a significant improvement of performance is achieved at around 7 and 14 shifts. Furthermore, one can see that for very few bit shifts, LD performs worse than HD, which makes sense, since in order to benefit from the better nonlinear alignment, a sufficient amount of shifts is required (in the order of angular displacement of genuine pairs). Finally, Fig. 10.11 illustrates the resulting trade-off between EER and average comparison time.

10.3 Reliability-Based Comparators

In contrast to alignment-optimized comparators, reliability-based techniques employ a user-specific or global weighting of bits according to the entropy of each bit. For example, based on the observations in [196] weights can be assigned to iris-code bits depending on which part of the iris textures these originate from. Bits of iris-codes which originate from the inner bands of iris textures are found to be more consistent than those parts which originate from outer bands. Additionally, the top and bottom of the iris ring are often occluded by eyelashes or eyelids (315° to 45° and 135° to 225°). Hence, an adequate choice of weights is illustrated in Fig. 10.12 (high weights indicate high consistency) and employed as a reference technique in [427]. In contrast to global weights, which are assessed in modified form in *incremental iris recognition* [438], the *bit reliability-driven comparator* employs user-specific learning of weights. The employed recognition mode represents the

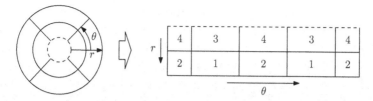

Fig. 10.12 Global weights: Bits in iris-codes originating form the inner bands of iris textures reveal higher consistency than those of outer bands

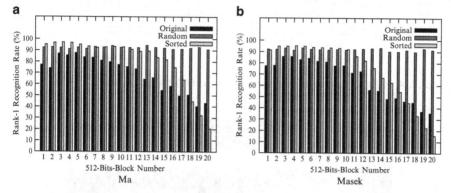

Fig. 10.13 RR-1 for 512-bit blocks using 7 shifts for (**a**) Ma and (**b**) Masek for the incremental-iris comparator on CASIA.v3-I-Testing

key difference between the two reliability-based comparators to be evaluated in this section: *incremental iris recognition* targets a speed-up of identification and is not applicable to verification mode, while the *bit reliability-driven comparator* is a verification mode comparator.

In case of the *incremental iris comparator*, instead of multiplying each bit with some factor (which is a rather costly process), bits are re-arranged with descending information reliability. In a first test, it is examined if the introduced reliability masks in Sect. 9.2.2 concentrate more reliable information in the first bits of an iris-code. After obtaining the reliability mask and ideal permutation from set *CASIA.v3-I-Training*, block-wise partial matching is tested on set *CASIA.v3-I-Testing*, see Fig. 10.13 (10,240-bit iris-codes are divided into 20 adjacent 512-bit blocks). For the unaltered configuration (*Original*), bits in early 512-bit blocks tend to exhibit more information with respect to RR-1 than later blocks; however, there is no clear monotonicity for both algorithms. Indeed, if block size is further reduced, a typical sawtooth-pattern becomes visible as can be seen in the according reliability masks in Fig. 10.14, which define the reliability at each bit position as previously described. It turns out that reliable bits are not uniformly distributed (as observed in [196]), but rather follow a specific pattern. Experiments show that this pattern can be learned by relatively few training samples (87 images) and reproduces the desired sorting behavior in a distinctive set (1,220 images). Recognition rates for

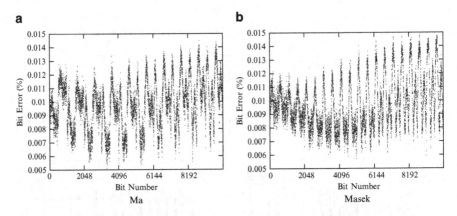

Fig. 10.14 Reliability masks for the feature extraction of (**a**) Ma and (**b**) Masek

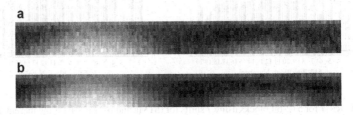

Fig. 10.15 Distribution of reliable bits: Schematical impression of reliability textures for (**a**) Ma, and (**b**) Masek

the partial matching variant (*Sorted*) stay rather high until about 50 % of the iris-code (92 %–97 % for Ma, 91 %–95 % for Masek), and then decrease rapidly. When applying *Random* (partial matching using random permutation), (1) an almost equal RR-1 is obtained (92.3 % with standard deviation 0.9 for Ma, 91.8 % with standard deviation 1.0 for Masek) for each 512-bit block; (2) this rate is higher than for each other block in the original iris-code, i.e. in case no training data is available random permutations are suggested.

Regarding the distribution of reliable parts over iris textures for different iris recognition algorithms, Fig. 10.15 illustrates the back-mapping of bit errors to the localized area of origin within the iris texture revealing similarities in the structure of different reliability masks and corresponding reliability textures. Shapes of reliability textures are rather expectable: Since reliability masks are computed on the whole iris texture without considering iris masks, usually masked areas should exhibit many errors, while unmasked areas should be free of errors. A typical two-dome pattern of nonreliable bits with stable middle bands (as reported in [196]) is clearly visible, especially for lower iris parts (right arm of the unrolled iris texture), probably due to less frequently occluding eyelashes.

Having obtained some insight in the distribution of reliable bits, evaluations now target the incremental iris comparator's ability of reducing matching time complexity while retaining high recognition accuracy. Incremental iris recognition

Table 10.7 RR-1 rates for diverse comparison techniques according to the amount of matched bits

Algorithm		Ma				Masek			
		0 shifts		7 shifts		0 shifts		7 shifts	
		RR-1	Bits	RR-1	Bits	RR-1	Bits	RR-1	Bits
Original	All Bits	79.8	100	98.6	100	86.8	100	95.7	100
	1 % Bits	19.4	1	19.2	1	20.5	1	18.4	1
	10 % Bits	64.8	10	87.0	10	72.8	10	81.8	10
	Best RR-1	79.8	100	98.8	70.7	87.5	70.7	97.4	70.7
Random	1 % Bits	56.6	1	61.6	1	66.3	1	65.6	1
	10 % Bits	76.0	10	96.5	10	85.0	10	95.2	10
	Best RR-1	79.8	100	98.6	84.1	87.0	59.5	95.9	42.0
Sorted	1 % Bits	69.8	1	77.9	1	66.7	1	67.5	1
	10 % Bits	83.6	10	97.7	10	86.0	10	94.9	10
	Best RR-1	84.1	14.9	99.2	35.4	88.6	50.0	97.3	70.7
Incremental	1 % Bits	76.5	1	79.7	1	75.1	1	67.5	1
	Best RR-1	82.7	3.2	99.2	4.8	87.7	3.8	97.2	5.0
	Non-partial	81.0	5.1	99.1	4.9	87.6	3.9	97.2	5.0

is tested for the algorithms of Ma and Masek in 2 different shifting variants: 0 shifts and 7 shifts. Table 10.7 lists all rates for the tested matching variants. For 0 shifts, the incremental iris comparator (*Incremental*) is able to reduce the total number of bit comparisons to 3.2 % at 82.7 % RR-1 for Ma and to 3.8 % at 87.7 % RR-1 for Masek. The obtained recognition rates are even slightly better than for unsorted iris-code (*Original*) utilizing all bits (79.8 % RR-1 for Ma and 86.8 % RR-1 for Masek) due to the property of reliability masks being able to identify nonreliable bits. The 7 shifts variant draws a similar picture with *Incremental* reducing the number of bit comparisons to 4.8 % at 99.2 % RR-1 for Ma and 5.0 % at 97.2 % RR-1 for Masek (*Original* reference rates: 98.6 % for Ma, 95.7 % for Masek). These rates refer to best RR-1 performance varying the maximum amount of bits. In addition, in case of taking all bits into account (non-partial) incremental iris recognition is a highly scalable technique.

The varying amount of bits to be compared for identification introduces a trade off between time complexity (in terms of bit comparisons) and recognition accuracy (RR-1), visualized in Figs. 10.16 and 10.17. This trade-off also exists for incremental matching since it is possible to abort the computation if a certain amount of bits has been compared. In this configuration however, it is no longer possible to directly control the amount of bit comparisons, since the list of potential matches is reduced dynamically. For partial iris matching, *Random* (employing randomly permuted bits) performs significantly better than *Original* over the entire range of bit comparisons and for all tested algorithm variants. Applying the *Random* technique it is possible to reduce the amount of bit comparisons to about 10 % without significant degradation of accuracy (maximum absolute RR-1 degradation of less than 5 % of the original value). Even without reordering (*Original*), partial matching tolerates a loss off about 50 % of bits without significantly degrading

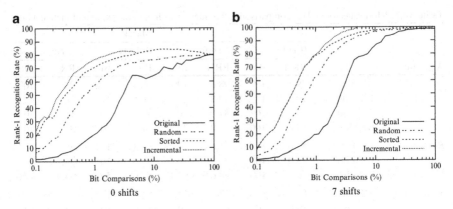

Fig. 10.16 Ma time complexity vs. recognition accuracy using (**a**) 0 shifts and (**b**) 7 shifts

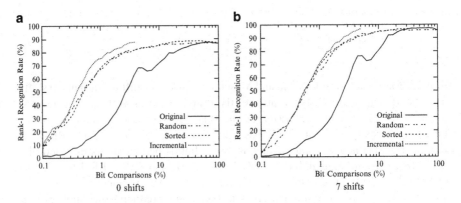

Fig. 10.17 Masek time complexity vs. accuracy using (**a**) 0 shifts and (**b**) 7 shifts

performance. But in this case, as can be seen from the graphs in Figs. 10.16 and 10.17, recognition rates decline rapidly if the amount of bits falls below 5 %. Utilizing reliability masks (*Sorted*), partial matching further optimizes recognition rates and even exceeds *Original* match performance using all bits (1 %–5 % better RR-1 at 15 %–70 % of bit comparisons, depending on the type of algorithm). This is the case, because the last bits in the code contain less discriminative information and may degrade total performance. *Incremental* consequently delivers the highest savings in terms of bit comparisons, only about 5 % of iris-code bits are required while all RR-1 values are at least as high as for a full iris-code match. However, additional savings obtained by partial matching are negligible.

Finally, in order to benefit of fast reduction of candidates while retaining high accuracy, parameter selection is a critical task within incremental iris recognition: there are two parameters to be selected, window sizes (positions within the iris-code where to combine and rank HD values) and the exclusion criterion (EC).

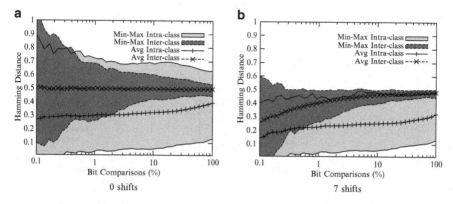

Fig. 10.18 Intra- and inter-class score distributions depending on bit comparisons for Ma using (**a**) 0 shifts and (**b**) 7 shifts

Regarding the first parameter it turns out that evaluations at positions with logarithmic spacing are well suited. This is because the RR-1 is sensitive to small changes for few bit comparisons, while tolerating larger changes if a high amount of bits is available. Also the additional worst case ranking overhead per match is in $O(log(n) * r)$ where n refers to the (partial) iris-code length and r is the time amount required to combine, resort, and reject HD measures.

In case of the second parameter, a natural approach is to define a maximum tolerance of HD deviation of candidate x with sample s from the best-matching candidate b at i percent of bit comparisons:

$$EC_i(x) := \begin{cases} keep & if\ HD_i(x,s) - HD_i(b,s) < \eta_i, \\ reject & otherwise. \end{cases} \quad (10.1)$$

Performance as well as intra- and inter-class scores depend on the amount of bit comparisons, see Fig. 10.18. This way, at each iteration step in the incremental computation, the probability that the current template may finally end up with a smaller HD value than the current best-matching candidate is assessed. An adequate choice for η_i is:

$$\eta_i := \max_{(a,b)\in G} |HD_i(a,b) - HD_{50}(a,b)| + \underset{(a,b)\in I}{\mathrm{avg}} |HD_i(a,b) - HD_{50}(a,b)| \quad (10.2)$$

obtained from intra-class comparisons G and inter-class comparisons I in the training set. Note that as reference rate the outcome after 50 % of the iris-code is selected in order to account for nonreliable bits. While there may be other (user-dependent) parameters achieving even higher savings in processing time, the presented choice is a straightforward approach and only a small amount of training data is needed to produce stable results.

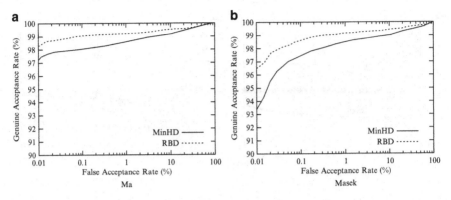

Fig. 10.19 ROCs for (**a**) Ma and (**b**) Masek applying the bit reliability-based comparator

Table 10.8 Experimental results for bit reliability-based comparison technique

		Masek		Ma	
		FRR at		FRR at	
Comparator	Shifts	FAR$\leq$0.01%	EER (%)	FAR$\leq$0.01%	EER (%)
HD	8	6.59%	1.29	2.54%	0.89
Bit reliability-based comparator	8	3.45%	0.89	1.78%	0.74

Following a completely different approach, namely the update of user-specific weights, the *bit reliability-driven comparator* presents an alternative to alignment-optimized operators, and is therefore evaluated using the same experimental setup employed for the 8 bits shifted variant. ROC curves of the *bit reliability-driven comparator* for each of the algorithms (Masek and Ma) after several numbers of authentications are plotted in Fig. 10.19. As can be seen, for both algorithms ROC are clearly superior to those where no or only a few genuine authentications have been performed. Additionally, it is observed that convergence is achieved relatively fast. This means, updating reliability masks may be stopped at a certain bit depth, reducing memory consumption (e.g., 3 or 4 bits per position).

Results for the reliability-driven comparator are illustrated in Table 10.8. In case of several authentication attempts user-specific reliability-masks (which require additional storage) are updated in order to perform a weighted comparison based on the most reliable bits in binary biometric feature vectors. According to ROC curves for the Ma and Masek algorithms are plotted in Fig. 10.19, achieving EERs of 0.74% and 0.89%, respectively. Obviously, the accuracy of the comparator highly depends on the number of successful authentication procedures, initial comparison scores are fractional HDs.

With respect to complexity, bit reliability-driven matching reveals the same performance as any weighted matching procedure, since updating user-specific reliability masks is performed after successful authentication (in case of identification only masks of rank-1 candidates are updated). However, as experiments demonstrate, by applying user-specific weights the performance is increased even more.

10.4   Comparators in the Image Domain

Apart from traditional iris comparators, general image metrics can be applied to normalized iris textures. For iris segmentation, this experiment uses textures normalized using the WAHET segmentation algorithm proposed in Chap. 6. At all authentication attempts, 7 circular texture-shifts are performed in each direction for all comparators. A summary of obtained EERs and FRR at FAR $\leq$ 0.01 % for the underlying image quality metrics is given in Table 10.9, applied image types are illustrated in Fig. 10.20. ROC curves are plotted in Fig. 10.21 for experiments evaluating (a) metrics, as well as (b) impact of the used image type: Original image, texture after segmentation, and enhanced texture after CLAHE normalization. Score distributions for each metric (normalized to $[0,1]$) with respect to genuine (intra-) and impostor (inter-personal) comparisons are illustrated in Fig. 10.22.

Table 10.9 Recognition performance of several different image quality metrics

Algorithm	Type	EER (%)	FRR at FAR $\leq$ 0.01 %	Threshold
SSIM	Enhanced	3.40	5.34 %	0.868
LEG	Enhanced	3.99	7.72 %	0.785
NICE	Enhanced	5.14	13.32 %	0.526
ESS	Enhanced	9.61	25.97 %	0.311
PSNR	Enhanced	4.21	10.33 %	0.592
PSNR	Texture	18.88	65.37 %	0.478
PSNR	Image	23.01	80.67 %	0.638

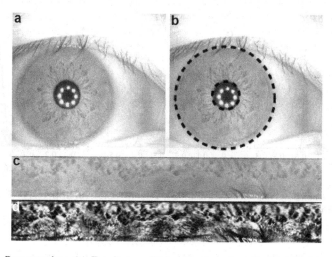

Fig. 10.20 Preprocessing: (**a**) Eye image; (**b**) localization of pupil and iris; (**c**) unrolled iris texture; (**d**) enhanced iris texture

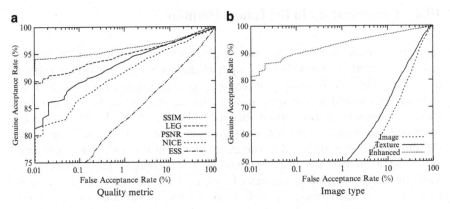

Fig. 10.21 Receiver operating characteristics by (**a**) quality metric, and (**b**) image type

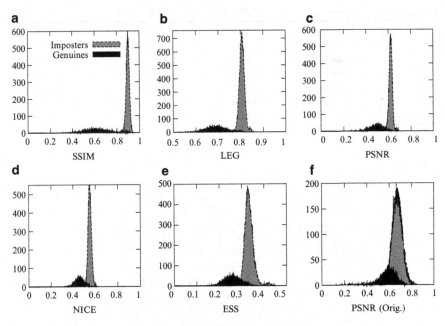

Fig. 10.22 Genuine and impostor score distributions for (**a**) SSIM, (**b**) LEG, (**c**) PSNR, (**d**) NICE, (**e**) ESS for enhanced textures and (**f**) PSNR on original images

While quality metrics clearly do not outperform specialized feature extractors, still accuracy is surprisingly high. The ranking of metrics with respect to EERs is as follows: SSIM, LEG, PSNR, NICE, and ESS, with the first three metrics exhibiting EERs of less than 5 %. It is interesting to see that PSNR with 4.21 % EER performs quite well on the enhanced textures, although it is the most simple metric. However, for high security applications with requested low FMR, SSIM with 5.34 % FRR at 0.01 % FAR compared to 10.33 % for PSNR is clearly the better alternative. Considering recognition accuracy, image metrics do not outperform feature-based techniques [44]. For instance, on the same dataset the USIT implementations of the approaches of Ma [323] and Ko [261], which extract binary iris-codes, obtain EERs of 1.83 % and 4.36 %, respectively (see Table 10.9). However, image metrics are rather useful as additional features in fusion scenarios. This type of fusion-based comparators will be examined in the next section explicitly targeting a combination of operators to improve accuracy.

In a second experiment, the effect of texture enhancement and segmentation on iris recognition accuracy of quality metrics is tested, applying the PSNR as reference metric, see Fig. 10.21b. Obtained results indicate a high degradation in case texture enhancement steps are skipped (18.88 % EER instead of 4.21 %). Recognition from the original eye images (without segmentation) further degraded results (23.01 % EER), thus normalization and enhancement steps accounting for different illumination enriching the texture in the image are extremely useful.

As opposed to the view that original iris textures exhibit too much noisy information to be used directly for comparison, it is found that some metrics perform quite well on enhanced and aligned texture patches. While being less accurate than feature-based techniques, still the presented approach has the advantage of alleviating the application of comparators on image data itself and improvements in image metrics can directly lead to advanced comparators.

10.5 Fusion-Based Approaches

Whereas some comparators, like shifting score fusion may itself be identified as a *fusion-based comparator*, this section explicitly refers to approaches combining proposed comparators or applying a comparator to multiple feature vectors combining results.

The *bit reliability score fusion* (BSF) operator combines the ideas of bit reliability with shifting score fusion and is evaluated using a joint dataset formed from CASIA.v3-Interval and IITD.v1 iris databases, allowing a comprehensive evaluation of the proposed systems. After applying USIT CAHT preprocessing (see Sect. 3.4) and texture normalization using block-wise brightness estimation, common features (as proposed by Ma and Masek) are extracted. At each authentication 8 circular bit-shifts are performed in each direction for both feature extraction methods and proposed comparators.

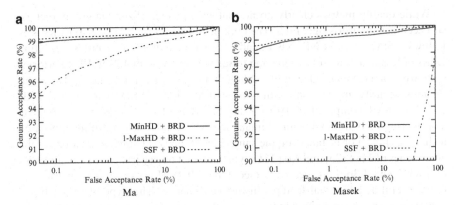

Fig. 10.23 ROC curves for the BSF comparator on (**a**) Ma and (**b**) Masek

Table 10.10 Experimental results for bit reliability score fusion comparison on CA-SIA.v3+IITD.v1

Comparator	Shifts	Ma		Masek	
		FRR at FAR$\leq$0.01 %	EER (%)	FRR at FAR$\leq$0.01 %	EER (%)
Min(HD)	8	1.48 %	0.69	3.65 %	1.04
1-Max(HD)	8	5.69 %	2.25	81.84 %	16.91
Bit reliability-driven	8	1.24 %	0.62	2.54 %	0.91
Shifting score fusion	8	1.11 %	0.59	2.66 %	0.93
BSF	8	1.09 %	0.58	2.23 %	0.86

While the comparator does not significantly affect the inter-class score distribution, intra-class distances are further reduced achieving FRRs of 1.09 % at 0.01 % FARs combining bit reliability-driven (1.24 %) and shifting score fusion (1.11 %) comparators. Also enhanced EER values with relative improvements of 16 % (0.58 % instead of 0.69 % for HD-based comparison) for Ma and 17 % (0.86 % instead of 1.04 % for HD-based comparison) for Masek are obtained. It is observed that convergence for the bit reliability-driven comparator is achieved relatively fast, i.e. updating reliability masks may be stopped at a certain bit depth, reducing memory consumption (e.g., 2 or 3 bits per position).

For the proposed *bit reliability score fusion* comparator, ROC curves compared with the minimum HD and one minus the maximum HD (to illustrate improvement from the SSF approach) are plotted in Fig. 10.23. Obtained performance rates for the entire experimental evaluation for the feature extraction method of Masek and Ma are summarized in Table 10.10. The bit reliability-driven comparator and the shifting score fusion comparator significantly improve the recognition accuracy of both feature extraction methods.

In contrast to *bit reliability score fusion*, *selective bits fusion* targets not a combination of comparators, but a fusion of different feature extraction algorithms.

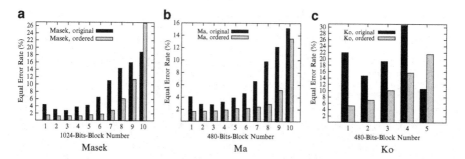

Fig. 10.24 EERs for bit-blocks in ascending order using different feature extraction. (**a**) Masek, 1,024-bits blocks, (**b**) Ma, 1,024-bits blocks, (**c**) Ko, 480-bits blocks

Since this comparator—like reliability-based operators—makes use of reliability masks to combine bits from different algorithms, for training purposes of reliability masks, images of the first 20 classes in CASIA.v3-Interval are used for parameter estimation purposes. In order to test the proposed bit fusion framework, all three feature extraction algorithms (Ma, Masek, and Ko) are employed. Since the algorithms by Ma and Masek are rather different to the iris-code version by Ko as they process texture regions of different size, extract different features, and produce iris-codes of different length, we paired up each of the two algorithms with the latter one.

Regarding reliability concentration in early bits, for each algorithm and for each bit position the probability of a bit switch is assessed in order to be able to identify reliable bits. For this parameter estimation the inter- and intra-class comparisons of the training set are used. Results in form of reliability measures for each bit induced a permutation for each algorithm with the goal of moving reliable bits to the front of the iris-code while more unstable bits should be moved to the end of the iris-code. This approach is more generic than area-based exclusion of typically distorted regions as executed by many feature extraction algorithms including the applied version by Masek (e.g., by ignoring outer iris bands or sectors containing eyelids). Like for incremental iris recognition which, in contrast to the proposed approach does not combine bits from multiple algorithms, the ability to concentrate reliable information in early bits on unseen data has been assessed for each of the applied algorithms and is illustrated in Fig. 10.24. It is found that EER performance of Ma and Masek already increases in the original (unsorted) iris-code. This behavior is not too surprising, since early iris-code bits correspond to inner bands of iris textures, which typically contain rich and discriminative information. However, it is clearly visible that the second 1,024-bits block exhibits a better (lower) EER than the first block, which can be explained by segmentation inaccuracies due to varying pupil dilation. EERs for different 480-bits blocks in the Ko algorithm do not seem to follow a specific pattern (due to the code layout grouping upward and downward slopes). While for Masek and Ma EERs stay low at approximately 2 % for two thirds of the total number of blocks and then increase quickly, Ko's EERs increase almost linearly for the new block order, see Fig. 10.25.

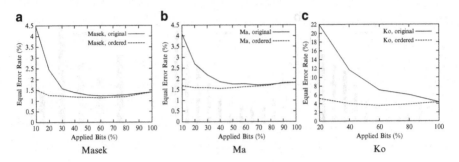

Fig. 10.25 Trade-off between EERs and bits for partial matching using different feature extraction. (**a**) Masek, (**b**) Ma, (**c**) Ko

Reliability masks are utilized in order to restrict the size of the combined template. By rejecting unstable bits one can (1) avoid degradation of results; (2) accelerate comparison time; (3) reduce storage requirements. But how many bits should be used for the combination and which mixing proportion should be employed for the combined features? At this point we clearly state that an exhaustive search for optimal parameters is avoided in order not to run into overfitting problems. Instead, we prefer an evaluation of two reasonable heuristics. Again, with this approach a fast and almost parameterless (except for the computation and evaluation of reliability masks) integration into existing iris-code-based solutions is alleviated. Emphasizing the usability of *selective bits fusion* we will show that even this simple approach will outperform traditional score-based fusion using the sum rule. Bits are selected from single algorithms according to the following two strategies:

1. *Zero-cost*: This heuristic simply assumes that all algorithms provide a similar information rate per bit, thus, the relative proportion in bit size is retained for the combined template. The maximum feature vector bit size is adopted as the new template size and filled according to the relative size of the algorithm's template compared to the total sum of bits, i.e. for combining the total 10,240 Masek bits and 2,400 Ko bits, we extract the most reliable 8,296 Masek and 1,944 Ko bits and build a new template of size 10,240 bits.
2. *Half-sized*: When assessing the trade-off between EER and bit count in Fig. 10.25 it can be seen, that for the reordered versions already very few bits suffice to obtain low EERs with a global optimum at approximately half of iris-code bits for all tested algorithms. Interestingly, even for the original (unordered) case 50 % of bits seems to be a good amount to get almost the same performance as for a full-length iris-code. The new template consists of a concatenation of the best half-sized iris-codes of each algorithm rounded to the next 32 bits (in order to be able to use fast integer-arithmetics for the computation of the HD). This yields, e.g., 6,336 bits for the combination of the algorithms of Ko and Masek.

Table 10.11 Accuracy vs.
number of bit comparisons
for tested fusion algorithms

Algorithm		EER (%)	Bits
Original	Masek	1.41	10,240
	Ko	4.36	2,400
	Ma	1.83	10,240
Sum rule fusion	Masek + Ko	1.38	10,240
	Ko + Ma	1.72	2,400
	Masek + Ma	1.54	10,240
Selective bits fusion	Masek + Ko	1.15	6,336
	Ko + Ma	1.52	6,336

Finally, selective bits are compared in both zero-cost and half-sized configurations with traditional sum rule fusion: the latter technique simply calculates the sum (or average) of individual comparison scores of each of n classifiers C_i for two biometric samples a, b:

$$S(a,b) = \frac{1}{n} \sum_{i=1}^{n} C_i(a,b). \qquad (10.3)$$

Results of the tested combinations are outlined briefly in Table 10.11 (selective bits fusion lists results by the better half-sized variant).

Highest accuracy of the original algorithms with respect to EER is provided by Masek's algorithm (1.41 %) closely followed by Ma (1.83 %). The almost five times shorter iris-code by Ko provides the least accurate EER results (4.36 %). In the experiments pairwise combinations of these algorithms are tested. It is worth to notice that improvement in score-level biometric fusion is not self-evident but depends on if algorithms assess complementary information. Indeed, if the similar algorithms of Ma and Masek are combined, an EER value (1.54 %) right in between values for both single algorithms is achieved at the cost of the iris-code being twice as long as for a single algorithm. For this reason only the combinations between the complementary algorithm pairs Masek and Ko as well as Ko and Ma are considered.

For the combination of Masek and Ko, sum rule yields only slightly superior EER (1.38 %) than for the better single algorithm, but still despite the worse single performance of Ko, information could still be exploited and the ROC curve is superior to both algorithms over almost the entire range (Fig. 10.26). If selective bits fusion is employed, much more improvement than for the traditional combination with EERs as low as 1.15 % for the half-sized version (and 1.21 % for the zero-cost variant) is achieved. Indeed it is even better to discard more bits, which is most likely caused by the fact that there is a significant amount of unstable bits present in each of the codes degrading the total result. Especially for high-security applications with requested low FMRs, selective bits fusion performed reasonably well.

When employing fusion for Ko and Ma results indicate a similar picture. Again, the sum rule yields slightly better EER results than the best individual classifier

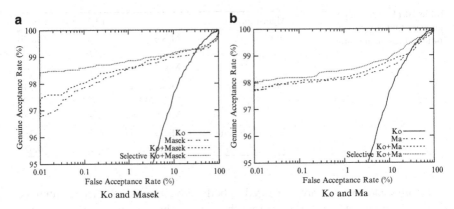

Fig. 10.26 Fusion scenarios: (**a**) Ko and Masek, and (**b**) Ko and Ma

(1.72 %) which is beaten by selective bits fusion (1.52 %). The zero-cost selective bits fusion variant is slightly worse (1.59 % EER).

Apart from building templates from multiple algorithms, it is also possible to combine multiple algorithms in a serial manner, which is useful for identification mode evaluations. In *rotation-invariant preselection*, efficient reductions are achieved by using pre-screening techniques, i.e. a fast but less accurate algorithm is employed to quickly reduce the gallery set of likely identities, and more time-consuming (but accurate) algorithms are employed for final decision ranking. In order to illustrate the behavior on multiple databases, three iris datasets are employed: CASIA.v1, CASIA.v3, and MMU. For CASIA.v1, which consists of 756 images acquired from 108 eyes (7 images per eye), the first subset contains 630 iris images and the second subset combines 126 images. For the CASIA.v3, the first subset consists of 1,705 iris images acquired from 341 different eyes (5 images for each eye). The second subset includes 117 images from 53 eyes with various numbers of images per eye. For MMU, the first dataset is composed of 400 iris images from 80 eyes, while the second set contains 50 images (again 5 images per eye). For all three databases, the first dataset is used to serve as database of enrolled persons and the second dataset contains images that are unknown to the recognition system (which are needed in the open-set scenario).

With respect to serial classifier combination, the proposed scheme is investigated for different reduction sizes, $p \in \{5, 10, 15\}$. Rotation compensation for Masek (see Sect. 3.4 is conducted with 8 shifts, Du et al.'s feature extraction is rotationally invariant and therefore does not need any bit shifting for alignment. Table 10.12 illustrates the time consumption (AMD Athlon 2200+ processor, 512 MB RAM, Windows XP and MatLAB R2007b) and accuracy for single and the serially combined techniques. When conducting only a single HD computation (instead of already 5 in the case of two shifts), the iris-code algorithm would be only slightly slower compared to the Du approach, but rotation compensation degrades its performance significantly.

Table 10.12 RR-1 vs. time consumption of serial fusion on different datasets

Algorithm	Shifts	Reduct. Size	CASIA.v1		CASIA.v3		MMU	
			RR-1	Time	RR-1	Time	RR-1	Time
Masek	8	–	90.9	176.3	68.3	507.1	84.5	111.5
Du et al.	0	–	81.6	12.5	69.2	32.1	49.8	8.1
Fusion	0+8	5	88.1	21.3	76.1	56.6	68.8	14.1
		10	90.3	30.3	65.5	79.7	73.8	19.8
		15	91.9	39.3	66.2	104.7	76.8	25.5

As expected, it is confirmed that the serial approach is much faster than classical methods. For example, for 1D signatures with $p = 10$, the serial approach is more than a factor of 6 faster and still provides comparable accuracy. We notice that the CASIA.v1 dataset yields overall better results than the CASIA.v3 and MMU datasets, probably due to post-processing of the CASIA.v1 dataset [393], which eases the segmentation process and therefore reduces segmentation errors. For CASIA.v1, only the $p = 15$ serial variant yields better identification rates than Masek. In CASIA.v3, the $p = 5$ serial variant yields the best identification rate (76.1 %) and also Du's algorithm itself is surprisingly better than the iris-code approach. The decreasing identification accuracy for increasing values of p may be surprising at first; however, these results are due to the fact that a larger set of preselected templates can increase the chance for false positives which have been excluded for lower values of p. For both datasets these recognition results are not obvious since a coarse preselection could be expected to exclude potential genuine templates, too. In contrary, the preselection helps to avoid false-positive matches. This may be explained by the fact that the Du approach yields good results for partial iris recognition (e.g., heavy eyelid occlusion or segmentation errors) and noisy images [135]. In contrast, the results for the MMU dataset are worse for the serial combinations as compared to the classical iris-code approach for all values of p. It is also noticed that recognition accuracy increases monotonically with increasing p.

Finally, the combination of *image metrics with traditional feature-based techniques* has been investigated. Image metric scores are normalized in a way that mean impostor scores are 0.5 and low scores indicate high similarity. Obtained performance rates in terms of EERs for single and paired combination of comparators are summarized in Table 10.13. According ROC curves of individual image metrics, feature extraction algorithms, as well as selected fusion scenarios are plotted in Fig. 10.27. It is important to note that all combinations (Iris-code + metric and metric + metric) represent a challenging single-sensor multi-algorithm fusion scenario.

Regarding the obtained EERs, most individual image metrics do not represent an alternative to traditional iris-based feature extraction algorithms (see Table 10.13). While an exclusive application of best image metrics yield EERs greater than 2 %, traditional feature extraction algorithms obtain EERs less than 1.5 %. However, as shown in Fig. 10.27, distinct combinations of image metrics yield significant improvement in accuracy, e.g., a fusion of LFBVS and VIF yields an EER of 1.86 %.

Table 10.13 Obtained results for the proposed biometric fusion scenarios

	EER (%)							
	Ma	Masek	PSNR	SSIM	LEG	ESS	LFBVS	VIF
Ma	1.43	1.46	1.56	1.53	1.32	2.51	2.01	1.65
Masek		1.77	1.97	1.72	1.58	2.43	2.12	1.78
PSNR			4.21	3.08	3.34	4.69	3.60	2.11
SSIM				3.40	3.40	4.51	2.71	2.18
LEG					3.99	5.76	3.46	2.10
ESS						9.61	4.90	2.20
LFBVS							5.54	1.86
VIF								2.06

Regarding a combination of metrics and traditional algorithms, for the simple sum rule, a combination of applied feature extraction algorithms does not yield improvement with respect to recognition performance. In addition, image metrics do not supplement traditional iris recognition algorithms in general. While the incorporation of most image metrics (e.g., PSNR, ESS and LFBVS) decreases performance, certain image metrics represent adequate complements (e.g., SSIM and LEG). In particular, combinations of the LEG metric and the applied feature extractors show significant improvements achieving EERs of 1.32 % and 1.58 %, respectively. Obtained results appear promising since image metrics are applied without any adaption using the most simple fusion rule to the proposed application scenario, i.e. adjusted implementations of image metrics are expected to further improve recognition accuracy.

10.6 Discussion

Several comparator techniques have been presented and evaluated: *Context-based* techniques present a new way of comparing iris-codes based on local surrounding information of each bit. When considering not only the proposed comparator, but also simpler pixel-based feature extraction, the more complex matching procedure does not degrade performance in verification mode. Relative EER-improvements of up to 5 % could be achieved using this comparator on Masek's feature extraction. An adapted version of the *Levenshtein Distance* as comparator has been shown to be a useful matching technique to tolerate nonlinear deformations of iris textures with drastically reduced error rates (42 % relative EER-improvement for Ma in case of the challenging ICE dataset). With the introduction of alignment constraints, LD is only 4–5 times slower than HD with an equal amount of shifts. With the *shifting score fusion* operator, the variation of comparison scores between iris-codes at different shifting positions has been exploited as a new comparison technique. Since pairs of iris-codes from the same data subject exhibit an optimal comparison score at a distinct alignment, mis-alignments reveal rather low comparison scores

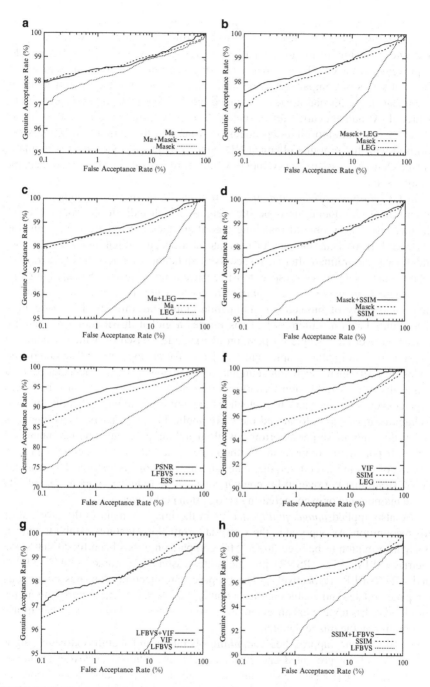

Fig. 10.27 ROC curves for traditional algorithms, image metrics, and selected fusion scenarios. (a) Traditional algorithms, (b-d) Iris-code + metric fusion, (e-f) Image metrics, (g-h) Metric + metric fusion

causing high variation. In contrast, pairs of non-genuine data subjects tend to yield low comparison scores regardless of shifting positions. These observations motivate a sensible fusion of comparison scores, yielding up to 5 % relative EER-improvements on CASIA.v3. When utilizing not only the worst alignment but the total series of comparison scores which are estimated at the time of template alignment, i.e. information loss is avoided, up to 24 % EER-improvement can be achieved. At authentication this so-called *Gaussian score fitting* fits the entire set of scores onto an algorithm-dependent Gaussian and the normalized fitting score is fused with the minimal obtained HD. Since bits in iris-codes are not mutually independent, successive improvements within scores are observed in case of genuine comparisons.

In *bit reliability-driven comparison*, information of successful authentications is leveraged introducing user-specific weights, which indicate the consistency of distinct bits. The proposed matching algorithm does not require the acquisition of several enrollment samples to generate user-specific reliability masks, rather these masks are refined after each successful authentication. Results of up to 31 % relative improvement with respect to EERs have been achieved when applying this technique. *Incremental iris recognition* refers to a generic approach to optimize time complexity of biometric identification employing different iris recognition algorithms. From a training set of iris images a global distribution of reliability is learned over each single bit position of iris-codes, based on which operational galleries of enrollment samples are reordered. By analogy, bits of acquired iris-codes are permuted, such that template comparison is highly accelerated in a single algorithm serial fusion scenario. This technique offers significant advantages over conventional bit-masking, which would represent binary reliability masks. Reliability masks are global and therefore applicable to all users. Thus, memory is saved (single mask per algorithm) while matching procedures remain unaltered for each pair-wise comparison. Furthermore, reliability masks define a precise ranking of bits in iris-codes, rather than ignoring parts of iris textures. Experiments demonstrate that the overall bit comparisons can be reduced to about 5 % of bits while maintaining or even increasing recognition performance.

We also applied *image quality metrics* in the image domain to the problem of iris recognition. As opposed to the view that original iris textures exhibit too much noisy information to be used directly for comparison, it has been found that some metrics (SSIM, LEG, PSNR) provide quite reasonable accuracy (3.4 %, 3.99 % and 4.21 % EER, respectively). The proposed architecture alleviates continuous template updates and enables a transparent replacement of comparators without re-enrollment. Iris texture enhancement is found to be essential to the accuracy of iris recognition in the image domain.

Finally, several approaches combining operators and feature extraction algorithms have been presented and evaluated: *Bit reliability score fusion* combines reliability-driven (BRD) and shifting score fusion (SSF) comparators and improves the recognition accuracy of each single comparator. *Selective best bits* applies the idea of template-reordering as executed in incremental iris recognition to multiple feature vectors: A sensible combination of diverse feature extraction algorithms tends to improve recognition accuracy. While in conventional biometric fusion scenarios improved accuracy comes at the cost of additional template storage as well as comparison time, selective bits fusion presents a generic approach to iris biometric fusion which does not require the storage of a concatenation of applied biometric templates. By combining the most reliable features only (extracted by different algorithms), storage is saved while the accuracy of the biometric fusion is even improved. Speed in identification mode can also be saved using the presented *preselection using rotation-invariant operator* technique. This serial classifier combination can save 70 %–80 % or even more computation time for identification (the actual value depends on the specific dataset considered) without severe degradations in accuracy. *Combining image metrics with iris-codes* is further able to significantly improve recognition accuracy of iris biometric systems.

Part III
Privacy and Security in Iris Biometrics

Chapter 11
Iris Biometric Cryptosystems

Biometric cryptosystems are designed to securely bind a digital key to a biometric or generate a digital key from a biometric [69]. The majority of biometric cryptosystems require the storage of biometric-dependent public information applied to retrieve or generate keys which is referred to as helper data [228]. Due to biometric variance it is not feasible for most biometric characteristics to extract cryptographic keys directly. Helper data, which must not reveal significant information about the original biometric templates, assists the key retrieval or key-generation process. Biometric comparisons are performed indirectly by verifying key validities, where the output of the authentication process is either a key or a failure message. The verification of keys represents a biometric comparison in the cryptographic domain [230]. The two most important aims of biometric cryptosystems are (1) application as a means of biometric template protection [228] and (2) introduction of biometrics to generic cryptosystems in order to replace key release based on passwords and personal identification numbers (PINs). The latter approach brings about substantial security benefits to traditional key release schemes since it is significantly more difficult to forge, copy, share, and distribute biometrics compared to passwords and PINs [229]. Furthermore, most biometrics provide an equal level of security across a user-group (one account is not easier to break than any other) since physiological biometric characteristics are not user selected. Motivated by these aspects, biometrics are utilized to release cryptographic keys dependent on biometric traits in order to enhance the security of conventional cryptosystems.

Due to the variance in biometric measurements, the combination of biometrics and cryptosystem turns out to be complex. Generic biometric systems perform a "fuzzy comparison" by applying decision thresholds which are set up based on intra- and inter-class distributions of genuine subjects and potential impostors. In contrast, biometric cryptosystems are designed to output stable cryptographic keys or hashes.

C. Rathgeb et al., *Iris Biometrics: From Segmentation to Template Security*,
Advances in Information Security 59, DOI 10.1007/978-1-4614-5571-4_11,
© Springer Science+Business Media, LLC 2013

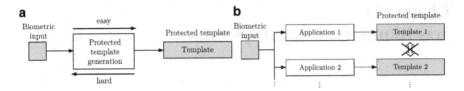

Fig. 11.1 The basic properties of irreversibility and unlinkability provided by biometric template protection schemes. (**a**) Unlinkability, (**b**) Irreversability

11.1   Irreversibility and Unlinkability

Biometric template protection schemes, which are commonly categorized as biometric cryptosystems (also referred to as helper data-based schemes), and cancelable biometrics (also referred to as feature transformation, see Chap. 12) are designed to meet two major requirements of biometric information protection (ISO/IEC FCD 24745):

- *Irreversibility*: It should be computationally hard to reconstruct the original biometric template from the stored reference data, i.e. the protected template, while it should be easy to generate the protected biometric template.
- *Unlinkability*: Different versions of protected biometric templates can be generated based on the same biometric data (renewability), while protected templates should not allow cross-matching (diversity).

Figure 11.1 illustrates the properties of irreversibility and unlinkability provided by biometric template protection technologies.

11.2   Categorization

Based on how helper data are derived, biometric cryptosystems are classified as key-binding or key-generation systems as shown in Fig. 11.2:

1. *Key-binding schemes*: Helper data is obtained by binding a chosen key to a biometric template. As a result of the binding process, a fusion of the secret key and the biometric template is stored as helper data. Applying an appropriate key retrieval algorithm, keys are obtained from the helper data at authentication [546]. Since cryptographic keys are independent of biometric features, the latter are revocable while an update of the key usually requires re-enrollment in order to generate new helper data.
2. *Key-generation schemes*: In a key-generation scheme the helper data is derived only from the biometric template so that the key is directly generated from the helper data and a given biometric sample [228]. While the storage of helper data is not obligatory the majority of proposed key generation schemes does store

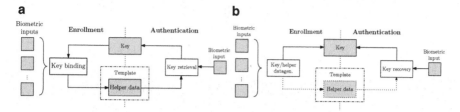

Fig. 11.2 The basic concept of biometric key-binding and key-generation. (**a**) Key-binding, (**b**) Key-generation

helper data (if key-generation schemes extract keys without the use of any helper data these are not updateable in case of compromise). Helper data-based key generation schemes are also referred to as "fuzzy extractors" or "secure sketches" as described in [132] (for both primitives, formalisms are defined). A fuzzy extractor reliably extracts a uniformly random string from a biometric input while stored helper data assists reconstruction. In contrast, in a secure sketch public helper data is applied to recover the original biometric template.

Several concepts of biometric cryptosystems can be applied as both key-generation and key-binding scheme (e.g., [239, 240]), respectively. Hybrid approaches which make use of both basic concepts (e.g., [42]) have been proposed as well. Furthermore, schemes which declare diverse goals such as enhancing the security of any kind of existing secret (e.g., [349, 352]) have been introduced. In contrast to biometric cryptosystems based on key-binding or key-generation, key-release schemes represent a loose coupling of biometric authentication and key release [546]. In case of successful biometric authentication a key release mechanism is initiated. While the loose coupling of biometric and cryptographic systems allows to exchange both components easily a great drawback emerges, since the separate storage of biometric templates and keys offers more vulnerabilities to conduct attacks. Key-release schemes are hardly appropriate for high security applications and usually not considered a biometric cryptosystem at all. Another way to classify biometric cryptosystems is to focus on how these systems deal with biometric variance. While some schemes apply error correction codes (e.g., [239, 240]), others introduce adjustable filter functions and correlation (e.g., [492]) or feature intervals (e.g., [146, 562]). Even though definitions for "biometric keys" and "biometric hashes" have been proposed (e.g., in [350, 559]), these terms are used as synonyms for any kind of key or hash dependent upon biometrics, i.e. biometric features take influence on the constitution of keys or hashes as opposed to key binding schemes.

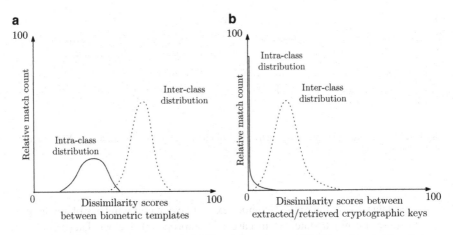

Fig. 11.3 Performance measurement in (**a**) biometric systems and (**b**) biometric cryptosystems

11.3   Performance Measurement

When measuring the performance of classical biometric systems widely used factors include FRR, FAR, and EER [227, 229] (defined in ISO/IEC FDIS 19795-1). As score distributions overlap, FAR and FRR intersect at a certain point, defining the EER of the system. According to intra- and inter-class distributions FRRs and FARs are adjusted by varying system thresholds (in general, decreasing the FRR increases the FAR and vice versa).

These performance metrics can be directly transferred to key release schemes only. In the context of biometric cryptosystems, the meaning of these metrics changes since threshold-based authentication is eliminated. In biometric cryptosystems acceptance requires the generation or retrieval of hundred percent correct keys. While conventional biometric systems response with "Yes" or "No," biometric cryptosystems retrieve or generate either correct or incorrect keys. The fundamental difference between performance measurement in biometric systems and biometric cryptosystems is illustrated in Fig. 11.3. The FRR of a biometric cryptosystem defines the rate of incorrect keys untruly generated by the system, that is, the percentage of incorrect keys returned to genuine users (correct keys are user-specific and associated with the according helper data). By analogy, the FAR defines the rate of correct keys untruly generated by the system, that is, the percentage of correct keys returned to non-genuine users. A false accept corresponds to an untrue generation or retrieval of keys bound to helper data or used to generate helper data at enrollment. Tolerance levels (FRRs and FARs) are adjusted using key generation and binding algorithms in several ways, for example, by stretching or tightening ranges in which features are arranged to generate correct keys [425, 559]. Compared to biometric systems, biometric cryptosystems generally exhibit noticeably inferior performance [546]. This is because within biometric cryptosystems, in most cases the enrolled template is not seen and, therefore, cannot be aligned properly at comparison. In addition, the majority of biometric cryptosystems introduces a higher degree of quantization at feature extraction compared to conventional biometric systems. Furthermore, conventional biometric systems are capable of setting thresholds more precisely to adjust the system performance.

11.4 Biometric Key-Binding

Key-binding schemes (see Fig. 11.2a) bind chosen cryptographic keys with biometric data in order to generate a secure template (helper data), which, in the optimal case, does neither reveal information about the key nor about the biometric data. With the use of another biometric input and an appropriate key retrieval algorithm keys are extracted from the stored secure template. In the following subsections different approaches to biometric key-binding are described where emphasis is put on approaches applied to iris biometrics.

11.4.1 Mytec1 and Mytec2 (Biometric Encryption^{TM})

The first sophisticated approach to biometric key-binding based on fingerprints was proposed by Soutar et al. [488–490]. The presented system was called Mytec2, a successor of Mytec1 [492], which was the first biometric cryptosystem but turned out to be impractical in terms of accuracy and security. Mytec1 and Mytec2 were originally called Biometric Encryption^{TM}, the trademark was abandoned in 2005. The basis of the Mytec2 (and Mytec1) algorithm is the mechanism of correlation.

At enrollment, a filter function $H(u)$ is derived from $f_0(x)$, which is a two-dimensional image array (0 indicates the first measurement). Subsequently, a correlation function $c(x)$ is defined involving $f_0(x)$ and any other biometric input $f_1(x)$ obtained at verification: $c(x) = FT^{-1}\{F_1(u)F_0^*(u)\}$, which is the inverse Fourier transform of the product of the Fourier transform of a biometric input, denoted by $F_1(u)$, and $F_0^*(u)$, where $F_0^*(u)$ is represented by $H(u)$. The output $c(x)$ is an array of scalar values describing the degree of similarity. To provide distortion tolerance, the filter function is calculated using a set of T training images $\{f_0^1(x), f_0^2(x), \ldots, f_0^T(x)\}$. The output pattern of $f_0^t(x)$ is denoted by $c_0^t(x)$ with its Fourier transform $F_0^t(u)H(u)$. The complex conjugate of the phase component of $H(u)$, $e^{i\phi(H(u))}$, is multiplied with a random phase-only array of the same size to create a secure filter, $H_{\text{stored}}(u)$, which is stored as part of the template while the magnitude of $H(u)$ is discarded. The output pattern $c_0(x)$ is then linked with an N-bit cryptographic key k_0 using a linking algorithm: If the nth bit of k_0 is 0, then L locations of the selected part of $c_0(x)$ which are 0 are chosen and the indices of the locations are written into the nth column of a look-up table, which is stored as part of

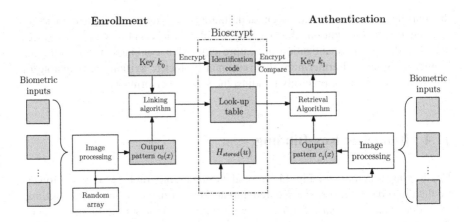

Fig. 11.4 Basic operation mode of Mytec1 and Mytec2: The mechanism of correlation is applied and biometric variance is overcome by means of error correction

the template, termed BioScrypt. During linking, redundancy is added by applying a repetitive code. Standard hashing algorithms are used to compute a hash of k_0, termed id_0 which is stored as part of the template, too. During authentication, a set of biometric images is combined with $H_{stored}(u)$ to produce an output pattern $c_1(x)$. With the use of the look-up table an appropriate retrieval algorithm calculates an N-bit key k_1 extracting the constituent bits of the binarized output pattern. Finally, a hash id_1 is calculated and tested against id_0 to check the validity of k_1. Figure 11.4 shows the concept of the Biometric Encryption^{TM} algorithm.

The algorithm was summarized in a patent [491], which includes explanations of how to apply the algorithm to other biometric characteristics, in particular to iris imagery. In all the publications performance measurements are omitted.

11.4.2 Fuzzy Commitment Scheme

In 1999 Juels and Wattenberg [240] combined techniques from the area of error correcting codes and cryptography to develop a type of cryptographic primitive referred to as fuzzy commitment scheme. A fuzzy commitment scheme consists of a function F, used to commit a codeword $c \in C$ and a witness $x \in \{0,1\}^n$. The set C is a set of error correcting codewords c of length n and x represents a bitstream of length n, termed witness (biometric data). The difference vector of c and x, $\delta \in \{0,1\}^n$, where $x = c + \delta$, and a hash value $h(c)$ are stored as the commitment termed $F(c,x)$ (helper data). Each x', which is sufficiently "close" to x, according to an appropriate metric, should be able to reconstruct c using the difference vector δ to translate x' in the direction of x. A hash of the result is tested against $h(c)$. With respect to biometric key-binding the system acquires a witness x at enrollment,

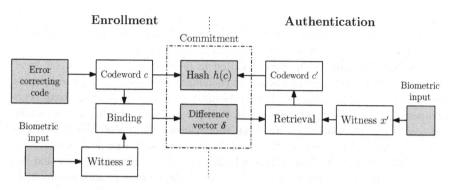

Fig. 11.5 Basic operation mode of the fuzzy commitment scheme: Chosen keys are prepared with error correction and bound to binary biometric templates

selects a codeword $c \in C$, calculates, and stores the commitment $F(c,x)$ (δ and $h(c)$). At the time of authentication, a witness x' is acquired and the system checks whether x' yields a successful decommitment. The basic operation mode of a fuzzy commitment scheme is illustrated in Fig. 11.5.

The fuzzy commitment scheme was applied to iris-codes by Hao et al. [184]. In their scheme 2,048-bit iris-codes are applied to bind and retrieve 140-bit cryptographic keys prepared with Hadamard and Reed–Solomon error correction codes (the C in the description above). Hadamard codes are applied to eliminate bit errors originating from the natural biometric variance and Reed–Solomon codes are applied to correct burst errors resulting from distortions. During enrollment, a 2048-bit iris code θ_{ref} is generated by applying 2D-Gabor wavelets according to Daugman's algorithm. Another 2,048-bit pseudo iris code θ_{ps}, which is a 140-bit cryptographic key k prepared with Hadamard and Reed–Solomon codes resulting in a 2,048-bit bitstream, is bitwise XORed with θ_{ref} to form the commitment $\theta_{\mathrm{lock}} = \theta_{\mathrm{ref}} \oplus \theta_{\mathrm{ps}}$. Additionally, a hash value of the key k, $H(k)$, is generated and stored. In the authentication process another iris code is extracted, denoted by θ_{sam}, and out of θ_{sam} and θ_{lock} a pseudo iris code denoted by $\hat{\theta}_{\mathrm{ps}}$ is calculated by XORing θ_{sam} with θ_{lock}. With the according Hadamard and Reed–Solomon decoding a 140-bit key $\hat{k}$ is reconstructed, hashed and if $h(\hat{k}) = h(k)$ the authentication is successful, otherwise the key will be deemed false and rejected. The system was tested with 700 iris images of 70 probands obtaining rather impressive results which were not achieved until then. In order to provide an error correction decoding in an iris-based fuzzy commitment scheme which gets close to a theoretical bound, two-dimensional iterative min-sum decoding is introduced by Bringer et al. [51,52]. In this approach a matrix is created where lines as well as columns are formed by two different binary Reed–Muller codes which enables a more efficient decoding. The proposed scheme was adapted to the standard iris recognition algorithm of Daugman to bind and retrieve 40-bit keys. Due to the fact that this scheme was tested on non-ideal iris images, a more significant performance evaluation is provided. Rathgeb and Uhl [526] provide a systematic approach to the construction of iris-based fuzzy commitment schemes. After analyzing error distributions among iris-codes of different iris recognition algorithms, customized Reed–Solomon and Hadamard codes are applied (similar to [184]). In other further work [424], the authors apply context-based reliable component selection in order to extract more stable keys from iris-codes which are then bound to Hadamard codewords. Further techniques to improve the performance of iris-based fuzzy commitment schemes have been proposed [211, 426, 611]. Cimato et al. [99] propose a system for the extraction of secure identifiers based on iris biometrics. During enrollment, these identifiers are extracted and two iris codes, I_1 and I_2, prepared with a random permutation are XORed to form δ. Additionally a hash value of the second iris code and the difference vector, denoted by $H(I_2, \delta)$, is stored. At the time of authentication, I_1' is presented and by applying the according inverse permutation, I_2' is decoded and a hash is calculated and tested against $H(I_2, \delta)$. A FAR of 0.204 % and a FRR of 16.799 % are reported. Zhang et al. [611] introduce a bit-masking scheme which is applied to a fuzzy commitment scheme based on iris biometrics. A simple bit-mask is additionally XORed with iris codes at the time of enrollment and authentication, thus, the total number of errors between iris codes is reduced. However, information is lost and the cumulations of genuine and non-genuine users will approximate if the bit-masking rate is too high. In contrast, Ignatenko et al. [211] suggest to apply reliable bit selection methods resulting in more discriminative iris codes yielding increased performance. Binary iris-codes are suitable to be applied in a fuzzy commitment scheme, in addition, template alignment is still feasible since it only involves a one-dimensional circular shift of a given iris-code. Besides iris, the fuzzy commitment scheme has been applied to other biometrics as well, which always requires a binarization of extracted feature vectors.

Teoh and Kim [515] applied a randomized dynamic quantization transformation to binarize fingerprint features extracted from a multichannel Gabor filter. Feature vectors of 375 bits are extracted and Reed–Solomon codes are applied to construct the fuzzy commitment scheme. The transformation comprises a non-invertible projection based on a random matrix derived from a user-specific token. It is required that this token is stored on a secure device. Similar schemes based on the feature extraction of BioHashing [163] (discussed later) have been presented in [15, 607]. Tong et al. [528] proposed a fuzzy extractor scheme based on a stable and order invariant representation of biometric data called Fingercode, reporting inapplicable performance rates. Nandakumar [363] applies a binary fixed-length minutiae representation obtained by quantizing the Fourier phase spectrum of a minutia set in a fuzzy commitment scheme, where alignment is achieved by a focal point of high curvature regions. Lu et al. [319] binarized PCA-based face features which they apply in a fuzzy commitment scheme. A method based on user adaptive error correction codes was proposed by Maiorana and Ercole [328], where the error correction information is adaptively selected based on the intra-variability of a user's biometric data. Applying online signatures, this seems to be the first approach of using behavioral biometrics in a fuzzy commitment scheme. In [324] another fuzzy commitment scheme based on online signatures is presented.

While in classic fuzzy commitment schemes [184, 240] biometric variance is eliminated by applying error correction codes, Zheng et al. [615] employ error tolerant lattice functions. In experiments an FRR of ~3.3% and an FAR of ~0.6% are reported. Besides the formalism of fuzzy extractors and secure sketches, Dodis et al. [132] introduce the so-called syndrome construction. Here an error correction code syndrome is stored as part of the template and applied during authentication in order to reconstruct the original biometric input. Table 11.1 summarizes performance measurements of key approaches to the fuzzy commitment scheme.

11.4.3 Shielding Functions

Tuyls et al. [315] introduced a concept which is referred to as shielding functions. It is assumed that at enrollment, a noise-free real-valued biometric feature vector X of fixed length is available. This feature vector is used together with a secret S (the key) to generate the helper data W applying an inverse δ-contracting function G^{-1}, such that $G(W,X) = S$. Like in the fuzzy commitment scheme [240], additionally, a hash $F(S) = V$ of the secret S is stored. The core of the scheme is the δ-contracting function G which calculates a residual for each feature, which is the distance to the center of the nearest even–odd or odd–even interval, depending on whether the corresponding bit of S is 0 or 1. W can be seen as correction vector which comprises all residuals. At authentication, another biometric feature vector Y is obtained and $G(W,Y)$ is calculated. In case $||X - Y|| \leq \delta$, $G(W,Y) = S' = S = G(W,X)$. In other words, noisy features are added to the stored residuals and the resulting vector is decoded. An additional application of error correction is optional. Finally, the hash value $F(S')$ of the reconstructed secret S' is tested against the previously stored one (V) yielding successful authentication or rejection. In further work [533] the authors extract reliable components from fingerprints reporting an FRR of 0.054 % and an FAR of 0.032 %. Figure 11.6 shows the operation mode of the shielding functions concept.

Buhan et al. [61] extend the ideas of the shielding functions approach by introducing a feature mapping based on hexagonal zones instead of square zones. No results in terms of FRR and FAR are given. Li et al. [304] suggest to apply fingerprints in a key-binding scheme based on shielding functions. So far, this concept has not been applied to iris biometrics.

11.4.4 Fuzzy Vault

One of the most popular biometric cryptosystems called fuzzy vault was introduced by Juels and Sudan [239] in 2002. The key idea of the fuzzy vault scheme is to use an unordered set A to lock a secret key k, yielding a vault, denoted by V_A. If another

Table 11.1 Experimental results of proposed fuzzy commitment schemes

Authors	Char.	FRR/ FAR	Remarks
Hao et al. [184]		0.47/ 0	Ideal images
Bringer et al. [52]	Iris	5.62/ 0	Short key
Rathgeb and Uhl [426]		4.64/ 0	–
Teoh and Kim [515]		0.9/ 0	User-specific tokens
Tong et al. [528]	Fingerprint	78/ 0.1	–
Nandakumar [363]		12.6/ 0	–
Ao and Li [15]	Face	7.99/ 0.11	–
Lu et al. [319]		~30/ 0	Short key
Maiorana and Ercole [328]	Online sig.	13.07/ 4	>1 enroll. sam.

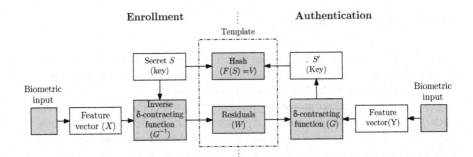

Fig. 11.6 Basic operation mode of shielding functions: Residuals are calculated for each feature element based on which intervals are constructed

set B overlaps largely with A, k is reconstructed, i.e. the vault V_A is unlocked. The vault is created by applying polynomial encoding and error correction. During the enrollment phase, a polynom p is selected which encodes the key k in some way (e.g., the coefficients of p are formed by k), denoted by $p \leftarrow k$. Subsequently, the elements of A are projected onto the polynom p, i.e. $p(A)$ is calculated. Additionally, chaff points are added in order to obscure genuine points of the polynom. The set of all points, R, forms the template. To achieve successful authentication, another set B needs to overlap with A to a certain extent in order to locate a sufficient amount of points in R that lie on p. Applying error correction codes, p can be reconstructed and, thus, k. The security of the whole scheme is based on the infeasibility of reconstructing the polynomial and the number of applied chaff points. The main advantage of this concept is the feature of order invariance, i.e. fuzzy vaults are able to cope with unordered feature set which occur in several biometric modalities (e.g., fingerprints [227]). The concept of a fuzzy vault scheme is shown in Fig. 11.7.

Clancy et al. [100] proposed the first practical and most apparent implementation of the fuzzy vault scheme by locking minutiae points in a "fingerprint vault." A set of minutiae points, A, is mapped onto a polynom p and chaff points are randomly added to construct the vault. During authentication, Reed–Solomon codes are applied to reconstruct the polynom p out of which a 128-bit key is recreated. A pre-alignment

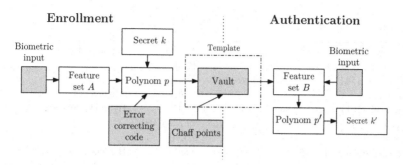

Fig. 11.7 Basic operation mode of the fuzzy vault scheme: If two unordered sets of features overlap enough, the vault is unlocked and the secret is retrieved

of fingerprints is assumed which is rarely the case in practice (feature alignment represents a fundamental step in conventional fingerprint recognition systems). To overcome the assumption of pre-alignment, Nandakumar et al. [365] suggest to utilize high curvature points derived from the orientation field of a fingerprint as helper data to assist the process of alignment. In their fingerprint fuzzy vault, 128-bit keys are bound and retrieved. Uludag et al. [544–546] propose a line-based minutiae representation which the authors evaluate on a test set of 450 fingerprint pairs. Several other approaches have been proposed to improve the alignment within fingerprint-based fuzzy vaults [97, 307, 596]. Rotation and translation invariant minutiae representations have been suggested in [232].

Numerous enhancements to the original concept of the fuzzy vault have been introduced. Moon et al. [353] suggest to use an adaptive degree of the polynomial. Nagar and Chaudhury [360] arrange encoded keys and biometric data of fingerprints in the same order into separate grids, which form the vault. Chaff values are inserted into these grids in an appropriate range to hide information. In other work Nagar et al. [361, 362] introduce the idea of enhancing the security and accuracy of a fingerprint-based fuzzy vault by exploiting orientation information of minutiae points. Dodis et al. [132] suggest to use a high degree polynomial instead of chaff points in order to create an improved fuzzy vault. Additionally, the authors propose another syndrome-based key-generating scheme which they refer to as PinSketch. This scheme is based on polynomial interpolation like the fuzzy vault but requires less storage space. Arakala [16] provides an implementation of the PinSketch scheme based on fingerprints.

Apart from fingerprints, iris biometrics have been applied in fuzzy vault schemes. Lee et al. [299] proposed a fuzzy vault for iris biometrics. Since iris features are usually aligned, an unordered set of features is obtained through independent component analysis. Wu et al. [584, 585] proposed a fuzzy vault based on iris as well. After image acquisition and preprocessing, iris texture is divided into 64 blocks where for each block the mean grayscale value is calculated resulting in 256 features which are normalized to integers to reduce noise. At the same time, a Reed–Solomon code is generated and, subsequently, the feature vector is

Table 11.2 Experimental results of proposed fuzzy vault schemes

Authors	Char.	FRR/ FAR	Remarks
Clancy et al. [100]		20–30/0	Pre-alignment
Nandakumar et al. [365]		4/0.04	–
Uludag et al. [544]	Fingerprint	27/0	–
Li et al. [307]		~7/0	Alignment-free
Nagar et al. [361]		5/0.01	Hybrid biometric cryptosystem
Lee et al. [299]		99.225/0.0/0	–
Wu et al. [585]	Iris	5.55/0	–
Reddy and Babu et al. [445]		9.8/0	Hardened vault
Wu et al. [586]	Palmprint	0.93/0	–
Kumar and Kumar [279]		~1/ 0.3	–
Wu et al. [587]	Face	8.5/0	–
Kholmatov and Yanikoglu [256]	Online sig.	8.33/2.5	10 subjects

translated to a cipher key using a hash function. In the decryption phase, another extracted feature vector is corrected applying the error correction code and the key is regenerated. In further work, Wu et al. [586] propose a system based on palmprints in which 362-bit cryptographic keys are bound and retrieved. A similar approach based on face biometrics is presented in [587]. PCA features are quantized to obtain a 128-bit feature vector from which 64 distinguishable bits are indexed in a look-up table while variance is overcome by Reed–Solomon codes. Hernandez et al. [190] proposed a fuzzy vault for iris biometrics as well. For extracting 192-bit keys, an FRR of $\sim 11\%$ and an FAR of $\sim 1.3\%$ was reported for a total number of 25 persons. Reddy and Babu [445] enhance the security of a classic fuzzy vault scheme based on iris by adding a password based on which the vault as well as the secret key is hardened. In experiments a system which exhibits an FRR of 8% and an FAR of 0.03% is hardened resulting in an FRR of 9.8% and an FAR of 0.0%. In case passwords are compromised, the systems security decreases to that of a standard one, thus, the according results were achieved under unrealistic preconditions. Kumar and Kumar [279, 280] present a fuzzy vault based on palmprints by employing real-valued DCT coefficients of palmprint images binding and retrieving 307-bit keys. Kholmatov and Yanikoglu [256] propose a fuzzy vault for online signatures. In Table 11.2 experimental results as given in literature are summarized for key approaches to the fuzzy vault scheme.

11.5   Biometric Key-Generation

In a key-generation scheme (see Fig. 11.2b), the structure of biometric characteristics affects the constitution of a generated key or hash, i.e., keys or hashes are extracted dependent on biometric data. Either keys are generated directly out of a persons biometric data [36], or additional helper data is stored in order to provide updateable keys or hashes [163, 559]. The prior idea of generating keys directly out of biometric templates was presented in a patent by Bodo [36]. An implementation of this scheme does not exist, and it is expected that most biometric characteristics do not provide enough information to reliably extract a sufficiently long and updateable key without the use of any helper data. Apart from that, the application of helper data is necessary in order to allow an update of the extracted key. In the following subsections approaches to biometric key-generation schemes are summarized, in particular, iris biometric key-generation schemes are emphasized.

11.5.1 Private Template Scheme

The iris-based private template scheme was proposed by Davida et al. [124, 125], in which the biometric template itself (or a hash value of it) serves as a secret key. The storage of helper data (i.e., error correction check bits) is required to correct faulty bits of given iris-codes.

In the enrollment process, M 2,048-bit iris codes are generated which are put through a majority decoder to reduce the HD between them. The majority decoder computes the vector $Vec(V) = (V_1, V_2, \ldots, V_n)$ for a n-bit code vector, denoted by $Vec(v_i) = (v_{i,1}, v_{i,2}, \ldots, v_{i,n})$, where $V_j = majority(v_{1,j}, v_{2,j}, \ldots, v_{M,j})$ is the majority of 0's and 1's at each bit position j of M vectors. A majority decoded iris code T, denoted by $Vec(T)$, is concatenated with check digits $Vec(C)$ to generate $Vec(T)||Vec(C)$. The check digits $Vec(C)$ are part of an error correction code. Subsequently, a hash value Hash(Name, Attr, $Vec(T)||Vec(C)$) is generated, where Name is the user's name, Attr are public attributes of the user and Hash($\cdot$) is a hash function. Finally, an authorization officer signs this hash resulting in Sig(Hash(Name, Attr, $Vec(T)||Vec(C)$)). During authentication, several iris-codes are captured and majority decoded resulting in $Vec(T')$. With the according helper data, $Vec(C)$, the corrected template $Vec(T'')$ is reconstructed. Hash(Name, Attr, $Vec(T'')||Vec(C)$) is calculated and compared against Sig(Hash(Name, Attr, $Vec(T'')||Vec(C)$)). The operation mode of the private template scheme is illustrated in Fig. 11.8. Experimental results are omitted, and it is commonly expected that the proposed system reveals poor performance due to the fact that the authors restrict to the assumption that only 10 % of bits of an iris-code change among different iris images of a single subject. However, in general, average intra-class distances of iris-codes lie within 20–30 %. Implementations of the proposed majority decoding technique (e.g., in [597]) were not found to decrease intra-class distances to that extent.

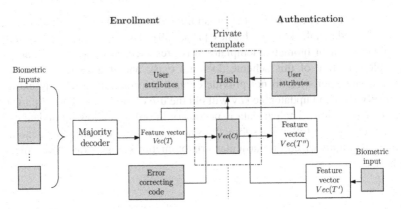

Fig. 11.8 Basic operation mode of the private template scheme: The biometric template itself (or a hash of it) serves as biometric key

11.5.2   Quantization Schemes

In this group of schemes, helper data is constructed in a way that assists in a quantization of biometric features in order to obtain stable keys. Quantization schemes, which have been applied to physiological as well as behavioral biometric characteristics, process feature vectors of several enrollment samples and derive appropriate intervals for each feature element (real-valued feature vectors are required). These intervals are encoded and stored as helper data. At the time of authentication, again, biometric characteristics of a subject are measured and mapped into the previously defined intervals, generating a hash or key. In order to provide updateable keys or hashes most schemes provide a parameterized encoding of intervals. Quantization schemes are highly related to shielding functions [315], since both techniques perform quantization of biometric features by constructing appropriate feature intervals. In contrast to the shielding functions, generic quantization schemes define intervals for each single biometric feature based on its variance. This yields an improved adjustment of the stored helper data to the nature of the applied biometrics. Figure 11.9 illustrates the basic concept of quantization schemes.

Feng and Wah [146] proposed a quantization scheme applied to on-line signatures in order to generate 40-bit hashes. To match signatures, dynamic time warping is applied to x and y-coordinates and shapes of x, y waveforms of a test sample are aligned with the enrollment sample to extract correlation coefficients where low ones indicate a rejection. Subsequently, feature boundaries are defined and encoded with integers. If a biometric sample passed the shape-matching stage, extracted features are fitted into boundaries and a hash is returned out of which a public and a private key are generated. Vielhauer et al. [559, 562] process online signatures to generate signature hashes, too. In their approach an interval matrix is generated for each subject such that hashes are generated by mapping every single feature against

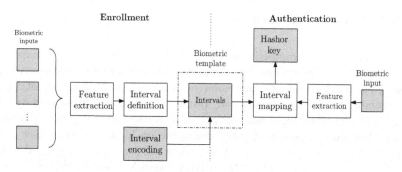

Fig. 11.9 Basic operation mode of quantization schemes: Intervals are constructed for each element of a feature vector and keys are generated by mapping features into intervals

Table 11.3 Experimental results of proposed quantization schemes from literature

Authors	Char.	FRR/ FAR	Remarks
Feng and Wah [146]	Online sig.	28/ 1.2	
Vielhauer et al. [562]		7.05/ 0	
Li et al. [310]	Fingerprint	20/ 1	>1 enroll. sam.
Sutcu et al. [502]	Face	5.5/ 0	
Rathgeb and Uhl [429]	Iris	4.91/ 0	

the interval matrix. In [471], the authors adapt the proposed feature extraction to an online signature hash generation based on a secure sketch. They report a decrease of the FRR but not of the EER. An evaluation of quantization-based key-generation schemes is given in [199]. Sutcu et al. [504] proposed a quantization scheme in which hash values are created out of face biometrics. Li et al. [310] study how to build secure sketches for asymmetric representations based on fingerprint biometrics. Furthermore, the authors propose a theoretical approach to a secure sketch applying two-level quantization to overcome potential pre-image attacks [309]. In [502], the proposed technique is applied to face biometrics. Regarding iris biometrics, Rathgeb and Uhl [425] extended the scheme of [504] generating 128-bit keys. By replacing Gaussian functions by polygonal chains, a more efficient way of encoding intervals is presented. In [429] the authors apply a context-based reliable component selection and construct intervals for the most reliable features of each subject. Experimental results of proposed schemes are summarized in Table 11.3.

11.6 Further Investigations

Besides the so-far described key concepts of biometric cryptosystems other approaches have been proposed. While some represent combinations of basic concepts, others serve different purposes. In addition, multi-biometric cryptosystems have been suggested.

11.6.1 Password Hardening

Monrose et al. [352] proposed a technique to improve the security of password based applications by incorporating biometric information into the password (an existing password is "salted" with biometric data). Keystroke dynamics of a user a are combined with a password pwd_a resulting in a hardened password $hpwd_a$, which can be tested for login purposes or used as cryptographic key. $\phi(a,l)$ denotes a single biometric feature ϕ acquired during the lth login attempt of user a. To initialize an account, $hpwd_a$ is chosen at random and $2m$ shares of $hpwd_a$, denoted by $\{S_t^0, S_t^1\}$, $1 \leq t \leq m$, are created by applying Shamir's secret sharing scheme. For each $b \in \{0,1\}^{\frac{a}{m}}$ the shares $\{S_t^{b(t)}\}$, $1 \leq t \leq m$, can be used to reconstruct $hpwd_a$, where $b(i)$ is the ith bit of b. These shares are arranged in an instruction table of dimension $2 \times m$ where each element is encrypted with pwd_a. During the lth login, pwd_a', a given password to access account a, is used to decrypt these elements (the correctness of pwd_a' is necessary but not sufficient). For each feature ϕ_i, comparing the value of $\phi_i(a,l)$ to a threshold $t_i \in \mathbb{R}$, indicates which of the two values should be chosen to reconstruct $hpwd_a$. Central to this scheme is the notion of *distinguishable features*: let μ_{ai} be the mean and σ_{ai} be the standard deviation of the measurement $\phi_i(a, j_1) \ldots \phi_i(a, j_h)$ where $j_1 \ldots j_h$ are the last h successful logins of user a. Then ϕ_i is a distinguishable feature if $|\mu_{ai} - t_i| > k\sigma_{ai}$ with $k \in \mathbb{R}^+$. Furthermore, the feature descriptor b_a is defined as $b_a(i) = 0$ if $t_i > \mu_{ai} + k\sigma_{ai}$, and 1 if $t_i < \mu_{ai} - k\sigma_{ai}$. For other features b_a is undefined. As distinguishing features ϕ_i develop over time, the login program perturbs the value in the second column of row i if $\mu_{ai} < t_i$, and vice versa. The reconstruction of $hpwd_a$ succeeds only if distinguishable features remain consistent. Additionally, if a subject's typing patterns change slightly over time, the system will adapt by conducting a constant-size history file, encrypted with $hpwd_a$, as part of the biometric template. In contrast to most biometric cryptosystems the initial feature descriptor is created without the use of any helper data. The operation mode of the password hardening scheme is shown in Fig. 11.10.

In several publications, Monrose et al. [349–351] apply their password hardening scheme to voice biometrics where the representation of the utterance of a data subject is utilized to identify suitable features. An FRR of approximately 6 % and a FAR below 20 % was reported. In further work [20, 22], the authors analyze and mathematically formalize major requirements of biometric key generators, and a method to generate randomized biometric templates is proposed [21]. Stable features are located during a single registration procedure in which several biometric inputs are measured. Chen and Chandran [77] proposed a key-generation scheme for face biometrics (for 128-bit keys), which operates like a password hardening scheme [352], using Radon transform and an interactive chaotic bispectral one-way transform. Here Reed–Solomon codes are used instead of shares. An FRR of 28 % and a FAR of 1.22 % are reported. Since the password hardening scheme is most suitable for behavioral biometric characteristics, this concept has not been applied to iris biometrics.

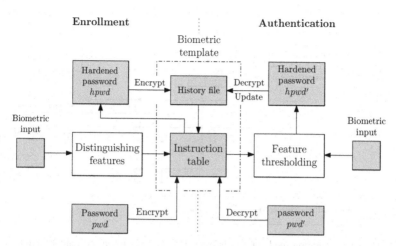

Fig. 11.10 Basic operation mode of the password hardening: The security of an existing password-based application is increased by "salting" passwords with biometrics

11.6.2 BioHashing

A technique originally applied to face biometrics called "BioHashing" was introduced by Teoh et al. [163, 164, 520, 521]. Basically, the BioHashing approach operates as key-binding scheme, however, to generate biometric hashes, secret user-specific tokens (unlike public helper data) have to be presented at authentication. Prior to the key-binding step secret tokens are blended with biometric data to derive a distorted biometric template, thus, BioHashing can be seen as an instance of "Biometric Salting." The original concept of BioHashing is summarized in two stages while the first stage is subdivided into two substages: First the raw image is transformed to an image representation in log-polar frequency domain $\Gamma \in \mathfrak{R}^M$, where M specifies the log-polar spatial frequency dimension by applying a wavelet transform, which makes the output immune to changing facial expressions and small occlusions. Subsequently, a Fourier–Mellin transform is applied to achieve translation, rotation and scale invariance. The generated face feature $\Gamma \in \mathfrak{R}^M$ is reduced to a set of single bits $b \in \{0,1\}^{l_b}$ of length l_b via a set of uniform distributed secret random numbers $r_i \in \{-1,1\}$, which are uniquely associated with a token. These tokenized random numbers, which are created out of a subject's seed, take on a central role in the BioHashing algorithm. First the user's seed is used for generating a set of random vectors $\{r_i \in \mathfrak{R}^M | i = 1, \ldots, l_b\}$. Then the Gram–Schmidt process is applied to the set of random vectors resulting in a set of orthonormal vectors $\{r_{\perp_i} \in \mathfrak{R}^M | i = 1, \ldots, l_b\}$. The dot product of the feature vector and all orthonormal vectors $\{\langle \Gamma | r_{\perp_i} \rangle \in \mathfrak{R}^M | i = 1, \ldots, l_b\}$ is calculated. Finally, an l_b-bit FaceHash $b \in \{0,1\}^{l_b}$ is calculated, where b_i, the ith bit of b is 0 if $\langle \Gamma | r_{\perp_i} \rangle \leq \tau$ and 1 otherwise, where τ is a predefined threshold. In the second stage of BioHashing a

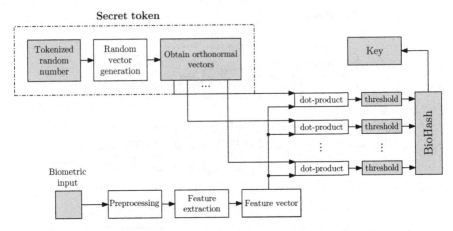

Fig. 11.11 Basic operation mode of BioHashing: User-specific tokenized random numbers are applied while transforming biometric feature vectors to binary BioHashes

key k_c is generated out of the BioHash b. This is done by applying Shamir's secret sharing scheme. Figure 11.11 shows the basic operation mode of the BioHashing technique.

For generating FaceHashes, an FRR of 0.93 % and a zero FAR are reported. In other approaches the same group adopts BioHashing to several biometric characteristics including fingerprints [487, 519], iris biometrics [93, 94] as well as palmprints [104] and show how to apply the generated hashes in generic key binding schemes [31, 487]. The authors reported zero EERs for several schemes.

Kong et al. [266] presented an implementation of FaceHashing and gave an explanation for the zero EER, reported in the first works on BioHashing. Zero EER were achieved due to the tokenized random numbers, which were assumed to be unique across subjects. In a more recent publication Teoh et al. [517] address the so-called "stolen-token" issue evaluating a variant of BioHashing, known as MRP. By applying a multi-state discretization, the feature element space is divided into 2^N segments by adjusting the user-dependent standard deviation. By using this method, elements of the extracted feature vector can render multiple bits instead of 1 bit in the original BioHash. As a result, the extracted bitstreams exhibit higher entropy and recognition performance is increased even if impostors are in possession of valid tokens. However, zero EERs were not achieved under the stolen-token scenario. Different improvements of the BioHashing algorithm have been suggested [321, 366]. With respect to iris biometrics, iris-based BioHashes could be used as biometric keys or applied within another template protection scheme, e.g. fuzzy commitment schemes.

11.6.3 Multi-biometric and Hybrid Biometric Cryptosystems

While multi-biometric systems have been firmly established [227] (e.g., combining iris and face in a single sensor scenario), a limited amount of approaches to biometric cryptosystems utilize several different biometric traits to generate cryptographic keys. Nandakumar and Jain [364] proposed the best performing multibiometric cryptosystem in a fuzzy vault based on fingerprint and iris. The authors demonstrate that a combination of biometric modalities leads to increased accuracy and, thus, higher security. An FRR of 1.8 % at an FAR of ∼0.01 % is obtained, while the corresponding FRR values of the iris and fingerprint fuzzy vaults are 12 % and 21.2 %, respectively. Several other ideas of using a set of multiple biometric characteristics within biometric cryptosystems have been proposed [99,225,243,245,341,503,565].

Nagar et al. [361, 362] proposed a hybrid fingerprint-based biometric cryptosystem. Local minutiae descriptors, which comprise ridge orientations and frequency information, are bound to ordinate values of a fuzzy vault applying a fuzzy commitment scheme. In experiments FRR of 5 % and an FAR of 0.01 % is obtained, without minutiae descriptors the FAR increased to 0.7 %. A similar scheme has been suggested in [73].

11.7 Entropy of Biometric Keys

Most biometric cryptosystems aim at binding or generating keys, long enough to be applied in a generic cryptographic system (e.g., 128-bit keys for AES). Obviously, to prevent biometric keys from being guessed, these need to exhibit sufficient entropy. While the issue of key entropy has been ignored in early approaches to biometric cryptosystems, recent works tend to provide key entropy estimations. System performance of biometric cryptosystems is mostly reported in terms of FRR and FAR. Since both metrics and key entropy depend on the tolerance levels allowed at comparison, these three quantities are highly inter-related.

Buhan et al. [60, 61] have shown that there is a direct relation between the maximum length k of cryptographic keys and the error rates of the biometric system. The authors define this relation as $k \leq -\log_2(\text{FAR})$, which has been established as one of the most common metrics used to estimate the entropy of biometric keys. This means that an ideal biometric cryptosystem would have to maintain an FAR $\leq 2^{-k}$ which appears to be a quite rigorous upper bound that may not be achievable in practice. Nevertheless, the authors pointed out the important fact that the recognition rates of a biometric system correlate with the amount of information which can be extracted, retaining maximum entropy. Based on their proposed quantization scheme [562], Vielhauer et al. [561] describe the issue of choosing significant features of online signatures and introduce three measures for feature evaluation: intrapersonal feature deviation, interpersonal entropy of hash value components, and the correlation between both. By analyzing the discriminativity of chosen features the authors show that the applied feature vector can be reduced by 45 % maintaining error rates [470]. This example underlines the fact that biometric cryptosystems may generate arbitrary long keys while inter-class distances (equals HD between keys) remain low. Ballard et al. [20, 22] propose a new measure to analyze the security of a biometric cryptosystem, termed guessing distance. The guessing distance defines the number of guesses a potential impostor has to perform in order to retrieve either the biometric data or the cryptographic key. Thus, the guessing distance directly relates to intra-class distances of biometric systems and, therefore, provides a more realistic measure of the entropy of biometric keys. Kelkboom et al. [250] analytically obtained a relationship between the maximum key size and a target system performance. An increase of maximum key size is achieved in various scenarios, e.g. when applying several biometric templates at enrollment and authentication or when increasing the desired false rejection rates. In theory-oriented work, Tuyls et al. [534] estimate the capacity and entropy loss for fuzzy commitment schemes and shielding functions, respectively. Similar investigations have been done by Li et al. [311, 501], who provide a systematic approach of how to examine the relative entropy loss of any given scheme, which bounds the number of additional bits that could be extracted if optimal parameters were used. A method for arranging secret points and chaff points in fuzzy vaults such that entropy loss is minimized is presented in [308].

Chapter 12
Cancelable Iris Biometrics

Cancelable biometrics consist of intentional, repeatable distortions of biometric signals based on transforms which provide a comparison of biometric templates in the transformed domain [418]. The inversion of such transformed biometric templates must not be feasible for potential impostors. In contrast to templates protected by standard encryption algorithms, transformed templates are never decrypted since the comparison of biometric templates is performed in transformed space which is the very essence of cancelable biometrics. Hence, the challenge is to construct transforms which provide secure biometric templates, while comparison procedures can still be adopted to compare transformed templates, maintaining recognition rates of the original biometric algorithm. The application of transforms provides irreversibility and unlinkability of biometric templates [69]. The intrinsic strength (individuality) of biometric characteristics should not be reduced applying transforms (constraint on FAR), while on the other hand transforms should be tolerant to intra-class variation (constraint on FRR) [418]. In addition, correlation of several transformed templates must not reveal any information about the original biometrics (unlinkability). In case transformed biometric data is compromised, transform parameters are changed, i.e. the biometric template is updated. To prevent impostors from tracking subjects by cross-matching databases, it is suggested to apply different transforms for different applications. Figure 12.1 shows examples of cancelable iris biometrics applied in the image domain. Obviously, cancelable biometrics are closely related to biometric cryptosystems.

12.1 Categorization

Cancelable biometrics are commonly categorized as non-invertible transforms and biometric salting:

1. *Non-invertible transforms*: In these approaches biometric data is transformed applying a non-invertible function (e.g., Fig. 12.1b,c). In order to provide

C. Rathgeb et al., *Iris Biometrics: From Segmentation to Template Security*,
Advances in Information Security 59, DOI 10.1007/978-1-4614-5571-4_12,
© Springer Science+Business Media, LLC 2013

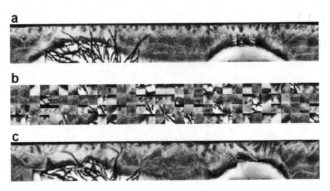

Fig. 12.1 Examples of cancelable iris biometrics applied in the image domain. (**a**) Original iris texture, (**b**) Block re-mapping, (**c**) Surface folding

updateable templates, parameters of the applied transforms are modified. The advantage of applying non-invertible transforms is that potential impostors are not able to reconstruct the entire biometric data even if transforms are compromised. However, applying non-invertible transforms mostly implies a loss of accuracy. Performance decrease is caused by the fact that transformed biometric templates are difficult to align (like in biometric cryptosystems) in order to perform a proper comparison and, in addition, information is reduced. These effects have been observed for several approaches (e.g., [418, 623]).

2. *Biometric salting*: Biometric salting usually denotes transforms of biometric templates which are selected to be invertible. Any invertible transform of biometric feature vector elements represents an approach to biometric salting even if biometric templates have been extracted in a way that it is not feasible to reconstruct the original biometric signal (e.g., [469]). As a consequence, the parameters of the transform have to be kept secret. In case user-specific transforms are applied, the parameters of the transform (which can be seen as a secret seed [517]) have to be presented at each authentication. Impostors may be able to recover the original biometric template in case transform parameters are compromised, causing a potential performance decrease of the system in case underlying biometric algorithms do not provide high accuracy without secret transforms. While approaches to biometric salting may maintain the recognition performance of biometric systems, non-invertible transforms provide higher security [228].

Approaches to cancelable biometrics can be classified further with respect to the parts of biometric systems in which transforms are applied. In the signal domain, transformations are either applied to raw biometric measurements (e.g., face image [418]) or to preprocessed biometric signals (e.g., iris texture [178]). In case transforms are applied in the signal domain, comparators do not need to be adapted. In case transforms are applied in the feature domain, the extracted biometric features (e.g., face features in [517]) are transformed, thus, a compromise of transforms requires further effort in reconstructing the original biometric from the template.

12.2 Issue of Result Reporting

While in the majority of the proposed approaches to cancelable biometrics template alignment is non-trivial and the applied transforms are selected to be non-invertible, still some schemes (e.g., in [445, 517]), especially biometric salting techniques, report an increase in performance as compared to the unmodified biometric scheme. In case user-specific transforms are applied at enrollment and authentication, by definition, two-factor authentication is yielded which may increase the security but does not effect the accuracy of biometric authentication.

A significant increase of recognition rates can be caused by unpractical assumptions during performance evaluations. If user-specific transforms are applied to achieve cancelable biometrics, these transforms have to be considered compromised during inter-class comparisons. Otherwise, biometrics becomes meaningless as the system could rely on secret tokens parameters without any risk [266]. Secret tokens, be it transform parameters, random numbers, or any kind of passwords are easily compromised and must not be considered secure [229]. Thus, performance evaluations of approaches to cancelable biometrics have to be performed under the so-called "stolen-token scenario," where each impostor is in possession of valid secret tokens (the same applies to biometric cryptosystems in case secret tokens are applied). Figure 12.2 illustrates how inter-class distances may change with or without considering the stolen-token scenario. If different tokens are applied for each subject, a clear separation of intra-class and inter-class distributions is achieved by adopting a new threshold. In contrast, if secret tokens are considered compromised, accuracy decreases. Performance is untruly gained if this scenario is ignored during experiments causing even more vulnerable systems in case of compromise [431].

12.3 Non-invertible Transforms

On the one hand, by definition, these approaches apply transforms which are noninvertible, i.e. irreversibility is provided for such techniques. On the other hand, any non-invertible transform implies information loss which is expected to decrease recognition accuracy. Approaches to non-invertible transforms which have been (or could be) applied to iris biometrics are summarized. Experimental results of key approaches to non-invertible transforms are summarized in Table 12.1.

12.3.1 IBM Approaches

Ratha et al. [418] were the first to introduce the concept of cancelable biometrics applying non-invertible transforms. At enrollment, non-invertible transforms are

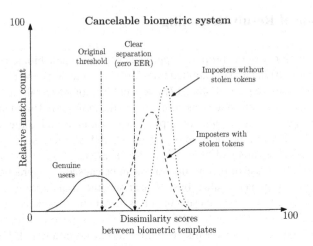

Fig. 12.2 Result reporting: The stolen-token scenario for cancelable biometrics

Table 12.1 Experimental results of proposed approaches to non-invertible transforms

Authors	Char.	FRR/ FAR	Remarks
Ratha et al. [422]	Fingerprint	$15/ 10^{-4}$	–
Boult et al. [39]		~0.08 EER	–
Hämmerle-Uhl et al. [178]	Iris	1.3 EER	–
Zuo et al. [623]		0.005/ 0	Perf. increase
Maiorana et al. [325]	Online Sig.	10.81 EER	–

applied to biometric inputs choosing application-dependent parameters. During authentication, biometric inputs are transformed and a comparison of transformed templates is performed. The basic operation mode is illustrated in Fig. 12.3.

Several types of transforms for constructing multiple cancelable biometrics from pre-aligned fingerprints and face biometrics have been introduced in [418, 421, 422] including Cartesian transform and functional transform. In further work [623], different techniques to create cancelable iris biometrics have been proposed. The authors suggest four different transforms applied in image and feature domains, where only small performance drops are reported. Hämmerle-Uhl et al. [178] applied classic transformations suggested in [418] to iris biometrics, which include block permutation and surface folding. Furthermore, in [143] it is shown that applying both transforms to rectilinear iris images, prior to preprocessing, does not work. Similar to [623], Rathgeb and Uhl [430] suggest to apply row permutations to iris-codes. Maiorana et al. [325, 329, 330] apply non-invertible transforms to obtain cancelable templates from online signatures. In their approach biometric templates, which represent a set of temporal sequences, are split into non-overlapping sequences of signature features according to a random vector which provides revocability. Subsequently, the transformed template is generated by linear convolution of sequences. The complexity of reconstructing the original data from the transformed template is computationally as hard as random guessing.

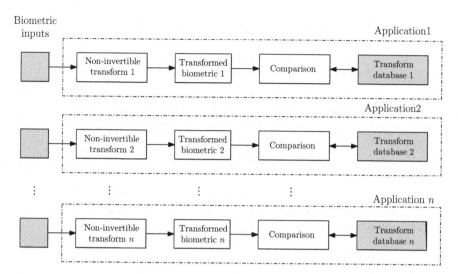

Fig. 12.3 The basic concept of cancelable biometrics based on non-invertible transforms

12.3.2 Revocable Biotokens

Boult et al. [39,42] proposed cryptographically secure biotokens which they applied to face biometrics and fingerprints. In order to enhance security in biometric systems, biotokens, which they refer to as Biotope^{TM}, are adopted to existing recognition schemes (e.g., PCA for face biometrics).

The basic concept of the revocable biotoken approach is shown in Fig. 12.4. Each measured biometric feature v is transformed via scaling and translation resulting in $v' = (v - t) \cdot s$. The key idea is to split v' into a stable part g termed integer and an unstable part r. For face biometrics, the authors suggest to simply split real feature values into an integer part and a fractional part (e.g., 15.4 is split into 15 and 0.4). Since g is considered stable, and a "perfect matching" is claimed to be feasible at authentication, comparisons can be performed in the encrypted domain. A one-way transform of g, denoted by w, is stored as first part of the secure biometric template. As second part of the template, the unencoded r, which has been obscured via the transform, as well as s and t are stored. After the transform, all data is "wrapped" to some position r within the residual, where several times the data is wrapped as given by g. At authentication, features are transformed applying s and t onto a residual region defined by r. Then the unencrypted r is used to compute the local distance within a "window," which is referred to as robust distance measure, to provide a perfect match of w. However, since a perfect match is required only for a number of features defined by the system threshold, biotokens are not matched exactly. Additionally, user-specific passcodes can be incorporated to create verification-only systems. Although the authors ideas seem promising, several questions with respect to the presented approaches are left open, for instance, the design of the

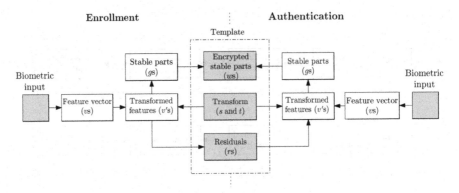

Fig. 12.4 Basic operation mode of revocable biotokens: Elements of biometric feature vectors are split into stable and unstable parts

helper function which separates biometric features into stable and unstable parts and the adoption of this scheme to other biometric characteristics (which is claimed to be feasible). In further work, bipartite biotokens [40, 41] are introduced and applied to fingerprints in order to provide secure communication via an untrusted channel, where cryptographic keys are released based on successful comparisons of biotokens.

12.4   Biometric Salting

Savvides et al. [469] generate cancelable face biometrics by applying so-called minimum average correlation filters which provide non-invertibility. User-specific secret PINs serve as seed for a random basis for the filters similar to [491]. As previously mentioned, BioHashing [163] without key-binding provides cancelable biometric templates, too. Early proposals of the BioHashing algorithm did not consider the stolen-token scenario. In more recent work [518] it is demonstrated that the EER for the extraction of cancelable 180-bit fingercodes increases from 0% to 5.31% in the stolen-token scenario. The authors address this issue by proposing a new method which they refer to as multistage random projection (MRP) [516, 522]. It is claimed that MRP (which is applied to face and speech) retains recognition performance in the stolen-token scenario. Furthermore, the authors proposed a method to generate cancelable keys out of dynamic signatures [278, 600] based on the random mixing step of BioPhasor and user-specific 2^N discretization. To provide cancelable biometrics, extracted features are randomly mixed with a token T using a BioPhasor mixing method. Kanadey[244] present a further method to generate cancelable iris biometrics. It is suggested to shuffle the bits of an extracted iris-code based on a shuffling key which is protected by a password.

Table 12.2 Experimental results of proposed approaches to biometric salting

Authors	Char.	FRR/ FAR	Remarks
Savvides et al. [469]		4.64 / 0	Non-stolen token
Teoh et al. [164]	Face	$2 \cdot 10^{-3}$ EER	Non-stolen token
Wang et al. [571]		6.68 EER	–
Zuo et al. [623]	Iris	0.005/ $<10^{-3}$	Perf. increase
Ouda et al. [382]		1.3 EER	–
Teoh et al. [518]	Fingerprint	5.31 EER	–

Additionally, iris-codes are prepared with Hadamard error correction codes to eliminate bit errors caused by natural variance. The authors claim to increase the performance of the original algorithm; however, it is not clear if the applied shuffling keys are user specific. Kim et al. [259] apply user-specific random projections to PCA-based face features followed by an error minimizing template transform. However, the authors do not consider a stolen-token scenario. Another approach to biometric salting was presented by Wang et al. [571] in which face features are transformed based on a secret key. Non-invertibility is achieved by means of quantization. Ouda et al. [381, 382] propose a technique to obtain cancelable iris-codes. Using several enrollment templates a vector of consistent bits (BioCode) and their respective positions are extracted. Revocability is provided by encoding the BioCode according to a selected random seed. Pillai et al. [395] achieve cancelable iris templates by applying sector random projection to iris images. Recognition performance is only maintained if user-specific random matrices are applied. Chin et al. [93] suggest an algorithm where they first create a feature vector from iris textures using 1D Log-Gabor filters, then extract a binary iris code (termed "S-Code") for use in matching. This binary code is the result of a non-invertible computation, obtained by thresholding inner products of the feature vector with randomly generated vectors. The random vectors are created by using a per-user token and a pseudo random number generator. Chong et al. [94] multiply iris pattern images with a random kernel in the frequency domain to create concealed feature vectors. They then create MACE filters using several training images for each enrolled user. These filters allow to get a similarity measure for each test image which also is multiplied with the user-specific random kernel. In Table 12.2 most notable experimental results of proposed approaches to biometric salting are shown.

12.5 Further Investigations

Jeong et al. [237] combine two different feature extraction methods to achieve cancelable face biometrics. PCA and ICA (independent component analysis) coefficients are extracted and both feature vectors are randomly scrambled and added in order to create a transformed template. Tulyakov et al. [531, 532] propose a method for generating cancelable fingerprint hashes. Instead of aligning fingerprint

Table 12.3 Experimental
results of proposed
approaches to other
cancelable biometrics

Authors	Char.	FRR/ FAR	Remarks
Jeong et al. [237]	Face	14 EER	–
Tulyakov et al. [531]	Fingerprint	25.9/ 0	–
Ang et al. [13]		4 EER	–

minutiae, the authors apply order invariant hash functions, i.e. symmetric complex
hash functions. Ang et al. [13] suggest to apply a key-dependent geometric
transform to fingerprints. In the first step a core point is selected in the fingerprint
image and a line is drawn through it where the secret key defines the angle of the
line ($0 \leq \mathrm{key} \leq \pi$). Secondly, all minutiae below the line are reflected above the
line to achieve a transformed template. Yang et al. [593] apply random projections
to minutiae quadruples to obtain cancelable fingerprint templates. In further work
[594], the authors address the stolen-token scenario by selecting random projection
matrices based on biometric features. Lee et al. [295] presented a method for generating alignment-free cancelable fingerprint templates. Similar to [531, 532, 596],
orientation information is used for each minutiae point. Cancelability is provided
by a user's PIN and the user-specific random vector is used to extract translation
and rotation invariant values of minutiae points. Hirata and Takahashi [191] propose cancelable biometrics for finger-vain patterns where images are transformed
applying a Fourier-like transform. The result is then multiplied with a random
filter where the client stores the inverse filter on some token. At authentication,
the inverse filter is applied to regenerate the transformed enrollment data and
correlation-based comparison is performed. A similar scheme is applied to fingerprints in [508]. Bringer et al. [54] presented an idea of generating time-dependent
cancelable biometrics to achieve untraceability among different identities across
time. Table 12.3 summarizes results obtained in other approaches to cancelable
biometrics.

12.6 Cancelable Biometrics vs. Biometric Cryptosystems

Approaches to cancelable biometrics offer solutions to use several secure biometric templates for different applications [418]. While cross-matching databases
is hardly feasible, single templates can be revoked in case of compromise. As
already mentioned, the feature of revocability is desirable for biometric keys
as well [546]. If an impostor gets to steal a cryptographic key released by a
biometric cryptosystem, it should be possible to update this key. This means
that the demand for updateable keys results in a strong interrelation between the
technologies of biometric cryptosystems and cancelable biometrics. In common
key-binding schemes, in which chosen keys are bound to biometric templates, keys
are updateable by definition. In most cases, revoking keys requires re-enrollment
(original biometric templates are discarded after enrollment). In case a key binding

systems can be run in secure sketch mode (e.g., [239, 240]), original biometric templates can be reconstructed from another biometric input. With respect to key generation schemes, revoking extracted keys requires more effort. If keys are extracted directly from biometric features without the application of any helper data (e.g., as suggested in [36]), an update of the key is not feasible. In helper data-based key generation schemes, the stored helper data has to be modified in a way that extracted keys are different from previous ones (e.g., changing the encoding of intervals in quantization schemes). Alternatively, the key generation process could comprise an additional stage in which biometric salting is performed prior to the key generation process [148, 158, 399]. Bringer et al. [53] suggest to combine a secure sketch with cancelable fingerprint templates. While cancelable biometrics protect the representation of the biometric data, the biometric template is reconstructed from the stored helper data. Several other approaches to generating cancelable biometric keys have been proposed in [291–293].

Chapter 13
Potential Attacks

With respect to generic biometric systems several different attacks have been encountered to infiltrate these [228, 418]. Recent work systematically identifies security threats against biometric systems and possible countermeasures [449] and discusses man-in-the-middle attacks and BioPhishing against a web-based biometric authentication system [606]. An illustration of the most common points of attacks against a conventional biometric system is shown in Fig. 13.1. Correspondingly, in their classical paper [418] Ratha et al. identified and described several stages at which a biometric system may be attacked by an intruder or impostor:

- *Fake physical biometric data*: An impostor may gain access to a biometric system by presenting fake biometric data to the sensor (e.g., a picture of another user's face). This attack is commonly referred to as "spoofing" and several techniques have been proposed to prevent from this type of attack (e.g., liveness detection of presented biometric data [475]).
- *Fake digital biometric data*: Infiltrating a biometric systems by presenting fake digital data requires access to the system at some point of attack. For instance, in a so-called "replay-attack" [420] data acquired by the biometric senor could be recorded and replayed to access the biometric system. In the "injection-attack" data acquired by a different sensor could be injected into the data transmission between sensor and feature extraction pretending to be recorded by the correct biometric sensor.
- *Substitution attacks*: In a substitution attack a biometric template, which is already registered with the system, is replaced by that of the potential impostor. Hence, the impostor will be able to access the system by presenting his own biometric data.
- *Masquerade attacks*: Another technique to gain access to biometric systems is to construct a "masquerade" of biometric data which produces a sufficiently high match score. This could be achieved, for instance, by reconstructing original biometric data from a stolen templates (e.g. in [455]) or synthesizing biometric data by observing internal match scores (e.g. in [4]). A straightforward type

C. Rathgeb et al., *Iris Biometrics: From Segmentation to Template Security*,
Advances in Information Security 59, DOI 10.1007/978-1-4614-5571-4_13,
© Springer Science+Business Media, LLC 2013

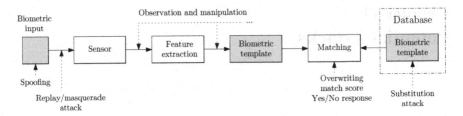

Fig. 13.1 Potential points of attack in generic (iris) biometric systems

of masquerade attack is the so-called "false acceptance attack" in which a sufficiently large number of different biometric samples is presented to the biometric system until a false accept is obtained.

- *Tampering*: A potential impostor may get access to the system and overwrite internal states of the biometric system such as internal match scores or final yes/no responses [418].

Spoofing a physiological biometric feature at the sensor site can be seen as counterpart to exposing a password. If a fraudulent duplicate is accepted by the sensor, breaking a biometric system is at least as easy as spying out a password. However, the illegitimate acquisition of biometric features belonging to a target person does not necessarily involve complicated spoofing techniques. It is a fact that some biometric modalities, e.g. fingerprint, face, iris, and hand-print, cannot be classified as being secret data. These data may be acquired quite easily: Fingerprint or even the full hand-print can be covertly lift off a glass, and current widespread digital cameras with telephoto lenses are able to take high-resolution images of faces unseen by the photographed (using state-of-the-art equipment may even provide enough resolution and sharpness to extract the iris out of a face image). Having acquired these "raw image data," a dedicated attack against the targeted person would be facilitated in case no further security mechanisms are employed.

The acquired image data could be presented to the sensor (spoofing) or could be inserted into the transmission of data between sensor and feature extractor (injection). Since also the feature set extraction might be possible given the raw image data, the computed feature set could eventually be injected into the data before being submitted to the matcher, which can also be applied to the communication channel between database and matcher. The latter attack supposes that the feature extraction scheme is publicly known and is not protected by some template protection technique [228].

Of course, several strategies have been developed to cope with some these problems. Liveness detection [475] helps to resolve the issue of fooling the sensor with prerecorded data. Encryption and authentication techniques have been suggested to secure the above-mentioned communication channels. However, the "public" availability of biometric data questions the necessity and appropriateness of encryption techniques for ensuring security/privacy of biometric data in the

Table 13.1 Potential attacks against different types of biometric cryptosystems

Technology	Proposed attack(s)
Biometric Encryption^{TM} [492]	Blended substitution attack, attack via record multiplicity, masquerade attack (hill climbing)
Fuzzy commitment scheme [240]	Attacks on error correcting codes
Shielding functions [315]	Attack via record multiplicity
Fuzzy vault scheme [239]	Blended substitution attack, attack via record multiplicity, chaff elimination
Key-gen. schemes [124, 561]	False acceptance attack, masquerade attack, brute force attack
Biometric hardend passwords [352]	Power consumption observation

data transmissions. Rather it is necessary to verify the sender (i.e., sensor and feature extractor) authenticity, as well as the integrity of the entire authentication mechanism.

Biometric template protection technologies do not prevent from classic spoofing attacks [420] (presenting fake physical biometrics). However, as previously mentioned there are other possibilities to detect fake biometric inputs which can be integrated, the same holds for replay attacks. Performing substitution attacks to biometric cryptosystems is more difficult compared to conventional biometric systems since biometric templates are either bound to cryptographic keys or used to extract helper data (the original biometric template is discarded). Substitution attacks against biometric cryptosystems require additional knowledge (e.g., of bound keys in case of key-binding schemes). In case of cancelable biometrics substitution attacks are feasible if impostors are in possession of secret transform parameters or secret keys in biometric salting approaches. Both technologies are more resilient to masquerade attacks [4, 70]. Since reconstruction of original biometric templates should not be feasible the synthetization of original biometric inputs is highly complicated (e.g., [5]). Performance rates of both technologies decrease compared to conventional biometric systems which makes biometric cryptosystems and cancelable biometrics even more vulnerable to false acceptance attacks. In contrast to cancelable biometrics, overriding final yes/no responses in a tampering scenario is hardly feasible within biometric cryptosystems as these return a keys instead of binary decisions (intermediate score-based attacks could still be applied [497]).

In Tables 13.1 and 13.2 overviews of specific attacks proposed against biometric cryptosystems and cancelable biometrics technologies are given.

13.1 Attacks Against Biometric Cryptosystems

Boyen [47] was the first to point out the vulnerability of secure sketches and fuzzy extractors in case an impostor is in possession of multiple invocations of the same secret which are combined to reconstruct secrets and, furthermore, retrieve

Table 13.2 Potential attacks against different types of cancelable biometrics

Technology	Proposed attack(s)
Non-invertible transforms [418]	Overwriting final decision, attack via record multiplicity, substitution attack (known transform)
Biometric salting [163]	Overwriting final decision, with stolen token: false acceptance attack, substitution attack, masquerade attack

biometric templates. This (rather realistic) scenario is considered as basis for several attacks against biometric cryptosystems and cancelable biometrics. Similar observations have been made in [472]. Moreover, it is pointed out that if the attacker has knowledge of the secret, the template can be recovered. In addition, a blended substitution attack is introduced in which a subjects and the attackers template are merged into one single template used to authenticate with the system. The Biometric Encryption^{TM} algorithm [492] is highly impacted or even compromised by these attacks. Adler [5] proposed a "hill-climbing" attack against the Biometric Encryption^{TM} algorithm in which a sample biometric input is iteratively modified while the internal comparison score is observed. Nearest impostor attacks [497] in which distinct parts of a large set of biometric templates is combined to obtain high match scores could be applied even more effectively.

Keys bound in fuzzy commitment schemes [240] have been found to suffer from low entropy (e.g., 44 bits in [184]) reducing the complexity for brute force attacks [515]. Attacks which utilize the fact that error correction codes underlie distinct structures have been suggested [70, 497]. In [212] privacy and security leakages of fuzzy commitment schemes are investigated for several biometric data statistics. It is found that fuzzy commitment schemes leak information in bound keys and non-uniform templates. Suggestions to prevent from information leakage in fuzzy commitment schemes have been proposed in [141]. In addition attacks via record multiplicity could be applied to decode stored commitments [62, 481]. Kelkboom et al. [252] introduce a bit-permutation process to prevent from this attack in a fingerprint-based fuzzy commitment scheme. In addition, it has been found that a permutation of binary biometric feature vectors improves the performance of fuzzy commitment schemes [52], i.e. not only the entropy of the entire biometric template (which is commonly estimated in "degrees-of-freedom" [115]) but also the distribution of entropy across feature vectors contributes to the security of the system. Attacks based on error correction code histograms have been successfully conducted against iris-based fuzzy commitment schemes in [435]. An adaption of biometric templates (e.g., [252]) or an improved use of error correction (e.g., [327]) is necessary.

Applying shielding functions to fingerprints, Buhan et al. [59] estimate the probability of identifying protected templates across databases. It is demonstrated that any kind of quantization approaches do not meet the requirement of unlinkability in general.

Several attacks have been discovered against fuzzy vaults [239]. Chang et al. [76] present an observation to distinguish minutiae from chaff points attacking fuzzy vaults based on fingerprints. Since chaff points are created one by one, those created later tend to reveal smaller empty surrounding areas which is verified experimentally, i.e. the security of a fuzzy vault highly relies on the methodology of generating chaff points. Scheirer and Boult [472] introduce an attack via record multiplicity. If more instances of a fuzzy vault (generated using different keys) are obtained minutiae are likely recoverable, i.e. unlinkability represents a major issue constructing fuzzy vaults. A method for inserting chaff points with a minimal entropy loss has been proposed in [308]. A brute force attack against fuzzy vaults was proposed in [346]. A collusion attack where the attacker is assumed to be in possession of multiple vaults locked by the same key is presented in [397]. It is demonstrated how to effectively identify chaff points which are subsequently remove to unlock the vault. In [197] vulnerabilities within the concept of a hardened fuzzy vaults are pointed out. In contrast to other concepts (e.g., the fuzzy commitment scheme) the fuzzy vault scheme does not obscure the original biometric template but hides it by adding chaff points, i.e. helper data comprises original biometric features (e.g., minutiae) in plain form. Even if practical key retrieval rates are provided by proposed systems impostors may still be able to unlock vaults in case the helper data does not hide the original biometric template properly, especially if attackers are in possession of several instances of a single vault.

Helper data-based key-generation schemes (e.g., [124, 561]) appear to be vulnerable to attack via record multiplicity in general. If an attacker is in possession of several different types of helper data and valid secret keys of the same user, a correlation of these can be utilized to reconstruct an approximation of biometric templates acquired at enrollment. Additionally, key-generation schemes tend to extract short keys which makes them easier to be guessed in brute force attacks within a realistic feature space. Methods to reconstruct raw biometric data from biometric hashes have been proposed in [281]. Since key-generation schemes tend to reveal worse accuracy compared to key-binding approaches (unless a large number of enrollment samples are applied) these are expected to be highly vulnerable to false acceptance attacks.

The password-hardening scheme [352] has been exposed to be vulnerable to power consumption observations. Side channel attacks to a key generator for voice [349, 350] were performed in [127]. Demonstrating another way of attacking biometric key generators, tolerance functions were identified, which decide to either authorize or reject a user. Another side channel attack against a biometric cryptosystem based on keystroke dynamics was presented in [512]. It is suggested to add noise and random bit-masks to stored parts of the template in order to reduce the correlation between the original biometric template and the applied key. A similar attack to initial steps of error correction decoding in biometric cryptosystems is proposed in [247].

13.2   Attacks Against Cancelable Biometrics

While in the vast majority of approaches security is put on a level with obtained recognition accuracy according to a reference system, analysis with respect to irreversibility and unlinkability (which are the actual security properties) is rarely done. With respect to irreversibility, i.e. the possibility of inverting the used transforms to obtain the original biometric template, the applied feature transformations have to be analyzed in detail. For instance, if (invertible) block permutation of biometric data (e.g., fingerprints in [422] or iris in [178]) is utilized to generate cancelable templates the computational effort of reconstructing (parts of) the original biometric data has to be estimated. While for some approaches analysis of irreversibility appear straightforward for others more sophisticated studies are required (e.g., in [329] irreversibility relies on the difficulty in solving a blind deconvolution problem).

In order to provide renewability of protected biometric templates, the applied feature transformations are performed based on distinct parameters, i.e. employed parameters define a finite key space (which is rarely reported). In general, protected templates differ more as more distant the respective transformation parameters are [325]. To satisfy the property of unlinkability, different transformed templates, generated from a single biometric template applying different parameters, have to appear as distinct as templates of different subjects. This implies that the amount of applicable parameters (key space) is limited by the requirement of unlinkability.

The main aim of attacking cancelable biometrics systems is to expose the secret transform (and parameters) applied to biometric templates. Thereby potential attackers are able to apply substitution attacks. If transforms are considered invertible original biometric templates may be reconstructed. In case of irreversible transforms attackers may reconstruct an approximation of the original biometric template. Comparison scores, calculated in the encrypted domain, could be overwritten [420] and hill climbing attacks [4] could be performed. In [412, 480] attacks against the block re-mapping and surface folding algorithm of [418] based on fingerprints are proposed. Similar to attacks via record multiplicity [472] against fuzzy vault schemes it is assumed that an attacker is in possession of several transformed versions of a single biometric template.

Since most approaches to biometric salting become highly vulnerable in case secret tokens are stolen [266] false accept attacks could be effectively applied. If the salting process is invertible templates may be reconstructed and applied in masquerade attacks. Approaches to biometric salting which do not comprise a keybinding step are vulnerable to overwriting final decisions. Several vulnerabilities in the original concept of the BioHashing algorithm [163] have been encountered in [321]. The main drawback of BioHashing (and other instances of biometric salting) resides in exhibiting low performance in case attackers are in possession of secret tokens.

Fig. 13.2 Example of (**a**) a permuted and (**b**) a re-mapped normalized iris texture

13.3 Security Analysis of Block Re-mapping: A Case Study

In the following, we conduct a security analysis of a cancelable iris recognition system using block re-mapping, assuming that an attacker is in possession of several transformed versions of a single iris template. For providing a classical iris-based cancelable recognition system [178], the normalized iris texture image is first partitioned into blocks of a fixed size (e.g., 64 × 10 pixels). Subsequently, two operations are carried out:

- *Permutation*: The blocks of the texture are rearranged according to a permutation key. In Fig. 13.2a a permutation of an iris texture is shown.
- *Re-mapping*: The former step of randomization of blocks is an invertible operation. Anybody in possession of the permutation key is able to undo this operation without any effort. To provide protection against a compromised key the re-mapping operation is performed. It duplicates some of the blocks atop of others eliminating them from the iris texture, thus making a full reconstruction of the iris texture impossible. The process takes two parameters: The number of blocks used as a source for duplication and the count of how many times these blocks should be reused as a source for the duplication process. In Fig. 13.2b a re-mapped iris texture is shown.

   Additionally, when selecting a source block an eventually computed bit mask can be consulted to determine how much valuable iris texture is concealed by an eyelash or lid. Blocks with too much concealed area can be ignored as a source for the re-mapping process. This ensures that a sensible amount of iris texture is provided to the matching process instead of duplicating eyelids and lashes all over the place.

Since the block permutation leaves a vulnerability in case of a compromised permutation key it has to be considered less secure (it is actually a salting approach). This is why the focus of the analysis is aimed onto the re-mapping process. Considering an acceptance threshold of 60% of coinciding bits for the system more than 40% of bits have to be removed to prevent an attacker from misusing a compromised template once the permutation has been inverted. Or more precisely, the corresponding amount of iris texture has to be eliminated by the re-mapping process. In addition to the information inferred from the compromised template, an attacker is able to guess missing binary template data by filling the gaps with random noise. Using this method it is expected that he/she will be able to guess about half of the missing feature bits (i.e., template) correctly. This implies that an attacker starting with 50% of known template bits and guessing additional 25% correctly will achieve access to the system since the attacker will be able to synthesize an iris template with 75% of correct bits. This observation requires removal of another 40% of iris texture settling the amount of "has to be removed" iris texture to over 80%. Thus, leaving less than 20% of the iris texture for the original matching process.

Now this will prevent an attacker from gaining access to the system if he/she was able to obtain a single iris template of a user. But what if he/she was able to obtain several templates, each of which containing different parts of the iris texture ("Collusion Attack")? It is most likely that some information the attacker extracts from the differently re-mapped iris templates is identical. In case of two differently re-mapped textures on average about half of the iris texture will be identical while the other half will provide new texture information.

Consequently, in case of a system with a threshold of 60%, a re-mapping process leaving little less than 20% of original iris texture to the system and an attacker who was able to obtain two iris templates of the same user with different re-mapping will have about 30% of iris texture at his hands. This is because he knows little less than 20% of the whole iris texture from the first template and additionally gains a little less than 10% from the second one (10% texture identical to the first template + 10% unknown texture). Thus, it is most likely that an impostor will succeed when attempting to gain unprivileged access since he will be able to guess about 35% of additional texture pushing it all up to 65% and past the acceptance threshold of the system. The formula,

$$c + \left(\frac{c}{n}\right) * (n-1),\tag{13.1}$$

allows to calculate the expected percentage of iris texture known to the attacker after he obtained n templates from an eye with c percent of texture left behind by the re-mapping process. With the first template the attacker gains c percent of the texture. Every additional iris template will potentially get the attacker about $c/n * (n-1)$ former unknown information. Equivalently the formula can be written as:

$$c * \left(2 - \frac{1}{n}\right).\tag{13.2}$$

In order to illustrate the expected progression of such a collusion attack some results for a given n and for a value of $c = 20\%$ are listed in Table 13.3. It can be seen in the table that the gain of iris texture stagnates at about 40%.

To prevent such an collusion attack from being successful this formula can be used to calculate the maximum amount of iris texture allowed to be left behind by the re-mapping process by inserting it into the equation:

$$t > c * \left(2 - \frac{1}{n}\right) + \frac{100\% - c * \left(2 - \frac{1}{n}\right)}{2}.\tag{13.3}$$

On the left-hand side of the equation the matching threshold of the system t is found, expressed in percent of matching bits. The right-hand side represents the

Table 13.3 Progression of the considered collusion attack against block re-mapping

No. of iris templates	Expected % of texture known by attacker
1	20
2	30
3	33.3
10	38
50	39.6
100	39.8

information usable to the attacker. Again c stands for the percent of texture left by the re-mapping process and n for the number of templates obtained by the attacker. Additionally, the right-hand side is extended to tribute the fact that the attacker is able to guess half of the iris texture. Transforming the formula it becomes:

$$2 * t - 100\% > c * \left(2 - \frac{1}{n}\right). \tag{13.4}$$

Now taken the case the attacker is able to get a hold on an infinite number of iris templates of a user we extend the formula to:

$$\lim_{n \to \infty} \left(2 * t - 100\% > c * \left(2 - \frac{1}{n}\right)\right). \tag{13.5}$$

Assuming further that 60% of matching bits serve as a threshold for the system, the maximum amount of texture allowed to be left by the re-mapping process is:

$$2 * 60\% - 100\% > 2 * c$$
$$\equiv 10\% > c. \tag{13.6}$$

So to be secure according to the expectation values this cancelable biometric system has to leave less than 10% of texture to the subsystem performing the matching. According to [418] odds are that this will influence the overall performance of the system negatively.

The subsequent experiments are conducted with the USIT implementation of the iris recognition scheme of Ma (see Sect. 3.4) applied to the CASIA.v3-Interval iris database. Before extracting templates, permutation and re-mapping is applied to the normalized iris texture images. In Fig. 13.3a, the ROC behavior of a test run with the original non-cancelable scheme is compared to a test employing permutations.

When introducing the permutation process into the system the performance does not significantly increase or decrease. Based on [178] for this run and all succeeding experiments a block-size of 64×10 pixel was chosen, partitioning the available normalized iris texture into 40 segments. The average EER for ten "permutation only" test runs was 1.223 with a minimum or maximum of 1.199 and 1.267.

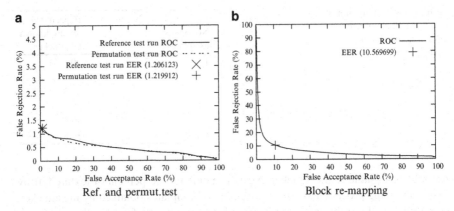

Fig. 13.3 Receiver operation characteristic behavior applied to CASIA.v3-Interval. (**a**) Reference and permutation-only test, (**b**) Block re-mapping with 5% texture

Table 13.4 Parameters and EERs showing improvements reducing the amount of iris texture

No.	Texture left (%)	EER	Source blocks	Reuses
1:	62.1	0.8526	10	2
2:	62.9	1.0942	10	1
3:	43.3	0.8147	10	3
4:	34.2	0.8266	13	3
5:	25.0	0.8408	10	4
6:	23.4	0.8169	6	6
7:	20.0	0.8588	8	5

When introducing the re-mapping process into the system the performance of the system increases surprisingly. In Table 13.4 the parameters and EER values of several test runs are listed. In columns two and three the amount of texture left behind by the re-mapping process and their EER values are listed. All EER values are below the score of the reference run of 1.2. The last two columns list the parameters passed to the re-mapping process. For instance, in the last listed run eight random blocks were selected and copied over five other randomly selected blocks leaving behind 20% of texture. The system still achieves an EER of 0.8588 with so little information left behind by the process. The increase in performance may be explained by the fact that the system uses a key per user (as opposed to a key per database). This introduces additional information into the system referencing a user besides his iris texture. Furthermore, it is well known that certain parts of an iris code are more reliable than other parts. So it comes as no surprise that the system seems to be strongly dependent on the selection of the source blocks. This can easily be observed when conducting several test runs with the same parameter set. For example, when the fifth test run from Table 13.4 was repeated ten times the EER values of those runs oscillated between 0.94 and 1.39 with a mean value of 1.12 and a variance of 0.02.

Table 13.5 Incorporation of the iris mask into block selection influencing EER

No.	Source blocks	Reuses	Allowed masked bits (%)	Unmasked bits (%)	Texture left (%)	EER
A1:	4	10	10.0	–	85.6	2.846
A2:	4	10	10.0	20	99.343	1.244
B1:	2	20	5.0	–	84.803	10.57
B2:	2	20	5.0	20	99.423	3.924
C1:	1	40	2.5	–	85.071	25.897
C2:	1	40	2.5	20	99.713	14.012

Table 13.6 Test runs with less than 20 % of textures left, show the escalation of EERs in this realm

No.	Source blocks	Reuses	Unmasked bits	Texture left (%)	EER
1:	8	5	83.247	20.0	1.49
2:	5	8	83.376	12.0	1.807
3:	4	10	85.600	10.0	2.846
4:	3	13	85.141	9.79	3.946
5:	2	20	84.803	5.0	10.57
6:	1	40	85.071	2.5	25.897

The influence of the block selection onto the EER gets even more evident when comparing test runs which incorporate information about the position of eyelids and lashes for block selection with runs using pure random selection. In Table 13.5 test runs with integration of the bit mask turned on and off are listed below each other. For instance, the test runs A1 and A2 use the same parameters for the re-mapping process (see column two, three and four) but A2 achieves a better EER due to the incorporation of the bit mask (see last column). As can be seen in column five, for A2 the maximum amount of masked bits allowed in a source block for the re-mapping process was 20%. Choosing this parameter value in test run A2, 99.4% of unmasked iris texture is left behind to the matching process while in A1 only 85.6% are left (see column six). Looking again at Table 13.4 it can be seen that as long as 100% to 20% of iris texture are left behind by the re-mapping process the system performs quite well when comparing the EER values to the initially given reference with an EER of 1.2. Unfortunately, this changes when entering the realm below the 20% barrier which has to be undercut as formerly pointed out to circumvent one-time attacks for a system with a threshold of 60% matching bits. And it gets worse when going below the 10% barrier which has to be undercut to prevent collusion attacks. In Table 13.6 the EER values and parameters of test runs below the 20% barrier are listed. It can bee seen that below the 10% barrier the EER increases rapidly. Figure 13.3b shows the ROC curve of a test run containing only 5% of original iris texture. All those test runs have been performed omitting the incorporation of the iris mask for block selection. It is presumed from the test runs

B1, B2 and C1, C2 found in Table 13.5 that the incorporation of the iris mask will improve the EER values of the test runs, but still they will be far from an EER of 1.2 achieved by the reference run.

Overall, the system has to be considered still vulnerable at texture values above and around 10% for a threshold of 60% matching bits. Adding extra security against collusion attacks recommends to leave less than 10% of texture behind going below 8% to 5% for this setup. Unfortunately, the EER values of the cancelable biometric system increase rapidly when leaving less then 10% of iris texture to the matching process increasing the FNMR as well as the FMR. Incorporating these two facts it is highly questionable if the system is suitable for practical and secure application.

Chapter 14
Experiments on Iris Biometric Template Protection

Experimental investigations comprise performance evaluations of different types of iris biometric cryptosystems as well as cancelable iris biometrics. All experiments are performed within a unified experimental scenario, giving an overview of different approaches to iris biometric template protection at a glance.

14.1 Experimental Setup

Experiments are carried out on the CASIA.v3-Interval iris database which comprises a total number of 2,639 320×280 pixel iris images of 250 persons yielding 396 classes allowing a comprehensive evaluation. For preprocessing, the USIT CAHT algorithm (see Sect. 3.4) is employed. Since some biometric template protection schemes require an extraction of biometric templates a priori, we use the USIT implementation of the algorithm of Masek [335] and the algorithm of Ma [323]. Both feature extraction techniques, which extract iris-codes of size 10,240 bit, are described in detail in Sect. 3.4. For both feature extraction methods the ROC curves and binomial distribution of HDs between pairs of iris-code extracted from different subjects are plotted in Fig. 14.1. The according means (p), standard deviations (σ), degrees of freedom (DoF), and recognition rates in terms of FRR, FAR, and EER are summarized in Table 14.1.

14.2 Iris Biometric Cryptosystems

The first scheme investigated represents an instance of biometric key-binding, following the fuzzy commitment scheme of Hao et al. [184]. In the original proposal a 140-bit cryptographic key is encoded with Hadamard and Reed–Solomon codes. For the applied feature extraction of Ma and Masek the application of Hadamard

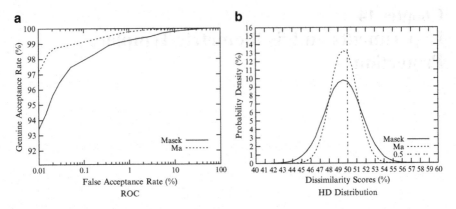

Fig. 14.1 Feature extraction: (**a**) ROC curves and (**b**) binomial distribution of HDs between different pairs of feature vectors for both feature extractors

Table 14.1 Feature extraction: Performance measurements for the feature extraction algorithms of Masek and Ma

Algorithm	p	σ	DoF (bit)	FRR/ FAR (%)	EER (%)
Masek	0.4958	0.0202	612	6.59/ 0.01	1.29
Ma	0.4965	0.0143	1232	2.54/ 0.01	0.89

DoF: degrees of freedom

codewords of 128-bit and a Reed–Solomon code $RS(16, 80)$ exhibits the best experimental results for committing 128-bit keys [526]. At key-binding, a $16 \cdot 8 = 128$-bit key is first prepared with an $RS(16, 80)$ Reed–Solomon code. The Reed–Solomon error correction code operates on block level and is capable of correcting $(80 - 16)/2 = 32$ block errors. Then the 80 8-bit blocks are Hadamard encoded. In a Hadamard code codewords of length n are mapped to codewords of length 2^{n-1} in which up to 25% of bit errors can be corrected. Hence, 80 8-bit codewords are mapped to 80 128-bit codewords resulting in a 10,240-bit bit stream which is bound with the iris-code by XORing both. Additionally, a hash of the original key is stored. At authentication, key retrieval is performed by XORing a given iris-code with the commitment. The resulting bit stream is decoded applying Hadamard decoding and Reed–Solomon decoding afterwards. The resulting key is hashed and compared to the stored one yielding successful key retrieval or rejection.

Another type of fuzzy commitment scheme was proposed in [52]. Motivated by the observation that the system in [184] does not maintain the reported performance rates on data sets captured under unfavorable conditions, a more effective error correction decoding is suggested. In the proposed technique, which is referred to as min-sum decoding, iris-codes of 2,048 bits are arranged in a two-dimensional manner. In the original system, a 42-bit key is encoded with a two-dimensional Reed–Muller code such that each 64-bit line represents a codeword and each 32-bit column represents a codeword, too. To obtain the helper data, the iris-code is XORed with the two-dimensional Reed–Muller code. It is shown that by applying a

Fig. 14.2 Biometric key generation: (**a**) preprocessed iris texture (45° to 135° and 225° to 315°) (**b**) feature extraction for 8 × 3 pixel blocks based on the approach in [424] and (**c**) in [429]

row-wise and column-wise min-sum decoding, the recognition performance comes near practical boundaries. In order to adapt the system to the applied feature extraction methods, 8,192 bits of iris-codes are arranged in 64 lines of 128 bits (best experimental results are achieved for this configuration). To generate the commitment, a 56-bit key is used to generate the error correction matrix. Since Reed–Muller codes are generated using Hadamard matrices and each line and each column of the resulting two-dimensional code represents a codeword, $2^n + 1$ codewords define a total number of 2^{n+1} codewords. Due to the structure of the error correction code, $2^{7 \cdot 8} = 2^{56}$ possible configurations of the $128 \times 64 = 8,192$-bit error correction code exist. At authentication, a given iris-code is XORed with the commitment and iterative min-sum decoding is applied until the correct key is retrieved or a threshold is reached.

In addition, the iris-biometric key generation schemes proposed in [424] and [429] are evaluated. Based on the idea of exploiting the most reliable parts of iris textures, biometric keys are extracted, long enough to be applied in common cryptosystems, i.e. cryptographic keys are directly derived from biometric data. After preprocessing, parts of the iris which mostly comprise eyelashes or eyelids are discarded (315° to 45° and 135° to 225°). It has been shown that distinct bits parts of biometric data exhibit higher reliability than others [196]. For both approaches, several enrollment images are captured and preprocessed in a common manner. Feature extraction based on discretization of blocks of preprocessed iris textures is performed detecting the most constant parts (those which rarely flip) in iris textures, which are encoded and subsequently concatenated in order to produce a key (masks which point at user-specific reliable parts are stored for each subject).

In the scheme proposed in [424] grayscale values of all included pixels in according blocks are mapped to a natural number in the range of [0,3] defining the codeword of the block. This process is schematically illustrated in Fig. 14.2b. A binary matching-code, pointing at matching codewords, is extracted from comparing all enrollment samples and large connected areas of matching codewords (clusters) are detected applying a context-based analysis. Finally, the most constant codewords of the extracted iris-codes are concatenated to generate the key, i.e. the key is formed by codewords of discretized pixel-blocks which are detected to be the most stable ones. In order to construct a secure template the resulting key is XORed with a randomly chosen codeword of a Hadamard code in order to provide some error tolerance, i.e. the proposed scheme represents a combination of key generation and key binding.

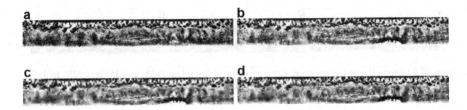

Fig. 14.3 Image compression: Different compression standards applied to an iris texture. (**a**) Original, (**b**) JPG, (**c**) J2K, (**d**) JXR

The biometric cryptosystems presented in [429] represents a pure key generation scheme. Real-valued feature vectors are obtained from texture analysis based on pixel-blocks, which is shown in Fig. 14.2c, and image quality measurement techniques are utilized to calculate appropriate intervals for these. Subsequently, the most reliable pixel-blocks are detected using context-based texture analysis and encoded in order to construct an according key. For each pixel-block of pairs of enrollment samples the peak signal-to-noise ratio (PSNR) is calculated and features within clusters of high PSNR values are detected. According to the obtained PSNR values, adequate intervals are defined and encoded using several bits. At the time of authentication, selected features of a given sample are mapped into intervals where according codewords are returned. By concatenating the bits of all returned codewords a biometric key is constructed.

14.3   Image Compression and Signal Degradation

Due to the sensitivity of template protection schemes it is generally conceded that deployments of biometric cryptosystems require a constraint acquisition of biometric traits. Therefore, any sort of signal degradation which may be caused by compression algorithms [70] is believed to endanger the reliability of such systems. In the following, different types of image compression standards are utilized to generate compact iris biometric data: JPG (ISO/IEC 10918), J2K (ISO/IEC 15444), and JXR (ISO/IEC 29199-2). In Fig. 14.3 iris textures compressed by these compression standards are illustrated. Additionally, the impact of signal degradation on the performance of template protection schemes is investigated. Two types of conditions, blur and noise, are considered. Regarding image acquisition, out of focus blur represents a frequent distortion while noise represents an undesirable but inevitable product of any electronic device. In Fig. 14.4 the applied signal degradation is shown for a sample iris texture.

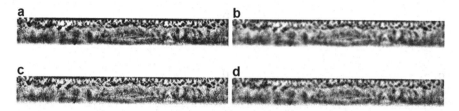

Fig. 14.4 Signal degradation: Different intensities of blur and noise applied to an iris texture. (**a**) Original, (**b**) Blur, (**c**) Noise, (**d**) Blur and Noise

14.4 Cancelable Iris Biometrics

Using a key to seed a pseudo-random-number generator, transformed versions of iris textures are constructed. In the first type of transformation, each block of the target texture is mapped to a block from the source texture. An actual example with a block size of 16×16 pixel is shown in Fig. 12.1b. As stated in [418], using a re-mapping of blocks instead of a permutation should be preferred for the application of cancelable biometrics, as it is not reversible. Source blocks which are not part of the mapping are not contained in the transformed texture at all, and therefore it is impossible to reconstruct the complete original.

The possible key space for n blocks are the n^n different mappings—however many mappings are not suitable as keys. Resulting textures can be close to the original—e.g. if the key corresponds to the identity mapping. In case the mapping is a permutation, as previously mentioned, it still contains all information from the source. The other kind of unwanted key is when it corresponds to a mapping which will not include enough information from the original texture to achieve sufficient matching performance—e.g. a mapping which maps all blocks to the same source block.

Distinct properties are required for mappings generated from a key in order to allow this key. The number of used source blocks should be within a reasonable choice of $[a;b], 1 < a \leq b < n$, and the re-mapped texture also should be sufficiently different from the original. Using 30 blocks was found to be a reasonable number according to experiments, there would be 30^{30} or about 2^{147} different mappings. When requiring a number of blocks to be present, the number of mappings will be reduced, down to 30! or about 2^{107} with only permutations. When, for example, using only derangements out of those, so no block retains its original position, the number would be further reduced to about 2^{106} possibilities. Treating them all as keys still has the problem that many keys are close to each other—so this cannot directly be seen as possible key strength. In the experiments, randomly generated keys out of all possibilities are applied, so they include a degradation in matching performance from such similar keys. Results from settings with a smaller number of overall blocks have a greater chance of containing similar keys, so the effect is more notable there.

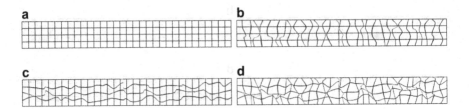

Fig. 14.5 Grid-based image wrapping technique applied to preprocessed iris textures. (**a**) Regular grid, (**b**) Wrapped horizontally, (**c**) Wrapped vertically, (**d**) Combined wrapping

The second type of transformation is a distortion called mesh warping [582]. In this approach the texture is re-mapped according to a distorted grid mesh laid over it. A key is used to specify one particular distortion, by offsetting each vertex in the original mesh by some amount. This is done by starting with a regular grid placed over the texture, in which the vertices are then randomly displaced using the key as seed to a pseudo-random-number generator.

The transformation distorts the texture by sampling each pixel in the target texture from the corresponding area in the source texture, so that each vertex of the source mesh is placed to its translated position in the target mesh, interpolating pixels inside grid cells accordingly. In the applied version, this works in two passes, distorting rows along the offset of vertical splines through the mesh vertices, and then columns along offsets of horizontal splines. In the case of miniaturization, a box-filter is applied to rows and columns, and linear interpolation is used in case of magnification. An illustration for the two passes is shown in Fig. 14.5, an example of the transformation applied to a sample iris texture is shown in Fig. 12.1c. Due to the interpolation strategies applied, the transformation is non-reversible as the original data may not be exactly recovered even if the warping parameters are known. The effect of non-revertability is more pronounced of course in the case of miniaturization.

The maximum theoretical key space is the number of different meshes we can generate by offsetting vertices. It is m^n if n is the number of vertices, and m is the number of possible offsets for one vertex. When choosing these parameters, the grid should not be distorted so much that large areas of the source texture are compressed to a single pixel in the target or are overlapped by other parts, as there may not be enough information left for matching. On the other hand, if the distorted picture resembles the original too closely, it is not useful as a key-dependent signal either.

A realistic size used in our experiments would be a grid of 32×32 pixel cells— for our 512×64 pixel texture a regular grid with 16×2 vertices inside the texture can then be fit over it. If each vertex can be moved by 8 pixels horizontally and vertically, there are 17^2 possibilities and a total of 289^{32} different transformations. Like in the case of re-mapped blocks, many transformations are very similar though. Using only 8 vectors with maximum offset as possible translations for each vertex, the total number of possible transformations would be $8^{32} = 2^{96}$. Like in the case

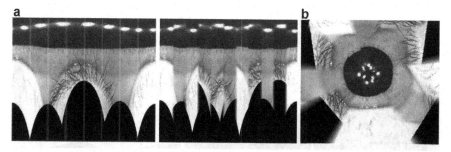

Fig. 14.6 Block-permutation in polar coordinates applied to a sample iris image. (**a**) Polar coordinates, (**b**) Polar permutation and result in image space

of re-mapped blocks, we use a pseudo-random-number generator to generate one of the possible transformations for each key and therefore the experimental results use random offsets out of all possibilities. The effect of similar keys is therefore again reflected in the results, especially when there is a small parameter space.

Typically, these transformations are applied to normalized iris textures as being suggested in [178, 623]. In this case, only feature extraction itself can be influenced by the transformed data; however, the unprotected sample data is subject to iris detection and texture unwrapping which can be seen as a part of the matching process (in this case, this process deals with data subject to privacy constraints).

When applying the transforms to rectilinear iris data we have the advantage that after having acquired the image, the transformation can be conducted immediately, eventually even integrated into the acquisition process. This is especially beneficial when viewing the biometric system as a "black box" we cannot trust—transformation is separated here from any further processing and specifically from the recognition process itself. A possible disadvantage are potential difficulties when detecting and unwrapping the iris texture from transformed image data as we shall see.

Running a block permutation or mesh warping on the rectilinear iris image would render the image useless for any further processing, especially iris texture segmentation would of course fail. Iris detection and texture unwrapping as implemented for almost all iris recognition techniques can only be successful if the quasi-circular nature of the iris texture boundaries (inner pupil and outer sclera boundary) is preserved. In order to accomplish this, we transform the image to polar coordinates using the center of the pupil as origin (see Fig. 14.6a).

In this polar space, permutations can be applied as follows. As depicted in Fig. 14.6a, the image data is cut into vertical stripes which can be subsequently permuted. To reduce the impact of high frequency block boundaries, we use a blurred edge overlay, which basically softens the edges before it overlays a block onto another block. By using the same block multiple times and carefully dropping other blocks out, it is possible to achieve a non-invertible block re-mapping. An example of a block permutation together with the corresponding reconstruction in the image domain can be seen in Fig. 14.6b.

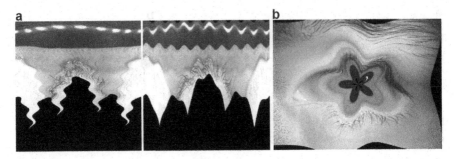

Fig. 14.7 Sinoid distortions in polar coordinates applied to a sample iris image . (**a**) Sine applied along x- and y-axis, (**b**) Image space: Sine along y-axis

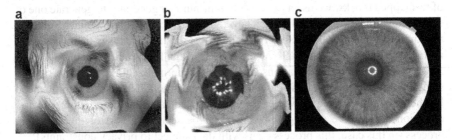

Fig. 14.8 Examples in image domain ((c) fits the proposed approach better). (**a**) Perm. and sinoid distortion, (**b**) Corrupted pupil border, (**c**) Optimal image

In addition to block re-mapping, a composition of arbitrary functions can be used as a warping function, still the pupil borders need to remain intact. Therefore, the warping needs to either leave these borders unchanged or apply translations only in direction of the axis which represents the angle in polar space. For simplicity and mere testing if warping would gain any further advantages, we apply a sine function with amplitude and frequency as parameters. An example can be seen in Fig. 14.7a—in the left image, the distortion is applied along the x-axis, which preserves the pupil borders. The right image shows a distortion parallel to the y-axis, which cannot be used, as it distorts the pupil border as can be seen in Fig. 14.7b.

A combination of sinoid distortion and block permutation in polar coordinates can be seen in Fig. 14.8a, which demonstrates that such a combination is feasible in principle. Contrasting to this, Fig. 14.8b reveals that in some cases even the pupil border is distorted (caused by inaccuracies in finding the pupil center and by the fact that those boundaries often do not exactly correspond to circles) and that eye lashes seem to get scattered over the entire image with obvious impact on iris texture segmentation.

Figure 14.8c shows an example image taken from the UPOL iris image database (see Sect. 3.1), which better fits our approach as there are no occlusions and as

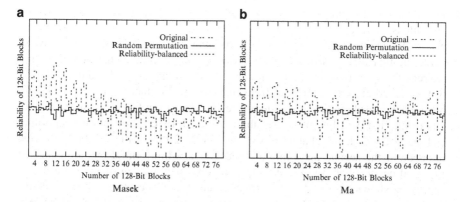

Fig. 14.9 Distributions of reliability within 128-bit blocks for unaltered templates, randomized templates, and the proposed BF for (**a**) Masek and (**b**) Ma (training set of 20 subjects)

almost the entire image is covered by iris texture. However, typical iris image data do not look like this. As shown in [143], recognition performance significantly suffers when applying the transformations to rectilinear iris image data taken from classical iris databases.

14.5 Performance Evaluation

We start with the evaluation of the described fuzzy commitment schemes.

Due to the fact that error correction codewords are designed to correct a fixed amount of errors, an equal level of biometric entropy across the entire binary template is desirable in order to utilize error correction capacities efficiently. In order to estimate per-algorithm distributions of block-wise bit-reliability, genuine and non-genuine comparisons are performed on a training set following the method described in [426, 441]. For each employed feature extraction method, the corresponding reliability is approximated in a separate training stage. Figure 14.9 illustrates distributions of reliability within 128-bit blocks. Subsequently, bits are reordered to obtain an equal level of reliability. These data also facilitate an efficient means of fusing iris templates from two different algorithms. The corresponding iris code bits are first rearranged in ascending order with respect to bit reliability. Based on a per-algorithm reliability distribution an ideal permutation of bit positions is derived for each algorithm and applied to reorder given samples such that the first bits represent the most reliable ones and the last bits represent the least reliable ones. To achieve a uniform distribution of errors per bit-block (with respect to the training set), bits at bit positions with low reliability have to be arranged in bit-blocks together with bits originating from bit positions which exhibit high reliability and vice versa. For this purpose the first $N/2$ bits of reliability-ordered iris codes of both algorithms are fused into a single template of length N. The fusion is performed in a way such that alternating single bits of each algorithm are set (bits are interleaved), while the first $N/2$ bits of reliability-ordered iris code bits of the first algorithm are read from left to right and the first $N/2$ bits of reliability-ordered iris code bits of the second algorithm are read from right to left. In other words, the first n-bit block of the resulting bits fusion template consists of the first $n/2$ (most reliable) bits of the first $N/2$ bits of the reliability-ordered iris code of the first algorithm and the last $n/2$ (least reliable) bits of the first $N/2$ bits of the reliability-ordered iris-code of the second algorithm and vice versa, while central bits are expected to reveal equal reliability. In addition, a random permutation of iris code bits is applied, as shown in Fig. 14.9. Performance rates with respect to different structures of iris-codes, based on the described feature extraction algorithms of Masek and Ma and the construction of fuzzy commitment schemes, are plotted in Fig. 14.10a–f. Compared to unaltered iris-codes, the random permutation (RP) and the reliable bit rearrangement (RB) achieve improved key retrieval rates since error correction is designed to correct a stable amount of bit errors within blocks of codewords. The improvement of key retrieval rates obtained from an adaption of biometric data to error correction configurations represents an important observation. Tables 14.2 and 14.3 summarize the resulting key retrieval rates for the feature extraction of Masek and Ma, respectively.

Performance rates for the fuzzy commitment scheme, in which min-sum decoding is applied, are illustrated in Fig. 14.11. In this approach, a limited number of line-wise and column-wise decoding iterations is performed. At FARs of $\sim$0.01%, FRRs of 6.94% and 3.01% are obtained for the algorithm of Masek and Ma, respectively, where for the Log-Gabor-based feature vector significantly less decoding iterations are required.

The constitution of biometric data with respect to reliability can cause vulnerabilities to stored commitments. Chunks of commitments which exhibit low average reliability scores are prone to statistical significant false acceptance. For both feature extraction methods binomial distributions of HDs between different pairs of iris-codes according to different feature vector sizes are plotted in Fig. 14.12a,b. Obviously, smaller parts of iris-codes exhibit higher variations in HDs. The according probabilities of obtaining HDs smaller than error correction capacities at bit-level, up to 25% for a single codeword, with respect to different lengths of chunks, are summarized in Table 14.4. As expected, the obtained probabilities are quite similar to cumulative probabilities of successes in Bernoulli trials of successive coin tosses derived from the according number of degrees of freedom.

In [435] an error correction code histogram attack has been presented. Soft decoding, i.e. the error correction decoding procedure always returns the nearest codeword or a list of nearest codewords, forms the basis of the proposed attack. Iris-codes generated by the applied feature extraction are randomly chosen from an impostor database and successive decommitment is performed for each chunk in soft decoding mode. The number of appearances of each possible codeword is counted,

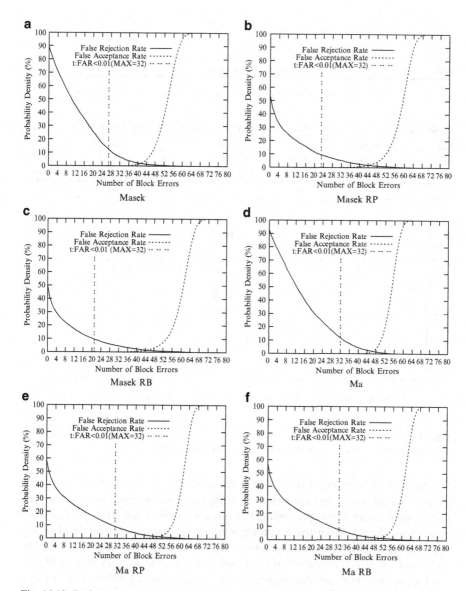

Fig. 14.10 Performance rates: fuzzy commitment schemes based on the algorithm of Masek and Ma applying different orders of bits. (**a**) Masek, (**b**) Masek RP, (**c**) Masek RB, (**d**) Ma, (**e**) Ma RP, (**f**) Ma RB

i.e. for each chunk a histogram is stored. After running an adequate amount of impostor templates against the commitment, histograms are analyzed. A bin which corresponds to the histogram maximum is identified for each chunk, yielding the most likely error correction codeword of the according chunk.

Table 14.2 Performance rates: Fuzzy commitment schemes for the algorithm of Masek

HD	FCS		FCS RP		FCS RB	
FRR at	FRR at	Corr.	FRR at	Corr.	FRR at	Corr.
FAR≤0.01	FAR≤0.01	blocks	FAR≤0.01	blocks	FAR≤0.01	blocks
6.59%	10.87%	27	9.56%	23	9.47%	21

Table 14.3 Performance rates: Fuzzy commitment schemes for the algorithm of Ma

HD	FCS		FCS RP		FCS RB	
FRR at	FRR at	Corr.	FRR at	Corr.	FRR at	Corr.
FAR≤0.01	FAR≤0.01	blocks	FAR≤0.01	blocks	FAR≤0.01	blocks
2.54%	11.93%	32	8.81%	31	7.64%	32

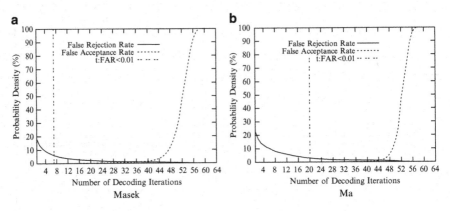

Fig. 14.11 Performance rates: fuzzy commitment schemes based on the algorithm of Masek and Ma applying the min-sum decoding scheme of [52]. (**a**) Masek, (**b**) Ma

The according probabilities of obtaining HDs smaller than error correction capacities at bit-level are summarized in Table 14.4. The obtained probabilities are quite similar to cumulative probabilities of successes in Bernoulli trials of successive coin tosses derived from the according number of degrees of freedom. For the constructed fuzzy commitment schemes target thresholds are set to $80 - 32 = 48$ codewords, where remaining errors are corrected by the Reed–Solomon block-level code. For both of the applied feature extraction algorithms the average number of required impostor templates in order to reach the target thresholds of correctly identified codewords are 124.38 and 251.19, respectively. For both types of fuzzy commitment schemes the error correction code histogram attack outperforms a conventional false acceptance attack, which would require more than 10,000 impostor attempts in the worst case (FAR $\leq$ 0.01%). Even though the applied feature extraction methods might exhibit enough entropy to bind and retrieve 128-bit keys at first glance, these are retrieved at alarmingly low effort. In the considered scenarios, 128-bit chunks of biometric templates would have to exhibit at least 24 degrees of freedom under the assumption that all incorrect codewords occur with

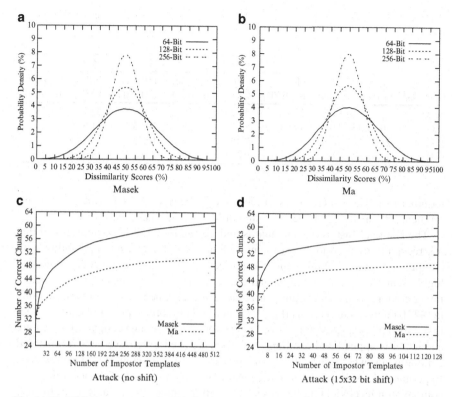

Fig. 14.12 ECC histogram attack: (**a**)–(**b**) binomial distributions of HDs between different pairs of feature vectors of various sizes (**c**)–(**d**) correctly identified codewords for the conducted attack

Table 14.4 Probabilities of HDs smaller than error correction capacities within chunks of both feature extraction algorithms

Length of chunks	$P(HD < 0.25)$ (%)		DoF per chunk	
	Masek	Ma	Masek	Ma
64-bit	5.57	3.61	3.83	7.7
128-bit	3.18	1.13	7.65	15.4
256-bit	1.12	0.13	15.3	30.8

$\sum_{i=0}^{0} B(4,i) \simeq 6.25\%$, $\sum_{i=0}^{1} B(8,i) \simeq 3.52\%$,
$\sum_{i=0}^{3} B(16,i) \simeq 1.06\%$, $\sum_{i=0}^{7} B(32,i) \simeq 0.11\%$

the same probability [435]. Different settings of the attack are considered in order to reduce the number of impostor templates necessary to retrieve secret keys. In [497] it is suggested to apply several circular shifts to binary feature vectors to construct diverse templates. In the applied feature extraction algorithms chunks of 512 bits originate from horizontal texture stripes, i.e. a circular shift of 256 bits corresponds to a rotation of the iris by 180°. In case 15 shifts of size 32 bit are applied to iris-codes prior to decommitment, significantly fewer impostor templates are

Table 14.5 Image compression: Summarized experiments for both feature extraction methods and fuzzy commitment schemes for various image compression standards

			Ma			Masek		
			HD	FCS		HD	FCS	
			FRR at	FRR at	Corr.	FRR at	FRR at	Corr.
Compress.	∅ PSNR	∅ Size	FAR≤0.01	FAR≤0.01	blocks	FAR≤0.01	FAR≤0.01	blocks
None	–	1.00	2.54%	5.90%	32	6.59%	8.01%	28
JPG	20.21 dB	0.05	5.55%	8.18%	32	10.93%	11.58%	27
J2K	21.92 dB	0.05	4.55%	7.49%	32	10.43%	10.23%	27
JXR	22.91 dB	0.05	5.18%	9.44%	32	11.60%	14.92%	26

required to retrieve secret keys, on average 21.98 and 78.64 for the fuzzy commitment scheme based on the algorithm of Masek and Ma, respectively.

The National Institute of Standards and Technology (NIST) demonstrated that iris recognition algorithms can maintain their accuracy and interoperability with compressed images. While template protection schemes are generally conceded highly sensitive to any sort of signal degradation, investigations on the impact of image compression on recognition accuracy have remained elusive. In the case study in [433], image compression (JPG, J2K, and JXR) is applied prior to feature extraction, i.e. to preprocessed normalized iris textures. After image compression, feature extraction is applied and resulting iris-codes are used to retrieve keys from stored commitments, where commitments are generated using un-compressed iris textures. Experimental results for both feature extraction methods and FCSs according to a compression level yielding file sizes of 5% are summarized in Table 14.5. Results include average peak signal-to-noise ratios (PSNRs) caused by image compression and the number of corrected block errors after Hadamard decoding. The according key retrieval rates are plotted in Fig. 14.13a–f. For both feature extraction methods and both types of fuzzy commitment schemes, characteristics of FRRs and FARs remain almost unaltered in case image compression is applied, i.e. surprisingly, fuzzy commitment schemes appear rather robust to a certain extent of image compression.

In [437], iris textures are successively blurred and noised in order to measure the impact of blur and noise to fuzzy commitment schemes. Again, signal degradation is applied to iris textures prior to key retrieval while iris-codes used to construct the commitment are extracted from unaltered textures. In the experiments, out-of-focus blur is simulated as a Gaussian convoluted with iris textures where B-1 corresponds to $\sigma = 1.2$ (B-0 represents no blur). Thermal noise is simulated as additive Gaussian noise where N-1 corresponds to $\sigma = 30$ (N-0 represents no noise). Experimental results for both feature extraction methods and fuzzy commitment schemes with respect to different combinations of blur and noise are summarized in Table 14.6 and according FRRs and FARs are plotted in Fig. 14.14a–f. In analogy to the compression case, we notice a certain extent of robustness against the signal degradations considered.

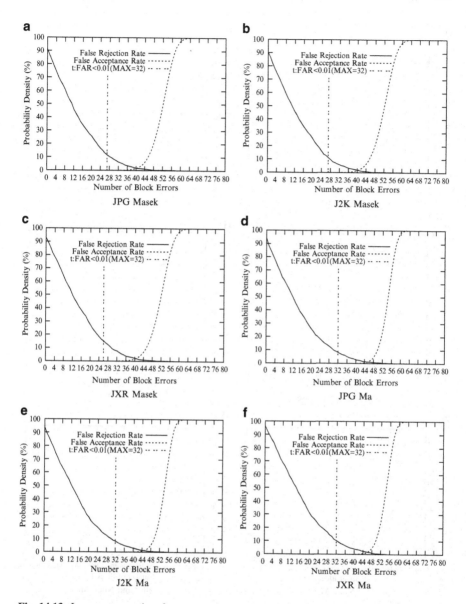

Fig. 14.13 Image compression: fuzzy commitment schemes based on the algorithm of Masek and Ma applying different image compression standards. (**a**) JPG Masek, (**b**) J2K Masek, (**c**) JXR Masek, (**d**) JPG Ma, (**e**) J2K Ma, (**f**) JXR Ma

In contrast to the fuzzy commitment scheme, which represents an instance of biometric key-binding, approaches proposed in [424, 429] implement the concept of key-generation. In [424] discretized blocks of three iris textures are analyzed to detect most stable parts in a context-based manner. Codewords which encode

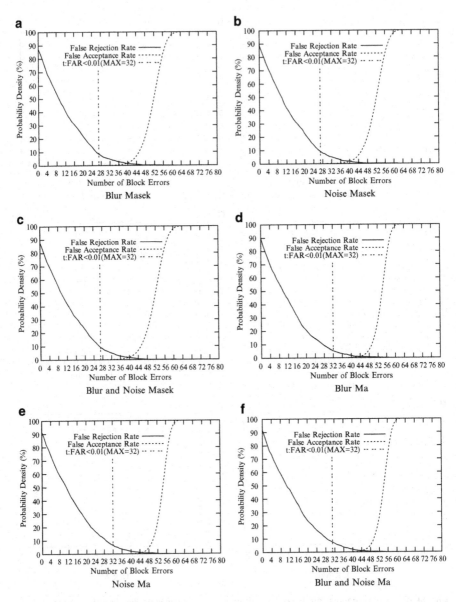

Fig. 14.14 Signal degradation: fuzzy commitment schemes based on the algorithm of Masek and Ma applying different combinations of blur and noise (**a**) Blur Masek, (**b**) Noise Masek, (**c**) Blur and Noise Masek, (**d**) Blur Ma, (**e**) Noise Ma, (**f**) Blur and Noise Ma

four grayscale values, i.e. 2 bits per codeword, are extracted from a given iris texture. At the time of enrollment three input samples are laid on top of another in order to detect matching codewords. Subsequently, the 64 greatest values of these are concatenated to form a 128-bit cryptographic key and according positions are

Table 14.6 Signal degradation: Summarized experiments for both feature extraction methods and fuzzy commitment schemes for various signal degradation conditions

			Ma			Masek		
			HD	FCS		HD	FCS	
Blur	Noise	∅ PSNR	FRR at FAR≤0.01	FRR at FAR≤0.01	Corr. blocks	FRR at FAR≤0.01	FRR at FAR≤0.01	Corr. blocks
B-0	N-0	–	2.54%	5.90%	32	6.59%	8.01%	28
B-1	N-0	19.62 dB	4.36%	5.22%	32	10.94%	8.61%	27
B-0	N-1	19.14 dB	4.36%	6.44%	32	10.33%	9.86%	28
B-1	N-1	16.19 dB	4.27%	6.58%	32	9.54%	9.29%	27

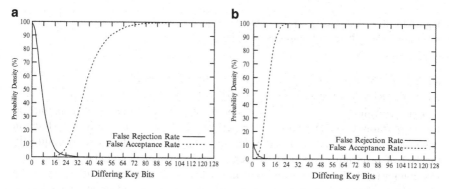

Fig. 14.15 Biometric key-generation: Performance rates for the proposed key-generation schemes in (**a**) [424] and (**b**) [429]

marked in a bit mask of dimension $256/12 \times 64/4 = 21 \times 16$ applying texture blocks of 12×4 pixels. The resulting key is XORed with a randomly chosen 128-bit error correcting codeword of a Hadamard code, capable of correcting up to 25% of occurring bit errors, i.e. the system is capable of correcting the remaining errors after key-generation. Performance rates of the proposed scheme are plotted in Fig. 14.15a where error correction is configured to correct 16 bit-errors yielding an FRR of 7.24% at an FAR less than 0.01%.

The system presented in [429] operates as pure key-generation scheme, i.e. extracted keys have to match exactly in order to achieve successful authentication. In this quantization scheme real-valued feature vectors are extracted by assigning mean grayscale values to texture blocks of size 12×6. In order to construct intervals for each element of the resulting feature vector the PSNR is calculated per block using several enrollment samples. Subsequently, the resulting intervals are encoded using 2 bits and chaff intervals are added. Again, a mask is stored for each subject pointing at the 64 most constant features in order to generate a 128-bit key. Performance rates of the scheme utilizing three enrollment images are shown in Fig. 14.15b achieving

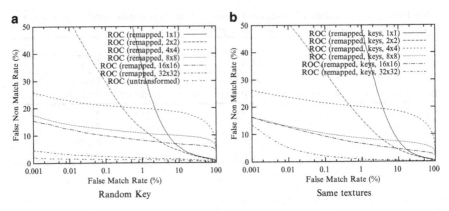

Fig. 14.16 ROC curves for the proposed block re-mapping with different block sizes. (**a**) Random key for each class, (**b**) Same textures for each class

an FRR of 9.83% at an FAR less than 0.01%. In case four or five enrollment textures are used, FRRs decrease to 7.79% and 4.91% at FARs less than 0.01%, respectively.

For the evaluation of cancelable iris biometrics based on block re-mapping and image warping, two different tests are performed on the entire CASIA.v3-Interval dataset: In the first test, a random key is assigned to each class, subsequently the HD of resulting iris-codes between any two images is calculated (3,517,878 iris comparisons, 9,008 of which are intra-class comparisons). If irises from the same class match worse after transformation, or irises from different classes match better after transformation, this is seen in the match results as increased FNMR and increased FMR, respectively. For feature extraction and matching, the USIT implementation of the algorithm of Ma is used (see Sect. 3.4). Corresponding results employing the feature extraction of Masek can be found in [143].

However, even if no degradation in matching performance is observed, this does not mean the key-dependent transformations increase security. For example, applying the same key to each class could lead to good results in the first test. Therefore, another test was performed in order to evaluate how discernible one transformation is from another, when they result from different keys (i.e., key-sensitivity is investigated). For this purpose, an iris class is copied multiple times, and each such class is then assigned a random key as before. If the key-dependent transformations do not lead to sufficiently distinct features, in this case it will show up as high FMR because features from different classes will match. For this second test, 20 classes with at least 10 samples are selected out of the dataset, and 50 random keys are created for each subject in order to perform a roughly similar number of comparisons to the first test (2,495,000 iris comparisons, 45,000 of which are intra-class).

Figure 14.16a shows the matching results using different block sizes for block re-mapping. For comparison, also the ROC curve for matching without any transformation applied is included. It is the lowest curve, obtaining an EER of

Table 14.7 EER with block re-mapping for different block sizes and random keys for each class

Size (pixel)	56×7	64×8	73×9	85×10	102×12	128×16
Blocks	81	64	49	36	25	16
EER (%)	1.3	1.6	1.2	1.2	1.2	1.6

Table 14.8 EER with block re-mapping for different block sizes and same textures for each class

Size (pixel)	56×7	64×8	73×9	85×10	102×12	128×16
Blocks	81	64	49	36	25	16
EER (%)	0.2	0.4	0.2	0.2	0.3	1.0

about 1.1% with the used data and according implementations. Applying random re-mappings of 32×32 pixel blocks (only 32 such blocks fit into the used 512×64 pixel textures), matching performance decreases, with a resulting EER of 1.6%. Matching performance decreases further using 16×16, 8×8 and 4×4 pixel sized blocks—which corresponds to 128, 512, and 2,048 blocks, respectively. The resulting EERs are 7.0%, 10.3%, and 17.6%. Surprisingly, for the case of 2×2 and 1×1 blocks, where the latter amounts to a random re-mapping of single pixels, EER values decrease again to 5.6% and 7.3%. This means that even textures looking like random noise can be classified by the matching algorithm to some extent. Instead of quadratic blocks, blocks also can be rectangles. Table 14.7 compares the matching results when using different rectangular grid sizes for the block re-mapping, from fitting 81 blocks of 56×7 pixels to the 512×64 texture, down to fitting 16 blocks of 128×16 pixel. The used sizes all obtain EERs below 1.6%. We notice that we are able to obtain almost identical behavior as compared to the original algorithm when choosing appropriate block re-mapping parameters.

Figure 14.16b shows the result of using the same block sizes as Fig. 14.16a, but now using the same images and only different keys for each class, to get an indication on the security of the keys, as described earlier. The big 32×32 pixel blocks obtain an EER of 0.8%, which in this case is an indicator for how distinct keys are from each other. As all classes use the same images, it means despite having different keys and therefore different block re-mappings, they were still close enough to match. In case actual eye classes are used instead of only copies with different keys, a block size of 4×4 pixels yields the worst results. The rectangular block sizes in Table 14.8 all result in an EER below 1%. Overall, the best results from the compared sizes are obtained when using 73×9 or 85×10 pixel sized blocks, with an EER of 1.2% for normal matching and 0.2% when only comparing different keys.

When using the mesh-warping transformation, the size of the used mesh as well as the range of random offsets available can be adjusted. Figure 14.17a compares matching performance when using a fixed grid with 128 vertices, consisting of 16×16-pixel sized blocks (note the expression 32 × 4 in the legend of the figure designates the number of 16×16 pixel blocks that can be accommodated in our texture patch). In the transformed grid, varying ranges for the horizontal and vertical

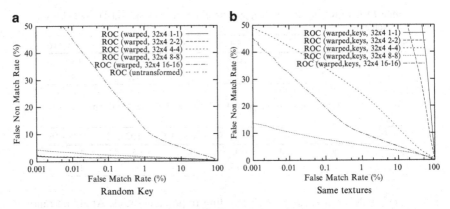

Fig. 14.17 ROC curves for Ma warping a grid of 32×32 pixel blocks by different amounts. (**a**) Random key for each class, (**b**) Same images for each class

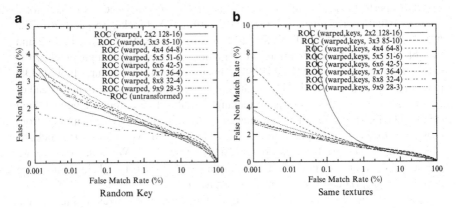

Fig. 14.18 ROC curves for Ma warping with different (*rectangular*) block sizes. (**a**) Random key for each class, (**b**) Same textures for each class

pixel offsets of each mesh vertex are used. An offset in the range of 8 pixels increases the EER to 1.6%, an offset of 16 pixels to over 6%. In the case of 8 pixels offset and a 16 pixel grid, in the worst case two vertices can coincide if they are offset by the maximum of 8 pixels towards each other. In the case of 16 pixels however, the grid will overlap often, which loses even more information and also introduces additional features to the transformed texture. Figure 14.17b shows the result when using the same iris textures in each class again. As expected, using only small translation offsets results in high FNMR, as transformations are too similar. The case of 8×8 pixel offsets with an EER of 4% has the best result of the compared offsets for 16×16 pixel blocks.

Always using half the block size as maximum offset, Fig. 14.18a and b compare different (rectangular) block sizes. The EER for matching always stays below 1.6% with the used sizes. Using a grid of only 4 nodes has the lowest EER with 1.2% for the matching test, but in Fig. 14.18b this results in high FNMR when keeping the same FMR, which means keys are often similar. Looking at all compared parameters, the best result is using a mesh with 9×9 vertices and offsets of up to 28×3 pixel—with an EER of 1.3% in Fig. 14.18a and an EER of 0.9% in Fig. 14.18b. The best parameters found for block re-mapping resulted in an EER of 1.2% when applying the transformation instead of 1.1% without transformations. For the mesh-warping transformation, our tests resulted 1.3% instead of 1.1% EER. This means that it is possible to maintain ROC values (only a very slight degradation is observed) when the key-dependent transformations are used in case appropriate parameters are chosen.

Chapter 15
Advances, Applications, and Challenges

Biometric cryptosystems and cancelable biometrics offer several advantages over generic biometric systems. The most important advantages are summarized in Table 15.1. These major advantages over conventional biometric systems call for several applications. In order to underline the potential of both technologies two essential use cases are discussed in detail. With respect to the design goals, biometric cryptosystems and cancelable biometrics offer significant advantages to enhance the privacy and security of biometric systems, providing reliable biometric authentication at a high security level. Techniques which provide provable security/privacy, while achieving practical recognition rates have remained elusive (even on small datasets). Additionally, several new issues and challenges arise deploying these technologies [70].

15.1 Encryption/ Decryption with Biometric Keys

Biometric cryptosystems aim at extracting a key from a biometric measurement or binding a key to a biometric template. The most apparent application of biometric cryptosystems is biometric-dependent key release for conventional cryptosystems. In order to replace insecure password- or PIN-based key release, biometric cryptosystems are introduced [546], be it key-binding or key-generation schemes. The operation mode "encryption/ decryption with biometric keys" is illustrated in Fig. 15.1. Once a user has registered with the biometric cryptosystem, cryptographic keys are released upon presenting biometric traits to the system. These biometric-dependent keys are then transferred to the applied cryptographic algorithm and plain data is encrypted. Several approaches to biometric cryptosystems fulfill the requirement of generating sufficiently long cryptographic keys to be used in symmetric cryptosystems (in most cases 128-bit keys [529]). Except for a few (e.g., [169]), most schemes fail to extract an adequate amount of information to construct public key infrastructures.

C. Rathgeb et al., *Iris Biometrics: From Segmentation to Template Security*, Advances in Information Security 59, DOI 10.1007/978-1-4614-5571-4_15, © Springer Science+Business Media, LLC 2013

Table 15.1 Major advantages of biometric cryptosystem and cancelable biometrics

Advantage	Description
Template protection	Within biometric cryptosystems and cancelable biometrics the original biometric template is obscured such that a reconstruction is hardly feasible
Secure key release	Biometric cryptosystems provide key release mechanisms based on biometrics
Pseudonymous auth.	Authentication is performed in the encrypted domain and, thus, is pseudonymous
Revocability of templates	Several instances of secured templates can be generated
Increased security	Biometric cryptosystems and cancelable biometrics prevent from several traditional attacks against biometric systems
More social acceptance	Biometric cryptosystems and cancelable biometrics are expected to increase the social acceptance of biometric applications

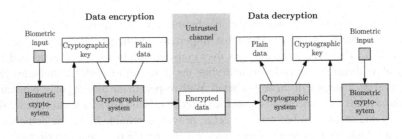

Fig. 15.1 Encryption and decryption of information with keys of biometric cryptosystems

Subsequently, encrypted data is transmitted via any untrusted channel. In order to decrypt the cipher text, again biometric data is presented to retrieve the correct key. It is important to point out that by using biometric keys in generic cryptosystems the generated cipher text is not harder to decipher (in fact it will be even easier to decipher since biometric keys often suffer from low entropy). Key release mechanism, which are in most cases implemented by introducing a second (weak) layer of authentication, represent the weakest link in a cryptographic system [546]. The introduction of biometric-dependent key release brings about substantial security benefits. Eliminating this weak link in cryptosystems, biometric-dependent key-release results in substantial security benefits making cryptographic systems more suitable for high security applications.

15.2   Pseudonymous Biometric Databases

Biometric cryptosystems as well as cancelable biometrics meet the requirements of launching pseudonymous biometric databases [69]. Both technologies provide a comparison of biometric templates in the encrypted domain. While in biometric cryptosystems comparison of biometric templates is performed indirectly by

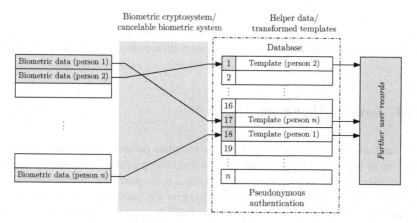

Fig. 15.2 The concept of pseudonymous biometric databases

comparing extracted keys, approaches to cancelable biometrics apply transforms which support the original comparison procedures. Stored templates (either helper data or transformed templates) do not reveal any information about the original biometric data. Additionally, several differently obscured templates can be used in different applications. At registration, the biometric data of the user is employed as input for a biometric cryptosystem or secured by applying cancelable biometrics. The user is able to register with several applications where different templates are stored in each database (as suggested in [418]). Depending on the type of application, further user records are linked to the template. These records should be encrypted where decryption could be applied based on a released key. In Fig. 15.2 the scenario of constructing a pseudonymous biometric database is illustrated.

Due to the fact that stored helper data or transformed biometric templates do not reveal information about the original biometric data high security in terms of template protection is provided. Since biometric comparisons are performed in the encrypted domain, biometric templates are not exposed during comparisons [228]. Since biometric templates are not exposed during comparisons [228], the authentication process is fully pseudonymous and, furthermore, the activities of any subject are untraceable.

15.3   Other Applications

Several other applications for the use of biometric cryptosystems and cancelable biometrics have been suggested. In [70], biometric ticketing, consumer biometric payment systems, and biometric boarding cards are suggested. VoIP packages are encrypted applying biometric keys in [17]. A remote biometric authentication scheme on mobile devices based on biometric keys is proposed in [255] and a framework for an alternative PIN service based on cancelable biometrics is presented in [183]. In [428], helper data-free key-generation is utilized for biometric database hashing. Privacy preserving video surveillance has been proposed in [551].

15.4   Issue of Alignment

One fundamental challenge with respect to template protection schemes represents the issue of alignment, which significantly affects recognition performance. Biometric templates are obscured in both technologies, i.e. alignment of obscured templates without leakage is highly non-trivial. Focusing on iris biometrics, alignment within a template protection scheme can still be feasible, e.g. within an iris biometric fuzzy commitment scheme template alignment can be achieved by applying de-commitments at various shifting positions. In case biometric data or templates are transformed in a non-row-wise manner, e.g. block permutation of preprocessed textures or a permutation of iris-code bits, alignment highly non-trivial. Additional information, which must not lead to template reconstruction, has to be stored. In conventional biometric systems align-invariant approaches have been proposed for several biometric characteristics. So far, hardly any suggestions have been made to construct align-invariant biometric cryptosystems or cancelable biometrics.

15.5   Biometric Characteristics

For a deployment of biometric template protection technologies it is not actually clear which biometric characteristics to apply in which type of application. In fact, it has been shown that even the iris may not exhibit enough reliable information to bind or extract sufficiently long keys providing acceptable trade-offs between accuracy and security. Best performing iris biometric schemes are based on fuzzy commitment and fuzzy vault against which several attacks have been proposed. Practical error correction codes which are essential for such schemes are designed for communication and data storage purposes, such that a perfect error correction code for a desired code length has remained evasive (optimal codes exist only theoretically under certain assumptions [581]). In addition, a technique to generate chaff points that are indistinguishable from genuine points has not yet been proposed. The fact that false rejection rates are lower bounded by error correction capacities [251] emerges a great challenge since unbounded use of error correction (if applicable) makes the system even more vulnerable [497].

Other characteristics such as voice or keystroke dynamics (especially behavioral characteristics) were found to reveal only a small amount of stable information [349, 352], but can still be applied to improve the security of an existing secret.

In addition, several characteristics can be combined to construct multi-biometric cryptosystems (e.g., [565]), which have received only little consideration so far. In these approaches security is enhanced and feature vectors can be merged to extract enough reliable data. While for some characteristics extraction of a sufficient amount of reliable features seems to be feasible, it still remains questionable if these features exhibit enough entropy. In case extracted features do not meet requirements of discriminativity, systems become vulnerable to several attacks (e.g., false acceptance attacks). However, key generation schemes which extract short (but rather discriminative) keys without the use of any helper data can be utilized for the purpose of biometric database indexing [428]. Stability of biometric features is required to limit information leakage of stored helper data. In addition, feature adaptation schemes that preserve accuracy have to be utilized in order to obtain common representations of arbitrary biometric characteristics (several approaches to extract binary fingerprint templates have been proposed, e.g. [55,591]) allowing fusion with iris biometrics in a form suitable for distinct template protection schemes.

15.6 Public Deployment

Biometric cryptosystems and cancelable biometrics represent a rather recent field of research, still several deployments are already available. Precise Biometrics[TM] [400] is a Swedish company which offers solutions to secure match-on-card fingerprint verification. Fingerprints are matched and stored on a smart card, i.e. biometrics act as PIN and password replacement, using the secure environment of the chip. SAFRAN Morpho [462] provides a multibiometric match-on-card technology combining fingerprints and finger vein. In 2011, the new priv-ID and GenKey [401] was formed as a result of a merger between the former GenKey, founded in 2001 and priv-ID B.V, founded in 2008 as a spin-off from Royal Philips Electronics. In order to provide template protection, binary fingerprint templates of 180 bytes are extracted which are referred to as BioHASH®. Extracted templates are renewable by applying "salting," while the small template size of 180 bytes gives the possibility to store templates on contactless RFID or in simple barcodes. PerSay [378], an originally Israeli company which was bought by Nuance in 2010, provides voice biometric speaker verification. The deployed technology represents a multi-factor instance of biometric password hardening which is referred to as VocalPassword[TM]. Securics: The science of security[TM] [477] provides revocable biometric tokens based on the BioToken approach [39] for fingerprints and face biometrics. The EU project TURBINE [128] has received a EU funding of over $9 million. Regarding iris biometrics so far no public deployments of template protection have been made.

15.7 Standardization

As plenty different approaches to biometric cryptosystems and cancelable biometrics have been proposed, a large number of pseudonyms and acronyms have been dispersed across literature such that attempts to represent biometric template protection schemes in unified architectures have been made [49]. Standardization on biometric template protection has been achieved in the ISO/IEC 24745 standard providing guidance on the protection of an individual's privacy during the processing of biometric information. With respect to iris biometrics, several template protection schemes providing practical performance rates (e.g., fuzzy commitment scheme, fuzzy vault scheme) can be mapped to the architecture of a template protection scheme presented in this standard. But, in order to comply with the ISO/IEC 19794 standard on "Biometric Data Interchange Formats," which represents one of the most relevant standards regarding public deployment of biometric systems, rigorous restrictions arise. Regarding iris biometrics (ISO/IEC 19794-6), iris biometric data is specified to be recorded and stored in (raw) image form, rather than in extracted templates which does not comply with any existing approaches to iris biometric template protection.

Chapter 16
Watermarking

In the first section of this chapter, the general relation between watermarking and biometrics is discussed in detail. The second section provides a systematic and critical view of the work done on applying watermarking to enhance biometric systems. In particular, several application scenarios described in literature using both, watermarking and biometric technologies, are reviewed [181, 182]. We follow the idea of distinguishing between template embedding and sample data watermarking schemes. For each scenario, the overall aim of the watermark (WM) technique is explained, required watermark properties, the types of attacks challenging the approach, and the possibility to replace the watermarking scheme by some alternative (cryptographic) approach are discussed. In the next sections, examples for the application of watermarking technology in iris recognition are discussed. First, problems arising in case robust WM is used to embed WM into iris sample data are discussed, in particular, eventual impact on iris recognition performance and an injection attack against robust embedding are shown. Then semi-fragile embedding of iris templates is described. The final section is devoted to the application of passive media security techniques (i.e., media forensics) in iris recognition systems as opposed to active ones (as represented by watermarking).

16.1 Watermarking in Biometric Systems

One of the first ideas to somehow combine biometric technologies and watermarking is "biometric watermarking." The aim of watermarking in this approach is not to improve any biometric system, but to employ biometric templates as "message" to be embedded in classical robust watermarking applications like copyright protection in order to enable biometric recognition after the extraction of the watermark. As a consequence, the WM has to be capable of carrying the template data (capacity requirement) and should not be perceived. The robust WM has to resist against unintentional and malicious cover data manipulations.

C. Rathgeb et al., *Iris Biometrics: From Segmentation to Template Security*,
Advances in Information Security 59, DOI 10.1007/978-1-4614-5571-4_16,
© Springer Science+Business Media, LLC 2013

Vielhauer et al. [560] introduce the general concept and notion of biometric watermarks, also discussed in [6]. One of the most interesting applications in this context is the "secure digital camera" [35], where an iris template of the photographer is embedded into digital images. Canon filed a corresponding patent recently (US Patent Application No. 2008/0025574). A similar idea (hiding iris data) also additionally addressing image integrity is proposed in [185]. Low et al. [318] suggest to embed offline signatures into digital images for copyright protection. Also for 3D graphics data, biometric watermarking has been suggested [356] by embedding an image of the copyright owners' biometric trait into a 3D mesh in a robust manner.

In order to motivate the use of watermarking in the biometric context with the aim of *improving security*, Jain et al. [230] suggest that if only traditional cryptographic techniques are used for the protection of biometric data, the data has to be decrypted somewhere along the way and therefore after decryption, security for the data is not maintained anymore—here (robust) watermarking comes in as a "second line of defense" similar to the digital rights management (DRM) scenario since a watermark is still present after decryption. In this manner, information carried by the watermark can still be retrieved even if cryptographic tools have already been defeated.

There has been a lot of work done during the last years proposing watermarking techniques to enhance biometric systems in some way. Dong et al. [133] try to give a systematic view of the situation in the case of iris recognition by distinguishing whether biometric template/sample data are embedded into some host data ("template embedding"), or biometric sample data is watermarked by embedding some data into them ("sample watermarking"). In the latter case, they only distinguish between robust embedding techniques for database ownership protection and fragile techniques for sample tampering detection. The impact of watermarking on the recognition performance of biometric systems has been investigated most thoroughly in the context of iris recognition also. While Dong et al. [133] do not report on performance degradations when investigating a single watermark embedding algorithm and one iris recognition technique only, Hämmerle et al. [179] find partially significant reductions in recognition accuracy (especially in case of high capacity) when assessing two iris recognition schemes and a couple of robust watermarking algorithms. Similar to the latter results, recognition impact has been observed as well for speech recognition [294] and fingerprint recognition [414] (the latter depending on the type of original which is employed in watermark extraction, thus, this is a non-blind approach).

For fingerprint recognition, watermarking techniques aiming at negligible impact on recognition performance have been designed. This is achieved, for example, by applying two blind robust spatial watermarking methods embedding a character bit string either sparing out fingerprint feature regions (i.e., close to minutiae data) or by maintaining the ridge gradient orientations [174, 543]. This approach has been followed by several other techniques (e.g., [98,354]). On the other hand, recent work by Zebbiche et al. [604, 605] proposes two robust WM schemes for fingerprint images where WM data is embedded into the ridge area ROI only. The aim is to increase robustness of WM due to the concentration onto the ROI, while of course, some impact on recognition performance may be expected by using this idea. In many papers covering the use of watermarking in biometric systems, the authors remain rather vague about the actual aim, content, and required property of the employed watermarking system. A good example is the paper by Hong et al. [198] (although many more do exist) which discusses the application of robust watermarking and symmetric encryption techniques for the exchange of compressed biometric sample data, where they also investigate the impact on accuracy of a fingerprint recognition scheme. Additionally, energy consumption of different variants with respect to the applied compression in a distributed authentication scenario with mobile sensors is investigated. It is not discussed, which functionality the watermark is aimed to fulfill and how a successful attack against the used watermarking system would look like. Consequently, there is also no information about which data is embedded and which attacks against the biometric scheme should be prevented by the usage of watermarking. As a second example, a quantization-based robust watermarking of off-line signatures is mentioned [210]—while robustness against compression is investigated, the actual aim of robustly embedding a watermark is not described.

16.2   Application Scenarios for Enhancing Biometric Systems

Watermarking techniques have been applied in several different application scenarios in order to enhance biometric systems. The following subsections present an overview of different approaches.

16.2.1   Covert (Template) Communication

The aim of watermarking in this approach is to transmit biometric data (not only typically template data but also sample data is considered) hidden into arbitrary carrier/host data (in this manner transmitted sample data cannot be sniffed since an attacker is not aware of the biometric data transmission). For example, a fingerprint image may carry face data or any arbitrary image could include fingerprint minutiae. An attacker should be unaware of the concealed (real) data transfer. Therefore, this is a typical *steganographic* application scenario, which is based on template (or even sample data) embedding.

- *Attack*: An attacker aims at *detecting* the WM in order to be able to intercept the template data transfer.
- *WM properties and content*: As a consequence, the WM has to be capable of carrying the template/sample data (capacity requirement) and has to be undetectable. In the passive wardenscenario, robustness of the WM is not an

issue; however, robustness contradicts the requirement of a non-detectable WM. Blind extraction is required as it is a must for all steganographic application scenarios.

- *Crypto alternative*: There is no cryptographic technique capable of replacing a steganographic approach.

A data hiding approach that targets this scenario is introduced by Jain et al. [226, 231] where fingerprint minutiae data are embedded into an arbitrary host image (scenario 1). A robust amplitude modulation-based watermarking method is used to embed a minutiae data set converted to a bitstream. Zebbiche et al. [603] introduce a robust wavelet-based watermarking method hiding fingerprint minutiae data in fingerprint images (based on a method proposed by Kundur et al. [283]). They argue that an intruder is likely only to treat the fingerprint image instead the embedded data as well, so the scope is also a steganographic one. Khan et al. [254] uses a robust embedding technique to hide fingerprint templates into audio signals. Surprisingly, all proposals use robust embedding techniques which actually destroys the most important steganographic property as outlined above (non-detectability). In order to be able support non-detectability, steganographic (fragile) WM needs to be applied instead of robust schemes. The remaining value of the proposed robust schemes is in communicating embedded templates in a way that the are not *perceived* by a human observer. When applying robust embedding as being proposed, embedded templates resist non-malicious cover data manipulations (which is an advantage over steganographic schemes in the case of an active warden). Thus, the application context has to determine if robust WM or steganographic embedding serves the actual aim of the WM embedding (inperceptability vs. non-detectability).

When considering the application context, we have doubts that it is steganography which is actually most suited or required. In a classical biometric system, a biometric sensor is typically expected to transmit biometric authentication data over a dedicated channel to the feature extraction/matching module and no other types of data, so that it is not clear what is to be gained by steganography under these circumstances. It seems that in many papers, authors rather have confidentiality of embedded template data in mind, but this can only be achieved by using encryption (which is also inconvenient since decryption of the data is required before further processing). So in this scenario, many proposed robust WM schemes seem to represent an attempt to achieve a weak concealment of template content by embedding the data into some host material thereby avoiding encryption. Unfortunately, in this manner, neither the steganographic nor the confidentiality aim can be met.

In a distributed biometric system (as opposed to the classical case discussed before) where authentication data is transmitted over networks where also other type of data is communicated, the idea of applying steganography definitely makes more sense. The work described in [411] is explicitly focused to this application context— after a correlation analysis between host image and two images of different biometric modalities,residual data (sample images subtracted from cover image) is embedded into the middle significant bit of the cover data. Since non-detectability is not plausible considering the embedding strategy, this proposal fits better into the next category (two images are embedded thus enabling multibiometric recognition).

16.2.2 Multibiometric Recognition

The aim of watermarking in this scenario is to embed biometric data into a biometric sample in order to facilitate the employment of a multibiometric technique. The aim is an increased recognition performance due to the use of two different modalities. By using WM techniques, both informations are fused into a single data item which can be transmitted as a whole; however, the aim of using WM for this purpose is hardly ever motivated clearly.

There are two variants: First, biometric template data is embedded into the sample data of a different modality. These template data need to be generated at the sensor site which makes this approach somewhat unrealistic, especially in case of distributed biometric systems with low power sensor devices. The second approach is to embed sample data into the sample data of a different modality, which puts significant pressure to the capacity of the WM scheme. Therefore, in this scenario, sample watermarking as well as template/sample data embedding is used.

- *Attack*: The resulting system is vulnerable in principle against all types of attacks endangering classical unimodal systems systems. In particular, an attacker needs to *embed* sniffed biometric data of one modality into sniffed sample data of a second modality when targeting an injection attack (e.g., face and iris biometric data can be extracted from a single high-resolution image of the subject to be attacked).
- *WM properties and content*: As a consequence, the WM has to be capable of carrying either template or sample data (capacity requirement) and extraction has to be blind, since otherwise, the advantage of transferring only a single data item would be lost by the required re-transmission of the original sample for extraction. It is of advantage if the WM resists unintentional image manipulations like compression or noise insertion, but robustness is not a required property here. In order to prevent an attacker to embed a stolen template, the embedding algorithm has to be dependent on a key. In this context the multibiometric approach also enhances the scheme with respect to resistance against injection attacks, since only samples which have correctly embedded WM data should be accepted by the system.
- *Crypto alternative*: The benefit of embedding additional authentication data with WMs over classical cryptographic schemes is that this may be done in a way where "allowed" manipulations can be conducted on the data. Application of encryption to a concatenation of sample and template data results in slightly more data to be transmitted, but unauthorized embedding of stolen biometric data is prevented by this technique. Furthermore, this approach definitely has no impact on recognition performance as opposed to WM embedding.

Bartlow et al. [24] proposed a framework that encodes voice feature descriptors in raw iris images stored in a database. An asymmetric watermarking and cryptographic method using a public key infrastructure is used. The watermarking method is based on the robust technique by Kutter et al. [284] and is used to track data origin of data stored in centralized biometric databases. Hoang et al. [192] embed fingerprint minutiae in facial images (with fragile watermarks), while Jain et al. [226] embed face data into fingerprint images using a technique classified as being robust. Chung et al. [98, 354] use the same embedding technique as well to embed fingerprint templates into facial images and vice versa, and compare the recognition performance of the resulting systems. They also use this embedding technique as the fragile part of a dual watermarking approach [257, 354] so that doubts remain about the actual robustness properties of the scheme. Vatsa et al. employ robust embedding techniques: in [557], they embed voice features in color facial images, the same group [377, 554, 558] propose to embed facial template data (and additional text data in the first work) into fingerprint sample data using a robust (multiple) watermarking approach. Park et al. [387] suggest to use robust embedding of iris templates into face image data to enable various functionalities, among them proof of database membership, steganographic issues, and of course multibiometric fusion. Kim et al. [258] propose a blind and robust spread spectrum watermarking technique for embedding face template data into fingerprint sample. Maiorana et al. [326] embed dynamic signature properties into the image of a static signature using a robust DCT-Radon transform-based embedding technique.

The approach of Zebbiche et al. [603], employing a robust wavelet-based watermarking method for hiding fingerprint minutiae data in fingerprint images actually fits better into this scenario than into the steganographic one it has originally been suggested for.

Most schemes propose to use robust WMs for embedding and therefore do not provide the capacity for sample embedding (for many modalities, not even for template data). It seems that for this application case, it would therefore be better to abandon the idea of providing robustness but to use fragile or steganographic embedding techniques (eventually protected by error correction coding to provide some limited resistance against channel errors or lightweight signal process-ing). Key-dependent embedding is discussed explicitly only in some algorithms (e.g., [98, 354, 377]) but has turned out to be of importance in this setting. It is somewhat questionable if WM is in fact a suited technology in this context due to its potential impact on recognition performance (since the aim of the entire technique is the improvement of recognition!) and the existence of a sound cryptographic alternative.

A variant of the described ideas is to embed (template or sample) data into samples of the same modality. In this case, two different biometric templates of a single subject can be used in biometric matching which can also lead to improved recognition performance. In this case, only a single sensor has to be applied. This approach will be discussed further in Sect. 16.4.

16.2.3 Two-Factor Authentication

The idea is to enable a two-factor authentication by requiring an additional token providing authentication data. Additional authentication data can be stored on a smart-card which has to be submitted by the holder at the access control site. The smart-card embeds the authentication data into the host sample data using WM technology which is sent to the biometric feature extraction/matching module. Another possibility for the second authentication factor could be a password which is submitted by the user. As a special case, the second authentication factor can be a biometric template stored on a smart-card. In this case, the advantages with respect to improved recognition performance due to the multibiometric nature of the scheme apply here as well.

Security of the overall system is increased simply by introducing an additional but different authentication scheme. The aim of watermarking in this scenario is similar as in the previous one since it is used to embed additional information into sample data (which in the present case comes from a smart-card or from a users' password, whereas in the former scenario data is generated by a different sensor). Again, the appropriateness of WM to be applied in this context is not obvious, for the same reasons as discussed before. This scenario is a case of sample watermarking, only as a special case template embedding can be applied.

- *Attack*: The attacker can utilize a stolen smart-card (or sniffed password) and additional sniffed sample data of the attackers' target subject to fool the system. He/she uses the biometric system pretending to be a legitimate user, but after WM embedding (e.g., of the data stored on the card), the attackers' sample data is *tampered* to match that of the sniffed sample data while not destroying the WM.
- *WM properties and content*: As a consequence, the WM has to be capable of carrying the additional authentication data (capacity requirement: pass phrase, ID, or template data) and extraction has to be blind, since otherwise, the advantage of transferring only a single data item would be lost by the required re-transmission of the original sample for extraction. In order to resist against a manipulation of the attackers' sample acquired by the sensor as described in [180], the WM scheme employed must not be robust. Therefore, only semi-fragile or fragile WMs fit all requirements.
- *Crypto alternative*: The situation is perfectly identical to the multibiometric scenario and shares all corresponding problems discussed before.

A scheme embedding additional classical authentication data with robust watermarking is described in [468]. Here, the embedded signature is used as an additional security token like an additional password. In principle, all techniques developed for the multibiometric scenario could be used in this context; however, the majority of all schemes proposed also employ robust embedding, which is subject to tampering as described before.

Jain and Uludag [226] propose to embed face template data stored on a smart-card in fingerprint images (called senario 2 in the paper while scenario 1 is a steganographic one). Instead of embedding an additional security token also biometric template data from a second sensor can be embedded—in [414] an encrypted palmprint template is embedded into a fingerprint image, where the key is derived from palmprint classes. Since these additional data are not used in multibiometric fusion but serve as independent second token coming from a second sensor, this approach can be interpreted as being both, a multibiometric recognition scheme or a two-factor authentication scheme. Since the employed WM system is a non-blind one, the applicability in a real system remains questionable.

It has to be pointed out that for this as well as for the former scenario, WM is not the only means (and probably not the best one) to communicate the "embedded" data in addition to sample data. Therefore, WM cannot be seen as the key-enabling technology for both of these scenarios. In case WM is selected as the means of transportation for the scenario investigated in this section, fragile or semi-fragile schemes have to be used which usually also have less or no impact on recognition performance.

16.2.4 Sample Replay Prevention

The aim of watermarking in this scenario is to prevent the use of sniffed sample data to fool the sensor. During data acquisition, the sensor (i.e., camera) embeds a watermark into the acquired sample image before transmitting it to the feature extraction module. In case an intruder interferes the communication channel, sniffs the image data and presents the fake biometric trait (i.e., the sniffed sample image) to the sensor (spoofing attack), it can detect the watermark, will deduce non-liveness and will refuse to process the data further. Therefore, the sensor needs to be capable of extracting the WM in addition to embedding it. As a consequence, all image data eventually additionally stored in the template database for some reason also carry the WM which stems from the enrollment process in this case. Consequently, image data from a compromised database cannot be used as fake biometric traits either. In this scenario, sample watermarking is applied.

- *Attack*: An attacker aims at *removing* the WM in order to be able to use sniffed data for replay attacks or as fake traits.
- *WM properties and content*: As a consequence, the WM has to be robust. It has to be detectable in the image as long as the image can be used in the recognition process (note that this corresponds well to the DRM scenario where a robust WM has to be detectable as long as the image is of sufficient quality). The extracted mark needs to carry at least the information "yes, I have been acquired by a sensor" (so eventually zero-bit WM could be used), but could also carry actual sensor IDs. The WM must be detected in blind manner, otherwise the sample would have to be sent unprotected a second time.
- *Crypto alternative*: Encrypting the data after acquisition for transmission provides similar functionality; however, the data needs to be decrypted for feature

extraction and matching, which is a severe disadvantage. In any case, the WM may serve as additional "second line of defence" as it is suggested in the DRM context as well. Generic liveness detection techniques also target the attempt of using sniffed image data to fool the sensor and are a possible alternative method, however, usually at a much higher cost.

The proposed solution by Bartlow et al. [24] exactly targets the database environment. All robust WM algorithms, e.g., those proposed by Uludag and Gunsel [174, 543] could be employed in this scenario. Of course, problems with respect to impact of robust WM on recognition performance are valid in this scenario as well.

16.2.5 Sensor and Sample Authentication

The aim of watermarking in this scenario is to ensure the integrity of the sample data acquisition and transmission process. During data acquisition, the sensor (i.e., camera) embeds a watermark into the acquired sample image before transmitting it to the feature extraction module. The feature extraction module only proceeds with its tasks if the WM can be extracted correctly (which means that (1) the data has not been tampered with and (2) the origin of the data is the correct sensor). If an attacker tries to inject a sniffed image into the communication channel between sensor and feature extraction module for a replay attack or modifies a correctly acquired image in some malicious manner, this is prevented by this approach. The same strategy can be applied to raw image data in the template database (if present). In this scenario, sample watermarking is applied.

- *Attack*: An attacker aims at *inserting* the WM in order to mimic correctly acquired sensor data.
- *WM properties and content*: In contrast to the previous scenario, the WM needs to be unique in the sense that it has to uniquely identify the sensor and carry a unique transaction number or timestamp. Resistance against a WM insertion attack can be achieved by sensor-key-dependent embedding. Since the watermarking scheme has to be able to detect image manipulations, semi-fragile techniques are the method of choice. The WM could also be fragile eventually resulting in every minor modification attempt to be detected. However, each channel error or compression after embedding during transmission will destroy the WM in this case leading to a high false negative rate during authentication which is a highly undesired effect. Therefore, fragile WM can only by used in definitely lossless environments. Especially in semi-fragile watermarking it was found to be highly advantageous to embed image-dependent watermark data in order to prevent an embedding of image-independent watermarks after modifications have been conducted. WM extraction should be blind, otherwise the sample would need to be sent a second time (which would be possible in principle but is undesired due to transmission overhead).

- *Crypto alternative*: Classical authentication protocols can be used to secure the communication between sensor and feature extraction module—a digital signature signed with the private key of the acquisition device can ensure the authenticity of the sensor and the integrity of the image data. However, digital signatures represent separate data which has to be taken care of separately. Cryptographic digital signatures are not capable of providing any robustness against channel errors and unintentional signal processing "attacks" like compression, which is the same as with fragile WM. Additionally, WM eventually provide information about the location where image data tampering has occurred, which could be used to determine if recognition-critical data has been affected (e.g., the iris texture in rectilinear eye images) or to gain information if an intentional attack is the cause of the damaged WM (e.g., if the image data is corrupted by transmission noise "only," we result in evenly distributed tamper locations).

Yeung et al. [598, 599] propose a fragile watermarking technique to add the ability for integrity verification of the captured fingerprint images against altering during transmission or in a database. Also, the method is shown to have little impact on recognition performance. Ratha et al. [419, 423] propose to embed a response to an authentication challenge sent out by a server into a Wavelet Scalar Quantization (WSQ) compressed fingerprint image in order to authenticate the sensor capturing the fingerprint image. If the (fragile) watermark cannot be extracted, either the image has been tampered with or the image does not come from the correct sensing device. Since the approach is bound to a specific format, it is not even robust against lossless format conversions. Wang et al. [567] also introduce a fragile watermarking scheme, however, they propose to embed image-dependent data (i.e., singular value decomposition data) into the image contrasting to the former to approaches by Yeung et al. and Ratha et al. Also, semi-fragile watermarking has been suggested to verify authenticity of biometric sample data. Two different embedding techniques for embedding both, a sample image-dependent signature and a template are proposed by Komninos et al. [265]. PCA features are used as embedded data in [303], the embedded data can as well be used for an approximate recovery of the sample data in [130], and [7] proposes the embedding of robust signatures into fingerprint images.

Finally, [296] use two embedding techniques, the first for checking integrity on a block level using CRC checks, the second providing reversible watermarking (i.e., the sample is reconstructed to the original before data embedding took place) in case the first rates the sample as being authentic. It has to be noted that a combination of the last two scenarios (sample replay prevention and sample and sensor authentication) seems to be highly sensible and desirable. This can also easily be done at low cost, since in both cases the sensor embeds WM information. Kim et al. [257, 354] is the first approach somewhat addressing this issue by proposing a dual WM scheme to protect fingerprint images by using a robust and fragile method.

Overall, it has to be stated that this scenario is not at all specific to biometric systems. The general discussion if (semi-)fragile WM is a sensible alternative to classical authentication protocols in case of image data to be protected applies to the discussed scenario, as well as all corresponding arguments do.

16.2.6 Discussion

While the majority of proposals in the field employs watermarking to enable multibiometric scenarios (with the primary aim of increasing recognition accuracy) or to facilitate steganographic-like scenarios (in order to conceal the transfer of biometric data), we have also identified three scenarios where watermarking has been suggested to help in improving the security of classical uni-modal biometric systems.

We have found that the WM schemes as suggested to be used in the context of biometric systems often exhibit somewhat ad hoc properties and specific requirements are not analyzed in detail. In many cases, the actual WM method proposed does not lead to the desired effect or at least not in an optimal manner. A more thorough analysis of concrete attack scenarios is desirable for many environments in order to tailor required WM properties better to specific demands.

For most scenarios considered, WMs are not the only means to achieve the desired goals (and for some scenarios, WM are definitely not the best means to do so). For the covert (template) transmission scenario, we have found that the steganographic aim itself does only make sense under specific circumstances. In case of making sense, there is no other technique that achieves the same effect. If confidentiality is actually what the aim of WM is, only (additional) encryption can provide this in a sound manner.

Two scenarios use WM as a means to transport additional information embedded into sample data (i.e., multibiometric recognition and two factor authentication). Of course, this can be done in some classical way involving cryptography or not, however, these alternatives usually exhibit the classical disadvantages as compared to watermarking since they cannot provide any robustness even against format conversions. Since we have seen that robustness on the other hand potentially impacts on recognition performance and should therefore be avoided if possible, semi-fragile embedding techniques remain as the only sensible ones here. If schemes of this type can meet corresponding capacity requirements depends on the actual amount of data to be embedded.

With respect to sample replay prevention, WM is an attractive choice from the application viewpoint, since it prevents the encryption/decryption effort of classically securing template or sample confidentiality. However, sniffing of template data is not prevented and in case a different biometric system is not able to detect the embedded mark or does not even support this feature, the approach is flawed (contrasting to encrypting the data, where an attacker simply is not able to access the plaintext at all). Additionally, as already mentioned, in this approach robustness is absolutely a must, therefore caution needs to be paid not to degrade recognition.

For sample and sensor authentication, (semi-)fragile WM can be used as a means to provide the desired aims. The alternative cryptographic techniques provide more security, but on the other hand absolutely no robustness against the slightest modification of the data is achievable. In addition, the "classic" techniques are not able to localize possible data manipulations and authentication data has to be communicated separately.

With respect to WM properties, a disadvantage inherent in many (robust) watermarking schemes when applied to biometric sample data is that of possible negative impact on recognition performance [179]—besides the design of specific watermarking approaches taking this problem into account (e.g., [174, 543]) an entirely different solution is to rely on *reversible* WM schemes [147, 296] which enable to reconstruct the original signal after WM extraction. This property (which is important e.g., in applying WM to medical imagery) fits perfectly into the biometric scenario since it enables recognition with entirely unaffected sample data. However, such schemes typically do not provide enough capacity to embed template data. Another option is to use (semi-)fragile or steganographic embedding techniques, which do offer sufficient capacity and exhibit almost no impact on recognition accuracy. Therefore, in case robustness is not a vital requirement but only a desired property (i.e., multibiometric embedding), it should be either employed in a way not affecting recognition or avoided. Furthermore, blind WM extraction is a must for most scenarios and is highly desirable for the remaining ones. For the WM application cases where template data or even sample data has to be embedded, capacity turns out to be a critical and even limiting factor.

Summarizing, more thorough investigations are required in this field to (1) identify sensible application scenarios for watermarking in biometrics and to (2) select and/or design appropriate WM schemes to support the desired functionalities. We provide some corresponding examples for iris recognition in the subsequent chapter.

16.3 Robust Watermarking in Iris Recognition

As we have seen before, embedding of data with *robust* WM algorithms into iris sample data has been discussed already (e.g., [24, 133]). Overall, we have identified three different application scenarios, where robust WM have been proposed to be employed in order to embed information into sample data: First, embedding of sensor ID-information to prevent replay attacks of sniffed sample data. Second, embedding of signature information of a two-factor authentication system. And third (which also represents the most important application case), embedding of template data into sample data to enable a multibiometric system. In all three application scenarios, a degradation of biometric recognition performance caused by the embedded watermark is highly undesired.

Given the significant number of WM application scenarios where robust WM embedding into biometric sample data is considered, many more corresponding proposals involving *iris sample data* are to be expected. Therefore, it is highly relevant to consider the impact of such robust embedding strategies to iris recognition performance.

Since there is hardly any biometric application scenario where we have original (i.e., not-watermarked) sample data available to detect the WM in the marked image, only *blind* WM are applicable in the context considered here. We consider a variety of robust watermarking techniques in different flavors to assess the impact of robust WM on iris recognition performance [179, 181] in Sect. 16.3.1 and to validate the threat of a tampering attack against a two-factor authentication scheme involving watermarking [180] in Sect. 16.3.2 as follows. We have used some algorithms from the "Watermarking Toolbox" [342] developed by Meerwald for WM embedding and detection [343], additionally more recent wavelet-based schemes have been implemented as well (i.e., Barni, Cao, Chen, Pla, and Wu, see below). Using the WM techniques as listed subsequently, we have representatives for a variety of embedding domains (spatial domain, DCT domain, wavelet approximation domain, wavelet detail subbands), representatives for different embedding strategies (additive spread spectrum vs. quantization-based WM), as well as representatives for different types of WM (binary vs. Gaussian distributed values).

1. *Spatial and DCT-based algorithms*:

   - *Bruyndonckx (shorthanded Bruyn)*: This algorithm operates on 8×8 blocks with modifications on the luminance values where each block is able to obtain one bit of information. A binary sequence is used as watermark [58].
   - *Koch*: Uses a random sequence of concrete image positions. At this positions the DCT coefficients of 8×8 blocks are used for embedding imposing a strict ordering on coefficient triples. The watermark is a binary sequence [262].

2. *Wavelet-based algorithms*:

   - *Barni*: 4-level decomposition. Additive embedding in the 3 finest detail subbands with visual masking. The watermark is a pseudo-random binary sequence [23].
   - *Cao*: Uses a redundant wavelet transform and embeds in the 3 finest detail subbands. Additive embedding by creating a significance mask. A Gaussian distributed random sequence is used as watermark [67].
   - *Chen*: Embedding is done in the approximation subband depending on the watermark length via a bit selection algorithm. The watermark is a black/white image (i.e., a binary sequence) [82].
   - *Dugad*: 3-level decomposition. Uses a Gaussian-distributed watermark sequence. Additive embedding is applied only to a few significant coefficients using an image sized watermark in the detail subbands [139].
   - *Kundur*: 3-level decomposition. Uses a binary value sequence. Locations for embedding are pseudo-randomly selected in the detail subbands. A triple of coefficients at different subbands within the same spatial position is selected. The middle coefficient is quantized [282].
   - *Pla*: Additive proportional embedding in significant trees of coefficients in the detail subbands by visual modeling. The watermark is a Gaussian distributed random sequence [396].
   - *Wu*: 3-level decomposition. The quantization-based watermark is embedded in trees of coefficients. A random binary sequence is used as watermark [583].

- *Xie*: Embedding only in the approximation subband. Selecting the middle of three coefficients by a sliding window. The middle coefficient is then quantized. The watermark is a binary sequence [589].

The implementation of the Watermarking Toolbox (all algorithms but Chen, Barni, Cao, Pla and Wu) allows the free selection of the signature length. We chose either a "normal" standard signature length of 128 bits or 1,000 Gaussian-distributed or binary values, or a "long" signature length of 1,024 bits or 32,000 Gaussian-distributed or binary values to check the signature length influence. For "Xie" the length is limited by the size of the approximation subband (here 80 bits), therefore for this algorithm only the "normal" signature length is available. The same applies to the other algorithms (i.e., those not contained in the Watermarking toolbox), where the signature length is dependent on the image size.

Note that the question of WM capacity can be an important one in the biometric context—e.g., if we intend to embed iris template data, the Daugman schemes requires 2,048 bits to be embedded. Embedding other types of information like a camera ID to authenticate an admissible biometric sensor requires significantly lower capacity.

16.3.1   Impact on Recognition Performance

The tests actually conducted are based on the CASIA.v3-Interval iris image database. Out of this database we use the left-eyes of the "Interval"-samples only. We have computed about 800,000 intra-class comparisons on the basis of 894 images of 143 persons and a corresponding number of inter-class comparisons. For our tests, we trim the watermark embedding strength to achieve an average PSNR after embedding of about 42dB and 30dB—thereby we aim at covering scenarios with moderate (42dB) and high (30dB) WM robustness. The WM-signature is changed in every embedding process to blur its influence. So the result for one watermarking algorithm consists of 35,760 different signatures. Due to this enormous computational demand we were able to generate results for 10 runs with different watermarks only. The minimal and maximal values are given and can provide an estimation of the variation, though.

The following ROC curves are used to illustrate the iris recognition performance in case the data used in recognition has been watermarked (i.e., in the case of watermarking being applied, one of the two iris images involved in the matching process has been watermarked). Inside the plots, the "no watermark" curve shows the performance of the iris recognition algorithm without watermarking being applied to the iris images. In case watermarking being applied, the 42dB and 30dB curves are the average results, calculated over 10 test runs each. The min/max bars indicate the minimum and the maximum values to estimate variations due to different watermarking signatures applied. "Normal" and "long" refers to the signature lengths, respectively. On each ROC curve the EER is depicted as a single symbol (dot, square, star).

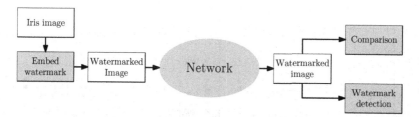

Fig. 16.1 Considered application scenario for watermarking in iris recognition

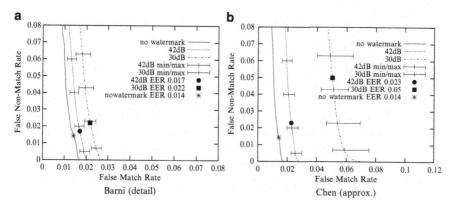

Fig. 16.2 ROC for Ma using watermarked authentication samples, normal signature length. (**a**) Barni, detail subband embedding, (**b**) Chen, approximation subband embedding

As example iris recognition algorithms, we use the USIT implementations (see Sect. 3.4) of the Ma et al. [323] and Masek [335] feature extraction and comparison—abbreviated as *Ma* and *Masek* in the following plots. Figure 16.1 illustrates our experimental scenario. The iris scan is acquired at the sensor site and the raw image is watermarked and transmitted over a network. At the receiver, WM detection is performed and finally, iris feature extraction and matching is done.

We first discuss the results of the *Ma* iris recognition algorithm. In Fig. 16.2 we compare the ROC curves of the Barni and Chen watermarking methods, respectively. Recall that the Barni technique embeds the WM into the wavelet detail subbands whereas Chen uses the approximation subband for embedding. The Barni WM approach does not degrade recognition results too much; however, we notice a slight reduction of recognition accuracy across the entire range of investigated matching rates, with higher impact when embedding with 30dB as compared to embedding with 42dB (as it is expected of course).

The situation is different with Chen WM. The ROC curve when embedding with 42dB is slightly worse as compared to that of Barni WM with 30dB (EER 0.023 vs. 0.022), as are the variations between best and worst cases as depicted in the plot. When embedding with 30dB, ROC behavior is significantly worse (EER 0.05) as are the fluctuations between different runs of the test.

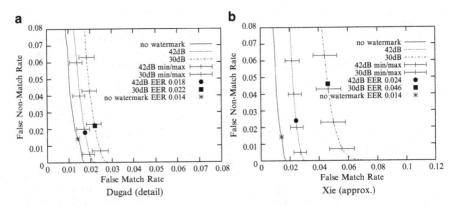

Fig. 16.3 ROC for Ma using watermarked authentication samples, normal signature length. (**a**) Dugad, detail subband embedding, (**b**) Xie, approximation subband embedding

Figure 16.3 displays a similar comparison. Dugad WM selects the embedding sites in the wavelet detail subbands while in Xie WM embedding takes place in the approximation subband. The results of Dugad WM is almost identical to Barni WM, whereas Xie WM again significantly degrades the recognition behavior in a similar manner as Chen WM does (in the Xie case, at 30dB the results are better, but this is hardly noticeable).

These results indicate that indeed using the approximation subband for WM embedding has a significantly higher impact as compared to detail subband embedding in case of wavelet-based WM. This is plausible, since the information contained in the approximation subband represents the basis for a correct representation of the iris texture. In particular, the approximation subband contains a low-resolution and averaged version of the iris texture with local details removed. In case of damage of this information by adding WM information, the incorrect data spreads out into the reconstruction of the texture, generating artificial details in many areas and thereby inhibiting good matching results. In contrast, modification of detail subband information affects the texture only locally and does not degrade results that much.

Figure 16.4 shows the ROC results for the spatial Bruyn WM algorithm and compares embedding a normal vs. a long WM. For embedding with 42dB, the results are competitive to the behavior of Barni and Dugad WM for both signature lengths considered. When embedding with 30dB we notice very different results comparing normal and long signatures. While for normal signature length recognition accuracy at 30dB is almost equivalent to Barni and Dugad WM, the long signature case behaves similar to Chen or Xie-type embedding.

The case of the block-DCT-based Koch WM is covered in Fig. 16.5. We find a behavior very similar to the Bruyn WM scheme discussed before; however, in case of normal signature length and 42dB embedding we obtain the best results of all WM schemes investigated (least impact on recognition accuracy). Also the other results are better compared to Bruyn, but the overall trend is identical (significant impact of the long signature at 30dB embedding).

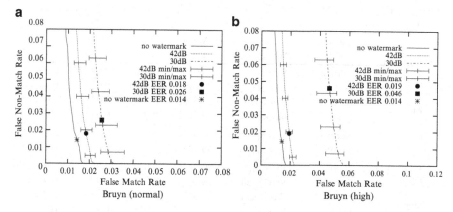

Fig. 16.4 ROC for Ma using watermarked authentication samples (Bruyn algorithm). (**a**) Normal signature length, (**b**) high signature length

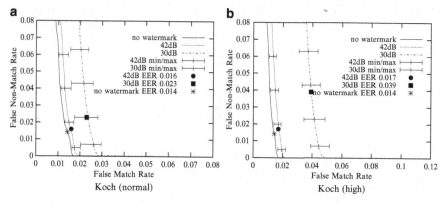

Fig. 16.5 ROC for Ma using watermarked authentication samples (Koch algorithm). (**a**) Normal signature length, (**b**) high signature length

The results of the Bruyn and Koch WM schemes indicate that no matter which embedding domain is selected, we notice an impact on recognition results with lower or higher extent. Both schemes operate in a block-based manner which means that for longer signatures, more blocks have to be manipulated for embedding. At 30dB embedding, this results in a significant impact on the recognition results. As we can observe in Table 16.1, for wavelet-based WM schemes using detail subband embedding, no additional recognition degradation caused by long signatures can be observed. In these techniques, longer signatures only affect single coefficients (as opposed to entire pixel blocks) which results in lower on recognition results. When comparing Wavelet-, DCT-, and Spatial-domain-based embedding we overall find localized embedding strategies showing the least impact on recognition performance (since here only single bits in the templates are affected), while the errors caused by the approximation subband-based embedding cause more burst-type errors causing much more significant impact on recognition.

Table 16.1 EER for Ma and Masek iris recognition algorithms under watermarking (EER is 0.014 and 0.028, respectively, without watermarking being applied)

Algorithm	Signature length	WM domain	Ma 42dB	30dB	Masek 42dB	30dB
Bruyn	Normal	Spatial	0.018	0.026	0.031	0.038
	Long	Spatial	0.019	0.046	0.032	0.062
Koch	Normal	blockDCT	0.016	0.023	0.028	0.036
	Long	blockDCT	0.017	0.039	0.030	0.053
Chen	Normal	WavApprox	0.023	0.050	0.037	0.097
Xie	Normal	WavApprox	0.024	0.046	0.039	0.084
Barni	Normal	WavDetail	0.017	0.022	0.030	0.034
Cao	Normal	WavDetail	0.018	0.029	0.030	0.041
Dugad	Normal	WavDetail	0.018	0.022	0.031	0.035
	Long	WavDetail	0.019	0.022	0.031	0.035
Kund	Normal	WavDetail	0.017	0.040	0.029	0.055
	Long	WavDetail	0.018	0.040	0.031	0.055
Pla	Normal	WavDetail	0.017	0.022	0.030	0.035
Wu	Normal	WavDetail	0.018	0.037	0.031	0.050

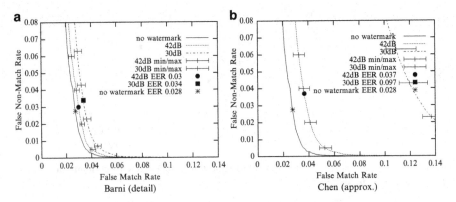

Fig. 16.6 ROC for Masek using watermarked authentication samples, normal signature length. (**a**) Barni, detail subband embedding, (**b**) Chen, approximation subband embedding

The results for the Masek iris recognition algorithm confirm the behavior observed so far. First, we provide detailed ROC results again for the comparison between wavelet-based approximation and detail subband embedding strategies. In Fig. 16.6, we notice that the overall results for the Masek scheme are worse compared to Ma (also without any WM applied). The results of Chen WM is even more degraded as compared to Barni WM as we have observed for the Ma approach. Here, at 30dB WM embedding strength, the scheme with WM employed does not lead to usable results any more. Moreover, Chen WM at 42dB embedding strength is even worse compared to the Barni scheme at 30dB embedding. Similar behavior may be observed when comparing Dugad and Xie WM as shown in Fig. 16.7. Xie WM at 42dB is clearly inferior to Dugad WM at 30dB which clearly confirms

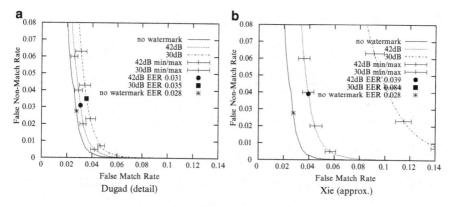

Fig. 16.7 ROC of Masek using watermarked authentication samples, normal signature length. (**a**) Dugad, detail subband embedding, (**b**) Xie, approximation subband embedding

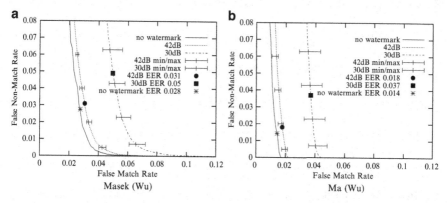

Fig. 16.8 ROC of Wu watermarked authentication samples, normal signature length. (**a**) Masek recognition, (**b**) Ma recognition

the observations made in case of Ma iris recognition. Also for Xie at 30dB the results are hardly useful any more. Contrasting to all the other WM techniques which embed in the detail subbands (Barni, Cao, Dugad, Pla), the Wu embedding approach suffers significantly from embedding with higher strength as shown in Fig. 16.8. This behavior is also confirmed for the Ma algorithm. As one shall see in Table 16.1, this effect can also be observed for a second algorithm which is based on detail coefficient embedding, i.e., the Kundur approach.

Turning to spatial and DCT-based embedding schemes we again focus on the potential effect of longer signatures. For the Bruyn embedding algorithm, the Ma results are confirmed in that we observe significant impact for stronger embedding with high signature length only (Fig. 16.9). At 42dB embedding, the results for normal and long signatures are almost identical.

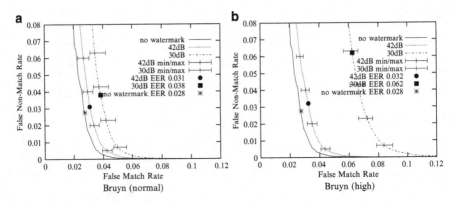

Fig. 16.9 ROC of Masek using watermarked authentication samples (Bruyn algorithm). (**a**) Normal signature length, (**b**) high signature length

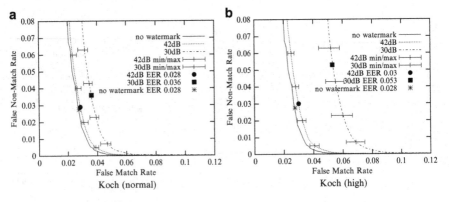

Fig. 16.10 ROC of Masek using watermarked authentication samples (Koch algorithm). (**a**) Normal signature length, (**b**) high signature length

For the Koch WM approach as shown in Fig. 16.10 we again find almost identical ROC for normal and long signatures while the recognition accuracy at 42dB is the best of all schemes considered. Again, the impact of 30dB embedding is significantly higher for long signatures as compared to "normal" ones. Since it is not sensible to display the ROC curves of all WM algorithms with all possible parameters we have selected the most interesting results for the displayed details so far. In order to provide a (more crude) overall view, Table 16.1 provides the Ma and Masek EER of all watermarking schemes investigated. We notice that the actual iris recognition scheme employed does not at all make any difference in the results, the effect of the WM schemes is entirely identical on Ma and Masek.

The WM schemes with lowest impact on recognition results at 42dB and 30dB embedding are Koch, Barni, and Pla. Considering the four schemes which enable long signatures to be embedded, Dugad WM shows the best behavior with almost no difference between normal and long signature.

Apart from the observation made so far with respect to wavelet-based approximation and detail subband embedding we notice an additional issue: The Kundur and Wu WM schemes also exhibit a higher impact on recognition results at 30dB embedding, although these techniques apply embedding in the wavelet detail subbands (as already observed for Wu in Fig. 16.8). However, there is an important difference as compared to the other detail subband embedding schemes (Barni, Cao, Dugad, Pla) concerning the underlying WM approach: while the latter four algorithms use an additive embedding rule, Kundur and Wu apply quantization-based embedding. Therefore, one might conjecture that quantization-based embedding results in higher impact on recognition results as compared to additive embedding.

16.3.1.1 Impact on Applicability of Robust Watermark Embedding

As to be expected, watermarking actually affects the iris recognition performance. For the two iris recognition algorithms considered, the observed trends are almost identical. We have found significant differences among the different WM algorithms with respect to impact on recognition results, ranging from almost no degradation to making the results almost useless. This implies that when designing a WM scheme for employment in a biometric context, it is important to consider those issues. While WM embedding at 42dB (high image quality but low robustness) results in minor impact on recognition performance for almost all WM schemes, embedding with 30dB (lower image quality but higher robustness) causes significant recognition degradations for some algorithms. It is a question of the specific application scenario, if high WM robustness is required for security or not.

While the results of these experiments are far from being conclusive with respect to the question which WM schemes are well suited for this application area and which are not, we have observed certain trends as follows. WM schemes exhibiting low impact on the recognition results can be designed in each embedding domain (e.g., spatial, DCT, and wavelet). Wavelet-based WM embedding schemes tend to degrade recognition results in case embedding is done in the approximation subband and to a lesser extent in case quantization-based embedding is applied (even in case the embedding locations are situated in the detail subbands). We have seen that some embedding strategies are fairly sensitive if long signatures are used: this is observed for block-based embedding (in the spatial and DCT domains, respectively) and again for quantization-based embedding. It has to be noted that we have not considered the different robustness properties of the WM schemes under investigation (or other properties of relevance in the biometric context like computational demand, etc.). Here, we have applied a normalization with respect to a fixed image degradation caused by embedding (i.e., 42dB and 30dB), an other option would be to normalize with respect to, e.g., a fixed robustness against a specific attack (resulting in a different image degradation for each WM scheme).

An entirely different approach is to rely on *reversible* WM schemes [147] which enable to reconstruct the original signal after WM extraction. This property (which is important, e.g., in applying WM to medical imagery) fits perfectly into the biometric scenario since it enables recognition with entirely unaffected sample data.

16.3.2 Attacking a Two-Factor Authentication Scheme

Two-factor authentication schemes in which the additional authentication data is embedded using robust WM have been suggested: in [468], additional classical authentication data is embedded while [226] embed face templates stored on a smart-card into fingerprint images. Also, the sample replay prevention scenario as described above (e.g., [24]) is subjected to the subsequent attack in case some sensor ID or similar data is embedded via the WM scheme.

The usage of robust embedding schemes in these proposals seems to indicate that both data (i.e., the sample data and the embedded WM information) need to be tightly coupled and that the entire transmitted data might be subject to various manipulations, since robust embedding is meant to make the embedded data robust against changes of the host data. Therefore it seems that an insecure channel between sensor and processing module is assumed in this context. In such an environment host data manipulations are to be expected, including even malicious tampering like cropping. While tampering is not a threat against the classical DRM scenario when robust watermarks are being used (in fact, these watermarks are actually designed to be robust against this type of attacks), in the biometric scenario considered here tampering can be used to fool the system. By demonstrating a corresponding attack we show that robust watermarking is not a suited technology for the purpose it is suggested for in this context.

For the actual attack, we focus on the watermarking approach as described before applied to iris sample data enabling two-factor authentication using a smart-card with stored template to facilitate template embedding or other authentication data. However, this idea carries over to the sample replay prevention scenario as well, since the attacker can also modify the sample data with embedded WM signature.

In case of the two-factor authentication technique, we suppose the attacker can utilize a stolen smart-card to fool the system. Additionally, she is in possession of sniffed sample iris data of the person owning the smart-card (the legitimate user) which could have been acquired with a telephoto lens or cropped from his high-resolution personal Facebook image for example.

Even if the WM embedding algorithm uses secret key information stored on the smart-card for embedding (which is the case for all watermarking schemes considered later), the following attack can be mounted since it is not the watermark that is being attacked. The attacker uses the biometric system pretending to be a legitimate user: her iris sample is acquired by the sensor, the (stolen) smart-card is inserted, and finally, the data on the smart-card (e.g., template of a second biometric modality like fingerprint minutiae data or classical authentication data) is secretly embedded as robust watermark. Now the attacker exploits the insecure

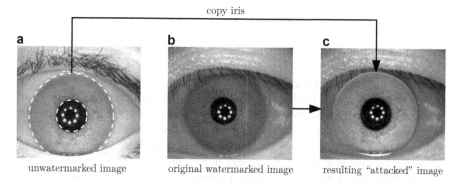

Fig. 16.11 Attack: (**a**) the image where the iris is copied out (with no signature or signature B); (**b**) the original watermarked image with signature A; (**c**) the resulting "attacked" image

channel and intercepts the transmission of the data to the matching module. She modifies the transmitted iris image such that the acquired attackers' sample data matches that of the sniffed sample data of the legitimate user while not destroying the embedded WM. We will show in the subsequent experiments that it is in fact possible to tamper/crop the iris image in a very crude manner without destroying the embedded data of the legitimate user. The result of this attack is an incorrect (i.e., false-positive) authentication of the attacker.

Robust watermarking techniques aim in keeping the signature information (e.g., the biometric template in our case) even if image data undergoes significant manipulations. Especially in case the image content after manipulation is similar from a perceptual viewpoint, the WM is expected to remain intact. So it may be possible to replace only the iris texture, not affecting the watermark detection capability. We will investigate if this is indeed the case for certain schemes.

Figure 16.11 illustrates the according attack. The iris texture of the middle image (Fig. 16.11b, attackers sample) is replaced by the iris texture of the left image (Fig. 16.11a, legitimate users' sniffed sample data), thus resulting in a new iris image as shown in the right (Fig. 16.11c, eventually still watermarked with the legitimate users' template).

16.3.2.1 Experiments

In the experiments we select two randomly chosen rectangular iris images from the CASIA.v3-Interval database. The watermarked image (Fig. 16.11b, with embedded signature A representing the legitimate users' template) will be attacked (i.e., their corresponding iris data are exchanged) by the attacker's image (Fig. 16.11a) which can either contain:

1. No watermark ("no signature").
2. Watermark embedded by the same algorithm but with different signature B ("other signature").

3. Watermark embedded by the same algorithm but with the same signature B ("same signature").

The different attacks correspond to different ways how the data to be inserted has been acquired. The first "no signature" attack can, e.g., occur in case an iris image of a target person has been covertly acquired thus it contains no embedded WM. The second and third attacks ("other signature","same signature") can occur in case an intruder has sniffed transmitted images from the communication channel between sensor and feature extractor/matcher and intends to replace the iris of one image with the other one. If the sensor embeds the same image-independent signature in all images (not recommended), this results in the third attack ("same signature") if the watermark is changed in every transmission being an image-dependent hash, the attack would be the second one ("other signature").

The experimental results are derived by examining 1,000 random watermarks for each attack. For our tests, we trimmed the watermark embedding strength to achieve an average PSNR of about 42dB and 30dB to model medium and high embedding strength.

To decide if the watermark is present or not, a threshold on the detection results has to be determined. In literature often a threshold is selected which results in a false alarm rate of 10^{-8} which is derived by detector responses of images not containing the watermark (hypothesis H_0) and is modeled by Generalized Gaussian distributions. In the plots the vertical line shows the calculated threshold, the x-axis shows the detector response value. All detector responses lying on the left side of the threshold line are interpreted as not indicating the watermark and on the right side as detecting the watermark.

The following figures show histograms (i.e., discrete distributions where on the y-axis the number of responses with a certain x-value is shown) of detector response values for all three attacks (no signature, other signature, same signature) as well as for the not attacked image (the "original" image with signature A—the hypothesis H_0), and for comparison a JPG compression with quality 50.

Figure 16.12 shows the only two algorithms/parameter settings where the watermark is not detected anymore in the attacked images. There is almost no difference among the results of the three attack types. Still, the effect of JPG compression is different in the two cases: while in case of Kund compression removes the watermark entirely, Xie is able to detect the signature even with these compression settings. This difference is due to the entirely different embedding strategies used in the two schemes, the former embedding into detail subbands, the latter into the approximation subband which makes the scheme obviously more robust.

Changing the employed parameters, however, results in very different results as shown in Fig. 16.13 where we display detection results of Kund using 42dB with normal signature length and 30dB with long signatures.

In the case of 42dB, in roughly 50% of all considered cases the WM cannot be extracted. For 30dB and long signatures, all types of embedded marks could be extracted. The latter result is a rather typical one. However, it is clearly visible that

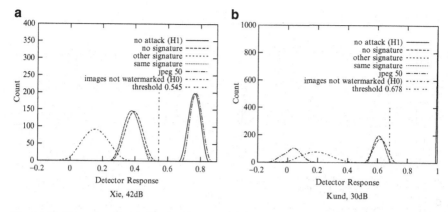

Fig. 16.12 Examples of algorithms and parameters not detecting the watermark. (**a**) Xie, 42dB, (**b**) Kund, 30dB

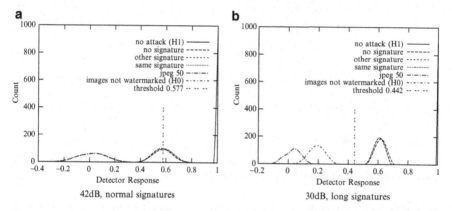

Fig. 16.13 Examples of Kund with selected parameters detecting the watermark. (**a**) 42dB, normal signatures, (**b**) 30dB, long signatures

detection values are clearly reduced for the attacked images as compared to the not attacked ones (H_1), which is true for all considered watermarking algorithms.

Figure 16.14 provides more examples where detection results are clearly reduced for the attacked images, but still indicate the presence of the watermark using the threshold leading to a false alarm rate of 10^{-8}.

In order to provide a better overview, we have calculated the probability of missing the WM by modeling generalized Gaussian distributions to the detector responses. A probability of zero means that each WM can be detected. A probability of, e.g. 0.5 means that in every second case the WM will be detected and 1 means that no WM will be detected. The results (for normal signature length) are shown in Table 16.2.

At 42dB, for Dugad and Xie the watermark will be destroyed with a probability of about 80% or higher (note that Dugad, on the other hand, exhibits a significant probability of miss for the H_1 data). For Barni, Cao, Chen, Koch, Pla, and Wu the

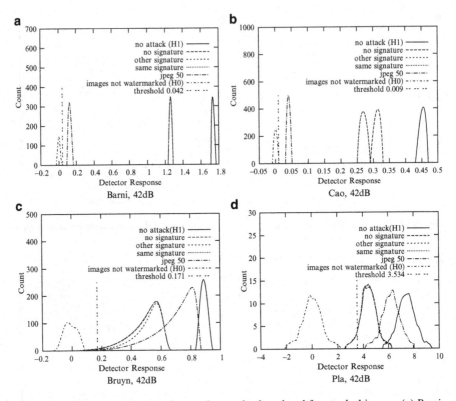

Fig. 16.14 Examples where detection results are clearly reduced for attacked images. (**a**) Barni, 42dB, (**b**) Cao, 42dB, (**c**) Bruyn 42dB, long signatures, (**d**) Pla, 42dB

attacks do not show significant influence, hence do not destroy the watermark. Using the higher embedding strength (30dB) the impact is quite similar. Only for Bruyn and Kund the detection miss probability raises from about 50% to 98% (where Bruyn again exhibits a significant probability of miss for the H_1 data).

16.3.2.2   Impact on Security of Two-Factor Authentication Watermarking

We have found that for most robust schemes, the embedded WM can be extracted although the iris texture has been changed. This is somewhat surprising at first sight since the iris texture covers about 30% of the watermarked image. However, when keeping in mind that robust WM schemes are intended to keep the WM in place even in case of cropping attacks, this result is not really entirely unexpected.

As a result of these experiments, we clearly find that robust watermarking techniques, although proposed in many watermarking-based two-factor authentication and multimodal biometric systems, are not appropriate as the only means of security in such schemes. While increasing the security in general due to the introduction of two-factor authentication, the issue of the protection of the sensor—matching module communication is not solved by just employing robust watermarking.

Table 16.2 Probability of missing the watermarks—normal signatures

Algorithm	Strength	No attack	No signature	Other signature	Same signature	JPG 50
Barni	42dB	0	0	0	0	1.89e-39
	30dB	0	0	0	0	0
Bruyn	42dB	1.69e-05	0.434	0.435	0.437	8.14e-20
	30dB	0.659	0.974	0.975	0.974	1.54e-05
Cao	42dB	0	0	0	0	2.93e-66
	30dB	0	0	0	0	0
Chen	42dB	0	5.71e-04	7.85e-04	4.41e-04	5.99e-29
	30dB	0	2.5e-05	1.11e-04	5.41e-05	1.6e-87
Dugad	42dB	0.045	0.795	0.806	0.807	0.286
	30dB	0.033	0.913	0.964	0.957	0.071
Koch	42dB	0	0.026	0.027	0.017	0
	30dB	0	0.014	0.009	0.014	0
Kund	42dB	0	0.540	0.479	0.482	1
	30dB	0	0.981	0.996	0.996	1
Pla	42dB	5.25e-10	0.045	0.043	0.043	1.09e-05
	30dB	5.75e-54	1.15e-29	4.18e-24	2.07e-24	7.22e-56
Wu	42dB	0	1.93e-116	1.42e-112	4.52e-110	4.04e-57
	30dB	0	9.38e-120	4.24e-106	2.17e-114	0
Xie	42dB	4.22e-18	1	1	1	2e-19
	30dB	0.770	1	1	1	0.787

How can we resolve the issues identified:

1. The method of choice for the target scenario is semi-fragile WM embedding as demonstrated in the subsequent section. These schemes allow for some robustness against unintentional image modifications like compression but are fragile against more severe intentional tampering. Exchanging iris texture as in our attack would lead to a destruction of the embedded template raising manipulation alarm. Of course, all fragile techniques discussed before can also be used, however, sacrificing robustness entirely. Another solution would be to employ the dual watermarking technique as proposed by Kim et al. [257] where the fragile part would detect the manipulation as conducted in the attacks used in this paper.

2. Recent work by Zebbiche et al. [604] proposes a watermarking scheme for fingerprint images where WM data is embedded into the ridge area (region of interest) only. This scheme can be applied to iris imagery by selectively watermarking the iris texture areas. Exchanging the iris leads to a destruction of the embedded template as well.

3. Protection of the sensor module—processing module communication by classical cryptographic means including authentication might represent a superior
   alternative to using watermarking. The small data overhead when concatenating
   sample and template data (and securing this concatenation with a signed hash)
   can probably be tolerated, since on the other hand, employing such a strategy we
   do not suffer from recognition performance decrease as caused by watermarking.
   However, this decision and the eventual demand for the robustness property as
   provided watermarking depends on the application scenario.

It has to be noted that the situation is different for the general multibiometric
approach without smart-card being applied (which is, on the other hand, unrealistic
due to required template generation at the sensor module as discussed before).
Tampering the sample data to match these of a legitimate user does not represent
a threat in this case, since still also the attackers' template would be embedded in
the data.

16.4 Semi-fragile Iris Template Embedding

In the sensor and sample authentication WM application scenario, semi-fragile WM
has been already suggested as an attractive alternative to other types of WM as
described before [7,130,265,303]. During data acquisition, the sensor (i.e., camera)
embeds a watermark into the acquired sample image before transmitting it to the
feature extraction module. The feature extraction module only proceeds with its
tasks if the WM can be extracted correctly (which means that (1) the data has not
been tampered with and (2) the origin of the data is the correct sensor). Choosing
a semi-fragile embedding scheme implies that the attack described in Sect. 16.3.2
cannot be conducted and that the embedded data is supposed to be robust to common
signal processing operations. Additionally, the impact of semi-fragile embedding is
expected to be lower as compared to robust embedding schemes.

In the considered semi-fragile WM scheme, we propose to embed biometric
template data instead of general purpose watermark information which can then be
used in the matching process in addition to checking integrity. Classical semi-fragile
schemes [140] embed generic robust image descriptors.

Embedding template data makes sense since, on the one hand, template data
are of course image-dependent data and therefore are able to prevent WM copy
attacks or similar. On the other hand, in case of tampering or other significant data
manipulations, the aim is not to reconstruct the sample data at first hand, but the aim
of the embedded data is to be able to generate template data from the sample data
required for matching. So data for reconstructing the sample data is suggested to be
replaced by data for directly generating template data. In the following, we describe
the WM embedding and extraction processes:

1. From the acquired sample data, a template is extracted.
2. The template is embedded into the sample data employing a semi-fragile embedding technique (this template is referred to as "template watermark" subsequently).
3. The data is sent to the feature extraction and matching module.
4. At the feature extraction module, the template watermark is extracted, and is compared to the template extracted from the sample (denoted simply as "template" in the following). In this way, the integrity of the transmitted sample data is ensured when there is sufficient correspondence between the two templates. In case of a biometric system operating in verification mode the template watermark can also be compared to the template in the database corresponding to the claimed identity (denoted "database template" in the following).
5. Finally, in case the integrity of the data has been proven, the watermark template and the template are used in the matching process, granting access if the similarity to the database template(s) is high enough.

When comparing this approach to previous techniques proposed in literature, we notice the following differences/advantages: As opposed to techniques employing robust template embedding watermarking (e.g., as proposed for enabling tightly coupled transport of sample and template data of different modalities), the proposed scheme can ensure sample data integrity. As opposed to techniques employing arbitrary (semi-)fragile watermarks for integrity protection (instead of the template watermark used here), the template watermark data can be used to provide a more robust matching process after data integrity has been assured. As opposed to fragile WM, robustness to signal processing like moderate compression can be provided.

However, some issues need to be investigated with respect to the proposed scheme (which will be done in the experiments):

- Does integrity verification indeed work in a robust manner?
- What is the impact of the embedded template watermark on the recognition performance using the template for matching only?
- Can biometric matching take advantage of the two different templates available for matching?

16.4.1 Experiments on Iris Recognition

The employed iris recognition system is Libor Masek's original Matlab implementation (see Sect. 3.4) of a 1-D version of the Daugman iris recognition algorithm. For the experiments, we have used 500 images from the CASIA.v3-Interval dataset, all 450 MMU.1 images, and 318 images from the UBIRIS.v1 dataset. All intra-class and inter-class matches possible with the selected respective image sets have been conducted to generate the experimental results shown.

As the baseline WM system, we employ the fragile watermarking scheme as developed by Yeung et al. (which will be transformed into a semi-fragile embedding

Table 16.3 PSNR without
and with error diffusion on
diverse iris databases

	CASIA.v3	MMU.1	UBIRIS.v1
PSNR [dB]	48.07	43.22	47.69
PSNR with ED [dB]	49.57	44.57	49.16

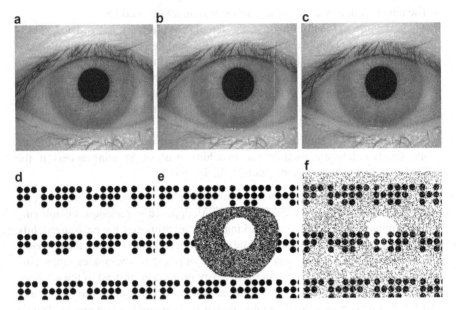

Fig. 16.15 Tamper localization examples of the original fragile scheme of Yeung. (**a**) Original,
(**b**) replaced iris, (**c**) compressed image, (**d**) original watermark, (**e**) WM of (b), (**f**) WM of (c)

scheme subsequently) and investigated in the context of fingerprint recognition
[599]. For this algorithm, the watermark embedded is binary and padded to the size
of the host image. Subsequently, the WM is embedded into each pixel according
to some key information. As a consequence, the WM capacity is 89,600 bits
for CASIA.v3-Interval, 76,800 bits for MMU.1, and 30,000 bits for UBIRIS.v1.
Table 16.3 shows PSNR values averaged over all images embedding 10 randomly
generated WM into each image. Obviously, the quality of the images remains very
high after embedding, especially with enabled error diffusion which is therefore
used in all subsequent experiments.

In Fig. 16.15 we display tampering localization examples of the original fragile
scheme. Figure 16.15b shows a doctored image corresponding to images as used in
the attack in Sect. 16.3.2—the attack is clearly revealed and the location is displayed
in exact manner. As expected, when applying compression to the image with JPEG
quality 75%, the WM indicates errors across the entire image (except for the pupil
area which is not affected by compression due to its uniform grayscale) as shown in
Fig. 16.15f.

The interesting question is the extent of influence an embedded watermark has on
the recognition performance of the system. In Fig. 16.16 we compare ROC curves of

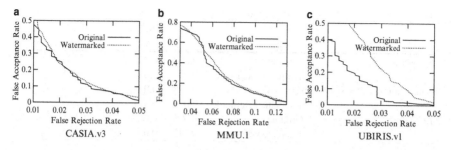

Fig. 16.16 ROC curves for the sample data with random embedded WMs and without. (**a**) CA-SIA.v3, (**b**) MMU.1, (**c**) UBIRIS.v1

Table 16.4 Error rates under different types of attacks for CASIA.v3

Attack	Signal	EER	FRR FAR $\leq 10^{-3}$	FAR FRR $\leq 5 \cdot 10^{-3}$
No attack	Original	0.045	0.091	0.650
	Template watermark	0.048	0.081	0.742
Mean filter	Original	0.035	0.061	0.644
	Template watermark	0.044	0.063	0.669
JPG Q98	Original	0.037	0.074	0.626
	Template watermark	0.049	0.086	0.617

the original data and ROC curves of sample data with embedded WMs—in the latter case, the average of ten embedded WMs is shown. While for the CASIA.v3 and MMU.1 there is hardly a noticeable impact, we notice significant result degradation in the case of the UBIRIS.v1 dataset.

A possible explanation for this effect is the already low quality of this dataset, in case of additional degradation results get worse quickly, while for the other datasets there is still room for slight quality reduction since the original quality is very high.

The situation changes when it comes to additional distortions: As shown in Tables 16.4 and 16.5, also in the case of the CASIA.v3 we notice some impact on recognition performance with embedded WMs as compared to the original sample data without WMs embedded. It is interesting to see that mean filtering and moderate JPG compression can even improve the recognition results of the data without WM embedded—this effect is due to the denoising capabilities of mean filtering and compression. In any case, we notice a slight result degradation for the variant with embedded WMs.

Since this technique is a fragile WM scheme, no robustness against any image manipulations can be expected of course. Table 16.6 demonstrates this property by displaying averaged bit error rates (BER) computed between original and extracted WMs for a subset of 100 images with randomly generated WMs. As can be observed, there is a certain amount of robustness against noise and JPG compression with quality 100. For the other attacks, the BER of 0.5 indicates that the extracted WMs are purely random and therefore entirely destroyed by the attack.

So far, randomly generated WM with size identical to the images have been embedded. The usually smaller size of biometric templates can be exploited to

Table 16.5 Error rates under different types of attacks for UBIRIS.v1

Attack	Signal	EER	FRR at FAR $\leq 10^{-3}$	FAR at FRR $\leq 5 \cdot 10^{-3}$
No attack	Original	0.032	0.062	0.764
	Template watermark	0.046	0.071	0.865
Gaussian noise $N = 0.001$	Original	0.038	0.068	0.871
	Template watermark	0.049	0.073	0.868
JPG Q95	Original	0.036	0.066	0.838
	Template watermark	0.045	0.070	0.975

Table 16.6 Bit error rates for six different attacks for diverse iris databases

Attack	CASIA.v3	MMU.1	UBIRIS.v1
Mean filtering	0.50	0.50	0.50
Gaussian Noise $N = 0.0005$	$4.6 \cdot 10^{-5}$	$5.6 \cdot 10^{-5}$	$6.1 \cdot 10^{-5}$
Gaussian Noise $N = 0.001$	0.03	0.03	0.03
JPG Q100	0.05	0.06	0.05
JPG Q95	0.43	0.45	0.45
JPG Q75	0.49	0.50	0.50

a
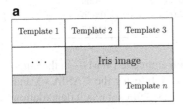

b
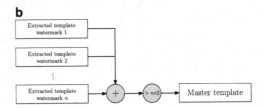

Fig. 16.17 The semi-fragile Yeung scheme: template watermarks are used in a majority voting. (**a**) Redundant embedding, (**b**) majority voting

embed the template in redundant manner, i.e. we embed the template several times as shown in Fig. 16.17a. After the extraction process, all template watermarks are used in a majority voting scheme which constructs a "master" template watermark as shown in Fig. 16.17b. We expect to result in higher robustness leading to an overall semi-fragile WM scheme for the template WMs.

In our implementation, the iris code consists of 9,600 bits; therefore, we can embed 9, 8, and 3 templates into images from the CASIA.v3, MMU.1, and UBIRIS.v1 databases, respectively. Note that instead of this embedding scheme, any semi-fragile WM scheme [140] with sufficient capacity to embed template information can be employed.

In Table 16.7 we show results for the robustness tests when applied to the database images with redundantly embedded template watermarks. When compared to Table 16.6, we clearly observe improved robustness against noise insertion and moderate JPG compression. It can be clearly seen that with an increasing amount of redundancy, robustness is improved which is to be expected due to the more robust

Table 16.7 Bit error rates for seven different attacks for diverse iris databases

Attack	CASIA.v3	MMU.1	UBIRIS.v1
Mean filtering	0.50	0.50	0.50
Gaussian Noise $N = 0.0005$	0	0	0
Gaussian Noise $N = 0.001$	0	0	0.003
JPG Q100	0	0	0.01
JPG Q99	0	0.01	0.05
JPG Q98	0.08	0.14	0.22
JPG Q95	0.35	0.40	0.43

Table 16.8 Bit error rates for seven different attacks for diverse iris databases

Attack	DB Template vs. Template WM			Template WM vs. Template		
	CASIA.v3	MMU.1	UBIRIS.v1	CASIA.v3	MMU.1	UBIRIS.v1
No attack	0.21	0.23	0.19	0.14	0.06	0.07
Mean filtering	0.49	0.50	0.50	0.49	0.50	0.50
Gauss. Noise $N = 0.0005$	0.21	0.23	0.19	0.14	0.06	0.07
Gauss. Noise $N = 0.001$	0.21	0.23	0.19	0.14	0.06	0.07
JPG Q100	0.21	0.23	0.19	0.14	0.06	0.08
JPG Q99	0.21	0.24	0.22	0.14	0.07	0.11
JPG Q98	0.25	0.30	0.32	0.20	0.18	0.26
JPG Q95	0.41	0.45	0.45	0.39	0.41	0.44

majority decoding (please recall that for CASIA.v3 redundancy is maximal among the three datasets).

After having experimentally assessed tampering localization capabilities and improved watermark template robustness, we further investigate integrity verification under conditions which require robustness properties.

- *Scenario S_1*: As a first scenario S_1 (restricted to the verification scenario), comparison between extracted template WM and database (DB) template is covered. We consider the case that 5 different templates are stored in the database out of which a single database template is generated by majority coding like explained before in the case of the template WM. Table 16.8 (left) shows the bit error rate (BER) for the different attacks considered.
- *Scenario S_2*: The second scenario S_2 is the comparison between extracted template WM and the template extracted from the watermarked sample data the results of which are shown in Table 16.8 (right).

The first thing to note is that even without attack, BER is clearly above zero. For S_2 this effect is solely due to the influence the embedded WM has on the extracted template—obviously the WM changes the sample in a way that about 10% of the bits are altered. For S_1 the differences are higher which is clear since the DB template is constructed from several distinct templates. We have to consider that a typical decision threshold value for the iris recognition system in use is at a BER in $[0.3, 0.35]$. When taking this into account, the extent of template similarity

Table 16.9 Bit error rates for the fused template under seven different attacks

Attack	CASIA.v3	MMU.1	UBIRIS.v1
No attack	0.21	0.21	0.21
Mean filtering	0.30	0.27	0.21
Gaussian Noise $N = 0.0005$	0.21	0.21	0.21
Gaussian Noise $N = 0.001$	0.21	0.21	0.21
JPG Q100	0.21	0.21	0.21
JPG Q99	0.21	0.21	0.21
JPG Q98	0.23	0.23	0.21
JPG Q95	0.27	0.26	0.21

is of course enough to decide on proven sample integrity. For both S_1 and S_2, adding noise and applying JPG compression with quality set to 100 (Q100) does not change the BER. When decreasing JPG quality to 98, BER starts to increase slightly. The situation changes drastically when applying JPG Q95 and mean filtering: BER is up to 0.4–0.5 which means that integrity cannot be verified successfully. We realize that integrity verification in our technique is indeed robust against moderate JPG compression and noise. On the other hand, mean filtering and JPG compression at quality 95% destroys the template WM and indicates modification. The distribution of incorrect bits can be used to differentiate between malicious attacks (where an accumulation of incorrect bits can be observed in certain regions) and significant global distortions like compression where incorrect bits are spread across the entire data.

S_1 and S_2 can be combined into a single integrity verification scheme. The idea is to combine the single templates extracted from the watermark and the template extracted from the watermarked sample into a weighted "fused template": in our example, we use 4 copies of the template and the embedded number of templates from the template WM in a majority voting scheme to generate the fused template. Table 16.9 shows the corresponding BER when comparing the fused template to the DB template.

It can be clearly seen that while the BER without attack and applying moderate attacks is higher as compared to S_2, we get much better robustness against JPG Q95 and even mean filtering. With the fusing strategy, robustness even against those two types of attacks can be obtained. Of course, the fusion scheme does only make sense in a biometric system in verification mode, since integrity verification is done against templates stored in the template database.

Besides integrity verification, the extracted template WM can be used in biometric matching. Therefore, we investigate iris recognition performance using the template extracted from the watermarked sample (W1) and the extracted template WM (W2), and compare the behavior to the "original" results using templates extracted from the original sample data (without embedded WM, W0). For this purpose, we compare ROC curves of the three cases with and without attacks

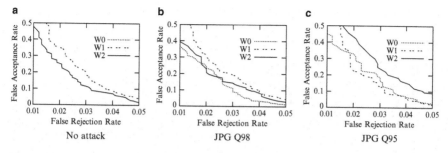

Fig. 16.18 Receiver operation characteristic curves of the CASIA.v3-Interval iris database. (a) No attack, (b) JPG Q98, (c) JPG Q95

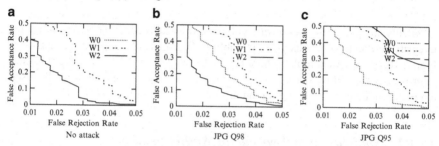

Fig. 16.19 Receiver operation characteristic curves of the UBIRIS.v1 iris database. (a) No attack, (b) JPG Q98, (c) JPG Q95

(i.e., JPG compression, noise insertion, and mean filtering) conducted against the sample data.

In both Figs. 16.18a and 16.19a the curve W0 is hidden by W2 and we clearly note that the embedded WM impacts on recognition performance since W1 shows clearly inferior ROC (note that this contrasts to the case of fingerprint matching reported in [599]). So without attack, using the template WM is beneficial over the template. This situation is also typical for moderate attacks being conducted as shown in Figs. 16.18b and 16.19b as an example for the case of JPG compression with Q98. While for the CASIA.v3 data W0 and W2 are close, both being superior to W1, for the UBIRIS.v1 data W2 is the best option. W0 is clearly inferior to W2, while W1 is the worst option. Obviously, the embedded template watermark is not yet severely impacted by the compression artifacts.

The situation changes when the attacks get more severe. As shown in Figs. 16.18c and 16.19c, under JPG compression with Q95 W2 is the worst option now since the robustness of the WM is not sufficient any more. While for the CASIA.v3 data W0 and W1 are close (so the impact of the WM is negligible), for UBIRIS.v1 the impact of the WM is quite significant (which can be explained by the fact that the UBIRIS.v1 data is of already quite low quality without any further degradation, the additional WM complicates template extraction). For mean filtering the result for W2 is even worse as shown in Fig. 16.20a, b, no recognition can be performed at all with the extracted template WM after this attack.

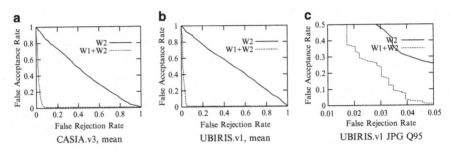

Fig. 16.20 Receiver operation characteristic curves for fused templates. (**a**) CASIA.v3, mean, (**b**) UBIRIS.v1, mean, (**c**) UBIRIS.v1, JPG Q95

Finally, the previous strategy of combining W1 and W2 into a fused template for integrity verification (results given in Table 16.9) can also be applied for matching. Figure 16.20 shows examples where the ROC behavior of W2 can be significantly improved by using this approach. In particular, in the case of mean filtering the fused template can be used for recognition purposes as shown in Fig. 16.20a, b.

16.4.2   Application to Two-Factor Authentication

One of the application scenarios described before involving watermarks actually represents a two-factor authentication scheme [226]: biometric data is stored on a smart-card and the actual biometric data acquired at the sensor is used to verify if the user at the sensor is the legitimate owner of the smart-card. In the reference above watermarking is used to embed data of a second modality into the sample data which is stored on the card (in the reference given, facial data is embedded into fingerprint images and at the access control site, a fingerprint sensor is installed). Therefore, watermarking is employed as a simple means of transportation data of two different modalities in an integrated manner.

Here we apply the semi-fragile WM iris template embedding approach described before to a two-factor authentication scheme using iris recognition (biometrics as the first factor) and smart-cards (a token as the second factor). Contrasting to most multibiometric approaches, we do not embed template data from a different modality, but the modality of sample data and template data do match. We demonstrate that in addition to enable tightly coupled transport, semi-fragile watermarking can also provide sensitivity against tampering and low impact on recognition performance as seen before. An additional advantage of the proposed scheme is the improved robustness in recognition accuracy under signal degradation due to the use of two templates in the matching process and increased security due to the two factor approach in general.

When a user is enrolled into the system, sample data are acquired, corresponding template data is extracted and stored in two different ways: first, in the centralized biometric database required for the actual recognition process, and second, on the

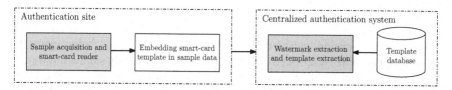

Fig. 16.21 Considered application scenario for two-factor biometric recognition

smart-card. In the authentication phase, the smart-card is submitted by the user to the access control site and the sensor acquires "new" sample data. The following actions are performed (Fig. 16.21 illustrates the scenario):

1. From the acquired sample data, a template is extracted and compared to the template on the smart-card. Only if there is sufficient correspondence, the following stages are conducted subsequently. Note that this is done at the sensor site, so there is no necessity to contact the centralized database.
2. The smart-card embeds its template into the sample data employing a semi-fragile embedding technique (this template is referred to as "template watermark" as in the previous section).
3. The data is sent to the feature extraction and matching module.
4. At the feature extraction module, the watermark template is extracted, and is compared to the template extracted from the sample (denoted simply as "template" in the following). In this way, the integrity of the transmitted sample data is ensured in case there is sufficient correspondence between the two templates. In case of a biometric system operating in verification mode the template watermark can also be compared to the template in the database corresponding to the claimed identity (denoted again "database template"). Note that in the latter case, the correspondence is expected to be higher since the template generated during enrollment has been extracted as template watermark—coming from the smart card—and is also extracted from the database.
5. Finally, in case the integrity of the data has been proven, the template watermark and the template are used in the matching process, granting access if the similarity to the database template is high enough.

Experimental results of the last section do carry over for most issues to this application scenario. Assuming the template embedding is done in the same way, results with respect to impact on recognition performance are perfectly in accordance.

The difference is that here the template watermark is actually identical to the database template and in the integrity verification scenario as discussed before the template watermark is generated by embedding the template extracted from the iris sample data. Therefore, for integrity verification at the feature extraction module between template and template watermark (which actually is the database template), higher BER need to be tolerated as in the case before, where the BER without attack comes only from the slight changes in the template caused by the embedded template watermark (both being derived from the identical sample data), while here, templates derived from different sample data are compared. Results are in perfect analogy to Table 16.8, where the left side corresponds to the results as obtained by the integrity verification and its robustness properties of the two-factor approach (only "template WM" is replaced by "template" which are highly similar anyway).

Also integrity verification with fused templates as shown in Table 16.9 can be done accordingly, again, slightly higher BER are to be expected due to the two sample data entities involved in the template generation. Biometric recognition with the single templates W1 and W2 (compare Figs. 16.18 and 16.19) can also be done, where the results of W1 remain unaffected while W2 results are even better as compared to W0 since the template watermark actually is the database template, against which matching is performed during the recognition process. Also, matching with a template generated by fusing the template extracted from the sample and the template watermark leads to better results as compared to those shown in Fig. 16.20.

Overall, we have found that applying iris template embedding with semi-fragile WM is an attractive option in the considered two-factor authentication approach where in addition to enhanced security as provided by introducing a second authentication factor, local authentication at the sensor site, sample data integrity verification at the feature extraction site, and improved recognition behavior with single and fused templates can be obtained.

16.5 Iris Sensor Authentication Using PRNU Sensor Fingerprints

As watermarks represent additional data which is inserted into sample data, impact on recognition accuracy is observed as we have seen in the last section, ranging from significant accuracy degradation in case of robust embedding with high capacity to moderate as well as hardly measurable impact in the case of (semi-)fragile embedding. For this reason, when it comes to authenticating biometric sample data, passive media security techniques come into play, typically termed "digital image forensics" [144]. The most interesting technique for our target scenario is that of sensor fingerprints based on a sensor's photo response non-uniformity (PRNU) [78, 79], since, besides image integrity, this technique can also provide authenticity by identifying the source sensor uniquely.

For this approach, important properties as required in a biometric scenario have been demonstrated recently: suitability to manage large datasets [167, 168], robustness against common signal processing operations like compression and malicious signal processing [10, 450], and finally methodology to reveal forged PRNU fingerprints which has been recently established [166].

We apply the PRNU sensor fingerprint methodology to iris datasets in order to investigate its usefulness in this application scenario. In particular, iris scans of the CASIA.v4 iris-sensors are used in our experiments. The subsequent subsection explains how an iris-sensor PRNU fingerprint is generated and how forgeries can be established. The following subsection presents experimental results with respect to those two issues.

16.5.1 Iris-Sensor Authentication Using Digital Image Forensics

The detection of a sensor fingerprint in an image implies knowledge about the sensor with which the image was taken. This could be useful in any case of uncertain origin or eventual tampering of biometric raw data. To estimate the sensor fingerprint the algorithm for calculating a sensor's PRNU as described by Fridrich [156] was chosen. The PRNU is unique to each single sensor. Thus, by setting up a database of iris templates it can be assured that all images are authentic by testing their provenience. This is a major advantage of this sensor fingerprint, since other algorithms are suited for distinguishing sensor models, only. The party responsible for the security of a biometric database will calculate the fingerprint of the sensors which are used to acquire the samples. Then, for each sample that is added, after its transmission it can be proven that it was actually taken with an authentic sensor by detecting the PRNU in the image.

The PRNU is based on the noise in an image that is inserted during acquisition of the image. For each image the noise residual W_I is estimated

$$W_I = I - F(I) \tag{16.1}$$

where F is a denoising filter and, consequently, $F(I)$ is a denoised version of the image I. The fingerprint $\hat{K}$ is then obtained by the maximum likelihood estimator for images I_i with $i = 1, \ldots, N$

$$\hat{K} = \frac{\sum_{i=1}^{N} W_I^i I^i}{\sum_{i=1}^{N} (I^i)^2} \tag{16.2}$$

Since the images under question have not undergone any geometrical transformation such as scaling or rotation we simply used the normalized cross-correlation (NCC) for detection of the sensor fingerprint in an image under question, and estimated the presence of a fingerprint $\hat{K}$ in an image J with

$$\rho_{[J,K]} = NCC(W_J, J\hat{K}) \tag{16.3}$$

Note that the fingerprint $\hat{K}$ is being weighted by the image's content J and W_J indicates the noise residual of image J. To estimate the detectability of a sensor's fingerprint in the respective images one can calculate the correlation ρ between the images of each sensor S_i not used to calculate the PRNU and the respective PRNU $\hat{K}_i$. On the other hand, to estimate the discriminative value of the fingerprint of sensor S_i, ρ between all images belonging to the sensors S_j, $j \neq i$ and the fingerprint of sensor S_i is calculated.

From these ρ values, a measure to evaluate the discriminative performance of the PRNU should be chosen. We estimated the EER and thresholds in discriminating each sensor from each other sensor in pairs. These values rely on a finite set of images. To estimate the real variability of these values, the interval of confidence (CI) at 95% was estimated. To do so, the calculation of EER and threshold was repeated 1,000 times on the respective set of m matching and n non-matching ρ values, by drawing m ρ values from the matching-data set and n ρ values from the non-matching data set, making use of sampling with replacement. That is, some values may not be drawn and others may be drawn twice or several times. As a result, one obtains 1,000 EERs and 1,000 thresholds. The range which contains 95% of these values is the CI. In other words, this range excludes the 2.5% lowest and 2.5% highest measures, that is, the most extreme values.

In the case of an intruder wanting to insert spoofed biometric samples into the transmission between sensor and feature extraction module, or if he wants to modify, replace, or add samples at the database, the somehow acquired sample data will not carry the correct PRNU fingerprint. Thus, with the method described before, the injected spoofed sample data can be detected. Thus, the attacker has to forge the sensor fingerprint into his spoofed sample data to be able to pretend that these data have been acquired with the correct sensor. For this forgery it is necessary that the attacker steals a sufficient number of images from which he can estimate the PRNU $\hat{K}$. This PRNU is then inserted in the spoofed sample data. To forge an image J, the image is first denoised with filter F [156] so that the intruder obtains a denoised version $F(J)$. According to the forgery-attack as described in [165], the additive forgery model is simply

$$J = F(J) + \alpha \hat{K} \qquad (16.4)$$

We chose this model since it turned out empirically that it was more simple to determine an adequate scaling factor α for the additive than the multiplicative model. The scalar α determines the strength of the forged fingerprint. α should be chosen so that the forgery does not contain a fingerprint that is too weak or too strong, that is, correlating the images taken with sensor S_i which are forged with the PRNU of sensor S_j ($j \neq i$) with the fingerprint of sensor S_j should yield similar values ρ as correlating images originally taken by sensor S_j and the PRNU of sensor S_j. Another criteria for choosing α is that the minimum of the forged ρ values should be larger than the threshold for the original ρ values. Otherwise the PRNU would not be detected in some forged images and thus the images would not be recognized as authentic iris scans of a specified database.

To obtain a good estimate for α, an adaptive procedure was applied. Images of a sensor S_i are forged with the PRNU of another sensor S_j, $j \neq i$. Then, the resulting distribution of correlation values is compared to the correlations of images I_j with sensor S_j. If the minimum of the forged ρ values is lower than the threshold for the original ρ values, α must be increased. However, the distance between the lowest forged ρ values and the threshold should be minimal. Note that this minimum-criteria is not a guarantee that an image is actually recognized as being taken with a specific sensor. To estimate α a certain subset of images was used to calculate the sensor's fingerprint. If a different subset of images is used, some of the correlation values of the forged images and this new fingerprint may drop below the threshold.

Table 16.10 EERs in first line and respective CIs in second line for all possible sensor comparisons

Data-set	Twins	Distance	Interval	Lamp
Thousand	1.68	1.13	20.68	11.74
	(1.26–1.97)	(0.84–1.47)	(19.36–21.74)	(10.81–12.7)
Lamp	14.39	7.42	22.42	
	(13.46–15.36)	(6.8–8.24)	(21.17–23.26)	
Interval	18.89	21.21		
	(17.84–19.94)	(20.05–22.5)		
Distance	0.37			
	(0.21–0.6)			

16.5.2 Experiments

As materials for experiments the CASIA.v4 database was used. Thus, the 5 different sensors of the data sets CASIA.v4-Interval, CASIA.v4-Lamp, CASIA.v4-Twins, CASIA.v4-Distance, and CASIA.v4-Thousand were examined. These sensors are the CASIA close-up iris camera, OKI IRISPASS-h (1), OKI IRISPASS-h (2), CASIA long-range iris camera, and Irisking IKEMB-100, respectively. CASIA.v4-Syn were not used because the images were not taken with a real sensor but were created with a synthetic algorithm. Of each data set, 1,000 images were randomly chosen.

Since the image-size varies between the data sets, we took 4 squares of 128×128 pixels in each corner for all images as proposed by Fridrich [156]. The PRNU was calculated with 50 reference images of each sensor. The remaining 950 images were used to calculate the NCC values. As a result, we got 950 matching correlations and $4 \times 1,000$ non-matching correlations for each of the 5 sensors to calculate the EER and thresholds. For each sensor S_i 100 images were forged with the PRNU estimated from the 50 reference images of each other sensor S_j. To detect the forgery, 50 innocent images were randomly chosen from the remaining 1,950 images and the triangle test was calculated with the PRNU of these 50 innocent images, the 100 forged images, the 50 images that were used for the forgery and a further 100 innocent images; that is, images that were not used for the forgery. The EERs, thresholds and respective CIs are shown in Tables 16.10 and 16.11.

From Table 16.10 it is obvious that the EERs vary highly between the several sensor comparisons. The EERs for the sensors Interval and Lamp compared with the other sensors are very high while the sensors Thousand, Distance, and Twins yield very low EERs in the comparisons with each other. The respective thresholds in Table 16.11 for the sensors Thousand, Distance, and Twins are higher than those for the sensors Interval and Lamp. If the PRNU were to be used to authenticate the iris scans this would be easier for sensors such as Thousand, Distance, and Twins. Sensors with poor discriminative power are more likely to produce errors in the authentication process. Results are somewhat difficult to interpret since it is not

Table 16.11 Thresholds in first line and CIs in second line for all possible sensor comparisons

Data-set	Twins	Distance	Interval	Lamp
Thousand	0.015	0.015	0.006	0.01
	(0.014–0.016)	(0.014–0.016)	(0.006–0.007)	(0.009–0.01)
Lamp	0.012	0.007	0.005	
	(0.011–0.012)	(0.006–0.007)	(0.004–0.005)	
Interval	0.005	0.007		
	(0.005–0.006)	(0.006–0.007)		
Distance	0.016			
	(0.015–0.017)			

clear if the CASIA.v4 datasets have been acquired with a single camera or with multiple cameras of the same model. If the latter is the case for some sets, this could explain the high EER for Interval and Lamp sensors.

Moreover, the images all contain very similar patterns of pixel-intensities. Therefore, the necessary content-variance to obtain a good estimate for the sensor's fingerprint cannot be reached. A poor estimate of the PRNU may not contain enough information to provide an acceptable level of distinctiveness. Less distinctive PRNUs result in higher EERs. The problem with the image's content is that certain pixel-ranges are very low-saturated in all images and therefore reflect very little of the sensor's fingerprint. To substantiate this assumption, new test-images are needed. Specifically, one would need images with highly saturated pixels, for example, images of a cloudy sky. Another possible explanation for EERs exceeding 10% or 20% as found for Interval and Lamp sensors is that the quality of a sensor's fingerprint depends on the irregularities a sensor actually has [156]. The less irregularities, the less information can be extracted by calculating the PRNU. This explanation would imply that the tested sensors are precisely constructed and contain only a few irregularities. This assumption could be verified by calculating the PRNU and respective EERs on images with similar content as the CASIA.v4 datasets, but which are taken with a set of sensors that are not specifically constructed for iris-scans, e.g., normal CCD cameras.

A further problem is the eventual presence of watermark information in the CASIA.v4 data. In Fig. 16.22 we display an example image where in which pixels suspicious for watermark presence are marked (these pixels are significantly different from their neighborhood). Since these pixels are not randomly distributed but can be arranged in a 8×8 pixels pattern, a block-based DCT watermarking scheme can be suspected.

For establishing a forgery, for each sensor, its largest threshold among the 4 comparisons to the other sensors was selected as the minimum that should be reached by the forged ρ values. In other words, α was chosen so that the minimal forged ρ was larger than this largest threshold (see Table 16.11 for the threshold values). When adapting the factors *alpha* for each forgery it turned out that these factors vary highly between the possible forgeries. Table 16.12 shows the values.

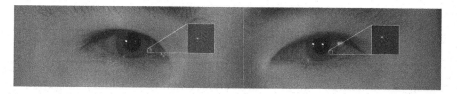

Fig. 16.22 CASIA.v4-Distance sensor; cropped example image with marked pixel position suspicious for watermark presence

Table 16.12 Factors α for pairwise forgeries (factors highly vary between possible forgeries)

PRNU from inserted in	Thousand	Twins	Distance	Interval	Lamp
Thousand		100	170	200	80
Twins	25		130	80	40
Distance	50	130		200	130
Interval	120	250	600		130
Lamp	50	110	270	370	

Embedding the Distance-PRNU requires higher α factors than embedding the Thousand-PRNU. This may or may not be due to the sensor's individual properties. Intuitively, we expected that a high-quality PRNU requires lower α values than a low-quality PRNU. Thus, if we assume that a high-quality PRNU corresponds to a low EER the Tables 16.10 and 16.12 should show some correspondence. Upon inspecting these tables, we can see that a low EER does not unequivocally correspond to a low α factor. While embedding the Thousand PRNU in images of the Twins or the Distance sensors requires relatively low α factors, when attempting this in the opposite direction, i.e. inserting the Twins or the Distance PRNU in images of the Thousand sensor, requires a higher embedding strength. Therefore, some other factor may also play a role in the determination of the embedding strength α.

One candidate for such a modulating factor is the different weighting of the images to calculate and insert a PRNU. Since the Distance-sensor takes images from some distance it captures a larger part of the face instead of one eye only. The insertion of a PRNU that is calculated with images that contain the whole face into images that contain only one eye could not succeed in certain image regions. For example, in regions where the Distance sensor captures skin, the other sensors capture the pupil. The Distance PRNU may contain significant information in this region, but embedding this information may not be possible in very dark image regions, such as is the case at the pupil.

Descriptive statistics (mean ρ and standard deviation, SD) of the forged image correlations and the actual correlations are shown in Table 16.13.

It can be seen that the forgery of some sensors tends to have a higher mean than the actual correlations while for other sensors (e.g., the Distance sensor) the mean

Table 16.13 Mean ρ and SD for actual image correlations (first column) and forged correlations

Data set	actual	Thousand	Twins	Forged Distance	Interval	Lamp
Thousand	0.0375		0.0560	0.0550	0.0904	0.0702
SD	0.0127		0.0107	0.0154	0.0199	0.0216
Twins	0.0474	0.0431		0.0537	0.0480	0.0582
SD	0.0140	0.0129		0.0139	0.0130	0.0191
Distance	0.5449	0.2454	0.3933		0.1263	0.1954
SD	0.0654	0.0706	0.0343		0.0192	0.0541
Interval	0.0100	0.0363	0.0292	0.0324		0.0705
SD	0.0110	0.0132	0.0059	0.0148		0.0254
Lamp	0.0170	0.0452	0.0448	0.0674	0.0406	
SD	0.0092	0.0131	0.0112	0.0203	0.0106	

of the forged correlations is lower than the mean of the actual image correlations. This variance rises from the criteria that the minimum correlation of the forged ones must exceed the chosen minimum-threshold (see Table 16.11). For the intruder the scenario where the forged correlations are lower than the actual correlations, but still higher than the threshold, is optimal. In such a setting the forged image would be authenticated but the correlation is so low that it would not raise any suspicion.

Thus, a high α factor does not necessarily coincide with a difficult situation for the intruder. The Distance sensor may require the highest embedding strength but yields a situation in which the forgery will probably not be detected due to high correlation values. On the other hand, since the distinctiveness of the Distance PRNU seems to be quite good, it should be possible to forge images and insert them into an iris database, since these forgeries would be considered to be authentic samples.

So far, we have been able to show that in principle, sensor PRNU fingerprints can be used to authenticate iris sample data. Also, the establishment of forgeries has been shown. However, in recent work [535] it has turned out that the produced forgeries cannot be distinguished from authentic images, which questions the reliability of this approach. Therefore, additional work in this direction is required to investigate if this particular passive media security technique can be used in real-world scenarios within biometric systems.

References

1. Aarabi, P., Lam, J., Keshavarz, A.: Face detection using information fusion. In: Proceedings of 10th International Conference on Information Fusion, pp. 1–8. IEEE, New York (2007). doi: 10.1109/ICIF.2007.4408078
2. Abhyankar, A., Schuckers, S.: Active shape models for effective iris segmentation. In: Flynn, P.J., Pankanti, S. (eds.) Biometric Technology for Human Identification III, Proceedings of SPIE, vol. 6202, pp. 62,020H.1–10. SPIE, Bellingham, WA (2006). doi: 10.1117/12.666435
3. Abhyankar, A., Schuckers, S.: Iris quality assessment and bi-orthogonal wavelet based encoding for recognition. Pattern Recogn. **42**, 1878–1894 (2009). doi: 10.1016/j.patcog.2009.01.004
4. Adler, A.: Sample images can be independently restored from face recognition templates. In: Proceedings of Canadian Conference on Electrical and Computer Engineering, vol. 2, pp. 1163–1166. IEEE, New York (2003). doi: 10.1109/CCECE.2003.1226104
5. Adler, A.: Vulnerabilities in Biometric Encryption Systems. In: Kanade, T., Jain, A., Ratha, N. (eds.) Proceedings of 5th International Conference on Audio- and Video-Based Biometric Person Authentication. LNCS, vol. 3546, pp. 211–228. Springer, New York (2005). doi: 10.1007/11527923_114
6. Ahmad, S., Lu, Z.M.: A joint biometrics and watermarking based framework for fingerprinting, copyright protection, proof of ownership, and security applications. In: Proceedings of International Conference on Computational Intelligence and Security Workshops, pp. 676–679. IEEE, New York (2007). doi: 10.1109/CISW.2007.4425586
7. Ahmed, F., Moskowitz, I.: Composite signature based watermarking for fingerprint authentication. In: Proceedings of 7th Workshop on Multimedia and Security, pp. 799–802. ACM, New York (2005). doi: 10.1145/1073170.1073195
8. Al-Raisi, A., Al-Khouri, A.: Iris recognition and the challenge of homeland and border control security in UAE. Telematics Inform. **25**(2), 117–132 (2008). doi: 10.1016/j.tele.2006.06.005
9. Alclear: Clear. URL http://clearme.com. Retrieved May 2012
10. Alles, E., Geradts, Z., Veenman, C.: Source camera identification for heavily jpeg compressed low resolution still images. J. Forensic Sci. **54**(3), 628–638 (2009). doi: 10.1111/j.1556-4029.2009.01029.x
11. Almeida, P.: A knowledge-based approach to the iris segmentation problem. Image Vis. Comput. **28**(2), 238–245 (2010). doi: 10.1016/j.imavis.2009.07.003
12. Alonso-Fernandez, F., Tome-Gonzalez, P., Ruiz-Albacete, V., Ortega-Garcia, J.: Iris recognition based on sift features. In: Proceedings of International Conf on Biometrics, Identity and Security, pp. 1–8. IEEE, New York (2009). doi: 10.1109/BIDS.2009.5507529

C. Rathgeb et al., *Iris Biometrics: From Segmentation to Template Security*, Advances in Information Security 59, DOI 10.1007/978-1-4614-5571-4, © Springer Science+Business Media, LLC 2013

13. Ang, R., Safavi-Naini, R., McAven, L.: Cancelable key-based fingerprint templates. In: Boyd, C., Nieto, J.G. (eds.) Proceedings of 10th Australasian Conference on Information Security and Privacy. LNCS, vol. 3574, pp. 242–252. Springer, New York (2005). doi: 10.1007/11506157_21

14. ANSI: Safe Use of Lasers and LEDs Used in Optical Fiber Transmission Systems, ANSI Z136.2 (1988)

15. Ao, M., Li, S.: Near infrared face based biometric key binding. In: Tistarelli, M., Nixon, M. (eds.) Proceedings of 3rd International Conference on Biometrics. LNCS, vol. 5558, pp. 376–385. Springer, New York (2009). doi: 10.1007/978-3-642-01793-3_39

16. Arakala, A.: Secure and private fingerprint-based authentication. Bull. Aust. Math. Soc. **80**(2), 347–349 (2009). doi: 10.1017/S0004972709000665

17. Arul, P., Shanmugam, A.: Generate a key for AES using biometric for VOIP network security. J. Theor. Appl. Inform. Tech. **5**(2), 107–112 (2009)

18. Arvacheh, E., Tizhoosh, H.: Iris segmentation: Detecting pupil, limbus and eyelids. In: Proceedings of IEEE International Conference on Image Processing, pp. 2453–2456. IEEE, New York (2006). doi: 10.1109/ICIP.2006.312773

19. Authenti-Corp: Iris Recognition Study 2006 (IRIS06) (2007). URL http://www.authenti-corp.com/iris06/report/IRIS06_final_report_v1-0_20070901.pdf. Retrieved May 2012

20. Ballard, L., Kamara, S., Monrose, F., Reiter, M.: On the requirements of biometric key generators. Tr-jhu-spar-bkmr-090707, JHU Department of Computer Science (2007)

21. Ballard, L., Kamara, S., Monrose, F., Reiter, M.K.: Towards practical biometric key generation with randomized biometric templates. In: Proceedings of 15th ACM Conference on Computer and Communications Security, pp. 235–244. ACM, New York (2008). doi: 10.1145/1455770.1455801

22. Ballard, L., Kamara, S., Reiter, M.: The practical subtleties of biometric key generation. In: Proceedings of 17th Conference on Security Symposium, pp. 61–74. USENIX (2008)

23. Barni, M., Bartolini, F., Piva, A.: Improved wavelet-based watermarking through pixel-wise masking. IEEE Trans. Image Process. **10**(5), 783–791 (2001). doi: 10.1109/83.918570

24. Bartlow, N., Kalka, N., Cukic, B., Ross, A.: Protecting iris images through asymmetric digital watermarking. In: IEEE Workshop on Automatic Identification Advanced Technologies, vol. 4432, pp. 192–197. IEEE, New York (2007). doi: 10.1109/AUTOID.2007.380618

25. Basit, A., Javed, M.: Iris localization via intensity gradient and recognition through bit planes. In: Proceedings of IEEE International Conference on Machine Vision, pp. 23–28. IEEE, New York (2007). doi: 10.1109/ICMV.2007.4469267

26. Belaroussi, R., Milgram, M., Prevost, L.: Fusion of multiple detectors for face and eyes localization. In: Proceedings of International Symposium Image and Signal Processing and Analysis, pp. 24–29. IEEE, New York (2005). doi: 10.1109/ISPA.2005.195378

27. Belaroussi, R., Prevost, L., Milgram, M.: Multi-stage fusion for face localization. In: Proceedings of International Conference on Information Fusion, pp. 1–8. IEEE, New York (2005). doi: 10.1109/ICIF.2005.1591996

28. Belcher, C., Du, Y.: A selective feature information approach for iris image-quality measure. IEEE Trans. Inform. Forensics Secur. **3**(3), 572–577 (2008). doi: 10.1109/TIFS.2008.924606

29. Belcher, C., Du, Y.: Region-based sift approach to iris recognition. Optic Laser Eng. **47**(1), 139–147 (2009). doi: 10.1016/j.optlaseng.2008.07.004

30. Belhumeur, P., Jacobs, D., Kriegman, D., Kumar, N.: Localizing parts of faces using a consensus of exemplars. In: Proceedings of IEEE Conference on Computer Vision and Pattern Recognition, pp. 545–552. IEEE, New York (2011). doi: 10.1109/CVPR.2011.5995602

31. Beng, A., Teoh, J., Toh, K.A.: Secure biometric-key generation with biometric helper. In: Proceedings of 3rd IEEE Conference on Industrial Electronics and Applications, pp. 2145–2150. IEEE, New York (2008). doi: 10.1109/ICIEA.2008.4582898

32. Berggren, L.: Iridology: A critical review. Acta Ophthalmol. **63**(1), 1–8 (1985). doi: 10.1111/j.1755-3768.1985.tb05205.x

33. Bertillon, A.: La couleur de l'iris. In: Annales de demographie internationale, pp. 226–246 (1886)

34. Bishop, C.: Pattern Recognition and Machine Learning (Information Science and Statistics), 1st edn. 2006. corr. 2nd printing edn. Springer, New York (2007)
35. Blythe, P., Fridrich, J.: Secure digital camera. In: Proceedings of Digital Forensic Research Workshop, pp. 1–12. Ithaca, NY (2004)
36. Bodo, A.: Method for producing a digital signature with aid of a biometric feature (1994). German patent DE 42 43 908 A1
37. Boles, W., Boashash, B.: A human identification technique using images of the iris and wavelet transform. IEEE Trans. Signal Process. **46**(4), 1185–1188 (1998). doi: 10.1109/78.668573
38. Bolle, R., Connell, J., Pankanti, S., Ratha, N., Senior, A.: Guide to Biometrics. Springer, New York (2004)
39. Boult, T.: Robust distance measures for face-recognition supporting revocable biometric tokens. In: Proceedings of 7th International Conference on Automatic Face and Gesture Recognition, pp. 560–566. IEEE, New York (2006). doi: 10.1109/FGR.2006.94
40. Boult, T., Scheirer, W.: Bio-cryptographic protocols with bipartite biotokens. In: Proceedings of IEEE Biometric Symposium, pp. 9–16. IEEE, New York (2008). doi: 10.1109/BSYM.2008.4655516
41. Boult, T., Scheirer, W.: Bipartite biotokens: Definition, implementation, and analysis. In: Tistarelli, M., Nixon, M. (eds.) Proceedings of 3rd International Conference on Biometrics. LNCS, vol. 5558, pp. 775–785. Springer, New York (2009). doi: 10.1007/978-3-642-01793-3_79
42. Boult, T., Scheirer, W., Woodworth, R.: Revocable fingerprint biotokens: Accuracy and security analysis. In: Proceedings of IEEE Conference on Computer Vision and Pattern Recognition, pp. 1–8. IEEE, New York (2007). doi: 10.1109/CVPR.2007.383110
43. Bowyer, K.: The results of the nice.ii iris biometrics competition. Pattern Recogn. Lett. **33**(8), 965–969 (2012). doi: 10.1016/j.patrec.2011.11.024
44. Bowyer, K., Hollingsworth, K., Flynn, P.: Image understanding for iris biometrics: A survey. Comput. Vis. Image Understand. **110**(2), 281–307 (2007). doi: 10.1016/j.cviu.2007.08.005
45. Bowyer, K., Hollingsworth, K., Flynn, P.: A survey of iris biometrics research: 2008–2010. In: Handbook of Iris Recognition. Springer, New York (2012)
46. Boyce, C., Ross, A., Monaco, M., Hornak, L., Li, X.: Multispectral iris analysis: A preliminary study. In: Proceedings of IEEE Conference on Computer Vision and Pattern Recognition Workshop, pp. 51–59. IEEE, New York (2006). doi: 10.1109/CVPRW.2006.141
47. Boyen, X.: Reusable cryptographic fuzzy extractors. In: Proceedings of 11th ACM Conference on Computer and Communications Security, pp. 82–91. ACM, New York (2004). doi: 10.1145/1030083.1030096
48. Braun, D.: How they found National Geographic's "Afgahn Girl" (2003). URL http://news. nationalgeographic.co.uk/news/2002/03/0311_020312_sharbat.html. Retrieved May 2012
49. Breebaart, J., Busch, C., Grave, J., Kindt, E.: A reference architecture for biometric template protection based on pseudo identities. In: Proceedings of Biometrics and Electronic Signatures, pp. 25–38. Ges. Informatik (2008)
50. Bresenham, J.: Algorithm for computer control of a digital plotter. IBM Syst. J. **4**(1), 25–30 (1965). doi: 10.1145/280811.280913
51. Bringer, J., Chabanne, H., Cohen, G., Kindarji, B., Zemor, G.: Optimal iris fuzzy sketches. In: Proceedings of IEEE 1st International Conference on Biometrics: Theory, Applications, and Systems, pp. 1–6. IEEE, New York (2007). doi: 10.1109/BTAS.2007.4401904
52. Bringer, J., Chabanne, H., Cohen, G., Kindarji, B., Zemor, G.: Theoretical and practical boundaries of binary secure sketches. IEEE Trans. Inform. Forensics Secur. **3**, 673–683 (2008). doi: 10.1109/TIFS.2008.2002937
53. Bringer, J., Chabanne, H., Kindarji, B.: The best of both worlds: Applying secure sketches to cancelable biometrics. Sci. Comput. Program. **74**(1-2), 43–51 (2008). doi: 10.1016/j.scico.2008.09.016

54. Bringer, J., Chabanne, H., Kindarji, B.: Anonymous identification with cancelable biometrics. In: Proceedings of 6th International Symposium on Image and Signal Processing and Analysis, pp. 494–499. IEEE, New York (2009)

55. Bringer, J., Despiegel, V.: Binary feature vector fingerprint representation from minutiae vicinities. In: Proceedings of IEEE 4th International Conference on Biometrics: Theory, Applications, and Systems, pp. 1–6. IEEE, New York (2010). doi: 10.1109/BTAS.2010.5634488

56. Broussard, R., Ives, R.: Using artificial neural networks and feature saliency to identify iris measurements that contain the most discriminatory information for iris segmentation. In: Proceedings of IEEE Workshop on Computational Intelligence in Biometrics: Theory, Algorithms, and Applications, pp. 46–51. IEEE, New York (2009). doi: 10.1109/CIB.2009.4925685

57. Broussard, R., Kennell, L., Soldan, D., Ives, R.: Using artificial neural networks and feature saliency techniques for improved iris segmentation. In: Proceedings of International Joint Conference on Neural Networks, pp. 1283–1288. IEEE, New York (2007). doi: 10.1109/IJCNN.2007.4371143

58. Bruyndonckx, O., Quisquater, J.J., Benoit, M.: Spatial method for copyright labeling of digital images. In: Pitas, I. (ed.) Proceedings of IEEE International Workshop on Nonlinear Signal and Image Processing, pp. 456–459. NAT, Thessaloniki (1995)

59. Buhan, I., Breebaart, J., Guajardo, J., de Groot, K., Kelkboom, E., Akkermans, T.: A quantitative analysis of indistinguishability for a continuous domain biometric cryptosystem. In: Proceedings of 1st International Workshop Signal Processing in the Encrypted Domain, pp. 82–99. SPEED, Lausanne (2009)

60. Buhan, I., Doumen, J., Hartel, P., Veldhuis, R.: Fuzzy extractors for continuous distributions. Technical report 06–72, University of Twente (2006)

61. Buhan, I., Doumen, J., Hartel, P., Veldhuis, R.: Constructing practical fuzzy extractors using qim. Technical report 07–52, University of Twente (2007)

62. Buhan, I., Guajardo, J., Kelkboom, E.: Efficient strategies to play the indistinguishability game for fuzzy sketches. In: Proceedings of IEEE Workshop on Information Forensics and Security, pp. 1–6. IEEE, New York (2010). doi: 10.1109/WIFS.2010.5711473

63. Burge, M., Bowyer, K.: Handbook of Iris Recognition. Springer, New York (2012)

64. Burl, M., Leung, T.K., Perona, P.: Face localization via shape statistics. In: Proceedings of International Workshop on Automatic Face and Gesture Recognition, pp. 154–159 (1995)

65. Camus, T., Wildes, R.: Reliable and fast eye finding in close-up images. In: Proceedings of 16th International Conference on Pattern Recognition, vol. 1, pp. 389–394. IEEE, New York (2002). doi: 10.1109/ICPR.2002.1044732

66. Canada Border Services Agency: NEXUS. URL http://www.cbsa-asfc.gc.ca/prog/nexus/menu-eng.html. Retrieved May 2012

67. Cao, J.G., Fowler, J., Younan, N.: An image-adaptive watermark based on a redundant wavelet transform. In: Proceedings of IEEE International Conference on Image Processing, vol. 2, pp. 277–280. IEEE, New York (2001). doi: 10.1109/ICIP.2001.958478

68. Cauchie, J., Fiolet, V., Villers, D.: Optimization of an hough transform algorithm for the search of a center. Pattern Recogn. 41(2), 567–574 (2008). doi: 10.1016/j.patcog.2007.07.001

69. Cavoukian, A., Stoianov, A.: Biometric encryption. In: Encyclopedia of Biometrics. Springer, New York (2009)

70. Cavoukian, A., Stoianov, A.: Biometric encryption: The new breed of untraceable biometrics. In: Biometrics: Fundamentals, Theory, and Systems. Wiley, London (2009). doi: 10.1002/9780470522356.ch26

71. Center for Identification Technology Research, West Virginia University: Biometric Dataset Collection. URL http://www.citer.wvu.edu/biometric_dataset_collections. Retrieved May 2012

72. Cha, S.H., Tappert, C., Yoon, S.: Enhancing binary feature vector similarity measures. J. Pattern Recogn. Res. 1(1), 63–77 (2006)

73. Chafia, F., Salim, C., Farid, B.: A biometric crypto-system for authentication. In: Proceedings of International Conference on Machine and Web Intelligence, pp. 434–438. IEEE, New York (2010). doi: 10.1109/ICMWI.2010.5648101

74. Chakraborty, A., Duncan, J.: Game-theoretic integration for image segmentation. IEEE Trans. Pattern Anal. Mach. Intell. **21**, 12–30 (1999). doi: 10.1109/34.745730

75. Chan, T., Vese, L.: Active contours without edges. IEEE Trans. Image Process. **10**(2), 266–277 (2001). doi: 10.1109/83.902291

76. Chang, E.C., Shen, R., Teo, F.: Finding the original point set hidden among chaff. In: Proceedings of 2006 ACM Symposium on Information, Computer and Communications Security, pp. 182–188. ACM, New York (2006). doi: 10.1145/1128817.1128845

77. Chen, B., Chandran, V.: Biometric based cryptographic key generation from faces. In: Proceedings of Digital Image Computing: Techniques and Applications, pp. 394–401. IEEE, New York (2007). doi: 10.1109/DICTA.2007.4426824

78. Chen, M., Fridrich, J., Goljan, M., Lukas, J.: Source digital camcorder identification using sensor photo-response non-uniformity. In: Delp, E., Wong, P. (eds.) Security, Steganography, and Watermarking of Multimedia Contents IX, Proceedings of SPIE, vol. 6505, pp. 65,051G.1–12. SPIE, Bellingham, WA (2007). doi: 10.1117/12.696519

79. Chen, M., Fridrich, J., Goljan, M., Lukas, J.: Determining image origin and integrity using sensor noise. IEEE Trans. Inform. Secur. Forensics **3**(1), 74–90 (2008). doi: 10.1109/TIFS.2007.916285

80. Chen, M., Zhang, S., Karim, M.: Modification of standard image compression methods for correlation-based pattern recognition. Opt. Eng. **43**(8), 1723–1730 (2004). doi: 10.1117/1.1765664

81. Chen, R., Lin, X., Ding, T.: Iris segmentation for non-cooperative recognition systems. IET Image Process. **5**(5), 448–456 (2011). doi: 10.1049/iet-ipr.2009.0234

82. Chen, T.S., Chen, J., Chen, J.G.: A simple and efficient watermark technique based on JPEG2000 codec. Multimed. Syst. **10**(1), 16–26 (2004). doi: 10.1007/s00530-004-0133-8

83. Chen, W.S., Chih, K.H., Shih, S.W., Hsieh, C.M.: Personal identification with human iris recognition based on wavelet transform. In: Proceedings of IAPR Conference on Machine Vision Applications, pp. 351–354 (2005)

84. Chen, W.S., Yuan, S.Y.: A novel personal biometric authentication technique using human iris based on fractal dimension features. In: IEEE International Conference on Acoustics, Speech, and Signal Processing, vol. 3, pp. 201–204 (2003). doi: 10.1109/ICASSP.2003.1199142

85. Chen, Y., Adjouadi, M., Barreto, A., Rishe, N., Andrian, J.: A computational efficient iris extraction approach in unconstrained environments. In: Proceedings of IEEE 3rd International Conference on Biometrics: Theory, Applications, and Systems, pp. 1–7. IEEE, New York (2009). doi: 10.1109/BTAS.2009.5339024

86. Chen, Y., Adjouadi, M., Han, C., Wang, J., Barreto, A., Rishe, N., Andrian, J.: A highly accurate and computationally efficient approach for unconstrained iris segmentation. Image Vis. Comput. **28**(2), 261–269 (2010). doi: 10.1016/j.imavis.2009.04.017

87. Chen, Y., Dass, S.C., Jain, A.K.: Localized iris image quality using 2-d wavelets. In: Zhang, D., Jain, A. (eds.) Proceedings of 1st International Conference on Biometrics. LNCS, vol. 3832, pp. 373–381. Springer, New York (2006). doi: 10.1007/11608288_50

88. Chen, Y., Wang, J., Han, C., Wang, L., Adjouadi, M.: A robust segmentation approach to iris recognition based on video. In: Proceedings of 37th Applied Imagery Pattern Recognition Workshop, pp. 1–8. IEEE, New York (2008). doi: 10.1109/AIPR.2008.4906441

89. Chinese Academy of Sciences, Institute of Automation: Biometrics Ideal Test. URL http://biometrics.idealtest.org. Retrieved May 2012

90. Chinese Academy of Sciences, Institute of Automation: Service Note on CASIA Iris Image Databases. URL http://www.cbsr.ia.ac.cn/HFB_Agreement/ServiceNoteOnCasiaIrisImageDatabases.pdf. Retrieved May 2012

91. Cho, D., Park, K., Rhee, D., Kim, Y., Yang, J.: Pupil and iris localization for iris recognition in mobile phones. In: Proceedings of 7th ACIS International Conference on Software Engineering, Artificial Intelligence, Networking, and Parallel/Distributed Computing, pp. 197–201. IEEE, New York (2006). doi: 10.1109/SNPD-SAWN.2006.58

92. Choi, S., Cha, S., Tappert, C.: A survey of binary similarity and distance measures. J. Systemics Cybern. Informat. **8**(1), 43–48 (2010)

93. Chong, S.C., Jin, A.T.B., Ling, D.N.C.: High security iris verification system based on random secret integration. Comput. Vis. Image Understand. **102**(2), 169–177 (2006). doi: 10.1016/j.cviu.2006.01.002

94. Chong, S.C., Jin, A.T.B., Ling, D.N.C.: Iris authentication using privatized advanced correlation filter. In: Zhang, D., Jain, A. (eds.) Proceedings of 1st International Conference on Biometrics. LNCS, vol. 3832, pp. 382–388. Springer, New York (2006). doi: 10.1007/11608288_51

95. Chou, C.T., Shih, S.W., Chen, W.S., Cheng, V.W.: Iris recognition with multi-scale edge-type matching. In: Proceedings of 18th International Conference on Pattern Recognition, pp. 545–548. IEEE, New York (2006). doi: 10.1109/ICPR.2006.728

96. Chu, C.T., Chen, C.H.: High performance iris recognition based on lda and lpcc. In: Proceedings of 17th IEEE International Conference on Tools with Artificial Intelligence, pp. 417–421. IEEE, New York (2005)

97. Chung, Y., Moon, D., Lee, S., Jung, S., Kim, T., Ahn, D.: Automatic alignment of fingerprint features for fuzzy fingerprint vault. In: Proceedings of Conference on Information Security and Cryptology. LNCS, vol. 3822, pp. 358–369. Springer, New York (2005). doi: 10.1007/11599548_31

98. Chung, Y., Moon, D., Moon, K., Pan, S.: Hiding biometric data for secure transmission. In: Khosla, R., Howlett, R.J., Jain, L.C. (eds.) Proceedings of KES 2005. LNCS, vol. 3683, pp. 1049–1057. Springer, New York (2005). doi: 10.1007/11553939_147

99. Cimato, S., Gamassi, M., Piuri, V., Sassi, R., Scotti, F.: A multi-biometric verification system for the privacy protection of iris templates. In: Corchado, E., Zunino, R., Gastaldo, P., Herrero, Á. (eds.) Proceedings of International Workshop on Computational Intelligence in Security for Information Systems, Advances in Soft Computing, vol. 53, pp. 227–234. Springer, New York (2008). doi: 10.1007/978-3-540-88181-0_29

100. Clancy, T.C., Kiyavash, N., Lin, D.J.: Secure smartcard-based fingerprint authentication. In: Proceedings of ACM 2003 Multimedia, Biometrics Methods and Applications Workshop, pp. 45–52. ACM, New York (2003). doi: 10.1145/982507.982516

101. Cogent 3M: CIS 202. URL http://www.cogentsystems.com/cis202.asp. Retrieved June 2012

102. Commission Int'l de l'Eclairage, TC 6-38: Photobiological Safety Standards for Safety Standards for Lamps, CIE 134-3-99 (1999)

103. Computer Vision Research Laboratory: CVRL Data Sets. URL http://www.nd.edu/~cvrl/CVRL/Data_Sets.html. Retrieved May 2012

104. Connie, T., Teoh, A., Goh, M., Ngo, D.: Palmhashing: a novel approach for cancelable biometrics. Inform. Process. Lett. **93**(1), 1–5 (2005). doi: 10.1016/j.ipl.2004.09.014

105. Cristinacce, D., Cootes, T., Scott, I.: A multi-stage approach to facial feature. In: Proceedings of British Machine Vision Conference, pp. 231–240. BMVA Press, Guildford (2004)

106. Crossmatch: I SCAN 2. URL http://www.crossmatch.com/de/i-scan-2.php. Retrieved June 2012

107. Cui, J., Wang, Y., Tan, T., Ma, L., Sun, Z.: A fast and robust iris localization method based on texture segmentation. In: Jain, A., Ratha, N. (eds.) Biometric Technology for Human Identification, Proceedings of SPIE, vol. 5404, pp. 401–408. SPIE, Bellingham, WA (2004). doi: 10.1117/12.541921

108. Daugman, J.: Two-dimensional spectral analysis of cortical receptive field profiles. Vis. Res. **20**(10), 847–856 (1980). doi: 10.1016/0042-6989(80)90065-6

109. Daugman, J.: High confidence visual recognition of persons by a test of statistical independence. IEEE Trans. Pattern Anal. Mach. Intell. **15**(11), 1148–1161 (1993). doi: 10.1109/34.244676

110. Daugman, J.: Biometric personal identification system based on iris analysis (1994). US Patent 5291560, WIPO Patent 9409446

111. Daugman, J.: Biometric decision landscapes. Technical report tr482, Cambridge University (2000)

112. Daugman, J.: Iris recognition. Am. Sci. **89**(4), 326–333 (2001). doi: 10.1511/2001.4.326

113. Daugman, J.: Statistical richness of visual phase information: Update on recognizing persons by iris patterns. Int. J. Comput. Vis. **45**(1), 25–38 (2001). doi: 10.1023/A:1012365806338

114. Daugman, J.: How the afghan girl was identified by her iris patterns (2002). URL http://www.cl.cam.ac.uk/~jgd1000/afghan.html. Retrieved May 2012

115. Daugman, J.: The importance of being random: statistical principles of iris recognition. Pattern Recogn. **36**(2), 279–291 (2003). doi: 10.1016/S0031-3203(02)00030-4

116. Daugman, J.: How iris recognition works. IEEE Trans. Circ. Syst. Video Tech. **14**(1), 21–30 (2004). doi: 10.1109/ICIP.2002.1037952

117. Daugman, J.: Probing the uniqueness and randomness of iriscodes: Results from 200 billion iris pair comparisons. Proc. IEEE **94**(11), 1927–1935 (2006). doi: 10.1109/JPROC.2006.884092

118. Daugman, J.: New methods in iris recognition. IEEE Trans. Syst. Man Cybern. B Cybern. **37**(5), 1167–1175 (2007). doi: 10.1109/TSMCB.2007.903540

119. Daugman, J.: Iris recognition at airports and border-crossings. In: Encyclopedia of Biometrics. Springer, New York (2009)

120. Daugman, J., Downing, C.: Epigenetic randomness, complexity and singularity of human iris patterns. In: Proceedings of the Royal Society (London): Biological Sciences, vol. 268, pp. 1737–1740. The Royal Society, London (2001)

121. Daugman, J., Downing, C.: Effect of severe image compression on iris recognition performance. IEEE Trans. Inform. Forensics Secur. **3**, 52–61 (2008). doi: 10.1109/TIFS.2007.916009

122. Daugman, J., Malhas, I.: Iris recognition border-crossing system in the uae. Int. Airport Rev. **2**, 49–53 (2004)

123. Daugman, J.G.: Uncertainty relation for resolution in space, spatial frequency, and orientation optimized by two-dimensional visual cortical filters. J. Opt. Soc. Am. A Opt. Image Sci. Vis. **2**(7), 1160–1169 (1985). doi: 10.1364/JOSAA.2.001160

124. Davida, G., Frankel, Y., Matt, B.: On enabling secure applications through off-line biometric identification. In: Proceedings of IEEE Symposium on Security and Privacy, pp. 148–157. IEEE, New York (1998). doi: 10.1109/SECPRI.1998.674831

125. Davida, G., Frankel, Y., Matt, B.: On the relation of error correction and cryptography to an off line biometric based identication scheme. In: Proceedings of Workshop on Coding and Cryptography, pp. 129–138 (1999)

126. De Marsico, M., Nappi, M., Daniel, R.: Isis: Iris segmentation for identification systems. In: Proceedings of 20th International Conference on Pattern Recognition, pp. 2857–2860. IEEE, New York (2010). doi: 10.1109/ICPR.2010.700

127. Delivasilis, D.L., Katsikas, S.K.: Side channel analysis on biometric-based key generation algorithms on resource constrained devices. Int. J. Netw. Secur. **3**(1), 44–50 (2005)

128. Delvaux, N., Chabanne, H., Bringer, J., Kindarji, B., Lindeberg, P., Midgren, J., Breebaart, J., Akkermans, T., van der Veen, M., Veldhuis, R., Kindt, E., Simoens, K., Busch, C., Bours, P., Gafurov, D., Yang, B., Stern, J., Rust, C., Cucinelli, B., Skepastianos, D.: Pseudo identities based on fingerprint characteristics. In: Proceedings of International Conference on Intelligent Information Hiding and Multimedia Signal Processing, pp. 1063–1068. IEEE, New York (2008). doi: 10.1109/IIH-MSP.2008.327

129. Determan, G.E., Jacobson, V.C., Jelinek, J., Phinney, T., Hamza, R.M., Ahrens, T., Kilgore, G.A., Whillock, R.P., Bedros, S.: Combined face and iris recognition system (2007). U.S. Patent 20080075334

130. Ding, S., Li, C., Liu, Z.: Protecting hidden transmission of biometrics using authentication watermarking. In: Proceedings of 2010 WASE International Conference on Information Engineering, pp. 105–108. IEEE, New York (2010). doi: 10.1109/ICIE.2010.120

131. Dobes, M., Martinek, J., Skoupil, D., Dobesova, Z., Pospisil, J.: A robust method for eye features extraction on color image. Optik **117**(10), 468–473 (2005). doi: 10.1016/j.patrec.2005.03.033

132. Dodis, Y., Ostrovsky, R., Reyzin, L., Smith, A.: Fuzzy Extractors: How to Generate Strong Keys from Biometrics and Other Noisy Data. In: Cachin, C., Camenisch, J. (eds.) Proceedings of International Conference on Theory And Applications of Cryptographic Techniques. LNCS, vol. 3027, pp. 523–540. Springer, New York (2004). doi: 10.1007/978-3-540-24676-3_31

133. Dong, J., Tan, T.: Effects of watermarking on iris recognition performance. In: Proceedings of 10th International Conference on Control, Automation, Robotics and Vision, pp. 1156–1161. IEEE, New York (2008). doi: 10.1109/ICARCV.2008.4795684

134. Dorairaj, V., Schmid, N.A., Fahmy, G.: Performance evaluation of iris-based recognition system implementing pca and ica encoding techniques. In: Jain, A.K., Ratha, N.K. (eds.) Biometric Technology for Human Identification II, Proceedings of SPIE, vol. 5779, pp. 51–58. SPIE, Bellingham, WA (2005). doi: 10.1117/12.604201

135. Du, Y.: Using 2D log-Gabor spatial filters for iris recognition. In: Flynn, P.J., Pankanti, S. (eds.) Biometric Technology for Human Identification III, Proceedings of SPIE, vol. 6202, pp. 62,020F.1–8. SPIE, Bellingham, WA (2006). doi: 10.1117/12.663834

136. Du, Y., Arslanturk, E., Zhou, Z., Belcher, C.: Video-based noncooperative iris image segmentation. IEEE Trans. Syst. Man Cybern. B Cybern. 41(1), 64–74 (2011). doi: 10.1109/TSMCB.2010.2045371

137. Du, Y., Ives, R., Etter, D., Welch, T.: A new approach to iris pattern recognition. In: Driggers, R.G., Huckridge, D.A. (eds.) Electro-Optical and Infrared Systems: Technology and Applications, Proceedings of SPIE, vol. 5612, pp. 104–116. SPIE, Bellingham, WA (2004). doi: 10.1117/12.578789

138. Dufaux, F., Sullivan, G.J., Ebrahimi, T.: The JPEG XR image coding standard. IEEE Signal. Process. Mag. 26(6), 195–199 (2009). doi: 10.1109/MSP.2009.934187

139. Dugad, R., Ratakonda, K., Ahuja, N.: A new wavelet-based scheme for watermarking images. In: Proceedings of IEEE International Conference on Image Processing, vol. 2, pp. 419–423. IEEE, New York (1998). doi: 10.1109/ICIP.1998.723406

140. Ekici, Ö., Sankur, B., Akcay, M.: Comparative evaluation of semi-fragile watermarking algorithms. J. Electron. Imag. 13(1), 209–216 (2003). doi: 10.1117/1.1633285

141. Failla, P., Sutcu, Y., Barni, M.: esketch: a privacy-preserving fuzzy commitment scheme for authentication using encrypted biometrics. In: Proceedings of 12th Workshop on Multimedia and Security, pp. 241–246. ACM, New York (2010). doi: 10.1145/1854229.1854271

142. Fancourt, C., Bogoni, L., Hanna, K., Guo, Y., Wildes, R., Takahashi, N., Jain, U.: Iris recognition at a distance. In: Kanade, T., Jain, A., Ratha, N. (eds.) Proceedings of 5th International Conference on Audio- and Video-Based Biometric Person Authentication. LNCS, vol. 3546, pp. 1–13. Springer, New York (2005). doi: 10.1007/11527923_1

143. Färberböck, P., Hämmerle-Uhl, J., Kaaser, D., Pschernig, E., Uhl, A.: Transforming rectangular and polar iris images to enable cancelable biometrics. In: Campilho, A., Kamel, M. (eds.) Proceedings of 7th International Conference on Image Analysis and Recognition. LNCS, vol. 6112, pp. 276–386. Springer, New York (2010). doi: 10.1007/978-3-642-13775-4_28

144. Farid, H.: Image forgery detection. IEEE Signal. Process. Mag. 26(2), 16–25 (2009). doi: 10.1109/MSP.2008.931079

145. fCoder Group: ImageConverter Plus. URL http://www.imageconverterplus.com/. Retrieved June 2012

146. Feng, H., Wah, C.C.: Private key generation from on-line handwritten signatures. Inform. Manag. Comput. Secur. 10, 159–164 (2002). doi: 10.1108/09685220210436949

147. Feng, J.B., Lin, I.C., Tsai, C.S., Chu, Y.P.: Reversible watermarking: current status and key issues. Int. J. Netw. Secur. 2(3), 161–171 (2006)

148. Feng, Y.C., Yuen, P.C., Jain, A.K.: A hybrid approach for face template protection. In: Kumar, B.V., Prabhakar, S., Ross, A.A. (eds.) Biometric Technology for Human Identification V, Proceedings of SPIE, vol. 6944, pp. 694,408.1–11. SPIE, Bellingham, WA (2008). doi: 10.1117/12.778652

149. Fenker, S.P., Bowyer, K.W.: Experimental evidence of a template aging effect in iris biometrics. In: Proceedings of IEEE Workshop on Applications of Computer Vision, pp. 232–239. IEEE, New York (2011). doi: 10.1109/WACV.2011.5711508

150. Filho, C., Costa, M.: Iris segmentation exploring color spaces. In: Proceedings of 3rd International Conference on Image and Signal Processing, vol. 4, pp. 1878–1882. IEEE, New York (2010). doi: 10.1109/CISP.2010.5647406

151. Fitzgibbon, A., Pilu, M., Fisher, R.B.: Direct least square fitting of ellipses. IEEE Trans. Pattern Anal. Mach. Intell. 21(5), 476–480 (1999). doi: 10.1109/34.765658

152. Flom, L., Safir, A.: Iris recognition system (1986). US Patent 4641349, WIPO Patent 8605018

153. Flynn, P.J.: Biometrics databases. In: Jain, A.K., Flynn, P., Ross, A.A. (eds.) Handbook of Biometrics, pp. 529–548. Springer, New York (2008)

154. Fong, W., Chan, S., Ho, K.: Designing JPEG quantization matrix using rate-distortion approach and human visual system model. In: Proceedings of IEEE International Conference on Communications, vol. 3, pp. 1659–1663. IEEE, New York (1997). doi: 10.1109/ICC.1997.595069

155. Forrester, J.V., Dick, A.D., McMenamin, P.G., Roberts, F.: The Eye: Basic Sciences in Practice, 3rd edn. Saunders, Philadelphia, PA (2008)

156. Fridrich, J.: Digital image forensic using sensor noise. IEEE Signal. Process. Mag. 26(2) (2009)

157. Frost, A.: FuturixImager. URL http://fximage.com/. Retrieved June 2012

158. Gaddam, S.V.K., Lal, M.: Effcient cancellable biometric key generation scheme for cryptography. Int. J. Netw. Secur. 11(2), 61–69 (2010)

159. Gan, J.Y., Liang, Y.: A method for face and iris feature fusion in identity authentication. Int. J. Comp. Sci. Netw. Secur. 6(2), 135–138 (2006)

160. Gentile, J.E., Ratha, N., Connell, J.: An efficient, two-stage iris recognition system. In: Proceedings of IEEE 3rd International Conference on Biometrics: Theory, Applications, and Systems, pp. 1–5. IEEE, New York (2009). doi: 10.1109/BTAS.2009.5339056

161. Gentile, J.E., Ratha, N., Connell, J.: Slic: Short-length iris codes. In: Proceedings of IEEE 3rd International Conference on Biometrics: Theory, Applications, and Systems, pp. 1–5. IEEE, New York (2009). doi: 10.1109/BTAS.2009.5339027

162. Georghiades, A.S., Belhumeur, P.N.: From few to many: Illumination cone models for face recognition under variable lighting and pose. IEEE Trans. Pattern Anal. Mach. Intell. 23(6), 643–660 (2001). doi: 10.1109/34.927464

163. Goh, A., Ngo, D.C.L.: Computation of cryptographic keys from face biometrics. In: Lioy, A., Mazzocchi, D. (eds.) Proceedings of 7th International Conference on Communications and Multimedia Security. LNCS, vol. 2828, pp. 1–13. Springer, New York (2003). doi: 10.1007/978-3-540-45184-6_1

164. Goh, A., Teoh, A.B.J., Ngo, D.C.L.: Random multispace quantization as an analytic mechanism for biohashing of biometric and random identity inputs. IEEE Trans. Pattern Anal. Mach. Intell. 28(12), 1892–1901 (2006). doi: 10.1109/TPAMI.2006.250

165. Goljan, M., Fridrich, J., Chen, M.: Sensor noise camera identification: Countering counterforensics. In: Memon, N.D., Dittmann, J., Alattar, A.M., Delp, E.J. (eds.) Media Forensics and Security II, Proceedings of SPIE, vol. 7541, pp. 75,410S.1–12. SPIE, Bellingham, WA (2010). doi: 10.1117/12.839055

166. Goljan, M., Fridrich, J., Chen, M.: Defending against fingerprint-copy attack in sensorbased camera identification. IEEE Trans. Inform. Secur. Forensics 6(1), 227–236 (2011). doi: 10.1109/TIFS.2010.2099220

167. Goljan, M., Fridrich, J., Filler, T.: Large scale test of sensor fingerprint camera identification. In: Delp, E.J., Dittmann, J., Memon, N.D., Wong, P.W. (eds.) Electronic Imaging, Security and Forensics of Multimedia Contents XI, Proceedings of SPIE, vol. 7254, pp. 72540I.1–12. SPIE, Bellingham, WA (2009). doi: 10.1117/12.805701

168. Goljan, M., Fridrich, J., Filler, T.: Managing a large database of camera fingerprints. In: Memon, N.D., Dittmann, J., Alattar, A.M., Delp, E.J. (eds.) Media Forensics and Security II, Proceedings of SPIE, vol. 7541, pp. 754,108.1–12. SPIE, Bellingham, WA (2010). doi: 10.1117/12.838378

169. Gong, Y., Deng, K., Shi, P.: Pki key generation based on iris features. In: Proceedings of International Conference on Computer Science and Software Engineering, vol. 6, pp. 166–169. IEEE, New York (2008). doi: 10.1109/CSSE.2008.1181

170. Gougelet, P.E.: XN-View. URL http://www.xnview.com/. Retrieved June 2012
171. Grabowski, K., Napieralski, A.: Hardware architecture optimized for iris recognition. IEEE Trans. Circ. Syst. Video Tech. **21**(9), 1293–1303 (2011). doi: 10.1109/TCSVT.2011.2147150
172. Grother, P., Quinn, G.W., Matey, J.R., Ngan, M., Salamon, W., Fiumara, G., Watson, C.: Irex iii performance of iris identification algorithms. Interagency report 7836, NIST (2012)
173. Grother, P., Tabasi, E., Quinn, G.W., Salamon, W.: Irex i performance of iris recognition algorithms on standard images. Interagency report 7629, NIST (2009)
174. Gunsel, B., Uludag, U., Tekalp, A.M.: Robust watermarking of fingerprint images. Pattern Recogn. **35**(12), 2739–2747 (2002). doi: 10.1016/S0031-3203(01)00250-3
175. Gupta, P., Sana, A., Mehrotra, H., Hwang, C.J.: An efficient indexing scheme for binary feature based biometric database. In: Prabhakar, S., Ross, A. (eds.) Biometric Technology for Human Identification IV, Proceedings of SPIE, vol. 6539, pp. 653,909.1–10. SPIE, Bellingham, WA (2007). doi: 10.1117/12.719237
176. Hämmerle-Uhl, J., Karnutsch, M., Uhl, A.: Recognition impact of JPEG2000 part 2 wavelet packet subband structures in polar iris image compression. In: Zovko-Cihlar, B., Rupp, M., Mecklenbräuker, C. (eds.) Proceedings of 19th International Conference on Systems, Signals and Image Processing, pp. 13–16. IEEE, New York (2012)
177. Hämmerle-Uhl, J., Prähauser, C., Starzacher, T., Uhl, A.: Improving compressed iris recognition accuracy using jpeg2000 roi coding. In: Tistarelli, M., Nixon, M. (eds.) Proceedings of 3rd International Conference on Biometrics. LNCS, vol. 5558, pp. 1102–1111. Springer, New York (2009). doi: 10.1007/978-3-642-01793-3_111
178. Hämmerle-Uhl, J., Pschernig, E., Uhl, A.: Cancelable iris biometrics using block re-mapping and image warping. In: Samarati, P., Yung, M., Martinelli, F., Ardagna, C. (eds.) Proceedings of 12th International Information Security Conference. LNCS, vol. 5735, pp. 135–142. Springer, New York (2009). doi: 10.1007/978-3-642-04474-8_11
179. Hämmerle-Uhl, J., Raab, K., Uhl, A.: Experimental study on the impact of robust watermarking on iris recognition accuracy. In: Proceedings of 25th ACM Symposium on Applied Computing, pp. 1479–1484. ACM, New York (2010). doi: 10.1145/1774088.1774405
180. Hämmerle-Uhl, J., Raab, K., Uhl, A.: Attack against robust watermarking-based multimodal biometric recognition systems. In: Vielhauer, C., Dittmann, J., Drygajlo, A., Juul, N., Fairhurst, M. (eds.) Proceedings of COST 2101 European Workshop on Biometrics and ID Management. LNCS, vol. 6583, pp. 25–36. Springer, New York (2011). doi: 10.1007/978-3-642-19530-3_3
181. Hämmerle-Uhl, J., Raab, K., Uhl, A.: Robust watermarking in iris recognition: application scenarios and impact on recognition performance. ACM SIGAPP Appl. Comput. Rev. **11**(3), 6–18 (2011). doi: 10.1145/2034594.2034595
182. Hämmerle-Uhl, J., Raab, K., Uhl, A.: Watermarking as a means to enhance biometric systems: A critical survey. In: Filler, T., Pevny, T., Craver, S., Ker, A. (eds.) Proceedings of 13th International Conference on Information Hiding. LNCS, vol. 6958, pp. 238–254. Springer, New York (2011). doi: 10.1007/978-3-642-24178-9_17
183. Han, B.J., Shin, Y.N., Jeun, I.K., Jung, H.C.: A framework for alternative pin service based on cancellable biometrics. In: Proceedings of Joint Workshop on Information Security, pp. 1–10 (2009)
184. Hao, F., Anderson, R., Daugman, J.: Combining Cryptography with Biometrics Effectively. IEEE Trans. Comput. **55**(9), 1081–1088 (2006). doi: 10.1109/TC.2006.138
185. Hassanien, A.E., Abraham, A., Grosan, C.: Spiking neural network and wavelets for hiding iris data in digital images. Soft Comput. Fusion Foundations Methodologies Appl. **13**(4), 401–416 (2008). doi: 10.1007/s00500-008-0324-x
186. He, X., Shi, P.: A new segmentation approach for iris recognition based on hand-held capture device. Pattern Recogn. **40**, 1326–1333 (2007). doi: 10.1016/j.patcog.2006.08.009
187. He, Y., Liu, T., Hou, Y., Wang, Y.: A fast iris image quality evaluation method based on weighted entropy. In: Zhou, L. (ed.) International Symposium on Photoelectronic Detection and Imaging, Proceedings of SPIE, vol. 6623, pp. 66,231R.1–8. SPIE, Bellingham, WA (2007). doi: 10.1117/12.791526

188. He, Z., Tan, T., Sun, Z.: Iris localization via pulling and pushing. In: Proceedings of 18th International Conference on Pattern Recognition, vol. 4, pp. 366–369. IEEE, New York (2006). doi: 10.1109/ICPR.2006.724

189. He, Z., Tan, T., Sun, Z., Qiu, X.: Toward accurate and fast iris segmentation for iris biometrics. IEEE Trans. Pattern Anal. Mach. Intell. 31(9), 1670–1684 (2009). doi: 10.1109/TPAMI.2008.183

190. Hernandez, A., Hernandez, E., Sanchez, A.: Biometric fuzzy extractor scheme for iris templates. In: Proceedings of International Conference on Security and Management, vol. 2, pp. 563–569 (2009)

191. Hirata, S., Takahashi, K.: Cancelable biometrics with perfect secrecy for correlation-based matching. In: Tistarelli, M., Nixon, M. (eds.) Proceedings of 3rd International Conference on Biometrics. LNCS, vol. 5558, pp. 868–878. Springer, New York (2009). doi: 10.1007/978-3-642-01793-3_88

192. Hoang, T., Tran, D., Sharma, D.: Remote multimodal biometric authentication using bit priority-based fragile watermarking. In: Proceedings of 19th International Conference on Pattern Recognition, pp. 1–4. IEEE, New York (2008). doi: 10.1109/ICPR.2008.4761869

193. Hofbauer, H., Rathgeb, C., Uhl, A., Wild, P.: Image metric-based biometric comparators: a supplement to feature vector-based hamming distance? In: Proceedings of IEEE International Conference of the Biometrics Special Interest Group, LNI, vol. 196. GI, Bonn (2012)

194. Hofbauer, H., Rathgeb, C., Uhl, A., Wild, P.: Iris recognition in image domain: Quality-metric based comparators. In: G. Bebis et al. (eds.) Proceedings of 8th International Symposium on Visual Computing. LNCS, vol. 7432, pp. 1–10. Springer, New York (2012). doi: 10.1007/978-3-642-33191-6_1

195. Hofbauer, H., Uhl, A.: An effective and efficient visual quality index based on local edge gradients. In: Proceedings of IEEE 3rd European Workshop on Visual Information Processing, pp. 162–167. IEEE, New York (2011). doi: 10.1109/EuVIP.2011.6045514

196. Hollingsworth, K.P., Bowyer, K.W., Flynn, P.J.: The best bits in an iris code. IEEE Trans. Pattern Anal. Mach. Intell. 31(6), 964–973 (2009). doi: 10.1109/TPAMI.2008.185

197. Hong, S., Jeon, W., Kim, S., Won, D., Park, C.: The vulnerabilities analysis of fuzzy vault using password. In: Proceedings of 2nd International Conference on Future Generation Communication and Networking, pp. 76–83. IEEE, New York (2008). doi: 10.1109/FGCN.2008.211

198. Hong, S., Kim, H., Lee, S., Chung, Y.: Analyzing the secure and energy efficient transmissions of compressed fingerprint images using encryption and watermarking. In: Proceedings of International Conference on Information Security and Assurance, pp. 316–320. IEEE, New York (2008). doi: 10.1109/ISA.2008.57

199. Hoque, S., Fairhurst, M., Howells, G.: Evaluating biometric encryption key generation using handwritten signatures. In: Proceedings of the 2008 Bio-inspired, Learning and Intelligent Systems for Security, pp. 17–22. IEEE, New York (2008). doi: 10.1109/BLISS.2008.8

200. Horvath, K., Stögner, H., Uhl, A.: Effects of jpeg xr compression settings on iris recognition systems. In: Real, P., Diaz-Pernil, D., Molina-Abril, H., Berciano, A., Kropatsch, W. (eds.) Proceedings of 14th International Conference on Computer Analysis of Images and Patterns. LNCS, vol. 6855, pp. 73–80. Springer, New York (2011). doi: 10.1007/978-3-642-23678-5_7

201. Horvath, K., Stögner, H., Uhl, A.: Optimisation of JPEG XR quantisation settings in iris recognition systems. In: Davies, P., Newell, D. (eds.) Proceedings of 4th International Conference on Advances in Multimedia, pp. 88–93. IARIA, Wilmington, DE (2012)

202. Horvath, K., Stögner, H., Uhl, A., Weinhandel, G.: Experimental study on lossless compression of biometric iris data. In: Proceedings of 7th International Symposium on Image and Signal Processing and Analysis, pp. 379–384. IEEE, New York (2011)

203. Horvath, K., Stögner, H., Uhl, A., Weinhandel, G.: Lossless compression of polar iris image data. In: Vitria, J., Sanches, J., Hernandez, M. (eds.) Proceedings of 5th Iberian Conference on Pattern Recognition and Image Analysis. LNCS, vol. 6669, pp. 329–337. Springer, New York (2011). doi: 10.1007/978-3-642-21257-4_41

204. Hosseini, S.M., Araabi, B.N., Soltanian-Zadeh, H.: Shape analysis of stroma for iris recognition. In: Lee, S.W., Li, S. (eds.) Proceedings of 2nd International Conference on Biometrics. LNCS, vol. 4642, pp. 790–799. Springer, New York (2007). doi: 10.1007/978-3-540-74549-5_83

205. Hough, P.V.C.: Machine Analysis of Bubble Chamber Pictures. In: Proceedings of International Conference on High Energy Accelerators and Instrumentation. CERN, Geneva (1959)

206. Huang, J., Wang, Y., Tan, T., Cui, J.: A new iris segmentation method for recognition. In: Proceedings of 17th International Conference on Pattern Recognition, vol. 3, pp. 554–557. IEEE, New York (2004). doi: 10.1109/ICPR.2004.1334589

207. Huang, Y.P., Luo, S.W., Chen, E.Y.: An efficient iris recognition system. In: Proceedings of 1st International Conference on Machine Learning and Cybernetics, pp. 450–454. IEEE, New York (2002). doi: 10.1109/ICMLC.2002.1176794

208. Huber, R., Stögner, H., Uhl, A.: Semi-fragile watermarking in biometric systems: template self-embedding. In: Real, P., Diaz-Pernil, D., Molina-Abril, H., Berciano, A., Kropatsch, W. (eds.) Proceedings of the 14th International Conference on Computer Analysis of Images and Patterns (CAIP 2011). LNCS, vol. 6855, pp. 34–41. Springer, New York (2011)

209. Huber, R., Stögner, H., Uhl, A.: Two-factor biometric recognition with integrated tamper-protection watermarking. In: DeDecker, B., Lapon, J., Naessens, V., Uhl, A. (eds.) Proceedings of the 12th IFIP TC6/TC11 International Conference on Communications and Multimedia Security (CMS 2011). LNCS, vol. 7025, pp. 72–84. Springer, New York (2011)

210. Hui, L., Yu-ping, H.: Wavelet tree quantization-based biometric watermarking for offline handwritten signature. In: Proceedings of International Asia Symposium on Intelligent Interaction and Affective Computing, pp. 71–74. IEEE, New York (2009). doi: 10.1109/ASIA.2009.19

211. Ignatenko, T., Willems, F.: Achieving secure fuzzy commitment scheme for optical pufs. In: Proceedings of International Conference on Intelligent Information Hiding and Multimedia Signal Processing, pp. 1185–1188. IEEE, New York (2009). doi: 10.1109/IIH-MSP.2009.310

212. Ignatenko, T., Willems, F.M.J.: Information leakage in fuzzy commitment schemes. IEEE Trans. Inform. Forensics Secur. 5(2), 337–348 (2010). doi: 10.1109/TIFS.2010.2046984

213. ImageMagick Studio LLC: ImageMagick. URL http://www.imagemagick.org/. Retrieved June 2012

214. Indian Institute of Technology Delhi: IIT Delhi Iris Database. URL http://www4.comp.polyu.edu.hk/~csajaykr/IITD/Database_Iris.htm. Retrieved May 2012

215. Intel, Willow Garage: Open Source Computer Vision Library. URL http://opencv.willowgarage.com. Retrieved May 2012

216. Iris ID: iCAM 4000. URL http://www.irisid.com/icam4000series. Retrieved May 2012

217. Iris ID: iCAM TD100. URL http://www.irisid.com/icamtd100. Retrieved May 2012

218. Iris ID: IrisAccess in Action. URL http://www.irisid.com/irisaccessinaction. Retrieved May 2012

219. IrisGuard: IG-AD100. URL http://www.irisguard.com/uploads/AD100ProductSheet.pdf. Retrieved May 2012

220. IrisKing Ltd. Co.: IKEMB-100. URL http://www.irisking.com/en/sdk.html. Retrieved May 2012

221. Ives, R., Bonney, B., Etter, D.: Effect of image compression on iris recognition. In: Proceedings of Conference on Instrumentation and Measurement Technology, pp. 2054–2058. IEEE, New York (2005). doi: 10.1109/IMTC.2005.1604535

222. Ives, R.W., Bishop, D.A., Du, Y., Belcher, C.: Iris recognition: The consequences of image compression. EURASIP J. Adv. Signal Process. 2010, 1–9 (2010). doi: 10.1155/2010/680845

223. Ives, R.W., Broussard, R.P., Kennell, L.R., Soldan, D.L.: Effects of image compression on iris recognition system performance. J. Electron. Imag. 17, 011015.1–8 (2008). doi: 10.1117/1.2891313

224. Ives, R.W., Guidry, A.J., Etter., D.M.: Iris recognition using histogram analysis. In: Proceedings of 38th Asilomar Conference on Signals, Systems, and Computers, pp. 562–566. IEEE, New York (2004). doi: 10.1109/ACSSC.2004.1399196

225. Jagadeesan, A., T.Thillaikkarasi, K.Duraiswamy: Cryptographic key generation from multiple biometric modalities: Fusing minutiae with iris feature. Int. J. Comput. Appl. **2**(6), 16–26 (2010)
226. Jain, A., Uludag, U.: Hiding biometric data. IEEE Trans. Pattern Anal. Mach. Intell. **25**(11), 1494–1498 (2003). doi: 10.1109/TPAMI.2003.1240122
227. Jain, A.K., Flynn, P., Ross, A.A.: Handbook of Biometrics. Springer, New York (2008)
228. Jain, A.K., Nandakumar, K., Nagar, A.: Biometric template security. EURASIP J. Adv. Signal Process. **2008**, 1–17 (2008). doi: 10.1155/2008/579416
229. Jain, A.K., Ross, A., Prabhakar, S.: An introduction to biometric recognition. IEEE Trans. Circ. Syst. Video Tech. **14**, 4–20 (2004). doi: 10.1109/TCSVT.2003.818349
230. Jain, A.K., Ross, A., Uludag, U.: Biometric template security: Challenges and solutions. In: Proceedings of European Signal Processing Conference, pp. 1–4 (2005)
231. Jain, A.K., Uludag, U.: Hiding fingerprint minutiae in images. In: Proceedings of 3rd Workshop on Automatic Identification Advanced Technologies, pp. 97–102 (2002)
232. Jeffers, J., Arakala, A.: Minutiae-based structures for a fuzzy vault. In: Proceedings of Biometric Consortium Conference, pp. 1–6. IEEE, New York (2006). doi: 10.1109/BCC.2006.4341622
233. Jenisch, S., Lukesch, S., Uhl, A.: Comparison of compression algorithms' impact on iris recognition accuracy II: revisiting JPEG. In: Delp, E., Wong, P., Dittmann, J., Memon, N. (eds.) Security, Forensics, Steganography, and Watermarking of Multimedia Contents X, Proceedings of SPIE, vol. 6819, pp. 68,190M.1–9. SPIE, Bellingham, WA (2008). doi: 10.1117/12.766360
234. Jenisch, S., Uhl, A.: Security analysis of a cancelable iris recognition system based on block remapping. In: Proceedings of IEEE International Conference on Image Processing, pp. 3274–3277. IEEE, New York (2011). doi: 10.1109/ICIP.2011.6115590
235. Jeong, D.S., Hwang, J.W., Kang, B.J., Park, K.R., Won, C.S., Park, D.K., Kim, J.: A new iris segmentation method for non-ideal iris images. Image Vis. Comput. **28**(2), 254–260 (2010). doi: 10.1016/j.imavis.2009.04.001
236. Jeong, G.M., Kim, C., Ahn, H.S., Ahn, B.J.: JPEG quantization table design for face images and its application to face recognition. IEICE Trans. Fund. Electron. Comm. Comput. Sci. **E69-A**(11), 2990–2993 (2006)
237. Jeong, M.Y., Lee, C., Kim, J., Choi, J.Y., Toh, K.A., Kim, J.: Changeable biometrics for appearance based face recognition. In: Proceedings of Biometric Consortium Conference, pp. 1–5. IEEE, New York (2006). doi: 10.1109/BCC.2006.4341629
238. Jin, L., Yuan, X., Satoh, S., Li, J., Xia, L.: A hybrid classifier for precise and robust eye detection. In: Proceedings of 18th International Conference on Pattern Recognition, pp. 731–735. IEEE, New York (2006). doi: 10.1109/ICPR.2006.81
239. Juels, A., Sudan, M.: A fuzzy vault scheme. In: Proceedings of IEEE International Symposium on Information Theory, p. 408. IEEE, New York (2002). doi: 10.1109/ISIT.2002.1023680
240. Juels, A., Wattenberg, M.: A fuzzy commitment scheme. In: Proceedings of 6th ACM Conference on Computer and Communications Security, pp. 28–36. ACM, New York (1999). doi: 10.1145/319709.319714
241. Kalka, N., Bartlow, N., Cukic, B.: An automated method for predicting iris segmentation failures. In: Proceedings of IEEE 3rd International Conference on Biometrics: Theory, Applications, and Systems, pp. 1–8. IEEE, New York (2009). doi: 10.1109/BTAS.2009.5339062
242. Kalka, N.D., Zuo, J., Schmid, N.A., Cukic, B.: Image quality assessment for iris biometric. In: Flynn, P.J., Pankanti, S. (eds.) Conference on Biometric Technology for Human Identification III, Proceedings of SPIE, vol. 6202, pp. 61020D.1–11. SPIE, Bellingham, WA (2006). doi: 10.1117/12.666448
243. Kanade, S., Camara, D., Petrovska-Delacrtaz, D., Dorizzi, B.: Application of biometrics to obtain high entropy cryptographic keys. World Acad. Sci. Eng. Tech. **52** (2009)

244. Kanade, S., Petrovska-Delacretaz, D., Dorizzi, B.: Cancelable iris biometrics and using error correcting codes to reduce variability in biometric data. In: Proceedings of IEEE Conference on Computer Vision and Pattern Recognition, pp. 120–127. IEEE, New York (2009). doi: 10.1109/CVPR.2009.5206646

245. Kanade, S., Petrovska-Delacretaz, D., Dorizzi, B.: Multi-biometrics based cryptographic key regeneration scheme. In: Proceedings of IEEE 3rd International Conference on Biometrics: Theory, Applications, and Systems, pp. 1–7. IEEE, New York (2009). doi: 10.1109/BTAS.2009.5339034

246. Kang, B.J., Park, K.R.: A study on iris image restoration. In: Kanade, T., Jain, A., Ratha, N. (eds.) Proceedings of 5th International Conference on Audio- and Video-Based Biometric Person Authentication. LNCS, vol. 3546, pp. 31–40. Springer, New York (2005). doi: 10.1007/11527923_4

247. Karakoyunlu, D., Sunar, B.: Differential template attacks on puf enabled cryptographic devices. In: Proceedings of IEEE Workshop on Information Forensics and Security, pp. 1–6. IEEE, New York (2010). doi: 10.1109/WIFS.2010.5711445

248. Kekre, H.B., Thepade, S.D., Jain, J., Agrawal, N.: Iris recognition using texture features extracted from haarlet pyramid. Int. J. Comput. Appl. **11**(12), 1–5 (2010). Found. Comp. Sci.

249. Kekre, H.B., Thepade, S.D., Jain, J., Agrawal, N.: Iris recognition using texture features extracted from walshlet pyramid. In: Prof. International Conference & Workshop on Emerging Trends in Technology, pp. 76–81. ACM, New York (2011). doi: 10.1145/1980022.1980038

250. Kelkboom, E.J.C., Breebaart, J., Buhan, I., Veldhuis, R.N.J.: Analytical template protection performance and maximum key size given a gaussian modeled biometric source. In: Biometric Technology for Human Identification VII, Proceedings of SPIE, vol. 7667, pp. 76670D.1–12. SPIE, Bellingham, WA (2010). doi: 10.1117/12.850240

251. Kelkboom, E.J.C., Molina, G.G., Breebaart, J., Veldhuis, R.N.J., Kevenaar, T.A.M., Jonker, W.: Binary biometrics: An analytic framework to estimate the performance curves under gaussian assumption. IEEE Trans. Syst. Man Cybern. A Syst. Humans **40**(3), 555–571 (2010). doi: 10.1109/TSMCA.2010.2041657

252. Kelkboom, E.R.C., Breebaart, J., Kevenaar, T.A.M., Buhan, I., Veldhuis, R.N.J.: Preventing the decodability attack based cross-matching in a fuzzy commitment scheme. IEEE Trans. Inform. Forensics Secur. **6**(1), 107–121 (2011). doi: 10.1109/TIFS.2010.2091637

253. Kennell, L.R., Ives, R.W., Gaunt, R.M.: Binary morphology and local statistics applied to iris segmentation for recognition. In: Proceedings of IEEE International Conference on Image Processing, pp. 293–296. IEEE, New York (2006). doi: 10.1109/ICIP.2006.313183

254. Khan, M., Xie, L., Zhang, J.: Robust hiding of fingerprint-biometric data into audio signals. In: Lee, S.W., Li, S. (eds.) Proceedings of 2nd International Conference on Biometrics. LNCS, vol. 4642, pp. 702–712. Springer, New York (2007). doi: 10.1007/978-3-540-74549-5_74

255. Khan, M.K., Zhang, J., Wang, X.: Chaotic hash-based fingerprint biometric remote user authentication scheme on mobile devices. Chaos Solitons Fractals **35**(3), 519–524 (2008). doi: 10.1016/j.chaos.2006.05.061

256. Kholmatov, A., Yanikoglu, B.: Biometric cryptosystem using online signatures. In: Levi, A., Savas, E., Yenigün, H., Balcisoy, S., Saygin, Y. (eds.) Proceedings of 21st International Symposium on Computer and Information Sciences. LNCS, vol. 4263, pp. 981–990. Springer, New York (2006). doi: 10.1007/11902140_102

257. Kim, T., Chung, Y., Jung, S., Moon, D.: Secure remote fingerprint verification using dual watermarks. In: Safavi-Naini, R., Yung, M. (eds.) Proceedings of 1st International Conference on Digital Rights Management. Technologies, Issues, Challenges and Systems. LNCS, vol. 6855, pp. 217–227. Springer, New York (2005). doi: 10.1007/11787952_17

258. Kim, W.G., Lee, H.: Multimodal biometric image watermarking using two-stage integrity verification. Signal Process. **89**(12), 2385–2399 (2009). doi: 10.1016/j.sigpro.2009.04.014

259. Kim, Y., Toh, K.: A method to enhance face biometric security. In: Proceedings of IEEE 1st International Conference on Biometrics: Theory, Applications, and Systems, pp. 1–6. IEEE, New York (2007). doi: 10.1109/BTAS.2007.4401913

260. Kittler, J., Hatef, M., Duin, R.P., Matas, J.: On combining classifiers. IEEE Trans. Pattern Anal. Mach. Intell. **20**(3), 226–239 (1998). doi: 10.1109/34.667881
261. Ko, J.G., Gil, Y.H., Yoo, J.H., Chung, K.I.: A novel and efficient feature extraction method for iris recognition. ETRI J. **29**(3), 399–401 (2007)
262. Koch, E., Zhao, J.: Towards robust and hidden image copyright labeling. In: Proceedings of IEEE International Workshop on Nonlinear Signal and Image Processing, pp. 452–455 (1995)
263. Koh, J., Govindaraju, V., Chaudhary, V.: A robust iris localization method using an active contour model and hough transform. In: Proceedings of 20th International Conference on Pattern Recognition, pp. 2852–2856. IEEE, New York (2010). doi: 10.1109/ICPR.2010.699
264. Kollias, N.: The spectroscopy of human melanin pigmentation. In: Zeise, L., Chedekel, M.R., Fitzpatrick, T.B. (eds.) Melanin: Its Role in Human Photoprotection, pp. 31–38. Valdenmar Publishing, Overland Park, KS (1995)
265. Komninos, N., Dimitriou, T.: Protecting biometric templates with image watermarking techniques. In: Lee, S.W., Li, S. (eds.) Proceedings of 2nd International Conference on Biometrics. LNCS, vol. 4642, pp. 114–123. Springer, New York (2007). doi: 10.1007/978-3-540-74549-5_13
266. Kong, A., Cheunga, K.H., Zhanga, D., Kamelb, M., Youa, J.: An analysis of BioHashing and its variants. Pattern Recogn. **39**(7), 1359–1368 (2006). doi: 10.1016/j.patcog.2005.10.025
267. Kong, W., Zhang, D.: Accurate iris segmentation based on novel reflection and eyelash detection model. In: Proceedings of of 2001 International Symposium on Intelligent Multimedia, Video and Speech Processing, 2001. pp. 263–266 (2001). doi: 10.1109/ISIMP.2001.925384
268. Konrad, M., Stögner, H., Uhl, A.: Custom design of jpeg quantization tables for compressing iris polar images to improve recognition accuracy. In: Tistarelli, M., Nixon, M. (eds.) Proceedings of 3rd International Conference on Biometrics. LNCS, vol. 5558, pp. 1091–1101. Springer, New York (2009). doi: 10.1007/978-3-642-01793-3_110
269. Konrad, M., Stögner, H., Uhl, A.: Evolutionary optimization of JPEG quantization tables for compressing iris polar images in iris recognition systems. In: Proceedings of 6th International Symposium on Image and Signal Processing and Analysis, pp. 534–539. IEEE, New York (2009)
270. Konrad, M., Stögner, H., Uhl, A., Wild, P.: Computationally efficient serial combination of rotation-invariant and rotation compensating iris recognition algorithms. In: Proceedings of 5th International Conference on Computer Vision Theory and Applications, vol. 1, pp. 85–90. SciTePress, Lynnfield, MA (2010)
271. Kostmajer, G., Stögner, H., Uhl, A.: Custom jpeg quantization for improved iris recognition accuracy. In: Gritzalis, D., Lopez, J. (eds.) Proceedings of 24th IFIP International Information Security Conference, IFIP, vol. 297, pp. 78–86. Springer, New York (2009). doi: 10.1007/978-3-642-01244-0_7
272. Kovesi, P.: Image features from phase congruency. Videre J. Comput. Vis. Res. **1**(3), 1–26 (1999)
273. Krichen, E., Dorizzi, B., Sun, Z., Garcia-Salicetti, S.: Iris recognition. In: Petrovska-Delacretaz, D., Dorizzi, B., Chollet, G. (eds.) Guide to Biometric Reference Systems and Performance Evaluation, pp. 25–49. Springer, New York (2009). doi: 10.1007/978-1-84800-292-0_3
274. Krichen, E., Garcia-Salicetti, S., Dorizzi, B.: A new probabilistic iris quality measure for comprehensive noise detection. In: Proceedings of IEEE 1st International Conference on Biometrics: Theory, Applications, and Systems, pp. 1–6. IEEE, New York (2007). doi: 10.1109/BTAS.2007.4401906
275. Krichen, E., Mellakh, A., Anh, P.V., Salicetti, S., Dorizzi, B.: A biometric reference system for iris. OSIRIS version 2.01 (2009). URL http://svnext.it-sudparis.eu/svnview2-eph/ref_syst/Iris_Osiris/
276. Kronfeld, P.: Gross anatomy and embryology of the eye. In: Davison, H. (ed.) The Eye. Academic, London (1962)

277. Kroon, B., Hanjalic, A., Maas, S.: Eye localization for face matching: is it always useful and under what conditions? In: Proceedings of International Conference on Content-based Image and Video Retrieval, pp. 379–388. ACM, New York (2008). doi: 10.1145/1386352.1386401

278. Kuan, Y.W., Teoh, A.B.J., Ngo, D.C.L.: Secure hashing of dynamic hand signatures using wavelet-fourier compression with biophasor mixing and discretization. EURASIP J. Appl. Signal Process. **2007**(1), 32–32 (2007). doi: 10.1155/2007/59125

279. Kumar, A., Kumar, A.: A palmprint based cryptosystem using double encryption. In: Kumar, B.V., Prabhakar, S., Ross, A. (eds.) Conference on Biometric Technology for Human Identification V, Proceedings of SPIE, vol. 6944, pp. 69,440D.1–9. SPIE, Bellingham, WA (2008). doi: 10.1117/12.778833

280. Kumar, A., Kumar, A.: Development of a new cryptographic construct using palmprint-based fuzzy vault. EURASIP J. Adv. Signal Process. **2009**, 967,046.1–11 (2009). doi: 10.1155/2009/967046

281. Kümmel, K., Vielhauer, C.: Reverse-engineer methods on a biometric hash algorithm for dynamic handwriting. In: Proceedings of 12th Workshop on Multimedia and Security, pp. 67–72. ACM, New York (2010). doi: 10.1145/1854229.1854244

282. Kundur, D.: Watermarking with diversity: Insights and implications. IEEE Multimed. J. **8**(4), 46–52 (2001). doi: 10.1109/93.959102

283. Kundur, D., Hatzinakos, D.: Digital watermarking using multiresolution wavelet decomposition. In: Proceedings of IEEE International Conference on Acoustics, Speech and Signal Processing, vol. 5, pp. 2969–2972. IEEE, New York (1998). doi: 10.1109/ICASSP.1998.678149

284. Kutter, M., Jordan, F., Bossen, F.: Digital signature of color images using amplitude modulation. In: Sethi, I.K., Jain, R.C. (eds.) Storage and Retrieval for Image and Video Databases V, Proceedings of SPIE, vol. 3022, pp. 518–526. SPIE, Bellingham, WA (1997). doi: 10.1117/12.263442

285. L-1 Identity Solutions: MobileEyes. URL http://www.l1id.com/files/708-2011-04-04_Mobile-Eyes_data-sheet.pdf. Retrieved May 2012

286. L-1 Identity Solutions: HIIDE Series 4. URL http://www.l1id.com/files/224-HIIDE_0908_final.pdf. Retrieved May 2012

287. L-1 Identity Solutions: Pier 2.4. URL http://www.aditech.co.uk/downloads/PIER24.pdf. Retrieved May 2012

288. L-1 Identity Solutions: Pier-T. URL http://www.l1id.com/files/205-PIER-T_0908_final.pdf. Retrieved May 2012

289. Labati, R.D., Scotti, F.: Noisy iris segmentation with boundary regularization and reflections removal. Image Vis. Comput. **28**(2), 270–277 (2010). doi: 10.1016/j.imavis.2009.05.004

290. Labati, R.D., Piuri, V., Scotti, F.: Agent-based image iris segmentation and multipleviews boundary refining. In: Proceedings of IEEE 3rd International Conference on Biometrics: Theory, Applications, and Systems, pp. 204–210. IEEE, New York (2009). doi: 10.1109/BTAS.2009.5339077

291. Lalithamani, N., Soman, K.: An effective scheme for generating irrevocable cryptographic key from cancelable fingerprint templates. Int. J. Comput. Sci. Netw. Secur. **9**(3), 183–193 (2009)

292. Lalithamani, N., Soman, K.: Irrevocable cryptographic key generation from cancelable fingerprint templates: An enhanced and effective scheme. Eur. J. Sci. Res. **31**, 372–387 (2009)

293. Lalithamani, N., Soman, K.P.: Towards generating irrevocable key for cryptography from cancelable fingerprints. In: Proceedings of International Conference on Computer Science and Information Technology, pp. 563–568. IEEE, New York (2009). doi: 10.1109/ICCSIT.2009.5234801

294. Lang, A., Dittmann, J.: Digital watermarking of biometric speech references: impact to the eer system performance. In: Delp, E., Wong, P. (eds.) Security, Steganography, and Watermarking of Multimedia Contents IX, Proceedings of SPIE, vol. 6505, pp. 650513.1–12. SPIE, Bellingham, WA (2007). doi: 10.1117/12.703890

295. Lee, C., Choi, J., Toh, K., Lee, S., Kim, J.: Alignment-free cancelable fingerprint templates based on local minutiae information. IEEE Trans. Syst. Man Cybern. B Cybern. **37**(4), 980–992 (2007). doi: 10.1109/TSMCB.2007.896999

296. Lee, H., Lim, J., Yu, S., Kim, S., Lee, S.: Biometric image authentication using watermarking. In: Proceedings of International Joint Conference SICE-ICASE, pp. 3950–3953. IEEE, New York (2006). doi: 10.1109/SICE.2006.314934

297. Lee, Y., Micheals, R.J., Filliben, J.J., Phillips, P.J.: Robust Iris Recognition Baseline for the Grand Challenge. Nistir report 7777, NIST (2011)

298. Lee, Y., Phillips, P.J., Micheals, R.J.: An automated video-based system for iris recognition. In: Tistarelli, M., Nixon, M. (eds.) Proceedings of 3rd International Conference on Biometrics. LNCS, vol. 5558, pp. 1160–1169. Springer, New York (2009). doi: 10.1007/978-3-642-01793-3_117

299. Lee, Y.J., Bae, K., Lee, S.J., Park, K.R., Kim, J.: Biometric key binding: Fuzzy vault based on iris images. In: Lee, S.W., Li, S. (eds.) Proceedings of 2nd International Conference on Biometrics, LNCS, vol. 4642, pp. 800–808. Springer, New York (2007). doi: 10.1007/978-3-540-74549-5_84

300. Levenshtein, V.I.: Binary codes capable of correcting deletions, insertions, and reversals. Sov. Phys. Dokl. **10**(8), 707–710 (1966)

301. LG Iris: Iris Access 2200. URL http://www.lgiris.com/ps/products/previousmodels/irisaccess2200.htm. Retrieved May 2012

302. LG Iris: Iris Access EOU3000. URL http://www.lgiris.com/ps/products/previousmodels/ia3k/eou3000.htm. Retrieved May 2012

303. Li, C., Ma, B., Wang, Y., Zhang, Z.: Protecting biometric templates using authentication watermarking. In: Qiu, G., Lam, K., Kiya, H., Xue, X.Y., Kuo, C.C., Lew, M. (eds.) Proceedings of 11th Pacific Rim Conference on Multimedia. LNCS, vol. 6297, pp. 709–718. Springer, New York (2010). doi: 10.1007/978-3-642-15702-8_65

304. Li, H., Wang, M., Pang, L., Zhang, W.: Key binding based on biometric shielding functions. In: Proceedings of International Conference on Information Assurance and Security, pp. 19–22. IEEE, New York (2009). doi: 10.1109/IAS.2009.305

305. Li, P., Liu, X., Xiao, L., Song, Q.: Robust and accurate iris segmentation in very noisy iris images. Image Vis. Comput. **28**(2), 246–253 (2010). doi: 10.1016/j.imavis.2009.04.010

306. Li, P., Ma, H.: Iris recognition in non-ideal imaging conditions. Pattern Recogn. Lett. **33**(8), 1012–1018 (2012). doi: 10.1016/j.patrec.2011.06.017

307. Li, P., Yang, X., Cao, K., Tao, X., Wang, R., Tian, J.: An alignment-free fingerprint cryptosystem based on fuzzy vault scheme. J. Netw. Comput. Appl. **33** (2010). doi: 10.1016/j.jnca.2009.12.003

308. Li, Q., Chang, E.C.: Hiding secret points amidst chaff. In: Vaudenay, S. (ed.) Proceedings of International Conference on Theory And Applications of Cryptographic Techniques. LNCS, vol. 4004, pp. 59–72. Springer, New York (2006). doi: 10.1007/11761679_5

309. Li, Q., Chang, E.C.: Robust, short and sensitive authentication tags using secure sketch. In: Proceedings of 8th Workshop on Multimedia and Security, pp. 56–61. ACM, New York (2006). doi: 10.1145/1161366.1161377

310. Li, Q., Guo, M., Chang, E.C.: Fuzzy extractors for asymmetric biometric representations. In: Proceedings of IEEE Conference on Computer Vision and Pattern Recognition Workshop, pp. 1–6. IEEE, New York (2008). doi: 10.1109/CVPRW.2008.4563113

311. Li, Q., Sutcu, Y., Memon, N.: Secure sketch for biometric templates. In: Lai, X., Chen, K. (eds.) Proceedings of 12th International Conference on Theory and Applications of Cryptology and Information Security. LNCS, vol. 4284, pp. 99–113. Springer, New York (2006). doi: 10.1007/11935230_7

312. Li, S.: Encyclopedia of Biometrics. Springer, New York (2009)

313. Liam, L.W., Chekima, A., Fan, L.C., Dargham, J.: Iris recognition using self-organizing neural network. In: Proceedings of Student Conference on Research and Development, pp. 169–172. IEEE, New York (2002). doi: 10.1109/SCORED.2002.1033084

314. Lienhart, R., Kuranov, A., Pisarevsky, V.: Empirical analysis of detection cascades of boosted classifiers for rapid object detection. In: Michaelis, B., Krell, G. (eds.) Proceedings of 25th DAGM Symposium, LNCS, vol. 2781, pp. 297–304. Springer, New York (2003). doi: 10.1007/978-3-540-45243-0_39

315. Linnartz, J.P., Tuyls, P.: New shielding functions to enhance privacy and prevent misuse of biometric templates. In: Kittler, J., Nixon, M. (eds.) Proceedings of 4th International Conference on Audio- and Video-Based Biometric Person Authentication. LNCS, vol. 2688, pp. 393–402. Springer, New York (2003). doi: 10.1007/3-540-44887-X_47

316. Liu, X., Bowyer, K., Flynn, P.: Experiments with an improved iris segmentation algorithm. In: Proceedings of 4th IEEE Workshop on Automatic Identification Advanced Technologies, pp. 118–123. IEEE, New York (2005). doi: 10.1109/AUTOID.2005.21

317. Lodin, A., Kovacs, L., Demea, S.: Interface of an iris detection program. In: Proceedings of 30th International Spring Seminar on Electronics Technology, pp. 555–558. IEEE, New York (2007). doi: 10.1109/ISSE.2007.4432918

318. Low, C.Y., Teoh, A.B.J., Tee, C.: Fusion of LSB and DWT Biometric Watermarking Using Offline Handwritten Signature for Copyright Protection. In: Tistarelli, M., Nixon, M. (eds.) Proceedings of 3rd International Conference on Biometrics. LNCS, vol. 5558, pp. 786–795. Springer, New York (2009). doi: 10.1007/978-3-642-01793-3_80

319. Lu, H., Martin, K., Bui, F., Plataniotis, K., Hatzinakos, D.: Face recognition with biometric encryption for privacy-enhancing self-exclusion. In: Proceedings of 16th International Conference on Digital Signal Processing, pp. 1–8. IEEE, New York (2009). doi: 10.1109/ICDSP.2009.5201257

320. Luengo-Oroz, M.A., Faure, E., Angulo, J.: Robust iris segmentation on uncalibrated noisy images using mathematical morphology. Image Vis. Comput. **28**, 278–284 (2010). doi: 10.1016/j.imavis.2009.04.018

321. Lumini, A., Nanni, L.: An improved BioHashing for human authentication. Pattern Recogn. **40**(3), 1057–1065 (2007). doi: 10.1016/j.patcog.2006.05.030

322. Ma, L., Tan, T., Wang, Y., Zhang, D.: Personal identification based on iris texture analysis. IEEE Trans. Pattern Anal. Mach. Intell. **25**(12), 1519–1533 (2003). doi: 10.1109/TPAMI.2003.1251145

323. Ma, L., Tan, T., Wang, Y., Zhang, D.: Efficient iris recognition by characterizing key local variations. IEEE Trans. Image Process. **13**(6), 739–750 (2004). doi: 10.1109/TIP.2004.827237

324. Maiorana, E.: Biometric cryptosystem using function based on-line signature recognition. Expert Syst. Appl. **37**(4), 3454–3461 (2010). doi: 10.1016/j.eswa.2009.10.043

325. Maiorana, E., Campisi, P., Fierrez, J., Ortega-Garcia, J., Neri, A.: Cancelable templates for sequence-based biometrics with application to on-line signature recognition. IEEE Trans. Syst. Man Cybern. A Syst. Humans **40**(3), 525–538 (2010). doi: 10.1109/TSMCA.2010.2041653

326. Maiorana, E., Campisi, P., Neri, A.: Biometric signature authentication using radon transform-based watermarking techniques. In: Proceedings of Biometrics Symposium, pp. 1–6. IEEE, New York (2007). doi: 10.1109/BCC.2007.4430543

327. Maiorana, E., Campisi, P., Neri, A.: User adaptive fuzzy commitment for signature templates protection and renewability. J. Electron. Imag. **17**(1), 011,011.1–12 (2008). doi: 10.1117/1.2885239

328. Maiorana, E., Ercole, C.: Secure Biometric Authentication System Architecture using Error Correcting Codes and Distributed Cryptography. In: Proceedings of Gruppo nazionale Telecomunicazioni e Teoria dell'Informazione, pp. 1–12 (2007)

329. Maiorana, E., Martinez-Diaz, M., Campisi, P., Ortega-Garcia, J., Neri, A.: Cancelable biometrics for hmm-based signature recognition. In: Proceedings of IEEE 2nd International Conference on Biometrics: Theory, Applications, and Systems, pp. 1–6. IEEE, New York (2008). doi: 10.1109/BTAS.2008.4699360

330. Maiorana, E., Martinez-Diaz, M., Campisi, P., Ortega-Garcia, J., Neri, A.: Template protection for hmm-based on-line signature authentication. In: Proceedings of IEEE Conference on Computer Vision and Pattern Recognition Workshop, pp. 1–6. IEEE, New York (2008). doi: 10.1109/CVPRW.2008.4563114

331. Malladi, R., Sethian, J., Vemuri, B.: Shape modeling with front propagation: a level set approach. IEEE Trans. Pattern Anal. Mach. Intell. **17**(2), 158–175 (1995). doi: 10.1109/34.368173

332. Maltoni, D., Maio, D., Jain, A., Prabhakar, S.: Handbook of Fingerprint Recognition. Springer, New York (2005)

333. Mao, Y., Wu, M.: Security evaluation for communication-friendly encryption of multimedia. In: Proceedings of IEEE International Conference on Image Processing, pp. 569–572. IEEE, New York (2004). doi: 10.1109/ICIP.2004.1418818

334. de Martin-Roche, D., Sanchez-Avila, C., Sanchez-Reillo, R.: Iris recognition for biometric identification using dyadic wavelet transform zero-crossing. In: Proceedings of 35th International Carnahan Conference on Security Technology, pp. 272–277. IEEE, New York (2001). doi: 10.1109/.2001.962844

335. Masek, L.: Recognition of human iris patterns for biometric identification. Master's thesis, University of Western Australia (2003)

336. Masek, L., Kovesi, P.: MATLAB Source Code for a Biometric Identification System Based on Iris Patterns (2003). URL http://www.csse.uwa.edu.au/~pk/studentprojects/libor/sourcecode.html. Retrieved May 2012

337. Matey, J., Naroditsky, O., Hanna, K., Kolczynski, R., LoIacono, D., Mangru, S., Tinker, M., Zappia, T., Zhao, W.Y.: Iris on the move: Acquisition of images for iris recognition in less constrained environments. Proc. IEEE **94**, 1936–1947 (2006). doi: 10.1109/JPROC.2006.884091

338. Matey, J.R., Broussard, R., Kennell, L.: Iris image segmentation and sub-optimal images. Image Vis. Comput. **28**(2), 215–222 (2010). doi: 10.1016/j.imavis.2009.05.006

339. Matschitsch, S., Stögner, H., Tschinder, M., Uhl, A.: Rotation-invariant iris recognition: boosting 1D spatial-domain signatures to 2D. In: Filipe, J., Cetto, J., Ferrier, J.L. (eds.) Proceedings of 5th International Conference on Informatics in Control, Automation and Robotics, pp. 232–235. SciTePress (2008)

340. Matschitsch, S., Tschinder, M., Uhl, A.: Comparison of compression algorithms' impact on iris recognition accuracy. In: Lee, S.W., Li, S. (eds.) Proceedings of 2nd International Conference on Biometrics, LNCS, vol. 4642, pp. 232–241. Springer, New York (2007). doi: 10.1007/978-3-540-74549-5_25

341. Meenakshi, V.S., Padmavathi, G.: Security analysis of password hardened multimodal biometric fuzzy vault. World Acad. Sci. Eng. Tech. **56**, 312–320 (2009)

342. Meerwald, P.: Watermarking Toolbox. URL http://www.cosy.sbg.ac.at/~pmeerw/Watermarking/source/. Retrieved June 2012

343. Meerwald, P., Uhl, A.: A survey of wavelet-domain watermarking algorithms. In: Wong, P.W., Delp, E.J. (eds.) Electronic Imaging, Security and Watermarking of Multimedia Contents III, Proceedings of SPIE, vol. 4314, pp. 505–516. SPIE, Bellingham, WA (2001). doi: 10.1117/12.435434

344. Mehrotra, H., Rattani, A., Gupta, P.: Fusion of iris and fingerprint biometric for recognition. In: Proceedings of International Conference on Signal and Image Processing, pp. 1–6. ACTA Press, Calgary, AB (2006)

345. Micilotta, A., Jon, E., Bowden, O.: Detection and tracking of humans by probabilistic body part assembly. In: Proceedings of British Machine Vision Conference, pp. 429–438. BMVA Press, Guildford (2005)

346. Mihailescu, P.: The fuzzy vault for fingerprints is vulnerable to brute force attack. Report arxiv:0708.2974v1, Cornell University (2007)

347. Miyazawa, K., Ito, K., Aoki, T., Kobayashi, K., Nakajima, H.: A phase-based iris recognition algorithm. In: Zhang, D., Jain, A. (eds.) Proceedings of 1st International Conference on Biometrics, LNCS, vol. 3832, pp. 356–365. Springer, New York (2006). doi: 10.1007/11608288_48

348. Monro, D.M., Rakshit, S., Zhang, D.: Dct-based iris recognition. IEEE Trans. Pattern Anal. Mach. Intell. **29**(4), 586–595 (2007). doi: 10.1109/TPAMI.2007.1002

349. Monrose, F., Reiter, M.K., Li, Q., Wetzel, S.: Cryptographic Key Generation from Voice. In: Proceedings of IEEE Symposium on Security and Privacy, pp. 202–213. IEEE, New York (2001). doi: 10.1109/SECPRI.2001.924299

350. Monrose, F., Reiter, M.K., Li, Q., Wetzel, S.: Using Voice to Generate Cryptographic Keys. In: Proceedings of Speaker Odyssey 2001, The Speech Recognition Workshop, pp. 237–242 (2001)

351. Monrose, F., Reiter, M.K., Lopresti, D.P., Shih, C.: Toward speech-generated cryptographic keys on resource constrained devices. In: Proceedings of 11th USENIX Security Symposium, pp. 283–296 (2002)

352. Monrose, F., Reiter, M.K., Wetzel, S.: Password hardening based on keystroke dynamics. In: Proceedings of 6th ACM Conference on Computer and Communications Security, pp. 73–82. ACM, New York (1999). doi: 10.1145/319709.319720

353. Moon, D., Choi, W.Y., Moon, K., Chung, Y.: Fuzzy fingerprint vault using multiple polynomials. In: Proceedings of IEEE 13th International Symposium on Consumer Electronics, pp. 290–293. IEEE, New York (2009). doi: 10.1109/ISCE.2009.5156914

354. Moon, D., Kim, T., Jung, S.H., Chung, Y., Moon, K., Ahn, D., Kim, S.: Performance evaluation of watermarking techniques for secure multimodal biometric systems. In: Hao, Y., Liu, J., Wang, Y.P., ming Cheung, Y., Yin, H., Jiao, L., Yong-Chang Jiao, J.M. (eds.) Proceedings of International Conference on Computational Intelligence and Security. LNCS, vol. 3802, pp. 635–642. Springer, New York (2005). doi: 10.1007/11596981_94

355. Morimoto, C.H., Santos, T.T., Muniz, A.S.: Automatic iris segmentation using active near infra red lighting. In: Proceedings of 18th Brazilian Symposium on Computer Graphics and Image Processing, pp. 37–43. IEEE, New York (2005). doi: 10.1109/SIBGRAPI.2005.14

356. Motwani, R.C., Harris, F.C., Bekris, K.E.: A proposed digital rights management system for 3d graphics using biometric watermarks. In: Proceedings of 7th IEEE Consumer Communications and Networking Conference, pp. 1075–1080. IEEE, New York (2010). doi: 10.1109/CCNC.2010.5421663

357. Multimedia University: MMU1 and MMU2 Iris Databases. URL http://pesona.mmu.edu.my/~ccteo/. Retrieved May 2012

358. Mumford, D., Shah, J.: Optimal approximations by piecewise smooth functions and associated variational problems. Comm. Pure Appl. Math. **42**(5), 577–685 (1989). doi: 10.1002/cpa.3160420503

359. Myers, C.S., Rabiner, L.R.: A comparative study of several dynamic time-warping algorithms for connected word recognition. Bell Syst. Tech. J. **60**(7), 1389–1409 (1981)

360. Nagar, A., Chaudhury, S.: Biometrics based Asymmetric Cryptosystem Design Using Modified Fuzzy Vault Scheme. In: Proceedings of 18th International Conference on Pattern Recognition, pp. 537–540. IEEE, New York (2006). doi: 10.1109/ICPR.2006.330

361. Nagar, A., Nandakumar, K., Jain, A.: A hybrid biometric cryptosystem for securing fingerprint minutiae templates. Pattern Recogn. Lett. **31**, 733–741 (2010). doi: 10.1016/j.patrec.2009.07.003

362. Nagar, A., Nandakumar, K., Jain, A.K.: Securing fingerprint template: Fuzzy vault with minutiae descriptors. In: Proceedings of 19th International Conference on Pattern Recognition, pp. 1–4. IEEE, New York (2008). doi: 10.1109/ICPR.2008.4761459

363. Nandakumar, K.: A fingerprint cryptosystem based on minutiae phase spectrum. In: Proceedings of IEEE Workshop on Information Forensics and Security, pp. 1–6. IEEE, New York (2010). doi: 10.1109/WIFS.2010.5711456

364. Nandakumar, K., Jain, A.K.: Multibiometric template security using fuzzy vault. In: Proceedings of IEEE 2nd International Conference on Biometrics: Theory, Applications, and Systems, pp. 1–6. IEEE, New York (2008). doi: 10.1109/BTAS.2008.4699352

365. Nandakumar, K., Jain, A.K., Pankanti, S.: Fingerprint-based Fuzzy Vault: Implementation and Performance. IEEE Trans. Inform. Forensics Secur. **2**, 744–757 (2007). doi: 10.1109/TIFS.2007.908165

366. Nanni, L., Lumini, A.: Random subspace for an improved biohashing for face authentication. Pattern Recogn. Lett. **29**(3), 295–300 (2008). doi: 10.1016/j.patrec.2007.10.005

367. Nanni, L., Lumini, A.: A combination of face/eye detectors for a high performance face detection system. IEEE Multimed. **PP**(99), 1–15 (2011). doi: 10.1109/MMUL.2011.57

368. Newman, C.: A life revealed. Natl. Geogr. **2002** (2002)

369. Nguyen, K., Fookes, C., Sridharan, S.: Fusing shrinking and expanding active contour models for robust iris segmentation. In: Proceedings of 10th International Conference on Information Sciences Signal Processing and their Applications, pp. 185–188. IEEE, New York (2010). doi: 10.1109/ISSPA.2010.5605546

370. Nishino, K., Nayar, S.K.: Eyes for relighting. ACM Trans. Graph. **23**, 704–711 (2004). doi: 10.1145/1015706.1015783

371. NIST: Face Recognition Vendor Test 2006. URL http://www.nist.gov/itl/iad/ig/frvt-2006. cfm. Retrieved May 2012

372. NIST: Iris Challenge Evaluation. URL http://iris.nist.gov/ice. Retrieved May 2012

373. NIST: IRIS Exchange Program. URL http://iris.nist.gov/irex/. Retrieved May 2012

374. NIST: Multiple Biometric Grand Challenge. URL http://www.nist.gov/itl/iad/ig/mbgc.cfm. Retrieved May 2012

375. NIST: VASIR Source Code Beta V1.0. URL http://www.nist.gov/itl/iad/ig/vasir.cfm. Retrieved May 2012

376. Noh, S.I., Bae, K., Park, Y., Kim, J.: A novel method to extract features for iris recognition system. In: Kittler, J., Nixon, M. (eds.) Proceedings of 4th International Conference on Audio- and Video-Based Biometric Person Authentication. LNCS, vol. 2688, pp. 862–868. Springer, New York (2003). doi: 10.1007/3-540-44887-X_100

377. Noore, A., Singh, R., Vatsa, M., Houck, M.: Enhancing security of fingerprints through contextual biometric watermarking. Forensic Sci. Int. **169**, 188–194 (2007)

378. Nuance, USA: URL http://www.nuance.com/. Retrieved June 2012

379. OKI: IrisPass-H. URL http://www.pro-4-pro.com/media/product_data/9354428_1_p4p0804/ download.pdf. Retrieved May 2012

380. OKI: IrisPass-M. URL http://www.oki.com/en/otr/2006/n205/pdf/otr-205-R06.pdf. Retrieved May 2012

381. Ouda, O., Tsumura, N., Nakaguchi, T.: Bioencoding: A reliable tokenless cancelable biometrics scheme for protecting iriscodes. IEICE Trans. Inform. Syst. **E93.D**, 1878–1888 (2010). doi: 10.1587/transinf.E93.D.1878

382. Ouda, O., Tsumura, N., Nakaguchi, T.: Tokenless cancelable biometrics scheme for protecting iris codes. In: Proceedings of 20th International Conference on Pattern Recognition, pp. 882–885. IEEE, New York (2010). doi: 10.1109/ICPR.2010.222

383. Palacky University of Olomouc: Iris Database. URL http://phoenix.inf.upol.cz/iris/. Retrieved May 2012

384. Panasonic: BM-ET200. URL http://www.aditech.co.uk/downloads/PanasonicBM-ET200. pdf. Retrieved May 2012

385. Panasonic: BM-ET330. URL ftp://ftp.panasonic.com/pub/Panasonic/cctv/SpecSheets/BM-ET330.pdf. Retrieved May 2012

386. Park, C.H., Lee, J.J.: Extracting and combining multimodal directional iris features. In: Zhang, D., Jain, A. (eds.) Proceedings of 1st International Conference on Biometrics, LNCS, vol. 3832, pp. 389–396. Springer, New York (2006). doi: 10.1007/11608288_52

387. Park, K.R., Jeong, D.S., Kang, B.J., Lee, E.C.: A study on iris feature watermarking on face data. In: Beliczynski, B., Dzielinski, A., Ribeiro, B. (eds.) Proceedings of 8th International Conference on Adaptive and Natural Computing Algorithms. LNCS, vol. 4432, pp. 415–423. Springer, New York (2007). doi: 10.1007/978-3-540-71629-7_47

388. Pavlov, I.: 7ZIP. URL http://www.7-zip.org/. Retrieved June 2012

389. Pennebaker, W., Mitchell, J.: JPEG – Still image compression standard. Van Nostrand Reinhold (1993)

390. Perona, P., Malik, J.: Scale-space and edge detection using anisotropic diffusion. IEEE Trans. Pattern Anal. Mach. Intell. **12**(7), 629–639 (1990). doi: 10.1109/34.56205

391. Phillips, P., Bowyer, K., Flynn, P., Liu, X., Scruggs, W.: The iris challenge evaluation 2005. In: Proceedings of IEEE 2nd International Conference on Biometrics: Theory, Applications, and Systems, pp. 1–8. IEEE, New York (2008). doi: 10.1109/BTAS.2008.4699333

392. Phillips, P.J., Flynn, P.J., Beveridge, J.R., Scruggs, W.T., O'Toole, A.J., Bolme, D., Bowyer, K.W., Draper, B.A., Givens, G.H., Lui, Y.M., Sahibzada, H., Scallan Iii, J.A., Weimer, S.: Overview of the multiple biometrics grand challenge. In: Tistarelli, M., Nixon, M. (eds.) Proceedings of 3rd International Conference on Biometrics. LNCS, vol. 5558, pp. 705–714. Springer, New York (2009). doi: 10.1007/978-3-642-01793-3_72

393. Phillips, P.J., Member, S., Bowyer, K.W., Flynn, P.J.: Comments on the casia version 1.0 iris dataset. IEEE Trans. Pattern Anal. Mach. Intell. **29**(10), 1869–1870 (2007). doi: 10.1109/TPAMI.2007.1137

394. Phillips, P.J., Scruggs, W.T., O'toole, A.J., Flynn, P.J., Kevin, W., Schott, C.L., Sharpe, M.: FRVT 2006 and ICE 2006 Large-Scale Results. NISTIR 7408 Report, NIST (2007)

395. Pillai, J.K., Patel, V.M., Chellappa, R., Ratha, N.K.: Sectored random projections for cancelable iris biometrics. In: Proceedings of IEEE International Conference on Acoustics Speech and Signal Processing, pp. 1838–1841. IEEE, New York (2010). doi: 10.1109/ICASSP.2010.5495383

396. Pla, O.G., Lin, E.T., Delp, E.J.: A wavelet watermarking algorithm based on a tree structure. In: Delp, E.J., Wong, P.W. (eds.) Security, Steganography, and Watermarking of Multimedia Contents VI, Proceedings of SPIE, vol. 5306, pp. 571–580. SPIE, Bellingham, WA (2004). doi: 10.1117/12.531459

397. Poon, H.T., Miri, A.: A collusion attack on the fuzzy vault scheme. ISC Int. J. Inform. Secur. **1**(1), 27–34 (2009)

398. Poursaberi, A., Araabi, B.N.: Iris recognition for partially occluded images: methodology and sensitivity analysis. EURASIP J. Appl. Signal Process. **2007**, 36751.1–12 (2007). doi: 10.1155/2007/36751

399. Prasanalakshmi, B., Kannammal, A.: A secure cryptosystem from palm vein biometrics. In: Proceedings of 2nd International Conference on Interaction Sciences, pp. 1401–1405. ACM, New York (2009). doi: 10.1145/1655925.1656183

400. Precise Biometrics AB, Sweden: URL http://www.precisebiometrics.com/. Retrieved June 2012

401. priv-ID B.V., The Netherlands: URL http://www.priv-id.com/. Retrieved June 2012

402. Proença, H.: Iris recognition: A method to segment visible wavelength iris images acquired on-the-move and at-a-distance. In: Bebis, G., Boyle, R.D., Parvin, B., Koracin, D., Remagnino, P., Porikli, F.M., Peters, J., Klosowski, J.T., Arns, L.L., Chun, Y.K., Rhyne, T.M., Monroe, L. (eds.) Proceedings of International Symposium on Visual Computing. LNCS, vol. 5358, pp. 731–742. Springer, New York (2008). doi: 10.1007/978-3-540-89639-5_70

403. Proença, H.: Iris recognition: On the segmentation of degraded images acquired in the visible wavelength. IEEE Trans. Pattern Anal. Mach. Intell. **32**(8), 1502–1516 (2010). doi: 10.1109/TPAMI.2009.140

404. Proença, H., Alexandre, L.: Iris segmentation methodology for non-cooperative recognition. IEE Proceedings of Vis. Image Signal Process. **153**(2), 199–205 (2006). doi: 10.1049/ip-vis:20050213

405. Proença, H., Alexandre, L.: A method for the identification of noisy regions in normalized iris images. In: Proceedings of 18th International Conference on Pattern Recognition, vol. 4, pp. 405–408. IEEE, New York (2006). doi: 10.1109/ICPR.2006.100

406. Proença, H., Alexandre, L.: Toward noncooperative iris recognition: A classification approach using multiple signatures. IEEE Trans. Pattern Anal. Mach. Intell. **29**(4), 607–612 (2007). doi: 10.1109/TPAMI.2007.1016

407. Proença, H., Alexandre, L.: Toward covert iris biometric recognition: Experimental results from the nice contests. IEEE Trans. Inform. Forensics Secur. **7**(2), 798–808 (2012). doi: 10.1109/TIFS.2011.2177659

408. Proença, H., Alexandre, L.A.: Iris recognition: Analysis of the error rates regarding the accuracy of the segmentation stage. Image Vis. Comput. **28**(1), 202–206 (2010). doi: 10.1016/j.imavis.2009.03.003

409. Proença, H., Filipe, S., Santos, R., Oliveira, J., Alexandre, L.A.: The ubiris.v2: A database of visible wavelength iris images captured on-the-move and at-a-distance. IEEE Trans. Pattern Anal. Mach. Intell. **32**(8), 1529–1535 (2010). doi: 10.1109/TPAMI.2009.66

410. Puhan, N., Sudha, N., Jiang, X.: Robust eyeball segmentation in noisy iris images using fourier spectral density. In: Proceedings of 6th International Conference on Information, Communications and Signal Processing, pp. 1–5. IEEE, New York (2007). doi: 10.1109/ICICS.2007.4449723

411. Qi, M., Lu, Y., Du, N., Zhang, Y., Wang, C., Kong, J.: A novel image hiding approach based on correlation analysis for secure multimodal biometrics. J. Netw. Comput. Appl. **33**(3), 247–257 (2010). doi: 10.1016/j.jnca.2009.12.004

412. Quan, F., Fei, S., Anni, C., Feifei, Z.: Cracking Cancelable Fingerprint Template of Ratha. In: Proceedings of International Symposium on Computer Science and Computational Technology, vol. 2, pp. 572–575. IEEE, New York (2008). doi: 10.1109/ISCSCT.2008.226

413. Qui, X., Sun, Z., Tan, T.: Coarse iris classification by learned visual dictionary. In: Lee, S.W., Li, S. (eds.) Proceedings of 2nd International Conference on Biometrics, LNCS, vol. 4642, pp. 770–779. Springer, New York (2007). doi: 10.1007/978-3-540-74549-5_81

414. Rajibul, M.I., Shohel, M., Andrews, S.: Biometric template protection using watermarking with hidden password encryption. In: Proceedings of International Symposium on Information Technology, pp. 296–303. IEEE, New York (2008). doi: 10.1109/ITSIM.2008.4631572

415. Rakshit, S., Monro, D.: Effects of sampling and compression on human iris verification. In: Proceedings of IEEE International Conference on Acoustics, Speech, and Signal Processing, vol. 2, pp. 337–340. IEEE, New York (2006). doi: 10.1109/ICASSP.2006.1660348

416. Rakshit, S., Monro, D.M.: An evaluation of image sampling and compression for human iris recognition. IEEE Trans. Inform. Forensics Secur. **2**, 605–612 (2007). doi: 10.1109/TIFS.2007.902401

417. Rakshit, S., Monro, D.M.: Pupil shape description using fourier series. In: Proceedings of IEEE Workshop on Signal Processing Applications for Public Security and Forensics, pp. 1–4. IEEE, New York (2007)

418. Ratha, N., Connell, J., Bolle, R.: Enhancing security and privacy in biometrics-based authentication systems. IBM Syst. J. **40**(3), 614–634 (2001). doi: 10.1147/sj.403.0614

419. Ratha, N.K., Connell, J.H., Bolle, R.M.: Secure data hiding in wavelet compressed fingerprint images. In: Proceedings of ACM Multimedia, pp. 127–130. ACM, New York (2000). doi: 10.1145/357744.357902

420. Ratha, N.K., Connell, J.H., Bolle, R.M.: An analysis of minutiae matching strength. In: Bigün, J., Smeraldi, F. (eds.) Proceedings of 3rd International Conference on Audio- and Video-Based Biometric Person Authentication. LNCS, vol. 2091, pp. 223–228. Springer, New York (2001). doi: 10.1007/3-540-45344-X_32

421. Ratha, N.K., Connell, J.H., Bolle, R.M., Chikkerur, S.: Cancelable biometrics: A case study in fingerprints. In: Proceedings of 18th International Conference on Pattern Recognition, pp. 370–373. IEEE, New York (2006). doi: 10.1109/ICPR.2006.353

422. Ratha, N.K., Connell, J.H., Chikkerur, S.: Generating cancelable fingerprint templates. IEEE Trans. Pattern Anal. Mach. Intell. **29**(4), 561–572 (2007). doi: 10.1109/TPAMI.2007.1004

423. Ratha, N.K., Figueroa-Villanueva, M.A., Connell, J.H., Bolle, R.M.: A secure protocol for data hiding in compressed fingerprint images. In: Maltoni, D., Jain, A. (eds.) Proceedings of International Workshop on Biometric Authentication. LNCS, vol. 3087, pp. 205–216. Springer, New York (2004). doi: 10.1007/978-3-540-25976-3_19

424. Rathgeb, C., Uhl, A.: Context-based texture analysis for secure revocable iris-biometric key generation. In: Proceedings of 3rd International Conference on Imaging for Crime Detection and Prevention, pp. 1–6. IET, London (2009). doi: 10.1049/ic.2009.0229

425. Rathgeb, C., Uhl, A.: An iris-based interval-mapping scheme for biometric key generation. In: Proceedings of 6th International Symposium on Image and Signal Processing and Analysis, pp. 511–516. IEEE, New York (2009)

426. Rathgeb, C., Uhl, A.: Adaptive fuzzy commitment scheme based on iris-code error analysis. In: Proceedings of 2nd European Workshop on Visual Information Processing, pp. 41–44. IEEE, New York (2010). doi: 10.1109/EUVIP.2010.5699103

427. Rathgeb, C., Uhl, A.: Bit reliability-driven template matching in iris recognition. In: Proceedings of 4th Pacific-Rim Symposium on Image and Video Technology, pp. 70–75. IEEE, New York (2010). doi: 10.1109/PSIVT.2010.19

428. Rathgeb, C., Uhl, A.: Iris-biometric hash generation for biometric database indexing. In: Proceedings of 20th International Conference on Pattern Recognition, pp. 2848–2851. IEEE, New York (2010). doi: 10.1109/ICPR.2010.698

429. Rathgeb, C., Uhl, A.: Privacy Preserving Key Generation for Iris Biometrics. In: Decker, B.D., Schaumüller-Bichl, I. (eds.) Proceedings of 11th International Conference on Communications and Multimedia Security. LNCS, vol. 6109, pp. 191–200. Springer, New York (2010). doi: 10.1007/978-3-642-13241-4_18

430. Rathgeb, C., Uhl, A.: Secure iris recognition based on local intensity variations. In: Campilho, A., Kamel, M. (eds.) Proceedings of 7th International Conference on Image Analysis and Recognition. LNCS, vol. 6112, pp. 266–275. Springer, New York (2010). doi: 10.1007/978-3-642-13775-4_27

431. Rathgeb, C., Uhl, A.: Two-Factor Authentication or How to Potentially Counterfeit Experimental Results in Biometric Systems. In: Campilho, A., Kamel, M. (eds.) Proceedings of 7th International Conference on Image Analysis and Recognition. LNCS, vol. 6112, pp. 296–305. Springer, New York (2010). doi: 10.1007/978-3-642-13775-4_30

432. Rathgeb, C., Uhl, A.: Context-based biometric key-generation for iris. IET Comput. Vis. 5(6), 389–397 (2011). doi: 10.1049/iet-cvi.2010.0176

433. Rathgeb, C., Uhl, A.: Image compression in iris-biometric fuzzy commitment schemes. Tech. Rep. 2011-05, University of Salzburg, Dept. of Computer Sciences (2011)

434. Rathgeb, C., Uhl, A.: The state-of-the-art in iris biometric cryptosystems. In: Yang, J., Nanni, L. (eds.) State of the art in Biometrics, pp. 179–202. InTech, New York (2011)

435. Rathgeb, C., Uhl, A.: Statistical attack against iris-biometric fuzzy commitment schemes. In: Proceedings of IEEE Conference on Computer Vision and Pattern Recognition Workshop, pp. 25–32. IEEE, New York (2011). doi: 10.1109/CVPRW.2011.5981720

436. Rathgeb, C., Uhl, A.: A survey on biometric cryptosystems and cancelable biometrics. EURASIP J. Inform. Secur. 2011(3) (2011). doi: doi:10.1186/1687-417X-2011-3

437. Rathgeb, C., Uhl, A.: Template protection under signal degradation: A case-study on iris-biometric fuzzy commitment schemes. Tech. Rep. 2011-04, University of Salzburg, Dept. of Computer Sciences (2011)

438. Rathgeb, C., Uhl, A., Wild, P.: Incremental iris recognition: A single-algorithm serial fusion strategy to optimize time complexity. In: Proceedings of IEEE 4th International Conference on Biometrics: Theory, Applications, and Systems, pp. 1–6. IEEE, New York (2010). doi: 10.1109/BTAS.2010.5634475

439. Rathgeb, C., Uhl, A., Wild, P.: Iris-biometric comparators: Minimizing trade-offs costs between computational performance and recognition accuracy. In: Proceedings of 4th International Conference on Imaging for Crime Detection and Prevention, pp. 1–6. IET, London (2011). doi: 10.1049/ic.2011.0110

440. Rathgeb, C., Uhl, A., Wild, P.: On combining selective best bits of iris-codes. In: Vielhauer, C., Dittmann, J., Drygajlo, A., Juul, N., Fairhurst, M. (eds.) Proceedings of COST 2101 European Workshop on Biometrics and ID Management, LNCS, vol. 6583, pp. 227–237. Springer, New York (2011). doi: 10.1007/978-3-642-19530-3_21

441. Rathgeb, C., Uhl, A., Wild, P.: Reliability-balanced feature level fusion for fuzzy commitment scheme. In: Proceedings of International Joint Conference on Biometrics, pp. 1–7. IEEE, New York (2011). doi: 10.1109/IJCB.2011.6117535

442. Rathgeb, C., Uhl, A., Wild, P.: Shifting score fusion: On exploiting shifting variation in iris recognition. In: Proceedings of 26th ACM Symposium On Applied Computing, pp. 1–5. ACM, New York (2011). doi: 10.1145/1982185.1982187

443. Rathgeb, C., Uhl, A., Wild, P.: Iris-biometric comparators: Exploiting comparison scores towards an optimal alignment under gaussian assumption. In: Proceedings of 5th International Conference on Biometrics, pp. 297–302. IEEE, New York (2012). doi: 10.1109/ICB.2012.6199823

444. Ravidá, S.: WinUHA. URL http://www.klaimsoft.com/winuha/. Retrieved June 2012

445. Reddy, E., Babu, I.: Performance of Iris Based Hard Fuzzy Vault. IJCSNS Int. J. Comput. Sci. Netw. Secur. 8(1), 297–304 (2008)

446. Reza, A.M.: Realization of the contrast limited adaptive histogram equalization (clahe) for real-time image enhancement. J. VLSI Signal Process. Syst. 38(1), 35–44 (2004). doi: 10.1023/B:VLSI.0000028532.53893.82

447. Ritter, N., Cooper, J.: Locating the iris: A first step to registration and identification. In: Proceedings of 9th IASTED International Conference on Signal and Image Processing, pp. 507–512. ACTA Press, Calgary, AB (2003)

448. Ritter, N., Owens, R., Van Saarloos, P.P., Cooper, J.: Location of the pupil-iris border in slit-lamp images of the cornea. In: Proceedings of 10th International Conference on Image Analysis and Processing, pp. 740–745. IEEE, New York (1999). doi: 10.1109/ICIAP.1999.797683

449. Roberts, C.: Biometric attack vectors and defenses. Comput. Secur. 26, 14–25 (2007). doi: 10.1016/j.cose.2006.12.008

450. Rosenfeld, K., Sencar, H.: A study of the robustness of prnu-based camera identification. In: Media Forensics and Security XI, Proceedings of SPIE, vol. 7254, pp. 72,540M.1–7. SPIE, Bellingham, WA (2009). doi: 10.1117/12.814705

451. Ross, A.: Information fusion in fingerprint authentication. Ph.D. thesis, Michigan State University (2003)

452. Ross, A.: Iris recognition: The path forward. Computer 43, 30–35 (2010). doi: 10.1109/MC.2010.44

453. Ross, A., Jain, A.K.: Information fusion in biometrics. Pattern Recogn. Lett. 24(13), 2115–2125 (2003). doi: 10.1016/S0167-8655(03)00079-5

454. Ross, A., Pasula, R., Hornak, L.: Exploring multispectral iris recognition beyond 900nm. In: Proceedings of IEEE 3rd International Conference on Biometrics: Theory, Applications, and Systems, pp. 1–8. IEEE, New York (2009). doi: 10.1109/BTAS.2009.5339072

455. Ross, A., Shah, J., Jain, A.K.: From template to image: Reconstructing fingerprints from minutiae points. IEEE Trans. Pattern Anal. Mach. Intell. 29(4), 544–560 (2007). doi: 10.1109/TPAMI.2007.1018

456. Ross A.; Shah, S.: Segmenting non-ideal irises using geodesic active contours. In: Proceedings of Biometric Consortium Conference, pp. 1–6. IEEE, New York (2006). doi: 10.1109/BCC.2006.4341625

457. Rouse, D., Hemami, S.S.: Natural image utility assessment using image contours. In: Proceedings of IEEE International Conference on Image Processing, pp. 2217–2220. IEEE, New York (2009). doi: 10.1109/ICIP.2009.5413882

458. Rouse, D., Hemami, S.S.: The role of edge information to estimate the perceived utility of natural images. In: Western New York Image Processing Workshop, pp. 1–4. IEEE, New York (2009)

459. Roy, K., Suen, C., Bhattacharya, P.: Segmentation of unideal iris images using game theory. In: Proceedings of 20th International Conference on Pattern Recognition, pp. 2844–2847. IEEE, New York (2010). doi: 10.1109/ICPR.2010.697

460. Ryan, W., Woodard, D., Duchowski, A., Birchfield, S.: Adapting starburst for elliptical iris segmentation. In: Proceedings of IEEE 2nd International Conference on Biometrics: Theory, Applications, and Systems, pp. 1–7. IEEE, New York (2008). doi: 10.1109/BTAS.2008.4699340

461. Rydgren, E., Ea, T., Amiel, F., Rossant, F., Amara, A.: Iris features extraction using wavelet packets. In: Proceedings of International Conference on Image Processing, vol. 2, pp. 861–864. IEEE, New York (2004). doi: 10.1109/ICIP.2004.1419435

462. SAFRAN Morpho, France: URL http://www.morpho.com/. Retrieved June 2012

463. Said, A., Pearlman, W.A.: A new, fast, and efficient image codec based on set partitioning in hierarchical trees. IEEE Trans. Circ. Syst. Video Tech. 6(3), 243–249 (1996). doi: 10.1109/76.499834

464. Sankowski, W., Grabowski, K., Napieralska, M., Zubert, M., Napieralski, A.: Reliable algorithm for iris segmentation in eye image. Image Vis. Comput. 28(2), 231–237 (2010). doi: 10.1016/j.imavis.2009.05.014

465. Santa-Cruz, D., Grosbois, R., Ebrahimi, T.: JJ2000: The JPEG 2000 Reference Implementation in Java. In: Proceedings of the First International JPEG 2000 Workshop, 46–49 (2003)

466. Santos, G., Proenca, H.: On the role of interpolation in the normalization of non-ideal visible wavelength iris images. In: Proceedings of International Conference on Computational Intelligence and Security, vol. 1, pp. 315–319. IEEE, New York (2009). doi: 10.1109/CIS.2009.113

467. Saragih, J., Lucey, S., Cohn, J.: Face alignment through subspace constrained mean-shifts. In: Proceedings of International Conference on Computer Vision, pp. 1034–1041. IEEE, New York (2009). doi: 10.1109/ICCV.2009.5459377

468. Satonaka, T.: Biometric watermark authentication with multiple verification rule. In: Proceedings of 12th IEEE Workshop on Neural Networks in Signal Processing, pp. 597–606. IEEE, New York (2002). doi: 10.1109/NNSP.2002.1030071

469. Savvides, M., Kumar, B., Khosla, P.: Cancelable biometric filters for face recognition. In: Proceedings of 17th International Conference on Pattern Recognition, vol. 3, pp. 922–925. IEEE, New York (2004). doi: 10.1109/ICPR.2004.228

470. Scheidat, T., Vielhauer, C.: Biometric hashing for handwriting : Entropy based feature selection and semantic fusion. In: Delp, E., Wong, P., Dittmann, J., Memon, N. (eds.) Security, Forensics, Steganography, and Watermarking of Multimedia Contents X, Proceedings of SPIE, vol. 6819, pp. 68,190N.1–12. SPIE, Bellingham, WA (2008). doi: 10.1117/12.766378

471. Scheidat, T., Vielhauer, C., Dittmann, J.: An iris-based interval-mapping scheme for biometric key generation. In: Proceedings of 6th International Symposium on Image and Signal Processing and Analysis, pp. 550–555. IEEE, New York (2009)

472. Scheirer, W., Boult, T.: Cracking Fuzzy Vaults and Biometric Encryption. In: Proceedings of Biometrics Symposium, pp. 1–6. IEEE, New York (2007). doi: 10.1109/BCC.2007.4430534

473. Schimke, S., Vielhauer, C., Dittmann, J.: Using adapted levenshtein distance for on-line signature authentication. In: Proceedings of 17th International Conference on Pattern Recognition, pp. 931–934. IEEE, New York (2004). doi: 10.1109/ICPR.2004.965

474. Schiphol: Iris scans at Amsterdam Airport Schiphol. URL http://www.schiphol.nl/Travellers/AtSchiphol/Privium/IrisScans.htm. Retrieved May 2012

475. Schuckers, S., Hornak, L., Norman, T., Derakhshani, R., Parthasaradhi, S.: Issues for liveness detection in biometrics. In: Proceedings of Biometric Consortium Conference. IEEE, New York (2002)

476. Schuckers, S., Schmid, N., Abhyankar, A., Dorairaj, V., Boyce, C., Hornak, L.: On techniques for angle compensation in nonideal iris recognition. IEEE Trans. Syst. Man Cyben. B Cybern. 37(5), 1176–1190 (2007). doi: 10.1109/TSMCB.2007.904831

477. Securics Inc., USA: URL http://www.securics.com/. Retrieved June 2012

478. Shah, S., Ross, A.: Iris segmentation using geodesic active contours. IEEE Trans. Inform. Forensics Secur. 4(4), 824–836 (2009). doi: 10.1109/TIFS.2009.2033225

479. Sheikh, H.R., Bovik, A.C.: Image information and visual quality. IEEE Trans. Image Process. 15(2), 430–444 (2006). doi: 10.1109/TIP.2005.859378

480. Shin, S.W., Lee, M.K., Moon, D., Moon, K.: Dictionary attack on functional transform-based cancelable fingerprint templates. ETRI J. 31(5), 628–630 (2009). doi: 10.4218/etrij.09.0209.0137

481. Simoens, K., Tuyls, P., Preneel, B.: Privacy weaknesses in biometric sketches. In: Proceedings of 30th IEEE Symposium on Security and Privacy, pp. 188–203. IEEE, New York (2009). doi: 10.1109/SP.2009.24

482. Skiljan, I.: IrfanView. URL http://irfanview.tuwien.ac.at/. Retrieved June 2012

483. SOCIA Lab, University of Beira Interior: Noisy Iris Challenge Evaluation Part I. URL http://nice1.di.ubi.pt/. Retrieved May 2012

484. SOCIA Lab, University of Beira Interior: Noisy Iris Challenge Evaluation Part II. URL http://nice2.di.ubi.pt/. Retrieved May 2012

485. SOCIA Lab, University of Beira Interior: UBIRIS.v1 Database. URL http://iris.di.ubi.pt/ubiris1.html. Retrieved May 2012

486. SOCIA Lab, University of Beira Interior: UBIRIS.v2 Database. URL http://iris.di.ubi.pt/ubiris2.html. Retrieved May 2012

487. Song, O.T., Teoh, A.B., Ngo, D.C.L.: Application-specific key release scheme from biometrics. Int. J. Netw. Secur. 6(2), 122–128 (2008)

488. Soutar, C., Roberge, D., Stoianov, A., Gilroy, R., Kumar, B.V.: Biometric Encryption - Enrollment and Verification Procedures. In: Casasent, D., Chao, T.H. (eds.) Optical Pattern Recognition IX, Proceedings of SPIE, vol. 3386, pp. 24–35. SPIE, Bellingham, WA (1998). doi: 10.1117/12.304770

489. Soutar, C., Roberge, D., Stoianov, A., Gilroy, R., Kumar, B.V.: Biometric Encryption using image processing. In: Renesse, R.V. (ed.) Optical Security and Counterfeit Deterrence Techniques II, Proceedings of SPIE, vol. 3314, pp. 178–188. SPIE, Bellingham, WA (1998). doi: 10.1117/12.304705

490. Soutar, C., Roberge, D., Stoianov, A., Gilroy, R., Kumar, B.V.: Biometric encryption. In: ICSA Guide to Cryptography, pp. 1–28. McGraw-Hill, New York (1999)

491. Soutar, C., Roberge, D., Stoianov, A., Gilroy, R., Kumar, B.V.: Method for secure key management using a biometrics (2001). U.S. Patent 6219794

492. Soutar, C., Tomko, G.J., Schmidt, G.J.: Fingerprint controlled public key cryptographic system (1996). U.S. Patent 5541994

493. SRI Sarnoff: IOM N-Glance. URL http://www.sarnoff.com/products/iris-on-the-move/compact-system. Retrieved May 2012

494. SRI Sarnoff: IOM PassPort. URL http://www.sarnoff.com/products/iris-on-the-move/portal-system. Retrieved May 2012

495. SRI Sarnoff: IOM RapID-Cam II. URL http://www.sarnoff.com/products/iris-on-the-move/handheld-system. Retrieved May 2012

496. Stögner, H., Uhl, A., Weinhandel, G.: Experiments on improving lossless compression of biometric iris sample data. In: Zovko-Cihlar, B., Behlilovic, N., Hadzialic, M. (eds.) Proceedings of 18th International Conference on Systems, Signals and Image Processing, pp. 217–220. IEEE, New York (2011)

497. Stoianov, A., Kevenaar, T., van der Veen, M.: Security issues of biometric encryption. In: Proceedings of Toronto International Conference on Science and Technology for Humanity, pp. 34–39. IEEE, New York (2009). doi: 10.1109/TIC-STH.2009.5444478

498. Storer, J.: Image and Text Compression. The Kluwer international series in engineering and computer science. Kluwer, Dordrecht (1992)

499. Sun, Z., Tan, T., Wang, Y.: Robust encoding of local ordinal measures: A general framework of iris recognition. In: Maltoni, D., Jain, A. (eds.) Proceedings of ECCV Workshop BioAW, LNCS, vol. 3087, pp. 270–282. Springer, New York (2004). doi: 10.1007/978-3-540-25976-3_25

500. Sun, Z., Wang, Y., Tan, T., Cui, J.: Improving iris recognition accuracy via cascaded classifiers. IEEE Trans. Syst. Man Cybern. C Appl. Rev. 35(3), 435–441 (2005). doi: 10.1109/TSMCC.2005.848169

501. Sutcu, Y., Li, Q., Memon, N.: How to Protect Biometric Templates. In: Delp, E., Wong, P. (eds.) Conference on Security, Steganography and Watermarking of Multimedia Contents IX, Proceedings of SPIE, vol. 6505, pp. 650514.1–11. SPIE, Bellingham, WA (2007). doi: 10.1117/12.705896

502. Sutcu, Y., Li, Q., Memon, N.: Protecting biometric templates with sketch: Theory and practice. IEEE Trans. Inform. Forensics Secur. **2**, 503–512 (2007). doi: 10.1109/TIFS.2007.902022

503. Sutcu, Y., Li, Q., Memon, N.: Secure biometric templates from fingerprint-face features. In: Proceedings of IEEE Conference on Computer Vision and Pattern Recognition, pp. 1–6. IEEE, New York (2007). doi: 10.1109/CVPR.2007.383385

504. Sutcu, Y., Sencar, H.T., Memon, N.: A secure biometric authentication scheme based on robust hashing. In: Proceedings of 7th Workshop on Multimedia and Security, pp. 111–116. ACM, New York (2005). doi: 10.1145/1073170.1073191

505. Szewczyk, R., Grabowski, K., Napieralska, M., Sankowski, W., Zubert, M., Napieralski, A.: A reliable iris recognition algorithm based on reverse biorthogonal wavelet transform. Pattern Recogn. Lett. **33**(8), 1019–1026 (2012). doi: 10.1016/j.patrec.2011.08.018

506. Tabassi, E., Grother, P., Salamon, W.: Irex ii - iqce iris quality calibration and evaluation. Interagency report 7820, NIST (2011)

507. Tajbakhsh, N., Araabi, B.N., Soltanian-Zadeh, H.: Robust iris verification based on local and global variations. EURASIP J. Adv. Signal Process. **2010**, 70:1–70:12 (2010). doi: 10.1155/2010/979058

508. Takahashi, K., Hirata, S.: Generating provably secure cancelable fingerprint templates based on correlation-invariant random filtering. In: Proceedings of IEEE 3rd International Conference on Biometrics: Theory, Applications, and Systems, pp. 1–6. IEEE, New York (2009). doi: 10.1109/BTAS.2009.5339047

509. Tan, C.W., Kumar, A.: Automated segmentation of iris images using visible wavelength face images. In: Proceedings of IEEE Conference on Computer Vision and Pattern Recognition Workshop, pp. 9–14. IEEE, New York (2011). doi: 10.1109/CVPRW.2011.5981682

510. Tan, T., He, Z., Sun, Z.: Efficient and robust segmentation of noisy iris images for non-cooperative iris recognition. Image Vis. Comput. **28**(2), 223–230 (2010). doi: 10.1016/j.imavis.2009.05.008

511. Tan, T., Zhang, X., Sun, Z., Zhang, H.: Noisy iris image matching by using multiple cues. Pattern Recogn. Lett. **33**(8), 970–977 (2012). doi: 10.1016/j.patrec.2011.08.009

512. Tao, Z., Ming-Yu, F., Bo, F.: Side-channel attack on biometric cryptosystem based on keystroke dynamics. In: Proceedings of 1st International Symposium on Data, Privacy, and E-Commerce, pp. 221–223. IEEE, New York (2007). doi: 10.1109/ISDPE.2007.48

513. Taubin, G.: Estimation of planar curves, surfaces, and nonplanar space curves defined by implicit equations with applications to edge and range image segmentation. IEEE Trans. Pattern Anal. Mach. Intell. **13**(11), 1115–1138 (1991). doi: 10.1109/34.103273

514. Taubman, D., Marcellin, M.: JPEG2000 — Image Compression Fundamentals, Standards and Practice. Kluwer, Dordrecht (2002)

515. Teoh, A., Kim, J.: Secure biometric template protection in fuzzy commitment scheme. IEICE Electron. Express **4**(23), 724–730 (2007)

516. Teoh, A.B.J., Chong, L.Y.: Secure speech template protection in speaker verification system. Speech Comm. **52**(2), 150–163 (2010). doi: 10.1016/j.specom.2009.09.003

517. Teoh, A.B.J., Kuan, Y.W., Lee, S.: Cancellable biometrics and annotations on biohash. Pattern Recogn. **41**(6), 2034–2044 (2008). doi: 10.1016/j.patcog.2007.12.002

518. Teoh, A.B.J., Ngo, D.C.L.: Biophasor: Token supplemented cancellable biometrics. In: Proceedings of International Conference on Control, Automation, Robotics and Vision, pp. 1–5. IEEE, New York (2006). doi: 10.1109/ICARCV.2006.345404

519. Teoh, A.B.J., Ngo, D.C.L., Goh, A.: Biohashing: two factor authentication featuring fingerprint data and tokenised random number. Pattern Recogn. **37**(11), 2245–2255 (2004). doi: 10.1016/j.patcog.2004.04.011

520. Teoh, A.B.J., Ngo, D.C.L., Goh, A.: Personalised cryptographic key generation based on FaceHashing. Comput. Secur. **2004**(23), 606–614 (2004). doi: 10.1016/j.cose.2004.06.002

521. Teoh, A.B.J., Ngo, D.C.L., Goh, A.: Biometric Hash: High-Confidence Face Recognition. IEEE Trans. Circ. Syst. Video Tech. **16**(6), 771–775 (2006). doi: 10.1109/TCSVT.2006.873780

522. Teoh, A.B.J., Yuang, C.T.: Cancellable biometrics realization with multispace random projections. IEEE Trans. Syst. Man Cybern. B Cybern. **37**(5), 1096–1106 (2007). doi: 10.1109/TSMCB.2007.903538

523. Thärna, J., Nilsson, K., Bigun, J.: Orientation scanning to improve lossless compression of fingerprint images. In: Kittler, J., Nixon, M. (eds.) Proceedings of 4th International Conference on Audio- and Video-Based Biometric Person Authentication. LNCS, vol. 2688, pp. 343–350. Springer, New York (2003). doi: 10.1007/3-540-44887-X_41

524. Thoonsaengngam, P., Horapong, K., Thainimit, S., Areekul, V.: Efficient iris recognition using adaptive quotient thresholding. In: Zhang, D., Jain, A. (eds.) Proceedings of 1st International Conference on Biometrics, LNCS, vol. 3832, pp. 472–478. Springer, New York (2006). doi: 10.1007/11608288_63

525. Tisse, C., Martin, L., Torres, L., Robert, M.: Person identification technique using human iris recognition. In: Proceedings of Vision Interface, pp. 294–299 (2002)

526. Tistarelli, M., Nixon, M. (eds.): Systematic Construction of Iris-based Fuzzy Commitment Schemes. LNCS, vol. 5558. Springer, New York (2009). doi: 10.1007/978-3-642-01793-3_95

527. Tong, L., Dai, F., Zhang, Y., Li, J.: Visual security evaluation for video encryption. In: Proceedings of International Conference on Multimedia, pp. 835–838. ACM, New York (2010). doi: 10.1145/1873951.1874091

528. Tong, V., Sibert, H., Lecoeur, J., Girault, M.: Biometric fuzzy extractors made practical: a proposal based on fingercodes. In: Lee, S.W., Li, S. (eds.) Proceedings of 2nd International Conference on Biometrics, LNCS, vol. 4642, pp. 604–613. Springer, New York (2007). doi: 10.1007/978-3-540-74549-5_64

529. Trappe, W., Washington, L.C.: Introduction to Cryptography with Coding Theory: 2nd Edition. Pearson Prentice Hall, Upper Saddle River (2006)

530. Tuceryan, M.: Moment based texture segmentation. In: Proceedings of 11th International Conference on Pattern Recognition, pp. 45–48. IEEE, New York (1992). doi: 10.1109/ICPR.1992.201924

531. Tulyakov, S., Farooq, F., Govindaraju, V.: Symmetric hash functions for fingerprint minutiae. In: Maltoni, D., Jain, A. (eds.) Proceedings of 3rd International Conference on Advances in Pattern Recognition. LNCS, vol. 3687, pp. 30–38. Springer, New York (2005). doi: 10.1007/11552499_4

532. Tulyakov, S., Farooq, F., Mansukhani, P., Govindaraju, V.: Symmetric hash functions for secure fingerprint biometric systems. Pattern Recogn. Lett. **28**(16), 2427–2436 (2007). doi: 10.1016/j.patrec.2007.08.008

533. Tuyls, P., Akkermans, A.H.M., Kevenaar, T.A.M., Schrijen, G.J., Bazen, A.M., Veldhuis, R.N.J.: Practical biometric authentication with template protection. In: Kanade, T., Jain, A., Ratha, N. (eds.) Proceedings of 5th International Conference on Audio- and Video-Based Biometric Person Authentication. LNCS, vol. 3546, pp. 436–446. Springer, New York (2005). doi: 10.1007/11527923_45

534. Tuyls, P., Goseling, J.: Capacity and examples of template-protecting biometric authentication systems. In: Maltoni, D., Jain, A. (eds.) Proceedings of International Workshop on Biometric Authentication. LNCS, vol. 3087, pp. 158–170. Springer, New York (2004). doi: 10.1007/978-3-540-25976-3_15

535. Uhl, A., Höller, Y.: Iris-sensor authentication using camera PRNU fingerprints. In: Proceedings of 5th International Conference on Biometrics, pp. 230–237. IEEE, New York (2012). doi: 10.1109/ICB.2012.6199813

536. Uhl, A., Wild, P.: Parallel versus serial classifier combination for multibiometric hand-based identification. In: Tistarelli, M., Nixon, M. (eds.) Proceedings of 3rd International Conference on Biometrics. LNCS, vol. 5558, pp. 950–959. Springer, New York (2009). doi: 10.1007/978-3-642-01793-3_96

537. Uhl, A., Wild, P.: Single-sensor multi-instance fingerprint and eigenfinger recognition using (weighted) score combination methods. Int. J. Biometrics **1**(4), 442–462 (2009). doi: 10.1504/IJBM.2009.027305

538. Uhl, A., Wild, P.: Enhancing iris matching using levenshtein distance with alignment constraints. In: Bebis, G., Boyle, R.D., Parvin, B., Koracin, D., Chung, R., Hammoud, R.I., Hussain, M., Tan, K.H., Crawfis, R., Thalmann, D., Kao, D., Avila, L. (eds.) Proceedings of 6th International Symposium on Advances in Visual Computing. LNCS, vol. 6453, pp. 469–479. Springer, New York (2010). doi: 10.1007/978-3-642-17289-2_45

539. Uhl, A., Wild, P.: Combining face with face-part detectors under gaussian assumption. In: Campilho, A., Kamel, M. (eds.) Proceedings of 9th International Conference on Image Analysis and Recognition. LNCS, vol. 7325, pp. 80–89. Springer, New York (2012)

540. Uhl, A., Wild, P.: Multi-stage visible wavelength and near infrared iris segmentation framework. In: Campilho, A., Kamel, M. (eds.) Proceedings of 9th International Conference on Image Analysis and Recognition. LNCS, vol. 7325, pp. 1–10. Springer, New York (2012)

541. Uhl, A., Wild, P.: Weighted adaptive hough and ellipsopolar transforms for real-time iris segmentation. In: Proceedings of 5th International Conference on Biometrics, pp. 283–290. IEEE, New York (2012). doi: 10.1109/ICB.2012.6199821

542. UK Border Agency: Iris recognition immigration system. URL http://www.ukba.homeoffice. gov.uk/customs-travel/Enteringtheuk/usingiris/. Retrieved May 2012

543. Uludag, U., Günsel, B., Ballan, M.: A spatial method for watermarking of fingerprint images. In: Proceedings of 1st International Workshop on Pattern Recognition in Information Systems, pp. 26–33. ICEIS Press (2001)

544. Uludag, U., Jain, A.K.: Fuzzy fingerprint vault. In: Proceedings of Workshop Biometrics: Challenges Arising from Theory to Practice, pp. 13–16 (2004)

545. Uludag, U., Jain, A.K.: Securing fingerprint template: Fuzzy vault with helper data. In: Proceedings of IEEE Conference on Computer Vision and Pattern Recognition Workshop, p. 163. IEEE, New York (2006). doi: 10.1109/CVPRW.2006.185

546. Uludag, U., Pankanti, S., Prabhakar, S., Jain, A.K.: Biometric cryptosystems: issues and challenges. Proc. IEEE **92**(6), 948–960 (2004). doi: 10.1109/JPROC.2004.827372

547. UNHCR: Iris testing of returning Afghans passes 200,000 mark. URL http://www.unhcr.org/ cgi-bin/texis/vtx/search?docid=3f86b4784. Retrieved May 2012

548. Unique Identification Authority of India: Aadhaar. URL http://uidai.gov.in/. Retrieved May 2012

549. Unique Identification Authority of India: Role of Biometric Technology in Aadhaar Enrollment. URL http://uidai.gov.in/images/FrontPageUpdates/role_of_biometric_technology_in_aadhaar_jan21_2012.pdf. Retrieved May 2012

550. University of Bath: Bath Iris Image Database. URL http://www.smartsensors.co.uk/ information/bath-iris-image-database. Retrieved May 2012

551. Upmanyu, M., Namboodiri, A.M., Srinathan, K., Jawahar, C.: Efficient privacy preserving video surveillance. In: Proceedings of IEEE International Conference on Computer Vision, pp. 1639–1646. IEEE, New York (2009). doi: 10.1109/ICCV.2009.5459370

552. US Department of Homeland Security: Independent Testing of Iris Recognition Technology (ITIRT), Report NBCHC030114/0002 (2005). URL http://www.hsdl.org/?view&did= 464567. Retrieved May 2012

553. Vatsa, M., Singh, R., Gupta, P.: Comparison of iris recognition algorithms. In: Proceedings of International Conference on Intelligent Sensing and Information Processing, pp. 354–358. IEEE, New York (2004). doi: 10.1109/ICISIP.2004.1287682

554. Vatsa, M., Singh, R., Noore, A.: Improving biometric recognition accuracy and robustness using DWT and SVM watermarking. IEICE Electron. Express **2**(12), 362–367 (2005)

555. Vatsa, M., Singh, R., Noore, A.: Reducing the false rejection rate of iris recognition using textural and topological features. Int. J. Signal Process. **2**(2), 66–72 (2005)

556. Vatsa, M., Singh, R., Noore, A.: Improving iris recognition performance using segmentation, quality enhancement, match score fusion, and indexing. IEEE Trans. Syst. Man Cybern. B Cybern. **38**(4), 1021–1035 (2008). doi: 10.1109/TSMCB.2008.922059

557. Vatsa, M., Singh, R., Noore, A.: Feature based RDWT watermarking for multimodal biometric system. Image Vis. Comput. **27**(3), 293–304 (2009). doi: 10.1016/j.imavis.2007.05.003

558. Vatsa, M., Singh, R., Noore, A., Houck, M., Morris, K.: Robust biometric image watermarking for fingerprint and face template protection. IEICE Electron. Express **3**(2), 23–28 (2006)
559. Vielhauer, C.: Biometric User Authentication for IT Security, vol. 18. Springer, New York (2006). doi: 10.1007/0-387-28094-4
560. Vielhauer, C., Steinmetz, R.: Approaches to biometric watermarks for owner authentification. In: Wong, P., Delp, E. (eds.) Security and Watermarking of Multimedia Contents III, Proceedings of SPIE, vol. 4314, pp. 209–219. SPIE, Bellingham, WA (2001). doi: 10.1117/12.435401
561. Vielhauer, C., Steinmetz, R.: Handwriting: feature correlation analysis for biometric hashes. EURASIP J. Appl. Signal Process. **2004**(1), 542–558 (2004). doi: 10.1155/S1110865704309248
562. Vielhauer, C., Steinmetz, R., Mayerhöfer, A.: Biometric hash based on statistical features of online signatures. In: Proceedings of 16th International Conference on Pattern Recognition, pp. 123–126. IEEE, New York (2002). doi: 10.1109/ICPR.2002.1044628
563. Viola, P., Jones, M.: Rapid object detection using a boosted cascade of simple features. In: Proceedings of IEEE Conference on Computer Vision and Pattern Recognition, pp. 511–518. IEEE, New York (2001). doi: 10.1109/CVPR.2001.990517
564. Viola, P., Jones, M.J.: Robust real-time face detection. Int. J. Comput. Vis. **57**(2), 137–154 (2004). doi: 10.1023/B:VISI.0000013087.49260.fb
565. Voderhobli, K., Pattinson, C., Donelan, H.: A schema for cryptographic key generation using hybrid biometrics. In: Proceedings of 7th Symposium on the Convergence of Telecommunications, Networking and Broadcasting, pp. 1–6 (2006)
566. Wallace, G.: The JPEG still picture compression standard. Comm. ACM **34**(4), 30–44 (1991). doi: 10.1145/103085.103089
567. Wang, D.S., Li, J.P., Hu, D.K., Yan, Y.H.: A Novel Biometric Image Integrity Authentication Using Fragile Watermarking and Arnold Transform. In: Li, J., Bloshanskii, I., Ni, L., Pandey, S.S., Yang, S.X. (eds.) Proceedings of International Conference on Information Computing and Automatation, pp. 799–802. World Scientific Publishing, Singapore (2007). doi: 10.1142/9789812799524_0203
568. Wang, F., Han, J., Yao, X.: Iris recognition based on multialgorithmic fusion. WSEAS Trans. Inform. Sci. Appl. **12**(4), 1415–1421 (2007)
569. Wang, K., Qian, Y.: Fast and accurate iris segmentation based on linear basis function and ransac. In: Proceedings of 18th IEEE International Conference on Image Processing, pp. 3205–3208. IEEE, New York (2011). doi: 10.1109/ICIP.2011.6116350
570. Wang, P., Green, M., Ji, Q., Wayman, J.: Automatic eye detection and its validation. In: Proceedings of IEEE Conference on Computer Vision and Pattern Recognition, pp. 164–171. IEEE, New York (2005). doi: 10.1109/CVPR.2005.570
571. Wang, Y., Plataniotis, K.: Face based biometric authentication with changeable and privacy preservable templates. In: Proceedings of Biometrics Symposium, pp. 11–13. IEEE, New York (2007). doi: 10.1109/BCC.2007.4430530
572. Wang, Y., Tan, T., Jain, A.: Combining face and iris biometrics for identity verification. In: Kittler, J., Nixon, M. (eds.) Proceedings of 4th International Conference on Audio- and Video-Based Biometric Person Authentication. LNCS, vol. 2688, pp. 805–813. Springer, New York (2003). doi: 10.1007/3-540-44887-X_93
573. Wang, Z., Bovik, A., Sheikh, H., Simoncelli, E.: Image quality assessment: from error visibility to structural similarity. IEEE Trans. Image Process. **13**(4), 600–612 (2004). doi: 10.1109/TIP.2003.819861
574. Wayman, J., Orlans, N., Hu, Q., Goodman, F., Ulrich, A., Valencia, V.: Technology assessment for the state of the art biometrics excellence roadmap vol. 2 ver. 1.3. Tech. rep., The MITRE Corporation (2009). US Gov Contr. J-FBI-07-164
575. Wayman, J.L.: Technical testing and evaluation of biometric identification devices. In: Biometrics: Personal Identification in a Networked Society, pp. 345–368. Kluwer, Dordrecht (1999)
576. Weinberger, M., Seroussi, G., Sapiro, G.: The LOCO-I lossless image compression algorithm: principles and standardization into JPEG-LS. IEEE Trans. Image Process. **9**(8), 1309–1324 (2000). doi: 10.1109/83.855427

577. Weinhandel, G., Stögner, H., Uhl, A.: Experimental study on lossless compression of biometric sample data. In: Proceedings of 6th International Symposium on Image and Signal Processing and Analysis, pp. 517–522. IEEE, New York (2009)

578. Wheeler, F., Perera, A., Abramovich, G., Yu, B., Tu, P.: Stand-off iris recognition system. In: Proceedings of IEEE 2nd International Conference on Biometrics: Theory, Applications, and Systems, pp. 1–7. IEEE, New York (2008). doi: 10.1109/BTAS.2008.4699381

579. Wildes, R.: Iris recognition: an emerging biometric technology. Proc. IEEE 85(9), 1348–1363 (1997). doi: 10.1109/5.628669

580. Wildes, R.P., Asmuth, J.C., Green, G.L., Hsu, S.C., Kolczynski, R.J., Matey, J.R., McBride, S.E.: A machine-vision system for iris recognition. Mach. Vis. Appl. 9(1), 1–8 (1996). doi: 10.1007/BF01246633

581. Willems, F., Ignatenko, T.: Identification and secret-key binding in binary-symmetric template-protected biometric systems. In: Proceedings of IEEE International Workshop on Information Forensics and Security, pp. 1–5. IEEE, New York (2010). doi: 10.1109/WIFS.2010.5711455

582. Wolberg, G.: Image morphing: a survey. Vis. Comput. 14(8/9), 360–372 (1998)

583. Wu, G.D., Huang, P.H.: Image watermarking using structure based wavelet tree quantization. In: Proceedings of 6th IEEE/ACIS International Conference on Computer and Information Science, pp. 315–319. IEEE, New York (2007). doi: 10.1109/ICIS.2007.111

584. Wu, X., Qi, N., Wang, K., Zhang, D.: An iris cryptosystem for information security. In: Proceedings of 2008 International Conference on Intelligent Information Hiding and Multimedia Signal Processing, pp. 1533–1536. IEEE, New York (2008). doi: 10.1109/IIH-MSP.2008.83

585. Wu, X., Qi, N., Wang, K., Zhang, D.: A novel cryptosystem based on iris key generation. In: Proceedings of 4th International Conference on Natural Computation, pp. 53–56. IEEE, New York (2008). doi: 10.1109/ICNC.2008.808

586. Wu, X., Wang, K., Zhang, D.: A cryptosystem based on palmprint feature. In: Proceedings of 19th International Conference on Pattern Recognition, pp. 1–4. IEEE, New York (2008). doi: 10.1109/ICPR.2008.4761117

587. Wu, Y., Qiu, B.: Transforming a pattern identifier into biometric key generators. In: Proceedings of International Conference on Multimedia and Expo, pp. 78–82. IEEE, New York (2010). doi: 10.1109/ICME.2010.5583388

588. Xiao, Q.: Face detection using information fusion. In: IEEE Workshop on Comp. Intell. in Biometrics and Identity Mgmnt., pp. 157–162 (2011)

589. Xie, L., Arce, G.R.: Joint wavelet compression and authentication watermarking. In: Proceedings of IEEE International Conference on Image Processing, vol. 2, pp. 427–431. IEEE, New York (1998). doi: 10.1109/ICIP.1998.723409

590. Xu, G., Zhang, Z., Ma, Y.: A novel method for iris feature extraction based on intersecting cortical model network. J. Appl. Math. Comput. 26, 341–352 (2008). doi: 10.1007/s12190-007-0035-y

591. Xu, H., Veldhuis, R.N.: Binary representations of fingerprint spectral minutiae features. In: Proceedings of 20th International Conference on Pattern Recognition, pp. 1212–1216. IEEE, New York (2010). doi: 10.1109/ICPR.2010.302

592. Xu, Z., Shi, P.: A robust and accurate method for pupil features extraction. In: Proceedings of 18th International Conference on Pattern Recognition, pp. 437–440. IEEE, New York (2006). doi: 10.1109/ICPR.2006.165

593. Yang, B., Busch, C., Gafurov, D., Bours, P.: Renewable minutiae templates with tunable size and security. In: Proceedings of 20th International Conference on Pattern Recognition, pp. 878–881. IEEE, New York (2010). doi: 10.1109/ICPR.2010.221

594. Yang, B., Hartung, D., Simoens, K., Busch, C.: Dynamic random projection for biometric template protection. In: Proceedings of IEEE 4th International Conference on Biometrics: Theory, Applications, and Systems, pp. 1–7. IEEE, New York (2010). doi: 10.1109/BTAS.2010.5634538

595. Yang, K., Du, E.: A multi-stage approach for non-cooperative iris recognition. In: Proceedings of IEEE International Conference on Systems, Man, and Cybernetics, pp. 3386–3391 (2011). doi: 10.1109/ICSMC.2011.6084192

596. Yang, S., Verbauwhede, I.: Automatic secure fingerprint verification system based on fuzzy vault scheme. In: Proceedings of IEEE International Conference Audio, Speech and Signal Processing, vol. 5, pp. 609–6012. IEEE, New York (2005). doi: 10.1109/ICASSP.2005.1416377

597. Yang, S., Verbauwhede, I.: Secure Iris Verification. In: Proceedings of IEEE International Conference on Acoustics, Speech and Signal Processing, vol. 2, pp. 133–136. IEEE, New York (2007). doi: 10.1109/ICASSP.2007.366190

598. Yeung, M.M., Pankanti, S.: Verification watermarks on fingerprint recognition and retrieval. In: Wong, P.W., Delp, E.J. (eds.) Security and Watermarking of Multimedia Contents, Proceedings of SPIE, vol. 3657, pp. 66–78. SPIE, Bellingham, WA (1999). doi: 10.1117/12.344704

599. Yeung, M.M., Pankanti, S.: Verification watermarks on fingerprint recognition and retrieval. J. Electron. Imag. 9(4), 468–476 (2000). doi: 10.1117/1.1287795

600. Yip, W.K., Teoh, A.B.J., Ngo, D.C.L.: Replaceable and securely hashed keys from online signatures. IEICE Electron. Express 3(18), 410–416 (2006). doi: 10.1587/elex.3.410

601. Yu, L., Wang, K., Zhang, D.: A novel method for coarse iris classification. In: Zhang, D., Jain, A. (eds.) Proceedings of 1st International Conference on Biometrics, LNCS, vol. 3832, pp. 404–410. Springer, New York (2006). doi: 10.1007/11608288_54

602. Zaim, A.: Automatic segmentation of iris images for the purpose of identification. In: Proceedings of IEEE International Conference on Image Processing, vol. 3, pp. 273–276. IEEE, New York (2005). doi: 10.1109/ICIP.2005.1530381

603. Zebbiche, K., Ghouti, L., Khelifi, F., Bouridane, A.: Protecting fingerprint data using watermarking. In: Proceedings of 1st NASA/ESA Conference on Adaptive Hardware and Systems, pp. 451–456. IEEE, New York (2006). doi: 10.1109/AHS.2006.61

604. Zebbiche, K., Khelifi, F.: Region-based watermarking of biometric images: Case study in fingerprint images. Int. J. Digit. Multimed. Broadcast. 2008, 492942.1–13 (2008). doi: 10.1155/2008/492942

605. Zebbiche, K., Khelifi, F., Bouridane, A.: An efficient watermarking technique for the protection of fingerprint images. EURASIP J. Inform. Secur. 2008, 918601.1–20 (2008). doi: 10.1155/2008/918601

606. Zeitz, C., Scheidat, T., Dittmann, J., Vielhauer, C.: Security issues of internet-based biometric authentication systems: risks of man-in-the-middle and BioPhishing on the example of BioWebAuth. In: Delp, E., Wong, P., Dittmann, J., Memon, N. (eds.) Security, Forensics, Steganography, and Watermarking of Multimedia Contents X, Proceedings of SPIE, vol. 6819, pp. 68190R.1–12. SPIE, Bellingham, WA (2008). doi: 10.1117/12.767632

607. Zeng, Z., Watters, P.A.: A novel face hashing method with feature fusion for biometric cryptosystems. In: Proceedings of European Conference on Universal Multiservice Networks, pp. 439–444. IEEE, New York (2007). doi: 10.1109/ECUMN.2007.2

608. Zhang, C., Zhang, Z.: A survey of recent advances in face detection. Tech. rep., Microsoft Research (2010). MSR-TR-2010-66

609. Zhang, G.H., Poon, C.C.Y., Zhang, Y.T.: A fast key generation method based on dynamic biometrics to secure wireless body sensor networks for p-health. In: Proceedings of 2010 International Conference of the IEEE Engineering in Medicine and Biology Society, pp. 2034–2036. IEEE, New York (2010). doi: 10.1109/IEMBS.2010.5626783

610. Zhang, G.H., Salganicoff, M.: Method of measuring the focus of close-up image of eyes (1999). U.S. Patent 5953440

611. Zhang, L., Sun, Z., Tan, T., Hu, S.: Robust biometric key extraction based on iris cryptosystem. In: Tistarelli, M., Nixon, M. (eds.) Proceedings of 3rd International Conference on Biometrics. LNCS, vol. 5558, pp. 1060–1070. Springer, New York (2009). doi: 10.1007/978-3-642-01793-3_107

612. Zhang, W., Chang, Y.J., Chen, T.: Optimal thresholding for key generation based on biometrics. In: Proceedings of International Conference on Image Processing, pp. 3451–3454. IEEE, New York (2004). doi: 10.1109/ICIP.2004.1421857

613. Zhang, X., Sun, Z., Tan, T.: Texture removal for adaptive level set based iris segmentation. In: Proceedings of 17th IEEE International Conference on Image Processing, pp. 1729–1732. IEEE, New York (2010). doi: 10.1109/ICIP.2010.5652941

614. Zhang, Z., Wang, R., Pan, K., Li, S., Zhang, P.: Fusion of near infrared face and iris biometrics. In: Lee, S.W., Li, S. (eds.) Proceedings of 2nd International Conference on Biometrics, LNCS, vol. 4642, pp. 172–180. Springer, New York (2007). doi: 10.1007/978-3-540-74549-5_19

615. Zheng, G., Li, W., Zhan, C.: Cryptographic key generation from biometric data using lattice mapping. In: Proceedings of 18th International Conference on Pattern Recognition, vol. 4, pp. 513–516. IEEE, New York (2006). doi: 10.1109/ICPR.2006.423

616. Zheng, Z., Yang, J., Yang, L.: A robust method for eye features extraction on color image. Pattern Recogn. Lett. **26**, 2252–2261 (2005). doi: 10.1016/j.patrec.2005.03.033

617. Zhou, Z., Du, Y., Belcher, C.: Transforming traditional iris recognition systems to work in nonideal situations. IEEE Trans. Ind. Electron. **56**(8), 3203–3213 (2009). doi: 10.1109/TIE.2009.2024653

618. Zhou, Z., Yingzi Du, E., Thomas, N., Delp, E.: Multi-angle sclera recognition system. In: IEEE Workshop on Computational Intelligence in Biometrics and Identity Management (CIBIM), 2011, pp. 103–108. IEEE, New York (2011). doi: 10.1109/CIBIM.2011.5949225

619. Ziauddin, S., Dailey, M.: Iris recognition performance enhancement using weighted majority voting. In: Proceedings of 15th International Conference on Image Processing, pp. 277–280. IEEE, New York (2008). doi: 10.1109/ICIP.2008.4711745

620. Zuiderveld, K.: Graphics Gems IV, chap. Contrast Limited Adaptive Histogram Equalization, pp. 474–485. Morgan Kaufmann, San Francisco (1994)

621. Zuo, J., Kalka, N., Schmid, N.: A robust iris segmentation procedure for unconstrained subject presentation. In: Proceedings of Biometric Consortium Conference, pp. 1–6. IEEE, New York (2006). doi: 10.1109/BCC.2006.4341623

622. Zuo, J., Ratha, N., Connell, J.: A new approach for iris segmentation. In: Proceedings of IEEE Conference on Computer Vision and Pattern Recognition Workshop, pp. 1–6. IEEE, New York (2008). doi: 10.1109/CVPRW.2008.4563109

623. Zuo, J., Ratha, N.K., Connel, J.H.: Cancelable iris biometric. In: Proceedings of 19th International Conference on Pattern Recognition pp. 1–4. IEEE, New York (2008). doi: 10.1109/ICPR.2008.4761886

624. Zuo, J., Schmid, N.: An automatic algorithm for evaluating the precision of iris segmentation. In: Proceedings of IEEE 2nd International Conference on Biometrics: Theory, Applications, and Systems, pp. 1–6. IEEE, New York (2008). doi: 10.1109/BTAS.2008.4699358

625. Zuo, J., Schmid, N.: On a methodology for robust segmentation of nonideal iris images. IEEE Trans. Syst. Man Cybern. B Cybern. **40**(3), 703–718 (2010). doi: 10.1109/TSMCB.2009.2015426

Appendix A
Credits: Copyrighted Material

The text of this book has been composed from both, published and unpublished resources from the authors, in order to form a unity to the reader. In the following, reference to the contributing copyright material is given.

- *Chapter 1*: The unsectioned part has been adapted with permission from [434] © InTech.
- *Chapter 4*: The unsectioned part and Sects. 4.1–4.4 have been adapted with permission from [539] © Springer.
- *Chapter 5*: The unsectioned part has been adapted with permission from [541] © IEEE. Section 5.1 has been adapted with permission from [540] © Springer.
- *Chapter 6*: The unsectioned part and Sects. 6.1–6.4 have been adapted with permission from [541] © IEEE and [540] © Springer.
- *Chapter 7*: The unsectioned part has been adapted with permission from [541] © IEEE. Section 7.1 has been adapted with permission from [541] © IEEE and [539] © Springer. Section 7.2 has been adapted with permission from [539] © Springer. Section 7.3 has been adapted with permission from [541] © IEEE and [540] © Springer.
- *Chapter 8*: Section 8.6.1 has been adapted with permission from [268, 271] © Springer, and [269] © IEEE. Section 8.6.2 has been adapted with permission from [177] © Springer. Section 8.6.3 has been adapted with permission from [200] © Springer and [201] © IARIA. Section 8.7 has been adapted with permission from [202] © IEEE and [203] © Springer.
- *Chapter 9*: The unsectioned part has been adapted with permission from [439] © IET. Section 9.1.1 has been adapted with permission from [432] © IET. Section 9.1.2 has been adapted with permission from [538] © Springer. Section 9.1.3 has been adapted with permission from [442] © ACM. Section 9.1.4 has been adapted with permission from [443] © IEEE. Section 9.2.1 has been adapted with permission from [427] © IEEE. Section 9.2.2 has been adapted with permission from [438] © IEEE. Section 9.3.1 has been adapted with permission from [194] © Springer. Section 9.4.1 has been adapted with permission from [439] © IET. Section 9.4.2 has been adapted with permission

C. Rathgeb et al., *Iris Biometrics: From Segmentation to Template Security*,
Advances in Information Security 59, DOI 10.1007/978-1-4614-5571-4,
© Springer Science+Business Media, LLC 2013

from [440] © Springer. Section 9.4.3 has been adapted with permission from [270] © SciTePress. Section 9.4.4 has been adapted with permission from [193] © GI

- *Chapter 10*: Section 10.2 has been adapted with permission from [442] © ACM, [538] © Springer, [443] © IEEE, and [432] © IET. Section 10.3 has been adapted with permission from [427,438] © IEEE. Section 10.4 has been adapted with permission from [194] © Springer. Section 10.5 has been adapted with permission from [439] © IET, [440] © Springer, [270] © SciTePress, and [193] © GI .
- *Chapter 11*: The unsectioned part and Sects. 11.1–11.7 have been adapted with permission from [436] © Springer.
- *Chapter 12*: The unsectioned part and Sects. 12.1–12.6 have been adapted with permission from [436] © Springer.
- *Chapter 13*: The unsectioned part and Sects. 13.1–13.2 have been adapted with permission from [436] © Springer. Section 13.3 has been adapted with permission from [234] © IEEE.
- *Chapter 14*: Section 14.2 has been adapted with permission from [429, 526] © Springer and [424] © IET. Section 14.4 has been adapted with permission from [143,178] © Springer. Section 14.5 has been adapted with permission from [426,435,441] © IEEE and [178] © Springer.
- *Chapter 15*: The unsectioned part and Sects. 15.1–15.7 have been adapted with permission from [436] © Springer.
- *Chapter 16*: Sections 16.1 and 16.2 have been adapted with permission from [182] © Springer. Section 16.3 has been adapted with permission from [179] © ACM and [180] © Springer. Section 16.4 has been adapted with permission from [208,209] © Springer. Section 16.5 has been adapted with permission from [535] © IEEE.

Appendix B
Authors' Biographies

Christian Rathgeb

Christian Rathgeb received his MSc and PhD degrees (both in Computer Science) from the University of Salzburg, Austria. He was a member of the Multimedia Signal Processing and Security Lab (WaveLab) at the same university and is currently a PostDoc researcher at the Center of Applied Security Research Darmstadt (CASED), Germany. His research interests are focused on IT security in particular, biometrics (with emphasis on iris recognition and template protection).

Andreas Uhl

Andreas Uhl received his MSc and PhD degrees (both in Mathematics) from the University of Salzburg, Austria. He is currently professor for computer science at the same university and leads the Multimedia Signal Processing and Security Lab (WaveLab). His research interests include multimedia signal processing (with emphasis on compression and security issues), biometrics, media security (watermarking and media encryption), medical image processing, and numbertheoretical methods in numerics.

C. Rathgeb et al., *Iris Biometrics: From Segmentation to Template Security*,
Advances in Information Security 59, DOI 10.1007/978-1-4614-5571-4,
© Springer Science+Business Media, LLC 2013

Peter Wild

Peter Wild received his MSc and is in the process of finalizing his PhD degree (both in Computer Science) from the University of Salzburg, Austria. He is a member of the Multimedia Signal Processing and Security Lab (WaveLab) and external lecturer at the same university. He is also an external lecturer at Fachhochschule Salzburg—University of Applied Sciences, and at Pädagogische Hochschule Salzburg—University of Education. His research interests include computer vision (with emphasis on object detection), biometrics (with emphasis on iris recognition), and media security.

Index

C. Rathgeb et al., *Iris Biometrics: From Segmentation to Template Security*,
Advances in Information Security 59, DOI 10.1007/978-1-4614-5571-4,
© Springer Science+Business Media, LLC 2013